WRITING
FROM
SOURCES
Second Edition

WRITING FROM SOURCES

Second Edition

Brenda Spatt

Office of Academic Affairs
City University of New York

ST. MARTIN'S PRESS   New York

cover design: Darby Downey
cover photo: Victor Schrager
text design: Levavi & Levavi

ISBN: 0-312-89470-8

Acknowledgments

"The Motor Industry" by J. D. Bernal. Reprinted from *Science and History*, Volume 3, by permission of The MIT Press, Cambridge, Massachusetts. Copyright © 1965 by The Massachusetts Institute of Technology.

Excerpt from *The Affluent Society* by John Kenneth Galbraith. Copyright © 1958, 1969, 1976 by John Kenneth Galbraith. Reprinted by permission of Houghton Mifflin Company.

Excerpt from "Degrees: Who Needs Them?" by Blanche Blank, Autumn, 1972, *AAUP Bulletin*, a publication of the American Association of University Professors. Reprinted by permission.

"Facing Violence" by Michael T. Kaufman, *The New York Times Magazine*, May 13, 1984. Copyright © 1984 by The New York Times Company. Reprinted by permission.

"Medicine's Second Revolution" by Lewis Thomas. From *Science84*, November, 1984, vol. 5, no. 9. Reprinted by permission of Harold Ober Associates, Incorporated. Copyright © 1984 by Lewis Thomas.

"Scientific Fraud and the Fight to Be First" by Robert K. Merton. From *The Times Literary Supplement*, November 2, 1984. Reprinted, by permission, from "The Times Literary Supplement," London. © Times Newspapers Limited, 1984.

"More People Waiting to Marry," *The New York Times*, August 27, 1984. Copyright © 1984 by The New York Times Company. Reprinted by permission.

"Must Doctors Serve Where They're Told?" by Harry Schwartz, *The New York Times*. © 1980 by the New York Times Company. Reprinted by permission.

"Holdup Man Tells Detectives How to Do It" by Selwyn Raab, *The New York Times*, March 5, 1975. © 1975 by The New York Times Company. Reprinted by permission.

"2-Year House Arrest Instead of Jail Term Is Ordered for Fraud" by Jesus Rangel, *The New York Times*, September 24, 1985. Copyright © 1985 by The New York Times Company. Reprinted by permission.

"The Social Responsibility of Scientists" by Bertrand Russell from *Fact and Fiction*. Reprinted by permission of Allen & Unwin.

Excerpt from "Heirs of General Practice" from *Table of Contents* by John McPhee. Copyrights © 1980, 1981, 1982, 1983, 1984, 1985 by John McPhee. Originally appeared in *The New Yorker*. Reprinted by permission of Farrar, Straus and Giroux, Inc.

Excerpt from "Terrorism and Public Policy" by Robert H. Kupperman from *American Violence and Public Policy: An Update on the Prevention of Violence*, edited by Lynn Curtis, Yale University Press. Reprinted by permission.

Acknowledgments and copyrights continue at the back of the book on pages 462–463, which constitute an extension of the copyright page.

Preface

When I wrote the first edition of *Writing from Sources* in the early 1980s, I derived its design from my experience teaching freshman composition courses at several colleges in the New York City area—Borough of Manhattan Community College, Montclair State College, the State University of New York at Purchase, and, primarily, Herbert H. Lehman College—over a period of eleven years. Most of the students who tested the original materials had completed (or been exempted from) a first term of freshman composition. Neither advanced nor remedial, they resembled the typical freshmen of the 1980s. Although intelligent, more often than not they had been poorly prepared for college work, were uncomfortable expressing themselves in writing, and lacked the skills to work with the disparate sources and abstract ideas encountered in college reading. Inexperienced in analysis and synthesis, such students tend to feel impotent and frustrated when confronted by term paper assignments, whether in English courses or in other disciplines. The object of *Writing from Sources* is to provide such students with the tools to do successful academic writing and thus to raise the standard of writing in all college courses.

Writing an essay based on sources depends on a complex group of skills. In most college courses, students are less often asked to do independent thinking than they are required to work with assigned sources—textbooks, lecture notes, and outside readings. The same is true of the professional writing that will be part of their future careers; occasionally they may be asked to initiate and develop original ideas, but far more often they will need to use skills of analysis and synthesis to explain, evaluate, and integrate opinions and facts taken from other sources. In eleven years of teaching composition, I rarely encountered a student who could—at the beginning of the term—pinpoint and paraphrase the key ideas of an essay, evaluate a group of readings, or undertake the extended synthesis necessary for presenting research. Rather, the freshman research essay typically contains "anthologies" of quotations strung together with little indication of their relationship. Few students know how to determine where the author's thought leaves off and their own interpretation begins or how to combine facts and ideas culled from several authors in a single paragraph.

Traditional methods of structuring the composition course have not been effective in teaching these skills. In the typical freshman course, as it was conceived when I was in college and as it is still taught today, the research essay is customarily regarded as a separate assignment, almost as an afterthought, to be saved for the end of the term. The skills required for working with source materials rarely get integrated into the first part of the course, which is often reserved for an exploration of rhetorical modes, with a single reading (or at most a comparison of two essays) serving as the basis of the early assignments. At the end of the term, when the research essay is suddenly introduced, students find the switch to multiple sources frightening, an unfair test of abilities that they have not been given the opportunity or the means to develop. Moreover, when the research essay is at last assigned, what is generally emphasized is library research. The locating of sources, however, is largely a mechanical process, unlikely in itself to teach students much about the skills connected with thinking or writing about what they have read. It is pointless to teach students how to compile an impressive bibliography if, when the time comes to select materials and integrate them into a coherent essay, they simply produce the familiar string of end-to-end quotations.

The last few weeks of the term is not the time to begin showing students how to understand, integrate, and present the fruits of their research. To make the research essay the natural conclusion to the composition course, the students' work should be structured around sources throughout the term, with major emphasis on the analysis and synthesis of ideas and evidence. *Writing from Sources* assumes that students learn best if skills are presented gradually, in lessons and assignments of progressive difficulty. Thus, comprehension and organizational skills are broken into isolated units and presented in discrete stages. In this sequential approach, each technique is first considered as an end in itself, to be explained, demonstrated, and practiced in isolation, like the skills necessary for mastering a sport. For example, the use of quotation is thoroughly taught and applied before the student learns about paraphrase. Simple operations get practiced again and again so that they have become automatic before the student goes on to attempt more complex variations.

Part I of the second edition—Making Your Sources Your Own—introduces students to all the skills necessary for working with written source materials: basic comprehension, including annotation; outlining a source's structure; summary; quotation; paraphrase; and avoiding plagiarism. After mastering the objective summary of a single source, students learn to incorporate quotation and paraphrase into their summaries.

In Part II—Writing from Sources—students are taught to write about a single source, using techniques of rebuttal, analysis, and interpretation, and eventually moving step-by-step through the stages of the writing process. Next, they are introduced to the synthesis of several sources in an essay controlled by the student's own thesis and voice. The chapter on the multiple-source essay is followed by a number of supplementary exercises and assignments, with relatively simple materials for synthesis taken from interviews, brief written statements by students, and newspaper articles. Since synthesis is the single most difficult skill in academic writing, the object here is to provide students with compatible materials and thus encourage accurate and coherent integration of sources.

Part III consolidates all the individual skills presented in the earlier chapters, as students turn to the formal research essay. By now, both the writing process and the handling of sources have become so familiar that students can focus on the evaluation and selection of sources gathered through research and, finally, on the various ways to document their sources. (Here again students are alerted to the danger of plagiarism.) While the chapter on documentation emphasizes the new MLA method of parenthetical notes, there is an appendix containing a detailed description of footnotes and endnotes, with examples, as well as a shorter explanation of APA documentation. Each of the major methods of documentation is illustrated in one of the three sample research essays, which comprise a historical narrative, an argument based on a contemporary issue, and an analysis of scientific explanations of a natural phenomenon. There is also an appendix containing a bibliography of useful source materials such as encyclopedias, indexes, and abstracts for a variety of disciplines, as well as an appendix describing how to write from sources on essay examinations.

This second edition of *Writing from Sources* has been improved in several ways. First, in response to suggestions from many instructors, the new edition is more streamlined. It still combines the advantages of a text, a reader, an exercise book, and a research-essay handbook. In the new edition, there are still more than enough assignments and exercises to keep the average class busy for a semester. However, many of the exercises contain fewer options and alternative versions, so that students—and instructors—will not feel overwhelmed by choice. The format of the most popular and effective exercises and assignments remains the same, but new reading materials have been provided for most of them.

In fact, about two-thirds of all the readings in this edition are new. *Writing from Sources* again contains a sufficient number of reprinted articles and essays to make supplements and handouts unnecessary. This time the authors range from Niccolo Machiavelli and Francis Bacon to Lewis Thomas, John McPhee, and Judith Crist. The readings and sample research essays illustrating typical academic writing are drawn from an even greater variety of disciplines than before; topics include deindustrialization (economics), the Lake Tunguskan phenomenon (astronomy), prison culture (sociology), the Crystal Palace Exhibition (history), the role of the modern doctor (biomedicine), terrorism (political science), grading standards and compulsory attendance (education), sports violence (psychology), criminal justice (philosophy), scientific fraud (history of science), and anorexia/bulimia (women's studies). As it did in the first edition, the text can serve as a case book, with enough articles on different themes for students to complete a "research" essay assignment without using the library. This time the two broad topics are sports and criminal justice.

Other changes in the second edition include strengthened coverage of the problem of plagiarism—a matter that many students need help with—and, as already mentioned, coverage of the new MLA method of documentation. The appendix on writing from sources during examinations expands upon the treatment of this topic in the previous edition.

Finally, the second edition omits the overview of the writing process—Part I in the first edition—containing a step-by-step description of how to write a short essay that is *not* based on sources. Many instructors found that their students were accustomed to writing essays based on their own ideas and experiences, and were eager to begin writing from sources. Skills such as topic narrowing, thesis writing, and outlining were, in fact, taught later in the text, in connection with the writing of the single- and multiple-source essays, as well as the research essay. And so a preliminary overview, while useful in some cases, was not really essential—and it certainly contributed to the weight of the text!

As I complete the second edition of *Writing from Sources*, I remain grateful to all of the hundreds of my students who first taught me how to teach the research essay and to all of the thousands of students using the first edition, who, through their instructors, suggested changes that have resulted in a more useful and effective textbook. I would especially like to thank the following instructors, who kindly offered advice during the preparation of the second edition: Paul Allen of the College of Charleston, Anita Anger of the University of Massachusetts—Boston, Lynn Bryce of St. Cloud State University, Mary Cermak of the University of the District of Columbia, Bill Farmer of Pasadena City College, Ellen Sprechman of Florida Atlantic University, Barbara Weaver of Ball State University, Deanna White of the University of Texas at San Antonio, and William Woods of Wichita State University. Others to whom I am grateful include my editors at St. Martin's Press—Nancy Perry, Michael Weber, and Julie Nord; my research assistants—Doris Hunt and Amy Mikula; and the friends who helped to sustain my erratic progress through the writing of this book—Richard Barsam, Diane Dettmore, Alice Morgan, Dane Morgan, William Myrick, Sondra Olsen, and Eve Zarin.

For the past two years, I have been a full-time administrator in the Office of Academic Affairs of the City University of New York. In some ways, I regret the loss of daily contact with students and their writing. But the daily preparation of professional memos, correspondence, and reports has reinforced the conviction derived from my teaching experience that the methods described in *Writing from Sources* actually work. I also followed my own step-by-step techniques as I worked on term papers for several recent courses in educational administration. The process was far easier and the essays—and grades—infinitely superior to anything that I produced in earlier incarnations as an undergraduate and graduate student. I can therefore cite my own example when I urge both instructors and students to become active participants in the process of writing from sources and to observe the increased facility—and pleasure—with which they pursue their academic and professional writing.

Brenda Spatt

Contents

Appendix C. Writing Essay Examinations   455

Index   465

List of Assignments, Examples, and Exercises (Including Readings)

CHAPTER 2

CHAPTER 3

CHAPTER 4

CHAPTER 5

CHAPTER 6

CHAPTER 7

CHAPTER 8

CHAPTER 9

CHAPTER 10

Introduction

Every day, as you talk, write, and work, you use sources. Most of the knowledge and many of the ideas that you express to others originate outside yourself. You have learned from your formal schooling and, even more, from observing the world around you, from reading, from watching television and movies, and from a multitude of other experiences. Most of the time, you use what you have learned from sources casually, almost automatically. You do not consciously think about where you got the information; you simply go about your activities, communicating with others and making decisions on the basis of your acquired knowledge.

In college, however, using sources becomes more concentrated and deliberate. Each course bombards you with countless new facts and ideas, coming from many places and all competing for your attention. Your success depends on how well you can develop certain skills—understanding what you read and hear in your courses, distinguishing the more important from the less important, relating new facts or ideas to what you already have learned, and, especially, communicating your findings to others. This book is intended to help you build all of those skills, with particular emphasis on the last.

Most college writing is both informative and interpretive; that is, it contains in varying proportions material that you take from sources and ideas that are your own. Depending on the individual course and assignment, a college paper may emphasize your own conclusions supported by knowledge you have gathered, or it may emphasize the gathered knowledge, showing that you have mastered a certain body of information. In any case it will contain something of others and something of you. If twenty students in your class are all assigned the same topic, the other nineteen papers will all be somewhat different from yours.

Instructors sometimes assign papers to test your knowledge, but that is not usually the primary reason. The main purpose of college writing assignments is to help you consolidate what you have learned and to expand your capacity for constructive thinking and clear communication—for making sense of things and conveying that sense to others. These are not merely academic skills; there are few careers in which success does not depend directly on these abilities. You will listen to the opinions of your boss, your colleagues, and your customers; or read the case histories of your clients or patients; or study the marketing reports of your salespeople or the product specifications of your suppliers; or perhaps even analyze the papers of your students! Whatever your job, the decisions that you make and the actions that you take will depend on your ability to understand and evaluate what your sources are saying (whether orally or in writing), to recognize any important pattern or theme, and to form conclusions. As you build on other people's ideas, you certainly will be expected to remember which facts and opinions came from which source and to give appropriate credit. Chances are that you will also be expected to be capable of drafting the memo, the letter, the report, the case history that will summarize your data and present and support your conclusions.

To help you see the connection between college and professional writing, here are some typical essay topics for various college courses, each followed by a parallel writing assignment that you might have to do on the job. Notice that all of the pairs of assignments call for much the same skills: the writer must consult a variety of sources, present what he or she has learned from those sources, and interpret that knowledge in the light of experience.

Assignment	Sources
For a political science course, you choose a law presently being debated in Congress or the state legislature, and argue for its passage.	debates Congressional Record
[As a lobbyist, consumer advocate, or public relations expert, you prepare a pamphlet to arouse public interest in your agency's program.]	editorials periodical articles your own opinions
For a health sciences course, you summarize present knowledge about the appropriate circumstances for prescribing tranquilizers and suggest some safeguards for their use.	books journals government reports pharmaceutical industry reports
[As a member of a medical research team, you draft a report summarizing present knowledge about a specific medication and suggesting likely directions for your team's research.]	

For a psychology course, you analyze the positive
and negative effects of peer group pressure.
[As a social worker attached to a halfway house
for adolescents, you write a case history of
three boys, determining whether they are to be
sent to separate homes or kept in the same facility.]

textbooks
journals
case studies
interviews
personal experi-
ences

For a business management course, you decide
which department or service of your college
would be the likeliest candidate for elimination
if the college budget were cut by 3 percent next
year; you defend your choice.
[As an assistant to a management consultant, you
draft a memo recommending measures to save a
manufacturing company that is in severe financial trouble.]

ledgers
interviews
newspapers
journals

For a sociology or history course, you compare
reactions to unemployment in 1980 with reactions in 1930.
[As a staff member in the social services agency of
a small city, you prepare a report on the social
consequences that would result from the closing of a major factory.]

newspapers
magazines
books
interviews

For a physical education course, you classify the
ways in which a team can react to a losing
streak and recommend some ways in which
coaches can maintain team morale.
[As a member of a special committee of physical-
education teachers for your area, you help plan
an action paper that will improve your district's
performance in interscholastic sports.]

textbooks
articles
observation and
personal
experience

For an anthropology course, you contrast the
system of punishment used by a tribe that you
have studied with the penal code used in your
home or college town.
[As assistant to the head of the local correction
agency, you prepare a report comparing the
success of eight minimum-security prisons
around the country.]

textbooks
lectures
articles
observation and
personal
experience

For a physics course, you write a definition of
"black holes" and explain why they were dis-

covered in the middle of the twentieth century—not earlier, not later.
[As a physicist working for a university research
team, you write a grant application based on an
imminent breakthrough in your field.]

books
journals

For a nutrition course, you explain why adolescents prefer junk food.
[As a dietician attached to the cafeteria of a local
high school, you write a memo that accounts
for the increasing waste of food and recom-
mends changes in the lunch menu.]

textbooks
articles
interviews
observation

For an engineering course, you describe changes
and improvements in techniques of American
coal mining over the last hundred years.
[As a mining engineer, you write a report determining whether it is cost-effective for your
company to take over the derelict mine that
you were sent to survey.]

books
articles
observation and
experience

Because you will need to use reading and writing skills throughout your academic and professional life, *Writing from Sources* will help you learn the basic procedures that are common to all kinds of academic and professional writing and will provide enough practice in these skills to enable you to write from sources confidently and successfully. Here are the basic skills.

1. *choosing a topic:* deciding what you are actually writing about; interpreting the requests of your instructor, boss, or client, and determining the scope and limits of the assignment; making the project manageable.
2. *finding sources and acquiring information:* deciding how much supporting information you are going to need (if any) and locating it; evaluating sources and determining which are most suitable and trustworthy for your purpose; taking notes on your sources and on your own reactions.
3. *deciding on a thesis:* determining the purpose and main idea of what you are writing and your probable conclusions; redefining the scope and objective in the light of what you have learned from your sources.
4. *taking notes:* presenting your sources through summary, outline, paraphrase, and quotation; learning when each skill is most appropriate.

5. *organizing your material:* determining what must be included and what may be eliminated; arranging your evidence in the most efficient and convincing way, so that your reader will reach the same conclusions as you; calling attention to common patterns and ideas that will reinforce your thesis; making sure that your presentation has a beginning, middle, and end, and that the stages are in logical order.

6. *writing your assignment:* breaking down the mass of information into easily absorbed units or paragraphs; constructing each paragraph so that the reader will receive a general idea that will advance your thesis, as well as providing supporting examples and details that will make the thesis convincing.

7. *giving credit to your sources:* ensuring that your reader knows who is responsible for which idea, distinguishing between the evidence of your sources and your own interpretation and evaluation; assessing the relative reliability and usefulness of each source so that the reader can appreciate your basis for judgment.

This list of skills may seem overwhelming right now. But remember: you will be learning these procedures gradually. In Part I, you will learn how to get the most out of what you read and how to use the skills of summary, quotation, and paraphrase to provide accurate accounts of your sources. In Part II you will begin to apply these skills as you prepare an essay based on a single reading and then a synthesis essay drawing on a group of sources. Finally, in Part III, you will go to the library to locate your own sources and begin the complex process of research. From the beginning to the end of the term, you will be practicing the same basic writing skills. The gradual increase in the number of sources will make each stage of the process more complex and demanding, but not essentially different.

The best way to gain confidence and facility in writing from sources is to master each skill so thoroughly that it becomes automatic, like riding a bicycle or driving a car. To help you break the task down into workable units, each procedure will first be illustrated with a variety of models and then followed by exercises to give you as much practice as you need before going on to the next step. As you go on to write essays for other courses, you'll discover that you can concentrate more and more on *what* you are writing and forget about *how* to write from sources, for these methods will have become natural and automatic.

WRITING
FROM
SOURCES
Second Edition

Part I
MAKING YOUR SOURCES YOUR OWN

Academic writers continually study and use the ideas of others. However good and original their own ideas may be, academic writers are obliged to explore the work of authorities in their field, to estimate its value and its relevance to their own work, and then to place the ideas and the words of others side by side with their own. The overall term that describes this procedure is *research*.

Except in creative writing courses, your college teachers will rarely ask you to write without a preliminary stage of careful reading and analysis. In order to make use of another person's ideas in developing your own work, you must be able to appreciate (and even temporarily share) that person's point of view. Naturally, you must be willing to read extensively and be able to understand what you read. In Chapter 1, you will learn to distinguish the main ideas of an essay and to grasp the strategy and the whole plan of its development. One useful measurement of your comprehension is the ability to sum up a group of related ideas briefly, yet completely. Chapter 1 ends with some practice in presenting a source through *summary*.

In order to make use of what you have learned from your reading and to write about your sources in essays, you must become familiar with the two other basic methods of presenting sources—

quotation and *paraphrase*. Your objective is fair representation. You must make it clear to your reader whether a specific idea, sentence, or group of sentences is the product of your work or that of another. By using quotation or paraphrase and by including the source's name, you avoid the dishonest "borrowings" associated with plagiarism, which can only occur when the reader cannot determine who is responsible for what and thus gives you credit for more work than you have actually done.

Distinguishing carefully between your sources and yourself serves to protect three major interests:

- it is in your own interest to receive credit for organizing and presenting an essay and for the original ideas within it;
- it is in your source's interest to receive credit for certain clearly identified contributions to your essay—both ideas and words;
- it is in your reader's interest to be able to read your essay easily and painlessly and to distinguish between your work and that of your sources without any confusion.

Chapter 2 discusses quotation and paraphrase. *Quotation* makes clear that someone else is responsible for the precise phrasing, as well as the ideas contained in the quoted sentences. Through *paraphrase*, you express the ideas of others in your own words and thus demonstrate your mastery of the source and your ability to integrate these ideas into your own work. But whether you paraphrase or you quote, you must always acknowledge your source by including a clear citation of the writer's name. Although these methods of presentation are somewhat technical, calling for a high standard of accuracy, they are used throughout the academic world and also in professional writing. You will use them again and again, and with practice they will become automatic.

These chapters do not assign essays for you to write. Rather, they show how to read a source, identify key facts and points, and extract them from the source in various forms. Later you will see how those facts and points can serve as material for your own writing.

1.
Reading for Understanding

Before class began, I happened to walk around the room and I glanced at some of the books lying open on the desks. Not one book had a mark in it! Not one underlining! Every page was absolutely clean! These twenty-five students had all read it. They all knew that there'd be an exam at the end of the week; and yet not one of them had had the sense to make a marginal note!

Teacher of an English honors class

Why should this teacher have been so horrified? The students had fulfilled their part of the college contract by reading the book and coming to class. Why write anything down, they might argue, when the ideas are already printed on the page. All you have to do is to read the assignment and, later on, review the material by skimming through it again. Sometimes it pays to underline an important point or two; but that's only necessary for very long chapters, so that you don't have to read every word all over again. Taking notes wastes a lot of time, and, anyway, there's never much space in the margins.

The last point is true: narrow margins discourage students from taking frequent and legible notes. But the other comments all come from passive readers who think that they are doing their work by letting their eyes rove over every page, line after line, chapter after chapter, until the entire assignment has been "read." In fact, they are *looking*, not reading. Effective reading—reading that is active, not passive—requires concentration and the deliberate application of your mind to the material that is being absorbed. Reading is hard work. To respond to what you are learning and to participate in a mental dialogue between yourself and the author of your source is challenging and difficult. But only this kind of participation can prevent your eyes from glazing over and your thoughts from wandering off to next weekend or next summer.

As with any job, doing it seems much less of a strain if you have a product to show for your labors. In active reading, this product is notes: the result of contact (even friction) between your mind and the author's. As you read and reread you should be alert to pick up ideas that make you react. You should pause frequently—not to take a break but to think about and respond to what you have read. If the reading has been difficult, these pauses will provide time for you to consider the problems and figure out the questions that you should ask yourself in order to achieve full understanding. And, as you read, your pencil should always be in your hand (assuming that you *own* the text), and a visible product should accumulate in the form of lines, checks, and comments in and around what you are reading. When you use borrowed books, take notes on paper.

UNDERLINING

Underlining can be a sophisticated analytical skill. Its primary purpose is selection and emphasis. You are distinguishing between what is important (and presumably worth rereading) and what you can skip past on later readings. Such discrimination is never easy. In fact, it cannot really be achieved on a first reading, since at that point you can have little idea of what is crucial to the work's main ideas.

On the other hand, underlining can also be the most primitive form of participation in reading. It can even be done while the reader is half-asleep: ideas do not have to register in the brain in order to make the pencil move across the page. Too often, underlining merely represents so many minutes spent on the task: the pencil running over the page documents the fact that the eyes have run over the same lines. Many pages are underlined or colored with "hi-liter" so extensively that there is hardly anything left over. Everything has been selected for review and retention—another product of passive reading.

Remember that the usefulness of underlining is selection. Some points are worth reviewing and some are not. Try underlining, and also circling and bracketing words and phrases that seem to you worth rereading and remembering, such as important generalizations and topic sentences, examples that have helped you understand a difficult point, or transitional phrases, where the argument changes. Or, in contrast, try "underlining" with an unobtrusive series of checks in the margin. Either way, deciding what to mark is the important part of the process.

ANNOTATING

Annotation refers to the comments written in the margins, specifically those notes in which the reader interprets, evaluates, or questions the author's meaning, defines a word or phrase, or clarifies a point. You are annotating when you insert short explanations, summaries, or definitions in the margin. You are also annotating when you introduce something of your own: a question or counter-argument, perhaps, or a point for comparison. Annotation is different from taking notes on a separate page (a procedure which will be discussed at length in Chapter Eight). Not every reading deserves to be annotated. Since the process takes a good deal of time and concentration, reserve your marginal notes for material that is especially difficult or stimulating.

Marginal notes work best if they serve as an aid to your memory, reminding you of ideas that you have already assimilated. Sometimes, for example, your notes will do no more than condense sentences and provide a short version of the major ideas of the text. At the other extreme, notes in the margin can remind you of where you disagreed with the author, looked at the ideas in a new way, or thought of fresh evidence.

Finally, no matter what kind of marginal notes you write, try always to use your own words instead of copying or abbreviating a phrase from the text itself. You will remember the point more easily if you have made the effort to express it yourself.

Here is an example of a passage that has been annotated. Certain difficult words have been defined; a few ideas have been summarized; some problems and questions have been raised.

THE MOTOR INDUSTRY

= untapped --
an instinct for travel?

Once the cheap car was available, the enormous latent demand hitherto unrealized for individual, family, and goods transport on the roads gave rise to a whole new industry. This should serve as an example of the lack of knowledge of the capitalist entrepreneur of where profits could be found. There is no way of assessing the real need for a new product unless a sufficient number of prototypes is available. But to supply these requires investment in plant, and the difficulty under capitalism has always been to finance such early stages. The result is that the great delay between first invention and first effective use is largely due to these purely financial considerations. *widespread? efficient?*

= risk-taker
= original model

The essential problem under capitalism of financing early stages of inventions depends on the expected return on investment. Even with as slow a return on capital as three percent, it will hardly pay to put up money for anything that has a reasonable chance of bringing in money only after thirty years. Even then the return would have to be at least ten times the original investment to make it worthwhile. If the devel-

true?
mar- ing make thing fitable rock -of out- ons f t of and ntial profit ence?
profitable?

opment is not a certainty the prospect of finding backers in the early stages is even less. Only quick-return prospects are really worthwhile, and except in fields like antibiotics rarely involve any radically new principle. With money doled out slowly the technical difficulties tend to hold up the new developments, and hence to make them still less profitable. For the ultimate profit has to be made quickly even for patented inventions, for afterwards it goes to the cautious investors, who will put their money only on proved successes. As a result, even in the twentieth century, the average time between the essential idea and the commercial pay-off remains about a generation. Whittle had the idea of the jet engine in the early thirties. It was developed slowly for lack of funds and, despite the military need, was hardly ready by the end of the war. The situation would be different if a very large investor, which in these days could be only the State, intervened. By putting more money in at the beginning, even though most of it would be lost on failures, the development time on the remainder would be cut so short that it would pay for everything even at high rates of interest. As socialist governments get into their stride they will win the race for industrial advances unless capitalist governments change their habits or even their natures to catch up with them.

Once the profitability of motor manufacture was proved capital flowed in readily enough. A new industry grew up which was in a few years to outstrip the older engineering industries, and in large measure to absorb them. The automobile industry was, from the moment of its popular success, highly concentrated, for only the very largest concerns could meet the market demand. Alongside the new chemical and electrical combines the automobile industry took its place at the very center of monopoly capitalism. It is interesting, but not very surprising, to note that the first large-scale development of the motor-car came practically at the end of the development of the internal-combustion engine, for, with minor modifications in performance, of an essentially technical nature, it still remains what it was in 1880. What is radically new is not the car itself, however its appearance may have changed, but the mass-production methods of manufacturing it, to which we return later. The further technical development of the internal-combustion engine into the internal-combustion turbine was to come from another quarter, that of aviation.

J. D. Bernal, from *Science in History, III*

Margin annotations:
cautious!
Is Bernal's tone at all critical? Contrary to speculator image, investors sound timid
or giant corporations are socialist gov'ts more likely to assume risks? why.
vicious cy
time 20 yrs
atom another exam
unh of 10 of ago
commercial development waits until product is refined? or marketable

---

EXERCISE 1

Read the following passage carefully. Then reread it, underlining and circling key ideas and inserting annotations in the margins.

The enjoyment of physical possession of things would seem to be one of the prerogatives of wealth which has been little impaired. Presumably nothing has happened to keep the man who can afford them from enjoying his Rembrandts and his home-grown orchids. But enjoyment of things has always been intimately associated with [another] prerogative of wealth which is the distinction that it confers. In a world where nearly everyone was poor, this distinction was very great. It was the natural consequence of rarity. In England, it is widely agreed, the ducal families are not uniformly superior. There is a roughly normal incidence of intelligence and stupidity, good taste and bad, and morality, immorality, homosexuality, and incest. But very few people are dukes or even duchesses, although the latter have become rather more frequent with the modern easing of the divorce laws. As a result, even though they may be intrinsically unexceptional, they are regarded with some residual awe. So it has long been with the rich. Were dukes numerous, their position would deteriorate irretrievably. As the rich have become more numerous, they have inevitably become a debased currency.

Moreover, wealth has never been a sufficient source of honor in itself. It must be advertised, and the normal medium is obtrusively expensive goods. In the latter part of the last century in the United States, this advertisement was conducted with virtuosity. Housing, equipage, female adornment and recreation were all brought to its service. Expensiveness was keenly emphasized. "We are told now that Mr. Gould's '$500,000 yacht' has entered a certain harbor, or that Mr. Morgan has set off on a journey in his '$100,000 palace car,' or that Mr. Vanderbilt's '$2,000,000 home' is nearing completion, with its '$50,000 paintings' and its '$20,000 bronze doors.'" The great houses, the great yachts, the great balls, the stables, and the expansive jewel-encrusted bosoms were all used to identify the individual as having a claim to the honors of wealth.

Such display is now passé. There was an adventitious contributing cause. The American well-to-do have long been curiously sensitive to fear of expropriation—a fear which may be related to the tendency for even the mildest reformist measures to be viewed, in the conservative conventional wisdom, as the portents of revolution. The Depression and especially the New Deal gave the American rich a serious fright. One consequence was to usher in a period of marked discretion in personal expenditure. Purely ostentatious outlays, especially on dwellings, yachts and associated females, were believed likely to incite the masses to violence. They were rebuked as unwise and improper by the more discreet. It was much wiser to take on the protective coloration of the useful citizen, the industrial statesman, or even the average guy.

However, deeper causes were at work. Increasingly, in the last quarter century, the display of expensive goods, as a device for suggesting wealth, has been condemned as vulgar. The term is precise. Vulgar means: "Of or pertaining to the common people, or to the common herd or crowd." And this explains what happened. Lush expenditure could be afforded by so many that it ceased to be useful as a mark of distinction. An elongated, richly upholstered and extremely high-powered automobile conveys no impression of wealth in a day when such automobiles are mass-produced by the thousands. A house in Palm Beach is not a source of distinction when the rates for a thousand hotel rooms in Miami Beach rival its daily upkeep. Once a sufficiently impressive display of diamonds could create attention even for the most obese and repellent body, for they signified membership in a highly privileged caste. Now the same diamonds are afforded by a television star or a talented harlot. Modern mass communications, especially the movies and television, insure that the populace at large will see the most lavish caparisoning on the bodies not only of the daughters of the rich but also on the daughters of coal miners and commercial travelers who have struck it rich by their own talents or some facsimile thereof. In South America, in the Middle East, to a degree in socialist India, and at Nice, Cannes and Deauville, ostentatious display by those of wealth is still much practiced. This accords with expectations. In these countries, most people are still, in the main, poor and unable to afford the goods which advertise wealth. Therefore, ostentation continues to have a purpose. In not being accessible to too many people, it has not yet become vulgar.

The American of wealth is not wholly without advantages in his search for distinction. Wealth still brings attention if devoted to cultural and technical pursuits or to hobbies with a utilitarian aspect. A well-to-do American may gain in esteem from an admirably run farm, although never from an admirably manicured estate. He will be honored for magnificent and imaginative cow stables, although rarely for luxurious horse stables. Although wealth aids a public career, those who too patently rely on it are regarded as slightly inferior public citizens. A Rockefeller or a Kennedy who is elected to public office enjoys a prestige far in excess of an Aldrich or a Whitney whose appointment to an ambassadorial position, however justified on merit, might have been less certain in the absence of sizable campaign contributions. In sum, although ostentatious and elaborate expenditure, in conjunction with the wealth that sustained it, was once an assured source of distinction, it is so no longer. The effect on attitudes toward inequality will be evident. Ostentatious expenditure focused the attention of the poor on the wealth of the wealthy, for this of course was its purpose. With the decline of ostentation, or its vulgarization, wealth and hence inequality were no longer flagrantly advertised. Being less advertised, they were less noticed and less resented. The rich had helped to make inequality an issue. Now they were no longer impelled to do so.

J. K. Galbraith, *The Affluent Society*, 1976

ASKING QUESTIONS

In order to read actively and to understand what you read, ask yourself questions about your source and try to answer them. Sometimes you may wish to write your answers down; sometimes answering your questions in your head is enough. The following questions are typical:

What does this word mean?
How should I understand that phrase?
What is the topic sentence of the paragraph?
What is the relationship between these two points?
What is this transitional word telling me?
This concept is difficult: how would I express it in my own words?
Is this point a digression from the main idea, or does it fit in with what I've already read?
Can the whole page be summarized briefly?
Does the essay have a main idea—a thesis? Is the writer trying to make a particular point?

As this partial list suggests, you can best understand what you read by sweeping your mind back and forth between a specific sentence on the page and the larger context of the whole paragraph, essay, or book. You can seriously mislead yourself and your reader if you interpret ideas out of context, ignoring the way in which they fit into the work as a whole.

Thorough comprehension takes time and careful reading. In fact, it is usually on the *second* reading, when you have some sense of the overall meaning and structure of the work, that questions begin to pop into your head and your reading rate slows down. Being a fast reader is not necessarily an advantage.

Read "A Question of Degree" once, and then go over it more slowly a second time. During your second reading, look at the comprehension questions that follow the essay and attempt to answer them in your head. Some of these questions may seem very subtle to you, and you may wonder whether you would have thought of all of them. But they are model questions, intended to demonstrate what *could* be asked in order to gain an especially thorough understanding of the essay. Think of your own answer to each question.

A QUESTION OF DEGREE

Perhaps we should rethink an idea fast becoming an undisputed   1
premise of American life: that a college degree is a necessary (and perhaps even a sufficient) precondition for success. I do not wish to quar-
rel with the assumptions made about the benefits of orthodox education. I want only to expose its false god: the four-year, all-purpose,
degree-granting college, aimed at the so-called college-age population
and by now almost universally accepted as *the* stepping-stone to
"meaningful" and "better" jobs.

What is wrong with the current college/work cycle can be seen in   2
the following anomalies: we are selling college to the youth of America
as a take-off pad for the material good life. College is literally advertised and packaged as a means for getting more money through "better" jobs at the same time that Harvard graduates are taking jobs as taxi
drivers. This situation is a perversion of the true spirit of a university, a
perversion of a humane social ethic and, at bottom, a patent fraud. To
take the last point first, the economy simply is not geared to guaranteeing these presumptive "better" jobs; the colleges are not geared to
training for such jobs; and the ethical propriety of the entire enterprise
is very questionable. We are by definition (rather than by analysis) establishing two kinds of work: work labeled "better" because it has a
degree requirement tagged to it and nondegree work, which, through
this logic, becomes automatically "low level."

This process is also destroying our universities. The "practical cur-   3
riculum" must become paramount; the students must become prisoners; the colleges must become servants of big business and big government. Under these conditions the university can no longer be an
independent source of scientific and philosophic truth-seeking and
moral criticism.

Finally, and most important, we are destroying the spirit of youth by   4
making college compulsory at adolescence, when it may be least congruent with emotional and physical needs; and we are denying college
as an optional and continuing experience later in life, when it might be
most congruent with intellectual and recreational needs.

Let me propose an important step to reverse these trends and thus   5
help restore freedom and dignity to both our colleges and our work-
places. We should outlaw employment discrimination based on college degrees. This would simply be another facet of our "equal-
opportunity" policy and would add college degrees to sex, age, race,
religion and ethnic group as inherently unfair bases for employment
selection.

People would, wherever possible, demonstrate their capacities on   6
the job. Where that proved impractical, outside tests could still serve.
The medical boards, bar exams, mechanical, mathematical and verbal
aptitude tests might still be used by various enterprises. The burden of

proof of their legitimacy, however, would remain with the *using* agencies. So too would the costs. Where the colleges were best equipped to impart a necessary skill they would do so, but only where it would be natural to the main thrust of a university endeavor.

The need for this rethinking and for this type of legislation may best 7
be illustrated by a case study. Joe V. is a typical liberal-arts graduate, fired by imaginative art and literature. He took a job with a large New York City bank, where he had the opportunity to enter the "assistant manager training program." The trainees rotated among different bank departments to gain technical know-how and experience and also received classroom instruction, including some sessions on "how to write a business letter." The program was virtually restricted to college graduates. At the end of the line, the trainees became assistant bank managers: a position consisting largely of giving simple advice to bank customers and a modest amount of supervision of employees. Joe searched for some connection between the job and the training program, on the one hand, and his college-whetted appetites and skills on the other. He found none.

In giving Joe preference for the training program, the bank had by- 8
passed a few enthusiastic aspirants already dedicated to a banking career and daily demonstrating their competence in closely related jobs. After questioning his superiors about the system, Joe could only conclude that the "top brass" had some very diffuse and not-too-well-researched or even well-thought-out conceptions about college men. The executives admitted that a college degree did not of itself ensure the motivation or the verbal or social skills needed. Nor were they clear about what skills were most desirable for their increasingly diverse branches. Yet, they clung to the college prerequisite.

Business allows the colleges to act as recruiting, screening and train- 9
ing agencies for them because it saves money and time. Why colleges allow themselves to act as servicing agents may not be as apparent. One reason may be that colleges are increasingly becoming conventional bureaucracies. It is inevitable, therefore, that they should respond to the first and unchallenged law of bureaucracy: Expand! The more that colleges can persuade outside institutions to restrict employment in favor of their clientele, the stronger is the college's hold and attraction. This rationale becomes even clearer when we understand that the budgets of public universities hang on the number of students "serviced." Seen from this perspective, then, it is perhaps easier to understand why such matters as "university independence," or "the propriety" of using the public bankroll to support enterprises that are expected to make private profits, can be dismissed. Conflict of interest is difficult to discern when the interests involved are your own. . . .

What is equally questionable is whether a college degree, as such, is 10
proper evidence that those new skills that *are* truly needed will be de-

livered. A friend who works for the Manpower Training Program feels that there is a clear divide between actual job needs and college-degree requirements. One of her chief frustrations is the knowledge that many persons with the ability to do paraprofessional mental-health work are lost to jobs they could hold with pleasure and profit because the training program also requires a two-year associate arts degree.

Obviously, society can and does manipulate job status. I hope that 11 we can manipulate it in favor of the greatest number of people. More energy should be spent in trying to upgrade the dignity of all socially useful work and to eliminate the use of human beings for any work that proves to be truly destructive of the human spirit. Outlawing the use of degrees as prerequisites for virtually every job that our media portray as "better" should carry us a long step toward a healthier society. Among other things, there is far more evidence that work can make college meaningful than that college can make work meaningful.

My concern about this degree/work cycle might be far less acute, 12 however, if everyone caught up in the system were having a good time. But we seem to be generating a college population that oscillates between apathy and hostility. One of the major reasons for this joylessness in our university life is that the students see themselves as prisoners of economic necessity. They have bought the media messages about better jobs, and so they do their time. But the promised land of "better" jobs is, on the one hand, not materializing; and on the other hand the student is by now socialized to find such "better" jobs distasteful even if they were to materialize.

One of the major improvements that could result from the proposed 13 legislation against degree requirements for employment would be a new stocktaking on the part of all our educational agencies. Compulsory schools, for example, would understand that the basic skills for work and family life in our society would have to be compressed into those years of schooling.

Colleges and universities, on the other hand, might be encouraged 14 to be as unrestricted, as continuous and as open as possible. They would be released from the pressures of ensuring economic survival through a practical curriculum. They might best be modeled after museums. Hours would be extensive, fees minimal, and services available to anyone ready to comply with course-by-course demands. Colleges under these circumstances would have a clearly understood focus, which might well be the traditional one of serving as a gathering place for those persons who want to search for philosophic and scientific "truths."

This proposal should help our universities rid themselves of some 15 strange and gratuitous practices. For example, the university would no longer have to organize itself into hierarchical levels: B.A., M.A.,

Ph.D. There would simply be courses of greater and lesser complexity in each of the disciplines. In this way graduate education might be more rationally understood and accepted for what it is—*more* education.

The new freedom might also relieve colleges of the growing practice of instituting extensive "work programs," "internships" and "independent study" programs. The very names of these enterprises are tacit admissions that the campus itself is not necessary for many genuinely educational experiences. But, along with "external degree" programs, they seem to pronounce that whatever one has learned in life by whatever diverse and interesting routes cannot be recognized as increasing one's dignity, worth, usefulness or self-enjoyment until it is converted into degree credits. 16

The legislation I propose would offer a more rational order of priorities. It would help recapture the genuine and variegated dignity of the workplace along with the genuine and more specialized dignity of the university. It should help restore to people of all ages and inclinations a sense of their own basic worth and offer them as many roads as possible to reach Rome. 17

Blanche D. Blank

Questions and Answers

Paragraph one

A. What does "false god" mean?	A. A false god is an idol that does not deserve to be worshiped.
B. In what context can a college degree be a false god?	B. Colleges are worshiped by students who believe that the degree will magically ensure a good career and a better life. Blank suggests that college degrees no longer have magic powers.
C. Why does Blank put "meaningful" and "better" in quotation marks?	C. Blank uses quotation marks around "meaningful" and "better" because she doesn't believe the adjectives are applicable; she is showing disagreement, disassociating herself through the quotation marks.

Paragraph two

D. What is an anomaly?

D. An anomaly is anything that is inconsistent with ordinary rules and standards.

E. What conclusion can be drawn from the "Harvard graduates" sentence? (Note that the obvious conclusion is not drawn at this point.)

E. If Harvard graduates are driving taxis, a degree does not ensure a high-level job.

F. What does "perversion" mean? How many perversions does Blank mention? Can you distinguish between them?

F. Perversion means distortion or corruption of what is naturally good or normally done. If degrees are regarded as vocational qualifications, the university's proper purpose will be perverted, society's conception of proper qualifications for promotion and advancement will be perverted, and, by implication, young people's belief in the reliability of rewards promised by society will be perverted.

G. In the last two sentences, what are the two types of "fraud" that are described? How would you define "fraud"?

G. One kind of fraud is the deception practiced on young college students who won't get the good jobs that they expect. A second type of fraud is practiced on workers without degrees whose efforts and successes are undervalued because of the division into "better" and "worse" jobs.

Paragraph three

H. What is the "practical curriculum"?

H. "Practical curriculum" refers to courses that will train college students for specific jobs; the term is probably being contrasted with "liberal arts."

I. What is the danger to the universities? (Use your own words.)

I. The emphasis on vocational training perverts the university's traditional pursuit of knowledge for its own sake, as it makes financing and curriculum very closely connected with the economic needs of the businesses and professions for which students will be trained.

J. What groups have suffered so far as a result of "compulsory" college?

J. Blank has so far referred to three groups: students in college; workers who have never been to college; and members of universities, both staff and students, interested in a liberal-arts curriculum.

Paragraph four

K. What new group, not mentioned before, does Blank introduce in this paragraph?

K. Blank introduces the needs of older people who might want to return to college after a working career.

Paragraph five

L. Can you explain " 'equal-opportunity' policy" in your own words?

L. Equal-opportunity policy for employment means that the only prerequisite for hiring should be the applicant's ability to perform the job.

M. What is Blank's contribution to "our 'equal-opportunity' policy?"

M. Blank suggests that a college degree does not indicate suitability for employment and therefore should be classed as discriminatory, along with sex, age, etc.

Paragraph six

N. What does "legitimacy" mean in this context?

N. If certain professions choose to test the qualifications of aspirants, professional organizations should prove that examinations are necessary and that the test results will measure the applicant's suitability for the job. These organizations should be responsible for the arrangements and the financing; at present, colleges serve as a "free" testing service.

Paragraphs seven and eight

O. What point(s) does the example of Joe help to prove?

O. Joe V.'s experience supports Blank's argument that college training is not often needed in order to perform most kinds of work. Joe V.'s expectations were also pitched too high, as Blank has suggested, while the experience of other bank employees whose place was taken by Joe exemplifies the plight of those workers without college degrees whose experience is not sufficiently valued.

Paragraph nine

P. What are the colleges' reasons for cooperating with business? (Explain in your own words.)

P. Colleges are competing for students in order to increase their enrollment; they therefore want to be able to assure applicants that many companies prefer to hire their graduates. Having become overorganized, with many levels of authority, the bureaucratic universities regard enrollment as an end in itself.

Q. What is the conflict of interest mentioned in the last sentence, and why is it hard to discern?

Q. The interests of an institution funded by the public might be said to be in conflict with the interests of a private, profit-making company; but the conflict is not apparent now that colleges choose to strengthen their connections with business.

Paragraph eleven

R. Can you restate the third sentence in your own words?

R. Instead of discriminating between kinds of workers and kinds of work, we should distinguish between work that benefits everyone and should therefore be considered admirable, and work that is degrading and dehumanizing and should, if possible, not be performed by people.

S. Is Blank recommending that everyone go to work before attending college (last sentence)?

S. Although Blanche Blank is not insisting that working is preferable to or should have priority over a college education, she implies that most people learn more significant knowledge from the work experience than from the college experience.

Paragraph twelve

T. Can you explain the meaning of "prisoners of economic necessity"?

T. Young people who believe that a degree will get them better jobs have no choice but to spend a four-year term in college, whether or not they are intellectually and temperamentally suited to the experience.

Paragraph thirteen

U. What are the "compulsory schools" and how would their role change if Blank's proposal were adopted?

U. Compulsory schools are grade and high schools, which students must attend up to a set age. If students were not automatically expected to go on to college, the lower schools would have to offer a more comprehensive and complete education than they do now.

Paragraph fourteen

V. What role does Blank envisage for the university in a healthier society? (Try not to use "museum" in your answer.)

V. Blanche Blank sees the colleges in a role quite apart from the mainstream of life. Colleges would be storehouses of tradition, to which people could go for cultural refreshment in their spare time, rather than training centers.

Paragraph fifteen

W. What are the "strange and gratuitous" practices of the universities? What purpose do they serve?

W. The universities divide the process of education into a series of clearly defined levels of attainment. Blanche Blank finds these divisions "gratuitous" or unnecessary perhaps because they are "hierarchical" and distinguish between those of greater or less achievements and status.

Paragraph seventeen

X. What, according to Blank, would be a "rational order of priorities"? Does she see any connection at all between the

X. Blanche Blank's first priority is the self-respect of the average member of society who presently may be

work experience and the educational experience?

disappointed and frustrated at not being rewarded for his work, whether at the job or at college. Another priority is the restoration of the university to its more purely intellectual role.

EXERCISE 2

Read the following essay twice, and then answer the comprehension questions that follow. (You will notice that some of the "questions" are really instructions, very much like examination questions, directing you to explain, define, or in other ways to annotate the reading.) Use complete sentences and use your own words as much as you can.

FACING VIOLENCE

1   Almost 20 years ago, when my oldest son was very young, I tried to shield the boy from violence and aggression, those alleged attributes of manliness. My wife and I had agreed to raise our children in an atmosphere of nonviolence, without playthings that simulated weapons. Then my uncle came to visit us from Israel. My uncle, unlike his wife and children, had survived Auschwitz, and he was surprised that my son had no toy guns. I tried to explain, but, asserting the moral authority of a war victim and survivor, he took my son off to Macy's to buy the biggest, noisiest toy machine gun he could find. My uncle said that if people do not go bang bang when they are young they go bang bang when they grow up.

2   Since then, we have lived in Africa and in Asia and I have seen and heard bang bang. I am not sure I fully understand what my uncle meant, but I no longer think that exposure to the symbols of death and violence causes little boys to grow up ethically impaired. In fact, now that I am living in North American civilization, where enormous energies are spent rendering death and violence either fictional or abstract, I think the greatest moral pitfall is not that we witness too much bang bang, but that, for the most part, we perceive it vicariously. We shield ourselves from real death and pain while paying to see these same things, sanitized and stylized, in the movies.

3   This idea crystallized in my mind after a conversation I had a short while ago with Jack Troake, a thoughtful man who, like his father, grandfather and great-grandfather, makes his living by fishing from his home port of Twillingate, Newfoundland. Like his ancestors and neighbors, he also used to spend the icebound winter months hunting

gray skin seals, but he does so no longer. The market for seal pelts in Europe and the United States has been destroyed because of protests launched abroad by animal-rights groups. The original protests were against the clubbing of baby white-furred seal pups, a hunt that Jack Troake never joined. Then the outcry spread to include all seals. Last year, a British supermarket chain declared it would no longer stock Canadian fish because of someone's belief that some fishermen either now hunt seals or once did.

As we sat on Mr. Troake's radar-equipped boat watching his sons 4 mend nets, he made it clear that he was flabbergasted and insulted by what he assumed to be the view of some foreigners that he and his neighbors were barbarians. "Look old boy, there's no doubt about it, I make my living killing things. We kill mackerel and cod and we used to kill seals. Now, there seems to be a bunch of people who do not like that. I imagine them sitting eating lamb chops and steak and chicken, thinking they all come neatly wrapped in plastic from some food factory. I wonder whether they have ever seen anything die or anything born, except on television and in the movies. But, to tell you the truth, old boy, I really feel sorry for those people who are so upset about this old Christian."

Me too. I left Twillingate, and in a motel that night I watched the 5 footage from Beirut. As I remember now, it contained what have become the current visual clichés of violence. Men firing bazookas around a corner at something. Smoke and rubble. Women with shopping bags walking fast across a street. Adolescent gunmen smiling into the camera from the backs of trucks. It conveyed a sense of destruction, but it stopped short of being horrible. I knew the images were authentic, but they did not seem real. They blurred into an already crowded memory bank of two-dimensional violence: Dirty Harry, the A Team, Beirut, Belfast, El Salvador, car crashes. And I thought how I, bombarded with such pictures of death, had, two years ago, backed away from the real drama of death when it touched me as something more than a witness. I had sent my own mother to die in a nursing home, among death specialists. I did not hold her as her life ebbed. Later, I consoled myself with the thought that this is what people do in a technological culture, and that, anyway, the room was clean and the doctors said she did not suffer greatly.

I recall how we used to hear that the images of the Vietnam War, 6 shown on television, sensitized the nation. Perhaps. I can recall the naked little girl running from napalm, and the man being shot by a police official in Saigon. But everything else has been jumbled in memory, and what remains are mostly recollections of what I now think of as my skin-deep shock and my pious responses. There were too many images. The only people I hear talking about Vietnam now are the ones who were there.

What I do remember is the first dead man I ever saw, a man shot and 7

aggression

bleeding on dirty stairs in New York. I remember victims of massacres in Zaire and Rhodesia, and I can recall where each of those bodies lay. I remember an Afghan freedom fighter in a hospital in Peshawar, his leg lost in a land-mine explosion. He had his rifle with him, and his 7-year-old son was on his bed touching the man's stump. The father was talking about returning to fight Soviet forces; he hoped that his son would continue the fight. For that small boy, perhaps, the moment was indeed too much bang bang, but I am no longer sure.

As for little boys playing with toy guns, I don't think it matters   8
much, one way or the other. What does matter, it seems to me, is that at some time in their formative years, maybe in high school, our children should bear witness to the everyday violence they could see, say, in an emergency ward of a big city hospital. I know it sounds extreme, but maybe our children could learn something valuable if they were taken for a day or two to visit a police station or an old-age home. It might serve as an antidote for the unreal violence on all our screens.

What would be learned, I think, is that, up close and in three dimen-   9
sions, the dead, the dying and the suffering are always to some extent "us." On the screens they always seem to be "them." I don't understand it, really, any more than my uncle's view of bang bang, but I know that as long as men die and men kill it is wrong to turn away too much. Also, I am certain that I would prefer to be judged by the hunter Jack Troake than by anyone who would judge him harshly.

Michael Kaufman, *The New York Times Magazine*,
13 May 1984

Paragraph One

A. In your own words, explain why Michael Kaufman's children were not allowed to have "playthings that simulated weapons." Distinguish between weapons and imitation weapons.
B. Why does Kaufman state that violence and aggression are "alleged" attributes of manliness?
C. In the same sentence, Kaufman tells us that his uncle was in a concentration camp and that he expected little boys to play with guns. What is the connection? Why are they in the same sentence?
D. Explain, in your own words, "the moral authority" of a war victim "survivor."
E. Contrast the two theories of child-raising contained in this paragraph.

Paragraph Two

F. "Bang bang" is a short method of expressing what?
G. What does "ethically impaired" mean?

H. Summarize Kaufman's point about the dangers ("moral pitfalls") of North American civilization (third sentence).
I. Define "vicarious." In what ways do movies provide a vicarious experience? Why does Kaufman imply that this is wrong?

Paragraphs Three and Four

J. Explain why Kaufman uses the example of a hunter. What does Mr. Troake represent?
K. What is Mr. Troake's argument? Summarize it, including an explanation of his reference to plastic-wrapped meat.

Paragraph Five

L. Explain the meaning of "current visual clichés of violence," considering the list of examples from Beirut that Kaufman cites.
M. Why does Kaufman include a description of his mother's death?
N. So far, Kaufman has provided four examples: his uncle and toy guns; Mr. Troake and antihunters; images of Beirut on TV; and the death of his mother. Can you explain why Kaufman uses the examples in that order? How is his argument being built?

Paragraph Six

O. Kaufman refers to "pious responses" to the Vietnam War. What does he mean?
P. In what sense were there "too many images" of the Vietnam War?

Paragraph Seven

Q. Summarize the point made by the examples listed in paragraph seven.
R. Kaufman once again refers to "bang bang" and its effect on small children. Compare the son of the Afghan freedom fighter and Kaufman's own son (both before and after he was given the toy machine gun).

Paragraph Eight

S. Explain what Kaufman means by "bear witness to violence."
T. In what way would experiences in an emergency ward or old-age home enable children to "bear witness to violence"?
U. In the context of the whole essay, how does Kaufman define violence?

Paragraph Nine

V. What point is Kaufman making in his contrast between "us" and "them"?

W. Why does Kaufman end the essay by accepting Jack Troake's moral authority?

X. Does the last paragraph contain the essay's main idea (thesis)? If not, write a brief summary of Kaufman's main idea.

EXERCISE 3

Read the following essay twice, and then make up a set of comprehension questions that would help a reader to gain a better understanding of the essay.

MEDICINE'S SECOND REVOLUTION

A sentimental 19th-century painting by Sir Luke Fildes, showing a physician seated at a child's bedside, is still being reproduced in the calendars mailed by pharmaceutical companies to doctors and graduating medical students. The picture, entitled *The Doctor*, illustrates what used to be the popular conception of medicine and is, to this day, a romantic version of the way the profession likes to view itself. The scene is a Victorian living room where a young child, stricken by an unspecified mortal illness, lies in a makeshift bed; at her side sits the elderly doctor in an attitude combining, all at once, concern, compassion, intelligence, understanding, and command. He is the painting's centerpiece. The child's parents are in the background, the father looking at the doctor with an expression of total trust. 1

The doctor in the painting is engaged in what was, for that period in medicine, the only course available at this stage of serious illness: He is monitoring the patient. He has already, presumably, arrived at the diagnosis. He knows the name of the child's illness, he has a solid working knowledge of the pathology, and from his lifetime of professional experience he is able to predict how the disease will run its course and what will happen at the end. He has explained all this to the parents in language that they can understand, and now, at the moment of the picture, he is engaged in the ancient art of medicine. This means, at its essence, that he is *there*, contributing his presence, providing whatever he can in the way of hope and understanding. 2

The illusion of the scene is that he is in control of the situation. He is not, of course. Beyond taking the pulse, examining the tongue, listening to the chest, palpating the abdomen, and making sure that what 3 was then regarded as good nursing care is available, there is nothing whatever that he can do to alter the course of the illness or affect its outcome. The diseases capable of producing the degree of prostration and lassitude indicated by the painting would include such things as lobar pneumonia, typhoid fever, bacterial meningitis, acute rheumatic fever, tuberculosis, or any of the other microbial infections that, for that time, were common causes of incapacitation and death during childhood.

The painting's scene is a very different picture from one that might   4
have been drawn of a doctor and his patient a century earlier. This man is practicing his art at a time when the first great revolution in medicine was already under way, and the lesson learned from the revolution was not to meddle.

It began around 1825, when a few sagacious doctors in Boston, Lon-   5
don, and Edinburgh began looking closely at the therapies then in use for serious illness, focusing their attention on the conventional treatment of typhoid fever and delirium tremens, a condition of frightening hallucinations and violent tremors. It had been taken for granted that patients with these afflictions would surely die unless heroic and strenuous efforts were undertaken for their rescue. Hence, they were subjected to vigorous bleeding, with the removal of several pints of blood—enough to produce the clinical manifestations of hemorrhagic shock. In addition, they received enormous doses of mercury and various plant purgatives, and blistering ointments were applied to the skin, all in the hope of reducing the volume of fluid in the body. The idea that congestion of internal organs was the underlying basis of every human disease dated back to the second-century physician Galen, who probably got it from observing congestion of the lungs and liver in patients dying of heart failure and then extrapolated the idea to include all disease.

It was not until around 1825 that serious questions were raised   6
about this kind of therapy, among them the central, scientific question: What would happen to patients with typhoid fever and delirium tremens if no treatment at all were given? The answer, once the question had been asked, was devastating in its implications. The untreated patients survived their illnesses at a significantly higher rate than those who were bled, purged, and blistered.

It was an unpopular piece of work, and it took the better part of the   7
century for the lesson to take hold. But take hold it did, and by the first decade of the 20th century medical practice had entered a period of conservative, non-meddling therapy, termed therapeutic nihilism by its critics. The active treatment of disease was restricted to a short list of things that really did seem to help: digitalis for heart failure, morphine for pain, a few others. But with these exceptions the main re-

sponsibilities of the physician were to learn enough about pathology and the natural history of disease to make an accurate diagnosis and a reasonably accurate prognosis, and then to stand by and care for the patient. "Caring for" didn't necessarily mean administering a drug or injecting fluids or, indeed, mobilizing any particular kind of technology. It meant, instead, long conversations with the patient and the family, frequent visits to the bedside, the enlistment of good nursing care, and as much comfort and reassurance as could honestly be mustered.

This is the kind of medicine I was taught in Boston 50 years ago. The terms *medical science* and *medical research* were not much used, and today's word *biomedical*, implying that medicine and biology are all of a piece, had not been invented. What science there was had as its mission the comprehension of disease mechanisms and the improvement of diagnostic procedures. Rabbit antiserum had just been introduced for the treatment of pneumococcal pneumonia, with limited success. But that was the only new topic to learn about in the therapy of disease. **8**

Shortly after the turn of the century, the German bacteriologist Paul Ehrlich had proposed that a new class of chemicals should be sought that could serve as magic bullets to destroy invading microorganisms. After years of research he emerged with the compound arsphenamine for syphilis, a useful but unpredictably toxic drug requiring many months, sometimes years, of intravenous injections. Even then it had little or no effect on the late and lethal manifestations of syphilis. Aside from this, and the new antiserum for pneumonia, there were no effective ways to alter the course of bacterial infection, and the notion that new ones might someday be discovered was dismissed as a pipe dream. **9**

As I recall, 50 years ago we believed that medicine had just about come its full distance. We might become more skilled at diagnosis, we might learn more details about the working of disease, but what we knew as facts in 1930 seemed, from our point of view, to be the final word. We saw no reason to expect more than marginal changes in the years ahead. **10**

Even then we ought to have known better. The dye sulfanilamide had been synthesized in 1908 in the German laboratories of I.G. Farben. But it wasn't until 1932 that a German bacteriologist, Gerhard Domagk, Farben's director of therapeutic research, tested a red dye derivative of sulfanilamide called prontosil for its action against streptococcal infection in mice and rabbits. The results were unequivocal: Prontosil could cure bacterial disease in living animals, although paradoxically it had no antibacterial action in the test tube. In 1933, the dye was first used in a human being for the successful treatment of **11** staphylococcal septicemia, or blood poisoning. If the investigators had limited their screening methods to *in vitro* tests of prontosil, the antibacterial properties of sulfanilamide would not have been recognized.

The way was now open for antibiotics, which would launch medicine's second revolution. The news that infectious bacteria could be killed off without harm to the cells of the host came as an astonishment to physicians everywhere. Alexander Fleming's discovery of penicillin in 1928, regarded up through the 1930s as a curiosity without practical applicability (due, as it turned out, to the instability of crude extracts of Fleming's mold), suddenly became of great interest. The isolation of pure penicillin by Howard Florey and Ernst Chain in 1939 and the devising of techniques for its mass production in 1941 finally convinced everyone that medicine had entered a new era of powerful, decisive therapy. It remained for Selman Waksman, in 1944, to demonstrate that even tuberculosis, the most resistant and irreversible of all common infections, could be brought under control by streptomycin. Medicine became a different profession, with its central and obsessive ambition the cure of disease through biomedical science, and it has never looked back. 12

In just the past 10 years, thanks to elegant basic research (much of it launched by the postwar expansion of the National Institutes of Health), more has been discovered about the underlying cellular mechanisms of cancer than could have been guessed by any earlier generation of scientists or physicians, and the younger investigators have high hopes that the disease will be solved before long. The same degree of optimism exists among the neuroscientists, who are encountering one astonishment after another in their studies of the brain and its disorders. The cardiologists, the rheumatologists, the endocrinologists and diabetes specialists, even the psychiatrists, are becoming convinced that nothing lies beyond reach if the efforts in basic research continue. If the future goes as it might, medicine will be transformed from the profession I was raised in, primarily a form of art, to a powerful and highly effective form of applied science. 13

It has not happened yet, of course, and we still have an agenda of unsolved and incurable diseases to cope with. Some of these, chronic nephritis and kidney failure, for instance, can be treated by feats of high technology—the artificial kidney and renal transplantation—and some of the patients can be rescued. The artificial heart, and transplants of hearts, lungs, and livers, are examples of applied medical science after the disease of one organ or another has run its course. These are halfway technologies, sometimes useful but always chancy and frightfully expensive, brought in at the end to shore up body functions that have been lost because of medicine's ignorance about the cellular mechanisms that caused the disease in the first place. The hope in the minds of the rising generation of biomedical scientists is that these 14 mechanisms can now be scrutinized firsthand, with the prospect of intervening to turn them around or preventing them at the outset of disease.

I tend to agree with the optimists, and I am on the side of those who   15
believe that we must have a deeply reductionist, totally scientific comprehension of the things gone wrong in disease before we can develop rational measures for effective therapy. At the same time, I acknowledge the point of view of the critics of today's medicine. They say that medicine is not yet all that much a science-based technology, that we are losing the essence of the old art, that we are so obsessed by the disease of the patient that we overlook the patient with the disease. But then they go on with extensions of the criticism with which I disagree. They claim that there is a new field called holistic medicine, which relies on nature for both the prevention and cure of disease, and they seem to disapprove of the kind of deep scientific research that I contend is needed for the future.

I come down on the middle ground. If I become ill with a disease   16
that is reasonably well comprehended by my specialist colleagues, then I want all the explanations and friendship I can get. But I do not mind at all being treated as a scientific puzzle by the clinicians around my bedside, as long as there is a hope of solving the puzzle and putting me back on my feet. Medicine is getting quite good at this, despite its limitations. It is, for sure, a totally different occupation from the profession I studied 50 years ago, vastly more knowledgeable, substantially more effective. It will continue to improve, if the basic research is kept up. As a physician and a potential patient, I want all the science that's going.

Lewis Thomas, from *Science 84*, November 1984

EXERCISE 4

Carefully read the following excerpt. Underline important ideas, and annotate key phrases, especially those with difficult vocabulary. Then make up a set of comprehension questions that would help a reader to understand the essay's vocabulary, structure, and meaning.

SCIENTIFIC FRAUD AND THE FIGHT TO BE FIRST

The culture of science has long put a premium on originality, on being   1
the first to make a scientific discovery. Being second, let alone a subsequent nth, hardly counts at all. Moreover, scientists know that much the same discovery is often made independently by two or more investigators at about the same time. They not only know it, but many of them act on that knowledge. This often brings about a rush for prior-

ity. So it is that the culture of science and its reward system combine with the fact of multiple discoveries to produce intense competition among scientists. The annals of science are punctuated by hundreds of disputes over priority during the past four centuries, and I shall suggest that that same premium on originality which has reinforced intrinsic motives for advancing the frontiers of scientific knowledge also contains pathogenic components. Self-assertive claims to have got there first, the hoarding of data to avoid being beaten to it, reporting only the data that support a favourite hypothesis, trimming and fudging the data to have them come in closer accord with theoretical expectations, falsely imputing plagiarism to others who have independently come upon the same results, occasional theft of ideas and, in rare known cases, the fabrication of data—all these have appeared in the history of science.

These examples of deviant behaviours which variously violate the   2
mores of science are responses to the gap between the emphasis placed upon original discovery and the great difficulty a good many scientists experience in making one, with the more inventive scientists confronting the ever-present risk of being preempted in their discoveries. Under such stressful conditions, a variety of would-be adaptive behaviours and misbehaviours is called into play. The recent spate of news stories about actual and alleged fraud in science has led to the belief that such deviant practices have greatly increased in our time.

I begin with a general question and a specific puzzle: how can we ac-   3
count for the great number of controversies centred on priority of discovery over the centuries and how can we solve the puzzle that even meek and unaggressive men and women, ordinarily slow to press their claims in other spheres of life, have often done so in the scientific work?

As I've hinted, I take this pattern of deep concern with establishing   4
priority to derive largely from the institutional values of science itself. On every side, scientists are reminded that it is their role to advance knowledge, and that originality is accordingly at a premium. When the institution of science works effectively—and, like other social institutions, it does not always do so—recognition accrues to those who have best fulfilled that role by making genuine contributions to the common stock of knowledge. Such recognition is communally validating testimony that one's ideas are truly new. And from these incessant appraisals of work by competent peers comes much of the self-image of individual scientists. As Darwin once wrote, "My love of natural science . . . has been much aided by the ambition to be esteemed by my fellow naturalists." Since such recognition is the coin of the scientific realm, we can understand how it is that, through the centuries, scientists, including the greatest among them, have been deeply concerned with safeguarding their priority.

Why, then, the frequent reluctance to acknowledge this drive for pri-   5 ority? Why the ambivalence expressed by Darwin, before he learned of Wallace's parallel ideas, in this way: "I rather hate the idea of writing for priority, yet I should certainly be vexed if anyone were to publish my doctrines before me"? Why the curious notion that a thirst for significant originality and for having that originality accredited by competent peers is rather depraved—somewhat like a thirst for, say, whisky and Coca-Cola? Or in Freud's self-deprecatory words, that that is an "unworthy and puerile" motive for doing scientific work?

In one aspect, the ambivalent attitude of a Darwin or Freud toward   6
his own acknowledged interest in priority is based upon the implicit assumption that behaviour is actuated by a single motive, which can then be appraised as good or bad, noble or ignoble. It is assumed that the truly dedicated scientist must be moved only by wanting to advance knowledge, whether the contribution is recognized or not. Deep interest in having one's priority acknowledged is seen as marring one's nobility of purpose (although it might be remembered that "noble" once meant being famous).

There is a grain of psychological truth in the suspicion enveloping   7
the drive for recognition. Any extrinsic reward—fame, money, position—is potentially subversive of socially esteemed values. For the extrinsic reward can displace the morally respected intrinsic motive: concern with recognition and its derivative rewards can displace the primary concern with advancing knowledge, as we observe at the extreme in cases of fraudulent practices in science.

Those mixed feelings about concern with priority often stem from   8
the superficial belief that it simply expresses naked self-interest. On the surface, the hunger for recognition appears a mere personal vanity, generated from within and craving satisfaction from without. But when we reach into the institutional complex that gives added edge to that hunger, it often turns out to have quite other functions. Vanity, so called, is then seen as the outer face of the inner need for reassurance that one's work has measured up to the demanding standards exacted by the scientists whose opinions one respects. As sociologists like to put it more generally, we each have our reference figures, those people whose opinion of us matters greatly.

Again, Darwin serves us well by way of example. He writes to Hux-   9
ley about *The Origin of Species* "with awful misgivings" that "perhaps I had deluded myself like so many have done, and I then fixed in mind three judges, on whose decision I determined mentally to abide. The judges were Lyell, Hooker and yourself." In choosing reference figures, Darwin was replicating the behaviour of many another scientist, both before and after him. Thus, before his feud with Newton, the astronomer John Flamsteed wrote: "I study not for present applause. Mr. Newton's approbation is more to me than the cry of all the ignorant in the world." In almost identical language, Schrödinger writes to Einstein that "your approval and Planck's mean more to me than that of

the world." And a Leo Szilard and a Max Delbrück, widely known as tough-minded judges who, all uncompromising, would not relax their standards of judgment even to provide momentary comfort to their associates, were reference figures whose approval of work accomplished had a multiplier effect, influencing in turn the judgments of many another scientist.

The now understandable concern with priority often takes the form   10 of a race for priority. For scientists know, at times from hard-won experience, that multiple independent discovery at about the same time is one of their occupational hazards. That the consequent rush to achieve priority is common in our time hardly needs documentation. The evidence is there on every side. Some years before James Watson reached his much wider audience with *The Double Helix*, Arthur Schawlow reported that Charles Townes and he had been "in a hurry, of course. We feared that it might be only a matter of time before others would come up with the same idea. So we decided to publish before building a working model. . . . Subsequently, Theodore Maiman won the frantic race between many experimenters to build the first laser. Our theory was verified." Townes in particular had ample reason to be in a hurry. In the early 1950s, he had been involved in that five-fold independent discovery of the maser, along with Willis Lamb, Joseph Weber, Nikolai Basov, and Aleksandr Prokhorov. . . .

As with Newton in his controversy with Leibniz over the invention   11 of the calculus, concern with establishing priority can lead to the use of dubious means to buttress valid claims. When the Royal Society finally provided a committee to adjudicate the rival claims, Newton, who was then president, packed the committee, helped direct its activities, anonymously wrote the preface for the second published report—the draft is in his handwriting—and included in that preface a disarming reference to the old legal maxim that "no one is a proper witness for himself [and that] he would be an iniquitous Judge, and would crush underfoot the laws of all the people, who would admit anyone as a lawful witness in his own cause." We can gauge the immense pressures for self-vindication that must have operated for such a man as Newton to have adopted these means for defence of his claims. It was not because Newton was so weak but because the institutionalized values were so strong that he was driven to such lengths.

In earlier times, as in our own, intense competition in science has   12 led to similar patterns of behaviour. It has led to what the English mathematician and adumbrator of computer technology, Charles Babbage, picturesquely described in *The Decline of Science in England* (1830) as "trimming" and "cooking." The trimmer clips off "little bits here and there from observations which differ most in excess from the mean, and [sticks] . . . them on to those which are too small . . . [for the unallowable purpose of] 'equitable adjustment'." The scientific cook makes "multitudes of observations" and selects only those which agree with a hypothesis and, as Babbage says, "the cook must be very unlucky if he cannot pick out fifteen or twenty which will do for serving up. . . ."

To bring matters to the more immediate present, we may take note of the recent rash of news reports about several cases of the fabrication of data, chiefly identified in the biomedical sciences, and grown painfully familiar through public reiteration: William Summerlin's inked-in mouse reminiscent of Paul Kammerer's inked-in midwife toad of half a century before, the forgeries of evidence by Marc Straus in his cancer research and by John Long in his research on Hodgkin's disease, the irreproducible findings reported by Melvin Simpson and the tampering with experimental equipment by the psychologist Jay Levy in his studies of extrasensory perception.   13

Such widely publicized cases have led some to conclude that the rate of these deviant practices has greatly increased in what is described as our competitive age. . . .   14

The impression that fraud has vastly increased may be the result of a heightened self-consciousness in society coupled with the strong moral expectation that scientists in pursuit of reliable knowledge will live up to the highest standards of probity. When those expectations are seen to have been violated in even a few cases, these statistically rare reports attract great public notice and become especially newsworthy. As the iconic sociologist, Emile Durkheim, might have said, the very rarity of these extreme violations of the mores of science only deepens the sense of moral outrage and intensifies the glare of publicity when they do occur.   15

The sociological moral of deviant behaviour in science can be put more generally. We have heard much recently about the precarious condition of a society in which people do not believe deeply enough or strongly enough. If there is a lesson to be learned from some of the consequences of a belief in the absolute importance of originality in science, it is that absolute beliefs have their dangers too. They can give rise to the kind of zeal in which anything goes. The absolutizing of aspirations can, in its way, be just as damaging as the decay of aspirations to life in civil society.   16

Robert K. Merton, from *Times Literary Supplement* (England), 2 November 1984

DRAWING INFERENCES

When you are actively reading and annotating a text, you may sometimes find yourself projecting your own thoughts and assumptions into what you are reading. After a while, it becomes difficult to differentiate between your own conjectures, inspired by what you have read, and the evidence that is actually to be found in the source. When such confusion occurs, you can easily attribute to your source ideas that are not there at all or—much more likely—ideas that you have *inferred* from your reading.

An inference means a conclusion drawn by reasoning from sound evidence. Inference is different from implication. The implications of a statement are quite easily found within the statement itself; they just are not explicitly expressed. In contrast, inference requires reasoning, not just suggestion, for the hidden idea to be observed. Murder *implies* violence; that a murder was committed can be *inferred* from the condition of the body.

It is perfectly correct to draw your own inferences from the sources that you are writing about, as long as you fulfill two conditions:

1. There must be a reasonable basis within the source for your inference.
2. The inferences should be clearly identified as yours, not the source's.

When in an essay you cite a specific work as the basis of an inference, your reader should be able to go to the source, locate the evidence there, and draw a similar inference. Thus, as preparation for presenting your ideas and your source's, you will find it useful to distinguish between what an essay or book actually *proves*, what it *states*, what it *implies*, and what can be *inferred* from it.

EXERCISE 5

Read "More People Waiting to Marry," and decide which of the following statements are *stated* or *proven*; which are *implied* (or suggested by the essay); which can be *inferred* from the essay; and which are *false* according to the information in the article.

MORE PEOPLE WAITING TO MARRY

More and more young Americans are putting off marriage, possibly to begin careers, according to a new Census Bureau report saying that three-quarters of American men and more than half of American women under 25 are still single.

"Many of these young adults may have postponed their entry into marriage in order to further their formal education, establish careers or pursue other goals that might conflict with assuming family responsibilities," said the bureau's study of households, families, marital status and living arrangements.

The report also found that Americans are once again forming new households at high rates after a decline, apparently recession-induced, last year.

A slight increase was noted in the number of unmarried couples living together; they totaled almost two million as of March and represent about 4 percent of the couples.

The trend toward postponed marriage has been growing steadily in recent years. The study found that 74.8 percent of men aged 20 to 24 had never married, compared with 68.8 percent in 1980 and 54.7 percent in 1970. Among women aged 20 to 24, 56.9 percent were single in this year's survey, as against 50.2 percent in 1980 and 35.8 percent in 1970.

Though the report said that most young people are expected to marry eventually, it noted that the longer marriage was delayed the greater the chance that it would not occur. "Consequently, the percentage of today's young adults that do not ever marry may turn out to be higher than the corresponding percentage of their predecessors," the report speculated.

Traditional married couples continue to make up the majority of family households in the United States, but the report documents the steady erosion of this group's dominance. The 50.1 million traditional families constitute 58.6 percent of American households, compared with 60.8 percent in 1980 and 70.5 percent in 1970.

Meanwhile, the number of one-person households has grown sharply as young people have entered the work force and set up housekeeping on their own. Single-person households totaled 19.9 million in the current report, or 23 percent of households, up a percentage point from 1980 and six percentage points from 1970.

Increasing rates of separation and divorce have contributed to the growth in families headed by women, which numbered 9.9 million, or 11.6 percent, as against 10.8 percent in 1980 and 8.7 percent in 1970. "About 25 percent of all households added since 1980 were families maintained by women," the report said.

The Census Bureau counted 85,408,000 households in March, consisting of 50,090,000 traditional families, 9,878,000 families headed by women, 2,030,000 families headed by men alone and 23,410,000 nonfamily households (mostly individuals).

The 1,988,000 unmarried couples may be relatively few, but their number has increased sharply over the last 14 years, from 523,000 counted in 1970. The makeup of this group has also changed: in 1970 a majority included a head of household aged 45 or more, while today 80 percent have a householder under 44.

Concerning the formation of households, the study found an increase of 1.5 million from 1983 to 1984, following a pattern common in the 1970's, after an increase of 391,000, much below normal, last year. Census officials said the 1983 slowdown seemed to be an aberration caused by the recession and cautioned against reading any trend into the data.

As the number of households grew, the average number of persons per household reached a record low, 2.71; it was 2.73 in 1983. "The disproportionate increase in one-person households has been a major factor in the decline of household size over the years," the report noted.

Average family size also reached a record low of 3.24, compared with 3.26 a year earlier. This reflects the decline in births in recent years, with the smaller family almost entirely due to the smaller population under age 18.

New York Times, 27 August 1984

1. More men than women are waiting until they are over 25 to marry.
2. Most households in the United States consist of unmarried couples.
3. Traditional married couples still make up a large majority of the family households in the United States.
4. In 1983 there was a large increase in the number of new households formed.
5. One-parent homes in the United States tend to be headed by divorced or separated women.
6. Economic conditions seem to be a factor in predicting how many new households are formed in the United States.
7. The longer a person remains single, the greater the chance that this person will never marry.
8. One reason why people are marrying later may be that they are living together as unmarried couples first.
9. Some people may be postponing marriage because they want to establish a career.
10. The increase in one-person households is part of a recent trend.
11. The age of persons heading households consisting of unmarried couples has increased sharply in the past ten years.
12. As a result of the growing number of single-person households, there will be a greater need for housing.
13. The age of the average unmarried couple is getting younger.
14. The trend to marry later in life may be a factor in the declining birth rate.
15. The decline in the birth rate is reflected by the smaller average family size.
16. If the trend toward later marriages continues at a steady rate, eventually there will be no more married couples in this country.

OUTLINING

In addition to making marginal notes and asking yourself comprehension questions, there is another way of fully understanding what you have read: outlining the author's main ideas. An outline is much more orderly and complete than marginal notes. When you outline, you are identifying the main points of a chapter or an essay, leaving them in roughly the same order as the original.

Outlines are built around the main ideas contained in an essay, the major points that the author is using to make the thesis convincing. In a short essay, the main ideas will probably all be parallel or of the same kind: the reasons why x is true, the ways in which y happens, the differences between x and y, the chief characteristics of z, and so on. In a longer, more complex essay there may be several sets of main ideas as the author shifts from one argument to another or from description of a problem to its solution, and so on.

Since the essay is built around these main ideas, they are given the most prominent place in the outline, usually in a numbered list at the left-hand margin. The supporting material—the secondary arguments, information, or examples being used to back up or prove each main idea—is generally grouped directly under the main idea and slightly to the right, to make a clear connection between main idea and supporting material. If there are different kinds of evidence presented or several examples, or both, each may be listed on a separate line and assigned letters of the alphabet to keep them in order. While this multilevel numbering and lettering can be helpful, it is not essential. The object is to show how the author has constructed the essay and to distinguish between main ideas and supporting material.

The wording of an outline may be taken directly from the original or may be expressed in your own words as inferences drawn directly from the essay. You may use complete sentences or fragmentary phrases for your outline, whichever is convenient, but it is helpful to be consistent in your choice and make all main ideas fragments or complete sentences.

Outlining is the most effective way to record the main points of an essay whose structure is clear and straightforward. In "Must Doctors Serve Where They're Told?" for example, Harry Schwartz presents the arguments for both sides in such an orderly sequence that underlining and numbering the key phrases in the essay would probably serve as an adequate record. (Each of the main points has been italicized in the essay.) However, since Schwartz moves back and forth from positive to negative reasons, the pairing of related arguments can be shown to best advantage if you outline them.

Read "Must Doctors Serve Where They're Told?" and then carefully examine the outline that follows. Notice that the outline is preceded by a *thesis*—a statement of the essay's central idea. A thesis is usually a substantial generalization that can stand by itself, forming the basis of an essay's development. In this essay, the thesis does no more than suggest the underlying issues, since Schwartz himself does not decisively support one side of the argument or the other.

MUST DOCTORS SERVE WHERE THEY'RE TOLD?

Should young doctors be "drafted" and forced to serve some years   1
in areas of physician shortage? Or, less drastically, should a portion of the places in the nation's medical schools be reserved for young people who promise that in return for government financial aid they will agree to serve where the government wants them to? These and related issues have been debated in Congress for the last two years and are still unresolved.

Currently, it costs an estimated average of about $13,000 a year to   2
train a medical student, but those students pay directly only about $1,000 to $6,000 in tuition. The remainder is paid by government funds, by return on endowments, by gifts and similar sources. Some lawmakers see a *compulsory service liability as a means of compensating the taxpayers for subsidizing the doctors' education.*

The specific proposals that have been debated in Congress have   3
ranged from Senator Edward M. Kennedy's suggestion for a universal draft for all medical school graduates to milder schemes that would give young doctors a choice between repaying the Federal Government or serving for several years in designated areas. In New York there is already a medical training program whose students have agreed to serve two years in doctor-short areas after graduating from medical school. Those who fail to meet this "service commitment" will be required to reimburse the city and state for up to $25,000 for their free undergraduate education.

Some conservative economists have argued that *physician incomes,*   4
which average around $50,000, remove all excuse for government subsidy. They would require medical students to pay the full cost, financing their way, if need be, by bank loans. Such an approach would remove the motive for any doctor draft, but many in Congress fear that this "solution" would close medical schools to children of the poor, the working class and minorities.

Proponents of some service requirements for young doctors usually   5
base their arguments on the *maldistribution of doctors in this country.* In 1973, for example, California had 265 doctors per 100,000 people, more than three times as many as South Dakota's 87 per 100,000. The actual disparities are even greater, because within each state physicians tend to congregate in metropolitan areas.

Opponents of forced service do not deny the existence of local   6
shortages, but they question the wisdom of *sending new physicians*

into shortage areas where they will have little or no help and consultation from older, more experienced doctors.

Opponents also ask *whether doctors serving in isolated areas* 7 *against their will are likely to give satisfactory service.* And they ask why young doctors and dentists should be *singled out for coercion* when government helps finance the education of most professionals and there are great inequalities in the current distribution of lawyers, accountants, architects and engineers as well.

But more is involved in this debate than the allocation of physicians. 8 The argument about young doctors is relevant to the broader national discussion about national economic planning and about the relative roles of government decision and market forces in directing the American economy.

On one side are those who emphasize the *obligation of government* 9 *to use all its resources to reach desirable goals for all Americans.* If one assumes, as Mr. Kennedy and others do, that every American has a "right" to health care, then it seems reasonable for government to take whatever actions are needed to make sure that doctors and related personnel and facilities are available everywhere. If market forces do not produce the desired result, this school is prepared to use either government coercion or government financial persuasion. Moreover, this school of thought wants to tailor the means to the end. Thus, instead of using government money just to expand the number of doctors in general, they want to assure that doctors are available wherever needed and available, moreover, in whatever distribution of specialties Congress or its servants decide is appropriate.

Opponents argue that such *regulation would be contrary to all* 10 *American history and tradition,* except for times of war or emergency when the military draft has been in effect. The *American emphasis, these opponents hold, is primarily upon the freedom of the individual and affords no warrant for infringing one person's freedom in order to benefit someone else.* The whole structure of publicly financed education in this country, from kindergarten to M.D. and Ph.D., it is pointed out, has developed over the decades without any related service requirement or repayment of any kind whatsoever. If doctors are drafted, it will provide a precedent for drafting other categories of Americans.

The issue is not peculiarly American, of course, nor is the problem 11 of physician maldistribution confined to the United States. *In the Soviet Union and its associated Communist states,* most graduates of higher educational institutions—not only physicians—are *assigned specific work locations* for the first few years after graduation.

Some non-Communist countries, like Mexico, have a requirement 12 for compulsory service for a limited time by doctors before they can go into normal practice. In Israel there is a universal service obligation for all young adults. *But in most countries of Western Europe there is no draft of young doctors.*

Most of the other democratic countries of the world are relatively   13
small, both in area and population, as compared with the United States. So the advocates of a doctor draft in the United States argue that the absence of such compulsion in other countries is no conclusive argument against it here.

Harry Schwartz

Thesis: A decision to draft young doctors for service throughout the country will have to consider the obligations and rights of the doctors, as well as the responsibility of the government to serve the public.

    I. Obligations of young doctors: public bears partial cost of education, entitled to compensation
        A. repayment of debt to public through service
            evidence: Kennedy plan; New York two-year term of service
        B. alternative: initial payment of medical school fees by bank loan
            evidence: extremely high incomes will allow ultimate repayment
            problem: possible difficulty in applying for initial loan
   II. Needs of the public: not enough doctors to serve the country
        A. "maldistribution" necessitates drafting: doctors tend to practice in certain populous states and cities
            evidence: California vs. South Dakota
        B. coercion would not ensure efficient service: inexperienced doctors would be isolated from guidance; unwilling doctors are inefficient
  III. Powers of the government vs. the rights of the individual
        A. the government is empowered to satisfy everyone's right to health care
        B. public policy shouldn't encourage coercion of individuals to benefit others; to draft doctors would be an unfortunate precedent
            evidence: other professions aren't subject to a draft; other beneficiaries of public education aren't forced to repay costs
  IV. Precedents in other countries
        A. drafting doctors is routine in some countries
            evidence: Communist countries, Mexico, Israel
        B. drafting doctors is not required in many countries with a democratic tradition similar to ours
            evidence: Western Europe

```
problem: these Western European countries are physically
smaller than the United States and therefore have differ-
ent requirements
```

Outlining Complex Essays

Most essays are not as clearly constructed as Harry Schwartz's. Often, the main ideas are not presented straightforwardly at the beginning of the paragraphs. If you read the Lewis Thomas essay in Exercise 3, then you will remember that his topic sentences tend to come at the ends of paragraphs, a decision related to the complex subject that Thomas is writing about. Michael Kaufman's essay in Exercise 2 is built around a se-ries of extended examples; Kaufman does not always supply a general-ization that sums up the point of the example, so that job is left to the reader.

Essays like Thomas's and Kaufman's are not bad essays or even badly constructed essays. They are loosely organized because they deal with complex subjects, which would probably spill out of more tightly con-structed paragraphs. However, Thomas and Kaufman are highly experi-enced writers and can afford to break the rules, for they continue to maintain control over the development of their ideas. Their essays can still be outlined; there is a plan, a structure linking up one idea with the next.

Essays that deal with more than one main idea at the same time are es-pecially difficult to outline, yet usually require and repay careful, point-by-point outlining. Such an essay is Blanche Blank's "A Question of De-gree." Since it is concerned with a controversial issue, and since Blank's arguments are certainly worth analyzing, outlining the essay becomes an interesting if complicated task.

"A Question of Degree": Establishing a Thesis

Unlike Harry Schwartz in "Must Doctors Serve Where They're Told?" Blank *is* attempting to convince her readers that a specific point of view is right. An accurate thesis, then, should convey some of her distaste for the excessive value placed on college degrees. But even with the full awareness of Blank's position that comes from thorough understanding, you may easily write an incomplete or an inadequate thesis. What is wrong with each of these?

```
1. According to Blanche Blank, universities need to change their
   outlook and curricula and return to a more traditional role.
2. Blanche Blank suggests that our present ideology about the purpose
   of college should be reconsidered and redefined.
3. I agree with Blanche Blank's belief that college degrees have too
   much importance.
```

4. Blanche Blank argues that employment discrimination arises from an emphasis on college degrees.
5. Blanche Blank believes that a college education isn't necessary at an early age.

A good thesis would be a generalization broad enough to cover most of Blank's argument without being so vague as to be meaningless. Consider the following criticisms of the five theses:

Thesis 1 accurately presents only one—and not the chief one—of Blank's points.

Thesis 2 is uninformative: what is "our present ideology" and what sort of redefinition is in order?

Thesis 3 is also vague: Blank may have convinced one reader, but which of her arguments did the reader find effective?

Thesis 4 is much too broad: Blank does not argue that degrees are the only cause of employment discrimination, nor does she suggest that employment is the only area adversely affected by the importance attached to degrees.

Thesis 5 is simply untrue: Blank is not urging all would-be freshmen to bypass college.

The following thesis is somewhat better than the first five: it conveys something of Blank's central idea, but it omits all reference to work and the self-respect of the worker, which are ideas crucial to the essay.

6. In Blanche Blank's view, acquiring a college degree immediately after high school should not be considered the best way to achieve a better life.

A thoroughly acceptable thesis would convey more precisely the dangers of overvaluing the college degree. Thesis 7 achieves this end:

7. The possession of a college degree cannot automatically lead to a better life and better earnings for a college graduate; the universal practice of regarding the degree as an essential for getting a "good" job can only discourage a more just and efficient system of employment.

Both parts of the thesis deal with the consequences of overvaluing the college degree: the first part is concerned with the effect on the individual, whose expectations may not be fulfilled; the second is concerned with the effect on social institutions and organizations, which may value credentials at the expense of merit.

"A Question of Degree": An Outline Based on Categories

Because the paragraphs of this essay are crowded with ideas, constructing an outline is difficult. For example, within the following single paragraph, Blank mentions most of her main points, some more than once, and in varying order. (The numbers here are keyed to the outline on pp. 42–43.)

What is wrong with the current college/work cycle can be seen in the following anomalies: we are selling college to the youth of America as a take-off pad for the material good life [IA]. College is literally advertised and packaged as a means for getting more money through "better" jobs at the same time that Harvard graduates are taking jobs as taxi drivers [IB]. This situation is a perversion of the true spirit of a university [III], a perversion of a humane social ethic [IVA], and, at bottom, a patent fraud. To take the last point first, the economy simply is not geared to guaranteeing these presumptive "better" jobs [IB]; the colleges are not geared to training for such jobs [III]; and the ethical propriety of the entire enterprise is very questionable [I and II]. We are by definition (rather than by analysis) establishing two kinds of work: work labeled "better" because it has a degree requirement tagged to it and non-degree work, which, through this logic, becomes automatically "low level" [IVA].

When dealing with a complex essay you must look for organizing principles and categories of ideas as you read and reread it. Experienced readers learn to watch for points that are repeated and emphasized, so that they will find a consistent way to organize and remember what they have read. Thus, the comprehension questions that analyzed "A Question of Degree" encouraged you to stop and review the points that Blanche Blank raised. You will remember that you were asked about the different groups of people who are affected by the unfortunate worship of college degrees. The easiest way to break down the mass of assertions in Blanche Blank's essay is to use those groups as a way to establish categories:

A. students who are in college unwillingly;
B. college graduates who work at frustrating jobs;
C. workers who have not been to college and are undervalued;
D. true scholars who resent the decline in the quality of university life.

If you combine the first two groups (both with career expectations and both disappointed by college), you have an outline with three major entries, plus a conclusion that sums up Blanche Blank's central ideas.

<u>Thesis:</u> The possession of a college degree cannot automatically lead to a better life and better earnings for a college graduate; the universal practice of regarding the degree as an essential for getting a "good" job can only discourage a more just and efficient system of employment.

I. The frustration of students with vocational expectations
    A. Whether or not they are suited to college, students believe that they must spend four years getting a degree to get a good job.
    B. Rewarding jobs are not necessarily available, even to those with degrees.
II. The frustration of working people without college degrees but with hopes for advancement
    A. Workers with experience and good qualifications are bypassed for promotion and denied their rightful status.
    B. Since college is considered the province of the young, it is unlikely that an experienced older person will seek a college education.
III. The frustration of students and teachers with traditional views of college
    A. Instead of continuing to emphasize the traditional pursuit of knowledge for its own sake, universities are trying to function as a service industry, preparing students for careers.
IV. Conclusion: deterioration of human values
    A. People are encouraged to make invidious comparisons between less and more desirable kinds of work.
    B. One form of educational experience is being elevated at the expense of the others.

There are a few important points to notice about the format of this outline. First, in some ways, this is a traditional outline: the main ideas are given Roman numerals and the secondary ideas are lettered. This has been done to refer more easily to each of the items and, in the case of the lettered supporting arguments, to separate them clearly from one another. Numbers and letters should be a convenience; if not, they should not be used. Next, the presentation need not be entirely consistent. In this outline, the main ideas are all written in sentence fragments and the supporting ideas are all complete sentences.

What is more important is that all the entries are on *roughly the same level of abstraction:* the main ideas are all very broad, while the secondary ideas suggest the more specific ways in which each paragraph in the essay will be developed. In contrast, here is an excerpt from an outline in which the main entries are both broad and specific:

```
 I. jobs aren't available
 II. Joe V. disappointed
III. college students feel cheated
```

The example of Joe V. is used in the essay only to illustrate important ideas, not as an end in itself. Thus, entry II is *evidence* in support of entries I and III, and therefore "Joe" belongs in a more subordinate position.

```
 I. jobs aren't available
 II. college students feel cheated
    A. Joe V. disappointed
```

All the entries in the complete Blank outline are *re-wordings* of ideas taken from the essay and are self-contained and self-explanatory. Outlines that retain the wording of the original very often fail to make sense by themselves, since phrases or sentences taken out of context usually cannot stand alone as representations of main ideas. Is this group of points easy to understand at a glance?

```
  I. Degree-granting colleges are like false gods.
 II. The college degree is regarded as a stepping-stone to "meaning-
     ful," "better" jobs.
III. The ethical propriety of the entire system is in question.
 IV. Students see themselves as prisoners of economic necessity.
```

How these four points relate to each other or how they serve as arguments to support the essay's thesis is not immediately clear. On the other hand, condensing sentences into brief phrases is usually not much help.

```
  I. destruction of adolescents
 II. vocational schools instead of universities
III. non-degree work menial
```

To appreciate Blanche Blank's argument from reading this group of entries would be impossible.

EXERCISE 6

Select one of the essays listed below, establish its thesis, and construct an outline of its main ideas. The number of entries and the number of levels, main and subordinate, in the outline will depend on the structure of the essay that you select. (For example, you may or may not need to have a subsidiary level for the presentation of evidence.)

Carl Singleton's "What Our Evaluation System Needs is More F's" on pp. 136–138.
Barbara Lerner's "Self-Esteem and Excellence: The Choice and the Paradox" on pp. 172–181.

WRITING A SUMMARY

When you underline and annotate a text, when you ask yourself questions about its contents, when you work out an outline of its structure, you are helping yourself to understand what you are reading. When you write a summary, you are *recording* your understanding for your own information; when you include the summary in an essay of your own, you are *reporting* your understanding to your reader.

A summary of a source is usually a condensation of ideas or information, and therefore to include every repetition and detail is neither necessary nor desirable. Rather, you are to extract only those points which you think are important—the main ideas, which in the original passage may have been interwoven with less important material. Thus, a summary of several pages can sometimes be as brief as one sentence.

In a brief summary, you should add nothing new to the material that is being presented, nor should there be any difference in emphasis or any new interpretation or evaluation. Although, for the sake of clarity and coherence, you may rearrange the order of the ideas, as summarizer you should strive to remain in the background.

The brief summary is often used as part of a larger essay. For example, you have probably summarized your own ideas in the topic sentence of a paragraph or in the conclusion of an essay. When you wish to discuss another piece of writing, you generally summarize the contents briefly, in order to establish for your reader the ideas that you intend to analyze. The writer of a research essay is especially dependent upon the summary as a means of referring to source materials. Through summary, you can condense a broad range of information, and you can present and explain the relevance of a number of sources all dealing with the same subject.

Writing a Summary of a Paragraph

Before you can begin to summarize a short reading—a paragraph, for example—you must, of course, read the passage carefully and become familiar with the significance of each idea and the way it is linked to the other ideas. A successful brief summary is never just a vague generalization, a "spin-off," loosely connected to the reading. The summary should above all be *comprehensive*, conveying as much as possible the totality of thought within the passage. Sometimes, you will find a single comprehensive sentence in the text itself, to be taken out verbatim and used as a summary. But, as a rule, you can find your summary in the text only when the passage is short and contains a particularly strong and comprehensive topic sentence.

The following paragraph *can* be summarized adequately by one of its own sentences. Which one?

> It is often remarked that science has increasingly removed man from a position at the center of the universe. Once upon a time the earth was thought to be the center and the gods were thought to be in close touch with the daily actions of humans. It was not stupid to imagine the earth was at the center, because, one might think, if the earth were moving around the sun, and if you threw a ball vertically upward, it would seem the ball should come down a few feet away from you. Nevertheless, slowly, over many centuries, through the work of Copernicus, Galileo, and many others, we have mostly come to believe that we live on a typical planet orbiting a typical star in a typical galaxy, and indeed that no place in the universe is special.
>
> Gordon Kane, from "Are We the Center of the Universe?"

Both the first and the last sentences are potential topic sentences, but the first is a broader generalization and a more comprehensive summary.

Usually, even when there is a strong sentence to suggest the main idea of the paragraph, you will need to tinker with that sentence, expanding its meaning by giving the language a more general focus. Here, for example, is a paragraph in which no one sentence is broad enough to sum up the main idea, but which contains a scattering of useful phrases:

> In a discussion [with] a class of teachers, I once said that I liked some of the kids in my class much more than others and that, without saying which ones I liked best, I had told them so. After all, this is something that children know, whatever we tell them; it is futile to lie about it. Naturally, these teachers were horrified. "What a terrible thing to say!" one said. "I love all the children in my class exactly the same." Nonsense; a teacher who says this is lying, to herself or to others, and probably doesn't like any of the children very much. Not that there is anything wrong with that; plenty of adults don't like children, and there is no reason why they should. But the trouble is that they feel they should, which makes them feel guilty, which makes them feel resentful, which in turn makes them try to work off their guilt with in-

dulgence and their resentment with subtle cruelties—cruelties of a kind that can be seen in many classrooms. Above all, it makes them put on the phony, syrupy, sickening voice and manner, and the fake smiles and forced, bright laughter that children see so much of in school, and rightly resent and hate.

John Holt, from *How Children Fail*

The object here is to combine key phrases: "a teacher who says" that she "loves all the children" "is lying to herself, or to others," and makes herself (and probably the children) "feel guilty" and "resentful." This summarizing sentence is essentially a patchwork, with the words and phrasing drawn straight from the original; therefore it is essential either to acknowledge the borrowings (by quotation marks, as above) or, preferably, to construct an entirely new sentence, such as this one:

> Although it is only natural for teachers to prefer some students to others, many cannot accept their failure to like all equally well and express their inadequacy and dissatisfaction in ways that are harmful to the children.

Finally, there are some diffuse paragraphs which offer no starting point at all for the summary and require the invention of a new generalization. How would you summarize this paragraph?

To parents who wish to lead a quiet life, I would say: Tell your children that they are very naughty—much naughtier than most children. Point to the young people of some acquaintances as models of perfection and impress your own children with a deep sense of their own inferiority. You carry so many more guns than they do that they cannot fight you. This is called moral influence, and it will enable you to bounce them as much as you please. They think you know and they will not have yet caught you lying often enough to suspect that you are not the unworldly and scrupulously truthful person which you represent yourself to be; nor yet will they know how great a coward you are, nor how soon you will run away, if they fight you with persistency and judgment. You keep the dice and throw them both for your children and yourself. Load them then, for you can easily manage to stop your children from examining them. Tell them how singularly indulgent you are; insist on the incalculable benefit you conferred on them, firstly in bringing them into the world at all, but more particularly in bringing them into it as your own children rather than anyone else's. Say that you have their highest interests at stake whenever you are out of temper and wish to make yourself unpleasant by way of balm to your soul. Harp much upon these highest interests. Feed them spiritually upon such brimstone and treacle as the late Bishop of Winchester's Sunday stories. You hold all the trump cards, or if you do not you can filch them; if you play them with anything like judgment you will find yourselves heads of happy, united God-fearing families, even as did my old friend Mr. Pontifex. True, your children will probably find out all about it some day, but not until too late to be of much service to them or inconvenience to yourself.

Samuel Butler, from The Way of All Flesh

A summary of this paragraph would recommend that parents intimidate their children and thus put them in their place. However, although such a generalization sums up the series of examples contained in the paragraph, it does not convey the fact that Butler is exaggerating outrageously. Butler's caricature of family life would not be taken very seriously. The summary, then, would have to include not only the essence of Butler's recommendations, but also his implied point: that he does not expect anyone to follow his advice. Irony is the term used to describe the conflict between Butler's real meaning—parents are not monsters—and the meaning apparently expressed by his words. Here is a possible summarizing sentence:

> When he ironically suggests that a parent can gain tranquillity and domestic happiness by tyrannizing over his children and making them feel morally inferior, Butler seems to be urging parents to treat their children with respect and justice.

Notice that the summarizing sentences include the author's name. Mentioning the author at the beginning of a summary is often an effective way to emphasize that what you are summarizing is not your own work.

There are, then, three ways to summarize a brief passage:

1. find a summarizing sentence within the passage (and, if you are using it in your own essay, put it in quotation marks);
2. combine elements within the passage into a new summarizing sentence;
3. write a summarizing sentence.

EXERCISE 7

Read the following paragraph and decide which of the sentences following it provides the most comprehensive summary. (Only one answer is correct: state your reason for rejecting each of the other sentences.)

Today, pornography attempts to make its audience focus their fantasies on specific people. The "Playmate of the Month" is a particular woman about whom the reader is meant to have particular fantasies. In my view, this has a more baneful effect on people—makes them demented, in fact, in a way that earlier pornography didn't. Today's pornography promises them that there exists, somewhere on this earth, a life of endlessly desirable and available women and endlessly potent men. The promise that this life is just around the corner—in Hugh Hefner's mansion, or even just in the next joint or the next snort—is maddening and disorienting. And in its futility, it makes for rage and self-hatred. The traditional argument against censorship—that "no one can be seduced by a book"—was probably valid when pornography was impersonal and anonymous, purely an aid to fantasizing about sexual utopia. Today, however, there is addiction and seduction in pornography.

Midge Decter

1. Pornography is responsible for all society's ills, including insanity, substance abuse, and violence.
2. Midge Decter points out that pornography today leads its readers into crime, violence, and delusion, while formerly it merely titillated the senses.
3. The explicit nature of pornography leads people to believe that available to them somewhere are others who exist only for sexual pleasure.
4. Pornography is dangerous because one can get addicted to fantasy.
5. According to Decter, the combination of pornography's explicit detail and its emphasis on fantasy can lead to a dangerous state of frustration where anything is possible.
6. Decter thinks that what is wrong with pornography is that it offers false promises.
7. Because pornography is more realistic now, using photographs of people with names and identities, Midge Decter thinks that it is more harmful to its readers and viewers, who can easily grow dissatisfied and frustrated with fantasies.

EXERCISE 8

Summarize each of the following paragraphs by doing *one* of three things:

A. underline a sentence which will serve as an adequate summary;

or

B. change an existing sentence or combine existing phrases to create an adequate summary;

or

C. invent a new generalization to provide an adequate summary.

1. Liars share with those they deceive the desire not to *be* deceived. As a result, their choice to lie is one which they would like to reserve for themselves while insisting that others be honest. They would prefer, in other words, a "free-rider" status, giving them the benefits of lying without the risks of being lied to. Some think of this free-rider status as for them alone. Others extend it to their friends, social group, or profession. This category of persons can be narrow or broad; but it does require as a necessary backdrop the ordinary assumptions about the honesty of most persons. The free rider trades upon being an exception, and could not exist in a world where everybody chose to exercise the same prerogatives.

Sissela Bok, from *Lying*

2. The neurotic individual may have had some special vulnerability as an infant. Perhaps he was ill a great deal and was given care that singled him out from other children. Perhaps he walked or talked much later— or earlier—than children were expected to, and this evoked unusual treatment. The child whose misshapen feet must be put in casts or the sickly little boy who never can play ball may get out of step with his age mates and with the expectations parents and other adults have about children. Or a child may be very unusually placed in his family. He may be the only boy with six sisters, or a tiny child born between two lusty sets of twins. Or the source of the child's difficulties may be a series of events that deeply affected his relations to people—the death of his mother at the birth of the next child or the prolonged illness or absence of his father. Or a series of coincidences—an accident to a parent, moving to a new town and a severe fright—taken together may alter the child's relationship to the world.

Margaret Mead, from *Some Personal Views*

3. The liberal arts will not simply provide a neatly packaged product such as a guaranteed job. All claims for instant education are counterfeit in that they pretend that learning is a possession. Education should be approached with caution. It is a transforming experience, not something that you purchase on the four-year installment plan. In other words, you don't *have* an education when you graduate as you would possess a stereophonic system or a VW Rabbit. On the contrary, you *are* the condensation of that shaking, transforming experience that we call learning. You will never again be the same, for you no longer need to trade in false wishes. You have found reality to be more enticing than fantasy. You have found, to paraphrase Robert Bolt in "A Man for All

Seasons,'' the ultimate armor against terrors and tragedy, a sense of selfhood without resort to the self-delusion of magic.

Sam A. Banks, from "The Magical Mystery
of the Liberal Arts"

4. A complete costume deliberately chosen may convey many different messages at once, providing us simultaneously with information about the age, sex, occupation, beliefs, tastes, desires, and mood of its wearer. In America a so-called fashion leader will have several hundred "words" at his or her disposal, many of them rare or specialized in other ways, and thus be able to form literally millions of "sentences" expressing a wide range and subtle variations of meaning, qualified with a great many elegant "adjectives" or accessories. The sartorial vocabulary of a migrant farm worker, by contrast, may be limited to some five or ten colloquial terms, from which it is mathematically possible to create only a comparatively few "sentences," almost bare of decoration and expressing the simplest concepts.

Alison Lurie, from "The Dress Code"

5. Play and toys are increasingly important to adults. Most work, in law or medicine or teaching, as on an assembly line, is repetitive. But variety is inexhaustible in play. Almost all work has almost always been drudgery. What is new is that many people are surprised by the drudgery. They have believed that all of life, and *especially* work, can be fun, or, in the current argot, "self-fulfilling." Such a strange idea could come only from institutions of higher learning, and when it is refuted by reality, people assuage their disappointment by turning with awesome intensity to the search for fun in consumption. In affluent societies, most people have acquired the "necessities" (*very* broadly construed), so the consumption that refreshes, briefly, is the consumption of adult toys.

George Will, from *The Pursuit of Virtue
and Other Tory Notions*

6. In modern America, it is a stock dilemma what to call the young man who shares an apartment with one's daughter, or the young woman with whom one's son happens to be cohabiting. "Lover" and "mistress" imply high passion where often enough a dominant concern is economy; "roommate," "companion," and "friend" ignore the sexual component entirely; they are euphemisms simon-pure. Some semi-humorous acronyms have been proposed, but none really satisfactory; the term which finally meets the need may be a euphemism to start, but it will not long be felt as one. If shacking up persists as a custom, the normal word will have to be created, no doubt with satellite euphemisms around it.

Robert Adams, from "Soft Soap and the Nitty-Gritty"

Writing a Brief Summary of an Article

When you want to summarize an essay in a few sentences, how are you to judge which points are significant and which are not? Some essays, especially newspaper articles, have a rambling structure and short paragraphs; thus, you do not even have fully developed paragraphs in which to search for summarizing topic sentences. Are there any standard procedures to help decide which points will need to be summarized? Read "Holdup Man Tells Detectives How to Do It," and observe your own method of pinpointing the key ideas.

HOLDUP MAN TELLS DETECTIVES HOW TO DO IT

His face hidden by a shabby tan coat, the career holdup man peeked out at his audience of detectives and then proceeded to lecture to them on how easy it was to succeed at his trade in New York.

"I don't think there's much any individual police officer can do," the guest lecturer told 50 detectives yesterday at an unusual crime seminar sponsored by the Police Department. "Once I knew what the police officer on the beat was up to I wasn't much concerned about the cops."

The holdup man, who identified himself only as "Nick," is serving a prison term of 6 to 13 years. He said his most serious arrest occurred after he was shot three times by a supermarket manager—not in any encounter with the police.

When asked by a detective taking a course in robbery investigations what the best deterrent would be against gunmen like himself, Nick replied crisply: "stiffer sentences."

After being seriously wounded in his last robbery attempt, Nick said he decided it was time to retire.

"I'm close to 40 and not getting any younger," he explained. "I just don't want to spend any more time in jail."

Nick also offered the detectives some tips on how robbers pick their targets and make their getaways in the city.

Except for wearing a hat, Nick said he affected no disguise. "I usually picked a store in a different neighborhood or in another borough where I was unknown."

Leads on places to hold up usually came from other criminals or from employees. There were no elaborate plannings or "casings," he said, adding:

"I liked supermarkets because there's always a lot of cash around. Uniformed guards didn't deter me because they're not armed, they usually just have sticks. It's better to pick a busy area rather than the suburbs. The chances of someone noticing you are greater in residential or suburban areas."

The detectives, sitting at desks with notepaper in front of them, were rookies as well as veterans. Besides city detectives, the audience included policemen from the Transit Authority, the Housing Authority, the Yonkers Police Department and from Seattle.

They listened carefully as Nick outlined how he or a confederate would inspect the area for signs of uniformed or plainclothes police officers.

The retired robber said he had preferred supermarkets or stores with large window advertisements or displays because these materials prevented him from being seen by passers-by on the street.

"I was always a little nervous or apprehensive before a job," he continued. "But once you're inside and aware of the reaction of the people and you know the possibilities then your confidence comes back."

Nick said he always made his escape in a car and he preferred heavily trafficked roads because it made the getaway vehicle less conspicuous than on little used side streets.

In New York, cheap handguns were selling from $15 to $70, he told the detectives. Such weapons as shotguns or automatic rifles, Nick said, could be rented for about $100 an hour.

Nick said he had been a holdup man since the age of 20 and had committed about 30 "jobs," but was uncertain of the exact number. The biggest robbery he had participated in netted a total of $8,000, and overall he got about $30,000 in his criminal activities.

Asked why he went back to robbing after his first arrest, Nick said: "I wanted whisky, women and big autos. Like most who rob I was not socially accepted. Big money elevates you above the people you think are looking down on you."

Short prison sentences, for first arrests, Nick asserted, probably do little to discourage holdup men. "I see them laying up in jail and it doesn't make any difference," he said. "They just go ahead planning the next one in a different way."

During his "on-and-off" criminal career, Nick said he had never fired any of the guns he carried.

After his one-hour appearance as a guest lecturer, Nick, his face still covered by his coat, was escorted out of the classroom back to his cell at an undisclosed prison.

Selwyn Raab, *New York Times*, 5 March 1975

Step One: Read the Entire Article More Than Once. This direction is not as simple as it sounds. Because you know that your purpose is to isolate main ideas, you may underline what you regard as the key sentences on first reading, and, from then on, look only at the "boiled-down" parts. But it would be a mistake to eliminate minor facts and interesting details too soon. They do have a function in the article, supporting and illuminating the central ideas. For example, the fact that Nick chose to hide his face during and after his "lecture" hardly seems worth underlining, and, in fact, would never *by itself* be regarded as a crucial point. But taken together with some of Nick's remarks, that "discardable" fact contributes to your recognition of a key point of the article: the robber's reliance on *anonymity* is his way of committing a successful crime, and Nick may at some point wish to resume his profession despite his "retirement."

Step Two: Ask Yourself Why the Article Was Written and Published. What does the newspaper want its readers to learn? An inquiry into basic intention is especially important in analyzing a news article, as the journal's and journalist's purpose is frequently two-fold—to describe an event and to suggest the event's significance—and so it is easy for you to confuse the *facts* being recorded with the underlying *reasons* for recording them. Here are two one-sentence summaries of the "Nick" article that are both off the mark because they concentrate too heavily on the event:

> Nick, a convicted retired criminal, was guest speaker at a police seminar and told detectives how robbers pick their targets and make their getaways in New York.

> Nick, after committing thirty robberies, suggested to detectives some possible methods of thwarting future robberies.

Both writers seem to be too concerned with Nick's colorful history and the peculiarity of his helping the police at all. They ignore the significance of what Nick was actually saying. The second summary—by emphasizing the phrase "thwarting future robberies"—is rather misleading and almost contradicts the point of the article; in fact, Nick is really suggesting that the police will continue to be ineffectual.

A news article can also mislead you into thinking that a headline is a summary: the headline "Holdup Man Tells Detectives How to Do It" does not summarize the material in the "Nick" article, but because it is broad and vague, it "sounds" good. What, for example, is meant by the "it" of the headline—robbery or its detection? What does Nick tell the detectives? Headlines are designed to include only as much "as fits the print," and they are often written by people who do not have time to read the article.

Step Three: Look for Repetitions of and Variations on the Same Idea. There is one concrete point that Selwyn Raab and his readers and the police and Nick himself are all interested in: ways of preventing criminals from committing crimes. Not only are we told again and again about Nick's contempt for the police, but we are also given his flat statement that only fear of imprisonment ("stiffer sentences") will discourage a hardened criminal.

A brief summary of this article, then, would mention tougher sentencing as a route to better crime prevention. But there is also the theme of the criminal's need for anonymity, something that ought, if possible, to be incorporated into a complete summary. In Nick's opinion, his career has been a (relatively) successful one because he has managed to appear normal and blend into the crowd. The primary and secondary ideas can be joined in a summary like this one:

> Observing with contempt that the police have rarely been able to penetrate his "anonymous" disguise, Nick, the successful robber, argues that the presence of policemen will not deter most experienced criminals and that only "stiffer sentences" will prevent crime.

EXERCISE 9

Carefully read "2-Year House Arrest Instead of Jail Term Is Ordered for Fraud." Determine the article's purpose and pick out the ideas that Rangel emphasizes; then write a comprehensive summary in two or three sentences.

2-YEAR HOUSE ARREST INSTEAD OF JAIL TERM IS ORDERED FOR FRAUD

A Federal judge in Brooklyn, in an unusual ruling, yesterday sentenced a woman convicted of insurance fraud to "house arrest," saying she must be confined to her home for two years.

The judge, Jack B. Weinstein of Federal District Court, said he had imposed the sentence because he doubted that the defendant could be rehabilitated in jail. He also said he believed that controls other than imprisonment were needed to halt the expanding prison population.

The concept of probation under house arrest has been applied in state cases in California and Florida, probation officials said, but has rarely been used in Federal courts.

Judge Weinstein directed the Federal Probation and Parole Office to develop a set of standards to be used in this case and in future cases. House arrest is detention in one's own house, often under guard.

Under Judge Weinstein's sentence, the defendant, Maureen Murphy, a 35-year-old legal secretary, is to be confined to her home in Elmhurst, Queens, and may leave it only to go to work, or to shop for food, or for medical or religious reasons. She may not change her place of residence or her job except with permission from probation officials and she must go home directly from work.

James F. X. Haran, the chief Federal probation officer for the Eastern District of New York, said that although no guard would be stationed at Miss Murphy's home, she would be subject to unannounced visits or telephone calls from probation officers seven days a week at any hour of the day or night.

"We still have to come up with written guidelines so she knows exactly what she is responsible for and the court knows exactly how we are approaching this," Mr. Haran said.

Miss Murphy and two lawyers, Jay Teitler of Brooklyn and Marc Shultz of Woodmere, L.I., were convicted on Aug. 15 of racketeering and conspiracy. They were among nine defendants indicted in April on charges of defrauding 19 insurance companies over a 10-year period by filing inflated and bogus accident claims. The two lawyers have not been sentenced yet.

Miss Murphy was also found guilty of obstruction of justice for encouraging two witnesses to lie to a grand jury.

She had faced up to 50 years in prison and a $56,000 fine. Judge Weinstein noted that Miss Murphy had been "raised in a close-knit, harmonious and religious family setting by hard-working parents" and was "an excellent and bright worker who has always been steadily employed."

He said the maximum term was "too long to even be considered seriously for this relatively young person." He also said the fine "could never be paid and would accomplish nothing except to make it impossible for the defendant to live and rehabilitate herself."

The judge placed her on five years' probation and ordered her to serve two of those years under house arrest.

"Putting her in prison for any substantial length of time will undoubtedly help to destroy her," Judge Weinstein said in a written statement that he released to explain his decision. "The conditions of imprisonment, even in the best of prisons for women, are reprehensible."

Citing the nation's prison population, which he said was approaching half a million inmates, the judge said that longer imprisonment for more people could not be borne indefinitely and that other controls and social policies to curb crime, along with alternative punishments, were "essential."

He added that while jailing those who were considered dangerous must continue to be judicial policy, deterrence among the nonprofessional criminals could be accomplished without long incarceration.

In another case, a Federal judge in Los Angeles sentenced David A. Wayte on Sept. 10 to a similar confinement in his grandmother's home for six months for refusing to register for the draft.

Judge Weinstein said the house-arrest sentence imposed in the New York case was used elsewhere in the world and was considered by some to be highly objectionable. "The difference, however, is that in other countries it is used to repress political dissent and before trial," he said. "Here it will be used after a full trial where the defendant has been found guilty of a serious offense."

Steven Kimelman, Miss Murphy's lawyer, said the sentence was an innovative idea that someday might be widely used as an alternative to jail. But he said his client was being used as a "guinea pig" and should have been placed under regular probation.

Mr. Kimelman said he would appeal the sentence on the ground that the judge had no authority to impose it.

More Humane and Economical

Mr. Haran, the chief probation officer, applauded the sentence, saying it was more humane and economical than a prison term. "It doesn't break up a family or cost a loss of employment, which means a saving on social-service costs," he said.

He estimated that it would cost the Government about $3,000 a year to administer having one person under this type of probation, while it cost $30,000 a year to keep a person in jail. His Eastern District office handles Federal probation cases in Brooklyn, Queens, Staten Island and Nassau and Suffolk Counties.

The United States Attorney for the Eastern District, Raymond J. Dearie, had recommended that Miss Murphy be given a prison term and the maximum fine because she was a "long-time, trusted member of this criminal venture." He refused to comment yesterday on the house-arrest sentence.

Jesus Rangel, *New York Times*, 24 September 1985

Writing a Summary of a Complex Essay

When you are asked to summarize a reading containing a number of complex and abstract ideas, a reading which may be disorganized, and therefore difficult to comprehend and condense, the best way to prepare for your summary is to isolate each important point and note it down in a list. Here is an essay by Bertrand Russell, followed by a preliminary list of notes, a statement of Russell's thesis, and the final summary. (The numbers in the margin are keyed to the preliminary list of notes on pp. 59–60.)

THE SOCIAL RESPONSIBILITY OF SCIENTISTS

Science, ever since it first existed, has had important effects in matters that lie outside the purview of pure science. Men of science have [1] differed as to their responsibility for such effects. Some have said that [2] the function of the scientist in society is to supply knowledge, and that he need not concern himself with the use to which this knowledge is put. I do not think that this view is tenable, especially in our age. The [3] scientist is also a citizen; and citizens who have any special skill have a public duty to see, as far as they can, that their skill is utilized in accordance with the public interest. Historically, the functions of the scientist in public life have generally been recognized. The Royal Society was founded by Charles II as an antidote to "fanaticism" which had plunged England into a long period of civil strife. The scientists of that time did not hesitate to speak out on public issues, such as religious toleration and the folly of prosecutions for witchcraft. But although science has, in various ways at various times, favored what may be called a humanitarian outlook, it has from the first had an intimate and sinister connection with war. Archimedes sold his skill to the Tyrant of Syracuse for use against the Romans; Leonardo secured a salary from the Duke of Milan for his skill in the art of fortification; and Galileo got employment under the Grand Duke of Tuscany because he could calculate the trajectories of projectiles. In the French Revolution the scientists who were not guillotined were set to making new explosives, but Lavoisier was not spared, because he was only discovering hydrogen which, in those days, was not a weapon of war. There have been some honorable exceptions to the subservience of scientists to warmongers. During the Crimean War the British government consulted Faraday as to the feasibility of attack by poisonous gases. Faraday replied that it was entirely feasible, but that it was inhuman and he would have nothing to do with it. 4

Modern democracy and modern methods of publicity have made the problem of affecting public opinion quite different from what it used to be. The knowledge that the public possesses on any important issue is derived from vast and powerful organizations: the press, radio, and, above all, television. The knowledge that governments possess is more limited. They are too busy to search out the facts for themselves, and consequently they know only what their underlings think good for them unless there is such a powerful movement in a different sense that politicians cannot ignore it. Facts which ought to guide the decisions of statesmen—for instance, as to the possible lethal qualities of fallout—do not acquire their due importance if they remain buried in scientific journals. They acquire their due importance only when they become known to so many voters that they affect the course of the elections. In general, there is an opposition to widespread publicity for such facts. This opposition springs from various sources, some sinister, some comparatively respectable. At the bottom of the moral scale there is the financial interest of the various industries connected with armaments. Then there are various effects of a somewhat thoughtless patriotism, which believes in secrecy and in what is called "toughness." But perhaps more important than either of these is the unpleasantness of the facts, which makes the general public turn aside to pleasanter topics such as divorces and murders. The consequence is that what ought to be known widely throughout the general public will not be known unless great efforts are made by disinterested persons to see that the information reaches the minds and hearts of vast numbers 5 6 7 8 of people. I do not think this work can be successfully accomplished except by the help of men of science. They, alone, can speak with the authority that is necessary to combat the misleading statements of those scientists who have permitted themselves to become merchants of death. If disinterested scientists do not speak out, the others will succeed in conveying a distorted impression, not only to the public but also to the politicians.

It must be admitted that there are obstacles to individual action in our age which did not exist at earlier times. Galileo could make his own telescope. But once when I was talking with a very famous astronomer he explained that the telescope upon which his work depended owed its existence to the benefaction of enormously rich men, and, if he had not stood well with them, his astronomical discoveries would have been impossible. More frequently, a scientist only acquires access to enormously expensive equipment if he stands well with the government of his country. He knows that if he adopts a rebellious attitude he and his family are likely to perish along with the rest of civilized mankind. It is a tragic dilemma, and I do not think that one should censure a man whatever his decision; but I do think—and I think men of science should realize—that unless something rather drastic is done under the leadership or through the inspiration of some part of the scientific world, the human race, like the Gadarene swine, will rush down a steep place to destruction in blind ignorance of the fate that scientific skill has prepared for it.

It is impossible in the modern world for a man of science to say with any honesty, "My business is to provide knowledge, and what use is made of the knowledge is not my responsibility." The knowledge that a man of science provides may fall into the hands of men or institutions devoted to utterly unworthy objects. I do not suggest that a man of science, or even a large body of men of science, can altogether prevent this, but they can diminish the magnitude of the evil.

There is another direction in which men of science can attempt to provide leadership. They can suggest and urge in many ways the value of those branches of science of which the important practical uses are beneficial and not harmful. Consider what might be done if the money at present spent on armaments were spent on increasing and distributing the food supply of the world and diminishing the population pressure. In a few decades, poverty and malnutrition, which now afflict more than half the population of the globe, could be ended. But at present almost all the governments of great states consider that it is better to spend money on killing foreigners than on keeping their own subjects alive. Possibilities of a hopeful sort in whatever field can best be worked out and stated authoritatively by men of science; and, since they can do this work better than others, it is part of their duty to do it.

As the world becomes more technically unified, life in an ivory tower becomes increasingly impossible. Not only so; the man who stands out against the powerful organizations which control most of human activity is apt to find himself no longer in the ivory tower, with a wide outlook over a sunny landscape, but in the dark and subterranean dungeon upon which the ivory tower was erected. To risk such a habitation demands courage. It will not be necessary to inhabit the dungeon if there are many who are willing to risk it, for everybody knows that the modern world depends upon scientists, and, if they are insistent, they must be listened to. We have it in our power to make a good world; and, therefore, with whatever labor and risk, we must make it.

12

Bertrand Russell, from *Fact and Fiction*

First Stage: List of Notes and Determination of the Thesis

1. Should scientists try to influence the way their discoveries are used?
2. One point of view: the scientist's role is to make the discovery; what happens afterwards is not his concern.
3. Russell's point of view: scientists are like any other knowledgeable and public-spirited people; they must make sure that the products of their knowledge work for, not against, society.
4. In the past, some scientists have made public their views on controversial issues like freedom of religion; others have been servants of the war machine.
5. The power to inform and influence the public is now controlled by the news media.
6. Government officials are too busy to be well-informed; subordinates feed them only enough information to get them reelected.
7. It is in the interests of various groups, ranging from weapons makers to patriots, to limit the amount of scientific information that the public receives.
8. The public is reluctant to listen to distasteful news.
9. Since the public deserves to hear the truth, scientists, who are respected for their knowledge and who belong to no party or faction, ought to do more to provide the public with information about the potentially lethal consequences of their discoveries. By doing so, they will correct the distortions of those scientists who have allied themselves with warmongers.
10. It is very difficult for scientists to speak out since they depend on government and business interests to finance their work.
11. While scientists cannot entirely stop others from using some of their discoveries for antisocial purposes, they can support other, more constructive kinds of research.

12. Speaking out is worth the risk of incurring the displeasure of powerful people; since the work of scientists is so vital, the risk isn't too great, especially if they act together.

Russell's Thesis: Contrary to the self-interested arguments of many scientists and other groups, scientists have a social responsibility to make sure that their work is used for, not against, the benefit of society.

Second Stage: Summary

Some scientists, as well as other groups, consider that they need not influence the way in which their discoveries are used. However, Bertrand Russell believes that scientists have a social responsibility to make sure that their work is used for, not against, the benefit of society. In modern times, it has been especially difficult for concerned scientists to speak out because many powerful groups prefer to limit and distort what the public is told, because government officials are too busy to be thoroughly informed, because scientists depend on the financial support of business and government, and because the public itself is reluctant to hear distasteful news. Nevertheless, scientists have the knowledge and the prestige to command public attention, and their work is too vital for their voices to be suppressed. If they act together, they can warn us if their work is likely to be used for an antisocial purpose and, at least, they can propose less destructive alternatives.

Guidelines for Writing a Summary

1. The summary must be comprehensive. You should review all the ideas on your list, and include in your summary all those that are essential to the author's development of his thesis.

2. The summary must be concise. Eliminate repetitions in your list, even if the author restates the same points. Your summary should be considerably shorter than the source. Notice that the Russell summary excludes points one, four, and five on the list of notes: point one is included in the presentation of points two and three; point four is an example, one which is not essential to an understanding of the essay; and point five is not directly related to Russell's argument.

3. The summary must be coherent. It should make sense as a paragraph in its own right; it should not be taken directly from your list of notes and sound like a list of sentences that happen to be strung together in a paragraph format. In the summary of Russell's essay, a framework is established in the first two sentences, which present the two alternative views of the scientist's responsibility. The next sentence, which describes the four obstacles to scientific freedom of speech, illustrates the rearrangement of ideas that is characteristic of summary. While reviewing the list of notes, the summarizer has noticed that points six, seven, eight, and ten each refers to a different way in which scientific truth is often suppressed; she has therefore brought them together and lined them up in a parallel construction based on the repeated word "because." Finally, the last two sentences contain a restatement of Russell's thesis and point out that the obstacles to action are not as formidable as they seem.

4. The summary must be independent. You are not being asked to imitate or identify yourself with the author whom you are writing about. On the contrary, you are expected to maintain your own voice throughout the summary. Even as you are jotting down your list of notes, you should try to use your own words. While you want to make it clear that *you* are writing the summary, you should be careful not to create any misrepresentation or distortion by introducing comments or criticisms of your own. (Such distortion is most likely to occur when you strongly disagree with the material that you are summarizing.) Thus, it would not be acceptable to point out in your summary the dangers of making scientific secrets public, for that would be arguing with Russell. On the other hand, within certain limits it is acceptable to go beyond point-by-point summary, to suggest the author's implied intention, and, in a sense, to interpret the work's meaning for your reader. You might state, for example, that ours is an age which encourages interdependence and discourages independent action. While Russell does not say so specifically, in so many words, the assertion is certainly substantiated by the material in the last two paragraphs. Such interpretations have to be supported by evidence from the reading, and you must make it clear to your reader when you are summarizing directly from the text and when you are commenting on or inferring or explaining what is being summarized.

ASSIGNMENT 1

Summarize one of the following passages in one or a few sentences. If it seems helpful to you, begin by making a preliminary list of points.

1. The age of medical technology began to pick up great momentum around the time of the First World War, and with it consequentially came the age of specialization. Beforehand, almost all doctors were general practitioners. As specialists and subspecialists began to de-

velop, the number of G.P.s went into a fifty-year decline, and by the middle nineteen-sixties G.P.s were becoming scarce, if not approaching extinction. To the layman—the neighbor, the patient—who looked back upon the old superhuman doctor with admiration, imagination, exaggeration, and nostalgia, it seemed that a form of giant had disappeared. It also seemed that, as in most human pursuits, when giants shuffle off the coil they are replaced by committees. Gynecologist, urologist, nephrologist, immunologist, pediatric oncologist, neuroophthalmologist, psychopharmacologist, coronary angiographist—through time the specialists had subdivided and subsubdivided, advancing and serving technology. The positive effects of this history—and of the research that created new machines and new procedures and new subspecialties to accompany them—were dramatic and considerable. In no way were they diminished by the concomitant eventuality that some effects were negative.

The committee—which seldom, if ever, met—took on the numbers of a crowd. No one seemed to be in charge. The patient, in the process, was not so much quartered as diced. People were being passed like bucks—or so it seemed to them—from doctor to doctor. Even such a traditionally one-on-one event as the "complete physical" might be subdivided, as internists who did not do pelvic or rectal examinations sent their patients on to gynecolgoists and urologists. Most people did not have access to a doctor who had the time—or maybe the inclination—not only to deal with them when they were sick but also to help keep them from getting sick in the first place. There was such an absence of doctors with varied general training that someone in, say, a small Maine town would have to travel large distances just to do something as natural as have a baby. For many people, the fees of specialists were prohibitive. People wanted health care. They wanted it locally, and they wanted it at a price they could afford. Also, they wanted something more on the other side of the Rx pad than a dispenser of penicillin. In growing numbers, they felt confused and used. Was there a doctor in the house who could still regard a patient as a person rather than a disease?

To many young doctors, a clearly defined niche of technical competence seemed preferable to the complexity of general practice. To varying extents, specialists could retreat into their specialties. As the medical technocracy grew, it reproduced itself, by contemplating the pool of medical students and choosing its own kind. In their concentration on a single topic, most doctors seemed more than willing to risk losing touch with medicine as a whole. The old doc of the magazine cover—magician, counselor, metaphysician—had been replaced by technicians with machines and clipboards.

John McPhee, from "Heirs of General Practice"

2. It may seem inconceivable that tactics of terror could be used successfully against a nation as powerful as the United States or indeed any industrial nation. No band of terrorists is a match for any metropolitan

police force, much less the smallest standing army. None can command the resources of the tiniest nation. Yet terrorism has been characterized as a worldwide menace. The terror event enjoys an unparalleled power simply because of its media value.

Of all the reasons for terrorist success, the platform offered by the enthusiastic media is by far the most important. Terrorists have used the media as a springboard onto the world stage. As a result, the terrorist assault has come to resemble highly choreographed theater, with the Western media inadvertently emerging as an adversary of liberal democracies by working in de facto partnership with terrorists.

Both government and terrorists operate in the glare of the media spotlight. Without that attention, the outcome of the incident becomes relatively insignificant. The militants in Iran recognized this as an essential ingredient of success and acted accordingly. By encouraging regular media coverage, the terrorists made the torment of the hostages an integral part of American daily life for 444 days. The fifty-four hostages quickly became so well known that any action by the United States that could have jeopardized their lives would have engendered severe political penalties.

The media mold public perceptions about the success or failure of the terrorist operation, about official competence in the face of the threat, and about the prowess of the terrorist organization. For example, Israel's desperate decision to resist escalating terrorist demands and its attempt at a high-risk rescue at Entebbe were depicted by the media as a major triumph. The German counterterrorist rescue force at Mogadishu basked in the same affirmative limelight. By contrast, the American military experience in the Iranian desert was presented not simply as a justified attempt that failed, but as a debacle, a symbol of American command weakness and presidential bungling. As a terror event unfolds, the media's involvement creates a peculiar synergy among the government, the public, and the terrorists. Each of the actors participates directly in the event, creating in effect a spectacle with a participatory audience. The problem for the terrorist comes when the level of violence loses its media sex appeal, when the next airline hijacking or "knee-capping" is no longer spellbinding news.

To maintain the media spotlight, terrorist organizations must heighten the threshold for the spectacular assault. Accepting the thesis that one of the terrorist's primary goals is governmental disruption and that there must be an aura of Broadway about the event, we can speculate about the next phase. Terrorists will be forced to change their methods, their tools, and their targets to stay ahead of government preparations and ensure front-page coverage.

Robert H. Kupperman, from "Terrorism and Public Policy"

3. Capital flight has always been a tactic that management wished to have at its disposal in order to "discipline" labor and to assure itself of a favorable business climate wherever it set up operations. But only in the

last two decades has systematic disinvestment become, from management's perspective, a *necessary* strategy, and from a technological perspective, a *feasible* one.

It is crucial to view this development in the light of post–World War II economic history. It was not only international competition that was threatening corporate profits. The postwar series of labor victories that successfully constrained the flexibility of management by regulating the workplace and forcing the corporate sector to underwrite part of the costs of the "social safety net" also contributed to the profit squeeze.

From the middle of the 1930s to the 1970s, organized labor in the United States won major concessions on a broad set of issues that ultimately limited capital's flexibility in its use of labor. One indicator of this loss in flexibility and of the subversion of unquestioned managerial discretion can be found in the sheer size of the contract documents negotiated between unions and employers. The initial agreement between the United Automobile Workers (UAW) and General Motors (GM), signed in 1937, covered less than one-and-a-half pages and contained only one provision: union recognition. By 1979 the UAW-GM contract, with its extensive array of provisions covering each of the company's 140 production units, contained literally thousands of pages printed in proverbial small type. In exacting detail the contract specifies hundreds of items from wage scales and a cornucopia of fringe benefits to limits on subcontracting and the pacing of each machine and assembly line; it even goes so far as to establish some rules governing the introduction of new technology.

Each of these rules and regulations was forced into place by labor for the explicit purpose of increasing job security and limiting the discretionary power of management. With the important—indeed absolutely critical—exception of limiting the right of management to reduce the aggregate size of its labor force, these incursions by organized labor were highly successful. As long as management *had* to deal with labor where workers were well organized, it was constrained to operate within the set of rules that Unions had long struggled to secure. Moreover, using the power of the State, labor won important concessions from industry through the regulatory process. Minimum wages, fair labor standards, occupational health and safety provisions, equal employment opportunity, extended unemployment benefits, and improvements in workers' compensation constitute only a partial list of the gains made by labor during this period. Taken together, these victories limited management's ability to extract the last ounce of productivity from labor and thus the last ounce of profit.

During the heyday of American economic power, from 1945 to about 1971, industrialists were able to reap healthy profits while affording these concessions to organized labor. The so-called social contract between labor and management even proved advantageous to the corporate sector, for it assured some semblance of labor peace needed for continued economic expansion. Corporations did not complain as bitterly in the early 1960s when they were earning an average annual real rate of return of 15.5 percent on their investments. Their attitudes changed dramatically, however, when profits began to slip near the end of the decade. By the late 1960s, the profit rate for non-financial corporations had declined to 12.7 percent. It fell further as a result of increased international competition. By the early 1970s, it never rose above 10 percent again.

Management found that it could no longer afford the social contract and maintain its accustomed level of profit. Instead of accepting the new realities of the world marketplace, one firm after another began to contemplate fresh ways to circumvent union rules and to hold the line on wages. Of course, labor was not initially ready to concede its hard-won victories; therefore to accomplish its goal of reasserting its authority, management had to find some mechanism for disarming organized labor of its standard weapons: the grievance process, various job actions, and work stoppages. The solution was capital mobility. If labor was unwilling to moderate its demands, the prescription became "move"—or at least threaten to do so. For one enterprise, this entailed disinvestment. When entire industries adopted this strategy, the result was deindustrialization.

Barry Bluestone and Bennett Harrison,
from *The Deindustrialization of America*

2.
Presenting Sources to Others

"I hate quotations. Tell me what you know."

Ralph Waldo Emerson (1849)

"By necessity, by proclivity, and by delight, we all quote."

Ralph Waldo Emerson (1876)

These quotations appear to be contradictory; but, in fact, they merely represent the development of one writer's understanding of his craft. Like Emerson in 1849, most writers hope to rely entirely upon what they know and to express their knowledge in their own words. But, as Emerson realized later, one rarely writes about an area of thought which has never before been explored. Someone has usually gone part of the way before; and it seems only common sense to make use of that person's discoveries.

Assuming that most of your writing in college will be based directly or indirectly upon what you have read, you will need to have a working knowledge of two more methods of presenting other people's ideas to your readers: *quotation* and *paraphrase*.

REASONS FOR QUOTING

In academic writing, presenting the words of another writer is a basic method of supporting your own ideas. Quotation is a pivotal skill. *Correct quotation* tells your reader that you respect your sources, that you know how to distinguish between your own work and theirs, and that you will not make unacknowledged use of another writer's words and ideas, which is called *plagiarism*. Writers who understand how to quote understand the need to give credit to their sources both for borrowed ideas and for borrowed words. *Appropriate quotation* tells your reader that you know when to quote and that you are not allowing your sources' words to dominate your writing. Quotations should not be used as a substitute for summary or paraphrase. Experienced writers hold quotation marks in reserve for those times when they think it essential to present the source's exact words.

Quoting for Support

You will often refer to another writer's work as evidence in support of one of your own points. To make sure that the evidence retains its full impact, you may decide to retain the author's original language, instead of putting the sentences in your own words. Very often, quoted material appears in an essay as an appeal to authority; the source being quoted is important enough or familiar enough with the subject (as in an eyewitness account) to make the original words worth quoting. For example, the only quotation in a *New York Times* article describing political and economic chaos in Bolivia presents the opinion of a government official:

> Even the Government acknowledges its shaky position. "The polity is unstable, capricious and chaotic," Adolfo Linares Arraya, Minister of Planning and Coordination, said. "The predominance of crisis situations has made the future unforeseeable."

The minister's words in themselves are not especially quotable, and they may not even be true; but his position as representative of the government makes his words useful evidence for the reporter's assessment of the Bolivian crisis.

Quoting Vivid Language

The wording of the source material may be so ingenious that, if you express it in your own words, the point will be lost. Quotation is often necessary for a sentence that is very compact or that relies on a striking image to make its point. For example, here is a paragraph from a review of a book about Vietnamese history.

> Not many nations have had such a history of scrapping: against Mongols and Chinese seeking to dominate them from the north, and to the south against weaker and more innocent peoples who stood in the way of the Vietnamese march to the rich Mekong Delta and the under-

populated land of Cambodia. Mr. Hodgkin [the author] quotes from a poem by a medieval Vietnamese hero: "By its tradition of defending the country/the army is so powerful it can swallow the evening star."

The quotation adds authentic evidence to the reviewer's discussion and provides a memorable image for the reader.

Quoting Another Writer in Order to Comment on the Quotation

As part of your essay, you may want to analyze or comment upon a statement made by another writer. Your readers should have that writer's exact words in front of them if they are to get the full benefit of your commentary; you have to quote it in order to talk about it. Thus, when a reviewer writing about Philip Norman's biography of the Beatles wants to criticize the biographer's style, he has to supply a sample so that his readers can make up their own minds.

Worst of all is the overwritten prologue, about John Lennon's death and its impact in Liverpool: "The ruined imperial city, its abandoned river, its tormented suburban plain, knew an anguish greater even than the recession and unemployment which have laid Merseyside waste under bombardments more deadly than Hitler's blitz." A moment's thought should have made Norman and his publishers realize that this sort of thing, dashed off in the heat of the moment, would quickly come to seem very embarrassing indeed.

Gaining Distance through Quotation

Writers generally use quotation to distinguish between the writer of the essay and the writer being cited in the essay. There are a few less important reasons for using quotation marks—reasons which also involve this concept of the distance between the writer and his sources of information. For example, you may want to use quotation marks to indicate that a word or phrase is not in common or standard use. A phrase may be *obsolete*, having been dropped from current usage—the young man announced his intention of "cutting a rug" at the party that evening—or *slang*, not having yet been absorbed into standard English—she tried to "cop out" of doing her share of the work. In effect, the writer wants to use the phrase and at the same time "cover" himself by signaling his awareness that the phrase is not quite right: he is distancing himself from his own vocabulary. It is usually better to take full responsibility for your choice of words and to avoid using slang or obsolete vocabulary, with or without quotation marks. But if the context requires such phrasing, you may use quotation marks to gain the necessary distance.

A different kind of distance can be achieved when quotation marks are used to suggest some form of irony: The actor was joined by his "constant companion." The quoted phrase is a familiar euphemism, a bland expression substituted for a more blunt term. Again, by placing it in quotation marks, the author is both calling attention to and distancing himself from the euphemism.

Quotation marks also serve as a means of disassociation for journalists who wish to avoid taking sides on an issue or making editorial comments.

> A fire that roared through a 120-year-old hotel and took at least 11 lives was the work of a "sick arsonist," the county coroner said today. Robert Jennings, the Wayne County coroner, said that he had told county officials that the building was a "fire trap."

The author of this article did not want the responsibility of attributing the fire to a "sick arsonist" or labeling the building a "fire trap"—at any rate, not until the findings of an investigation or a trial make the terminology unquestionably valid. Thus, he is careful not only to use quotation marks around certain phrases but also to cite the precise source of the statement.

USING QUOTATIONS

The apparatus for quotation is twofold: 1. by *inserting quotation marks*, you indicate that you are borrowing certain words, as well as certain ideas, that appear in your writing; 2. by *inserting a citation* containing the source's name, you give credit for both ideas and words to the original author.

Citation	*Quotation*
Somerset Maugham observed,	"To write simply is as difficult as to be good."

Direct Quotation: Separating the Quotation from Your Own Writing

The simplest way to quote is to combine the citation (written by you) with the words to be quoted (exactly as they were said or written by your source). This method—called direct quotation—joins together two quite separate statements, with punctuation (comma or colon) bridging the gap.

> St. Paul declared, "It is better to marry than to burn."

> In his first epistle to the Corinthians, St. Paul commented on lust: "It is better to marry than to burn."

In these forms of direct quotation, the quoted words are *not* fully integrated into the grammatical structure of your sentence. The comma or colon and the capital letter at the beginning of the quoted sentence, which are both separating devices, make clear that two voices are at work in the sentence: yours and your source's. In general, you should choose this kind of direct quotation when you want to differentiate between yourself and the quoted words. There are many reasons for wanting to emphasize this difference; an obvious example would be your own disagreement with the quotation.

The colon is used less frequently than the comma, partly because it usually follows a more formal introductory signal than a short citation; as a rule, it follows a clause that can stand alone as a complete sentence. As such, the colon separates a complete idea of your own from a complementary or supporting idea in your source.

Direct and Indirect Quotation: Running Quotations into Your Sentences

You can construct a much more integrated sentence if you regard the quoted statement as the direct object of the verb:

> St. Paul declared that "it is better to marry than to burn."

> Alvin Toffler defined future shock as "the shattering stress and disorientation that we induce in individuals by subjecting them to too much change in too short a time."

In this kind of quotation, only the quotation marks indicate the presence of someone else's words. There is no signal for the reader to separate citation from quotation—no comma or colon, no capital letter. The first word of the quoted material, in this second type of direct quotation, is *not* capitalized, even if it was capitalized in the source.

> Beware of all enterprises that require new clothes.
>
> Henry David Thoreau

> Thoreau warned his readers to "beware of all enterprises that require new clothes."

The effect is very smooth, and the reader's attention is not distracted from the flow of sentences.

Because integrating the quotation tends to blur the distinction between writer and source one must be careful to avoid confusion. Look, for example, at the various ways of quoting this first-person sentence, which was originally spoken (and not written) by a motorist: "I hate all pedestrians."

> The motorist said, "I hate all pedestrians."

> The motorist said that "I hate all pedestrians."

The first method, quoting with separation by punctuation, works well and requires no alteration in the original sentence. But in the second version, quoting with integration, the original wording does not quite fit: the first-person "I" conflicts with the third-person "motorist"; one wonders who "I" is—the motorist or the writer! The present-tense "hate" also conflicts with the past-tense "said," and "hate" must be turned into "hated." But once the person and the tense of the original statement have been altered for the sake of clarity and consistency, only two words—"all pedestrians"—are actually being quoted:

> The motorist said that she hated "all pedestrians."

If you decide not to put quotation marks around the two words taken from the original source, you are using *indirect quotation*:

> The motorist said that she hated all pedestrians.

In indirect quotation, you report rather than quote what has been said.

Direct quotation, without the use of "that," is probably the most appropriate method of presenting the motorist's opinion of pedestrians. The absence of quotation marks in the indirect quotation might in some cases lead to confusion: if one were collecting evidence for a libel suit, quotation marks would be necessary to indicate that the motorist was responsible for the precise wording. *As a rule, the writer has the obligation to insert quotation marks when using the exact words of his sources, whether written or oral.*

Direct quotation:

> Robert Ingersoll condemned those who deny others their civil liberties: "I am the inferior of any man whose rights I trample underfoot."

Indirect quotation:

> Robert Ingersoll proclaimed that he was the inferior of any man whose rights he trampled underfoot.

The indirect quotation does not indicate exactly who phrased this sentence. Changing ''I'' to ''he'' and the present to the past tense does not constitute using one's own words; the basic phrasing of the sentence remains Ingersoll's. To imply, as this sentence could, that the wording is the writer's, not Ingersoll's, is dishonest. For this reason, writers should use indirect quotation with great care. If one of the two forms of direct quotation does not seem appropriate, then you should invent your own phrasing—called paraphrase—to express the source's original statement.

Using the Historical Present Tense

Certain ideas and statements remain true long after their creators have died. By convention, or general agreement, writers often refer to these statements in the present tense.

> Thomas Mann writes, ''A man's dying is more the survivors' affair than his own.''

When you are devoting part of your own essay to a ''discussion'' with another writer, you may prefer to conduct the discussion on a common ground of time and use the present tense, called the *historical present*.

Punctuating Direct Quotations

You have already learned about punctuating the beginning of the quotation: in one type of direct quotation, the citation is followed by a comma or a colon; in the second type, quotations are completely integrated into your sentence and are introduced by no punctuation at all. There is a tendency to forget this second point and to include an unnecessary comma:

> Stendhal urged his readers to be silent about their pleasures, for, ''to describe happiness is to diminish it. ''

Remember that there should be no barriers between citation and quotation:

> Stendhal urged his readers to be silent about their pleasures, for ''to describe happiness is to diminish it. ''

Note also that, in the second type of direct quotation, the first letter of the quotation is not capitalized.

There is no easy way of remembering the proper sequence of punctuation for closing a quotation. The procedure has been determined by conventional and arbitrary agreement, for the convenience of printers. Although other countries abide by other conventions, in the United States the following rules apply—and *there are no exceptions.*

1. All periods and commas are placed inside the terminal quotation marks. It does not matter whether the period belongs to *your* sentence or to the quoted sentence: it must appear inside the marks. This is the most important rule, and the one most often ignored. (Don't resort to ambiguous devices like ".')

> P. T. Barnum is reputed to have said that "there's a sucker born every minute."

> P. T. Barnum is reputed to have said that "there's a sucker born every minute," and Barnum's circuses undertook to entertain each and every one.

Notice that, in the second example, the comma at the end of the quotation really belongs to the framework sentence, not to the quotation itself; nevertheless, it goes inside the marks.

2. All semicolons, colons, and dashes belong outside the quotation marks. They should be regarded as the punctuation for your sentence, and not for the quotation.

> George Santayana wrote that "those who cannot remember the past are condemned to repeat it"; today, we are in danger of forgetting the lessons of history.

Occasionally, when a semicolon or a colon or (most likely) a dash appears at the end of the material to be quoted, you will decide to include the punctuation in the quotation; in that case, the punctuation should be placed inside the marks.

> Lucretia Mott argued urgently for women's rights: "Let woman then go on--not asking favors, but claiming as a right the removal of all hindrances to her elevation in the scale of being--" so that, as a result, she might "enter profitably into the active business of man."

3. Question marks and exclamation points are sometimes placed inside the quotation marks and sometimes placed outside. If the quotation itself is a question or an exclamation, the mark or point goes inside the quotation marks; if your own sentence is an exclamation or a question, the mark or point goes outside a quotation placed at the very end of your sentence.

> In 1864, General Sherman signaled the arrival of his reinforcements: "Hold the fort! I am coming!"

> Can anyone in the 1980s agree with Dumas that "woman inspires us to great things and prevents us from achieving them"?

> Sigmund Freud's writings occasionally reveal a remarkable lack of insight: "The great question that has never been answered, and which I have not yet been able to answer despite my thirty years of research into the feminine soul, is: What does a woman want?"

> Freud was demonstrating remarkably little insight when he wrote, "What does a woman want?" citing his "thirty years of research into the feminine soul"!

To construct a sentence that ends logically in two question marks (or exclamation points) is possible: one for the quotation and one for your own sentence. In that case, one is enough—and, by convention, it should be placed *inside* the marks:

> What did Freud mean when he asked, "What does a woman want?"

These rules apply only to the quotation of complete sentences or reasonably long phrases. Whether it is a quotation or an obsolete, slang, or ironic reference, a single word or a brief phrase should be fully integrated into your sentence, without being preceded or followed by commas.

> Winston Churchill's reference to "blood, sweat and tears" rallied the English to prepare for war.

Interrupting Quotations

Sometimes it is desirable to break up a long quotation or to achieve variety in your sentences by interrupting a quotation and placing the citation in the middle.

> "I do not mind lying," wrote Samuel Butler, "but I hate inaccuracy."

Notice that you have divided Butler's statement into two separate parts, and therefore you need to use *four* sets of quotation marks: two introductory and two terminal. The citation is joined to the quotation by a comma on either side. The danger point is the beginning of the second half of the quotation: if you forget to use the marks there, then you are failing to distinguish your words from Butler's.

Quoting within a Quotation

Sometimes, the statement that you want to quote already contains a quotation. When a quotation incorporates a second quotation, you must use two sets of quotation marks, double and single, to help your reader to distinguish between the two separate sources. Single quotation marks are used for the words already quoted by your source (and this is the only time when it is appropriate to use single quotation marks). The more familiar double quotation marks are used around the words that *you* are quoting.

> Goethe at times expressed a notable lack of self-confidence: " 'Know thyself?' If I knew myself, I'd run away. "

> At the beginning of World War I, Winston Churchill observed that "the maxim of the British people is 'Business as usual.' "

The same procedure is used even when there is no author's name to be cited.

> A Yiddish proverb states that " 'for example' is not proof. "

Very occasionally, you may have to use triple quotation marks, usually to quote a source who is quoting another source who is using a quoted word or phrase. An article about the author Muriel Spark included the following statement by that novelist:

> I draw the line at "forever."

In the article, the author, Victoria Glendinning, quoted that statement using single and double quotation marks.

> Eternally inquiring and curious about places and people, "I draw the line at 'forever.'"

If you wanted to quote that sentence in an essay, you would need to distinguish between yourself, Victoria Glendinning, and Muriel Spark.

In her recent profile, Victoria Glendinning emphasizes Muriel
Spark's search for variety: "Eternally inquiring and curious about
places and people, 'I draw the line at "forever."'"

Notice that you would deliberately plan the quotation marks so that the
double marks are used for the largest, or framework, quotation.

EXERCISE 10

A. Correct the errors in the following sentences:

1. "Beggars should be abolished, said Friedrich Nietzsche. "It annoys one to give to them, and it annoys one not to give to them."
2. The *Chicago Times* asserted in 1861 that, "It is a newspaper's
   duty to print the news and raise hell."
3. The candidate said that, "He was not able to comment at this
   time."
4. James Brown wrote "Say it Loud: "I'm Black and I'm Proud."
5. According to Dr. Johnson; "a man is in general better pleased
   when he has a good dinner upon his table than when his wife
   talks Greek.
6. When he said "it'll play in Peoria", John Ehrlichman meant that
   most Americans would find it 'politically acceptable.
7. In Proust's view, "Everybody calls "clear" those ideas which
   have the same degree of confusion as his own".
8. Chesterton believed that "All men are ordinary men"; the extraordinary men are those who know it."
9. In *The Invisible Man*, Ralph Ellison noted that the fate of America, Is to become one, and yet many."
10. "Compassion is not weakness, stated Hubert Humphrey, and
    concern for the unfortunate is not socialism."

B. Use quotations from the group below in order to write three sentences:

   choose one quotation and write a sentence that introduces a direct
       quotation with separation;
   choose a second quotation and write a sentence that introduces a di-
       rect quotation with integration;
   choose a third quotation and write a sentence that interrupts a quota-
       tion with a citation in the middle.

1. In some sort of crude sense which no vulgarity, no humor, no over-statement can quite extinguish, the physicists have known sin; and this is a knowledge which they cannot lose. (J. Robert Oppenheimer, 1947)
2. Imprisoned in every fat man, a thin one is wildly signaling to be let out. (Cyril Connolly)
3. I hear much of people's calling out to punish the guilty, but very few are concerned to clear the innocent. (Daniel Defoe)
4. I do not believe that civilization will be wiped out in a war fought with the atomic bomb. Perhaps two-thirds of the people of the earth might be killed, but enough men capable of thinking, and enough books, would be left to start again, and civilization would be restored. (Albert Einstein)
5. Weapons are an important factor in war but not the decisive one; it is man and not materials that counts. (Mao Tse-Tung, 1938)
6. "We, the people." It is a very elegant beginning. But when that document was completed on the 17th of September in 1787 I was not included in that "We, the people." (Barbara Jordan, 1974)
7. This has always been a man's world, and none of the reasons hitherto brought forward in explanation of this fact has seemed adequate. (Simone de Beauvoir, 1950)
8. They were upon their great theme: "When I get to be a man!" Being human, though boys, they considered their present estate too commonplace to be dwelt upon. So, when the old men gather, they say: "When I was a boy!" It is the land of nowadays that we never discover. (Booth Tarkington)

Quoting Accurately

Quoting is not a collaboration in which you try to improve on the writing of your source. If you value a writer's words enough to want to quote them, you should respect the integrity of the sentence and leave it intact. Unless you are applying the conventional methods of presenting quotations, don't make minor changes or carelessly leave words out, but faithfully transcribe the exact words, the exact spelling, and the exact punctuation that you find in the original.

Original:

Those who corrupt the public mind are just as evil as those who steal from the public purse.

Adlai Stevenson

Inexact quotation:

Adlai Stevenson believed that "those who act against the public interest are just as evil as those who steal from the public purse."

Exact quotation:

> Adlai Stevenson believed that "those who corrupt the public mind are just as evil as those who steal from the public purse."

Even if you notice an error (or what you regard as an error), you must nevertheless copy the original wording accurately. Archaic spelling should be retained, as well as regional or national spelling conventions:

> One of Heywood's Proverbes tells us that "a new brome swepeth clean."

Standards of acceptable punctuation have also altered; if a comma or semicolon looks incorrect, remember that it may be correct for the *author's* era or locality.

> Dr. Johnson believed that "it is better to live rich, than to die rich."

To our eyes, the comma breaking into the flow of such a short sentence is intrusive and incorrect; but it is not the reader's place to edit Dr. Johnson's eighteenth-century prose.

The need to include the precise punctuation of the original, however, applies only to the material that gets placed *inside* quotation marks. The punctuation immediately preceding or following the quoted words in the original text may be omitted and, indeed, should be omitted if the quotation will thereby fit more smoothly into your sentence.

Original:

> It is better to be making the news than taking it; to be an actor than a critic.
>
> Winston Churchill

Incorrect quotation:

> Churchill observed, "It is better to be making the news than taking it;"

Correct quotation:

> Churchill observed, "It is better to be making the news than taking it."

You do not have to assume the blame if there are errors of syntax, punctuation, or spelling in the material that you are quoting. A conventional device can be used to point out such errors and inform the reader that the mistake was made, not by you, but by the author whom you are quoting. The Latin word *sic* (meaning "thus") is placed in square brackets and inserted immediately after the error. The [sic] signals that the quotation was "thus" and that you, the writer, were aware of the error, which was not the result of your own carelessness in transcribing the quotation.

In the following example, [sic] calls attention to an error in subject-verb agreement.

> Richard Farson points out that "increased understanding and concern has [sic] not been coupled with increased rights."

TAILORING QUOTATIONS TO FIT YOUR WRITING

There are several devices for making corrections and changes in quotations, so that the quoted material will fit in naturally with your own sentences. Like [sic], these devices are *conventional*, determined by generally accepted agreement: you cannot improvise; you must follow these rules. Usually, the conventional rules require you to inform your reader that changes are being made; in other words, to make clear the distinction between your wording and the author's. The first way of altering quotations, however, does not require identification and depends entirely on how and where the quotation fits into your sentence. When a quotation is incorporated completely into your sentence (for example, when your citation ends in "that"), except in the case of proper nouns and the pronoun "I," the first letter will be small, whether or not it is a capital in the original. On the other hand, when your citation ends in a comma or a colon, the first letter of the quotation will be large, whether or not it is a capital in the original.

> The poet Frost wrote that "good fences make good neighbors."

> The poet Frost wrote, "Good fences make good neighbors."

As a rule, it is not necessary to indicate to your readers that you have altered a letter from small to large, or from large to small.

Using Ellipses

It is permissible to *delete* words from a quotation, provided that you indicate to the reader that there is an omission. Once aware that there is a difference between your version and the original, any reader who wants to see the omitted portion can consult the original source. Your condensed version is as accurate as the original; it is just shorter. But you must remember to insert the conventional symbol for deletion, three spaced dots, called an *ellipsis*.

> It is not true that suffering ennobles the character; happiness does that sometimes, but suffering, for the most part, makes men petty and vindictive.
>
> W. Somerset Maugham

```
Maugham believes, "It is not true that suffering ennobles the charac-
ter; . . . suffering, for the most part, makes men petty and vindic-
tive."
```

Notice that the semicolon is retained, to provide terminal punctuation for the first part of the quotation. Notice also that the three dots are spaced equally. (The dots *must* be three—not two or a dozen.)

If you wish to delete the end of a quotation, and the ellipsis coincides with the end of your sentence, you must use the three dots, plus a fourth to signify the period.

```
Maugham believes, "It is not true that suffering ennobles the charac-
ter; happiness does that sometimes. . . . "
```

The first dot is placed immediately after the last letter. The sentence ends with quotation marks, as usual, with the marks placed *after* the dots, not before.

The three dots can serve as a link between two noncontinuous quotations from the same paragraph in your source, representing the deletion of an entire sentence or two, but *only* if the two sentences that you are quoting are fairly near each other in the original. Ellipses cannot cover a gap of more than a few sentences. If you do use ellipses to bridge one or more sentences, use only *one* set of quotation marks. Your full quotation, with an ellipsis in the middle, is still continuous—a single quotation—even though it is not complete. When an ellipsis is used following a quoted complete sentence, the period of the quoted sentence is retained so that a total of four dots is used, as in the following example.

> In one sense there is no death. The life of a soul on earth lasts beyond his departure. You will always feel that life touching yours, that voice speaking to you, that spirit looking out of other eyes, talking to you in the familiar things he touched, worked with, loved as familiar friends. He lives on in your life and in the lives of all others that knew him.
>
> Angelo Patri

Angelo Patri observes that "in one sense there is no death. The life of a soul on earth lasts beyond his departure. . . . He lives on in your life and in the lives of all others that knew him."

Misusing Ellipses

Ellipses should be used to make a quotation fit more smoothly into your own sentence. It is especially useful when you are working with a long passage which contains several separate points that you wish to quote. Ellipsis, however, cannot condense long, tedious quotations or replace summary and paraphrase. If all that you want to quote is a brief extract from a lengthy passage, then simply quote that portion and ignore the surrounding material. An ellipsis is poorly used when it calls attention to itself. To read a paragraph through dots can be very distracting.

The meaning of the original quotation must always be exactly preserved, despite the deletion represented by the ellipsis.

Original:

As long as there are sovereign nations possessing great power, war is inevitable.

Albert Einstein

To simplify Einstein's words might be tempting:

Inexact quotation:

Einstein believes that ". . . war is inevitable."

But it would not be accurate to suggest that Einstein believed in the inevitability of war, under all circumstances, without qualifications. To extract only a portion of this statement is to oversimplify and thus to falsify the evidence.

Another common consequence of misapplied ellipses is a mangled sentence. Deleting words from a quotation can distort and destroy its syntax and structure.

Original:

God created woman. And boredom did indeed cease from that moment—but many other things ceased as well! Woman was God's second mistake.

Friedrich Nietzsche

Inexact quotation:

> Women are certainly exciting. As Nietzsche declares, "God created woman . . . second mistake."

Altering Quotations: Brackets

Brackets have an opposite function: ellipsis signifies deletion; brackets signify addition or alteration. You have already seen how to use brackets with *sic*, which is in fact a quoter's addition to and comment on the quoted material. When you wish to explain a vague word, replace a confusing phrase, suggest an antecedent, correct an error in a quotation, or adjust a quotation to fit your own writing, you insert the information *inside* the quotation, placing it in square brackets. Brackets are not the same as parentheses. Parentheses are not suitable for this purpose, for the quotation might itself include a parenthetical statement, and the reader could not be sure whether the parentheses contained the author's insertion or yours. Instead, brackets, a relatively unusual form of punctuation, are a conventional method of indicating to the reader that material has been inserted.

The most common reason for using brackets is to clarify a vague word. You may, for example, choose to quote only the last portion of a passage, omitting an important antecedent:

> Man lives *by* habits, indeed, but what he lives *for* is thrills and excitement.
>
> William James

> William James argues that "what he [man] lives <u>for</u> is thrills and excitement."

You may also remove "he" entirely and replace it with *man*—in brackets:

> William James argues that "what [man] lives <u>for</u> is thrills and excitement."

The brackets will indicate that there has been a substitution. But, unless the presentation of both wordings seems very awkward and clumsy, it is better to quote the original as well as the clarification in brackets and thus provide your reader with all your source's words.

Brackets can also be used to complete a thought that has been obscured by the omission of an earlier sentence:

A well-trained sensible family doctor is one of the most valuable assets in a community. . . . Few men live lives of more devoted self-sacrifice.

Sir William Osler

> Osler had great respect for his less celebrated colleagues: "Few men live lives of more devoted self-sacrifice [than good family doctors]."

Here, the quotation marks are placed *after* the brackets, even though the quoted material ends after the word "self-sacrifice." The explanatory material inside the brackets is considered part of the quotation, even though it is in the quoter's own words.

Comments in brackets should be restricted to *brief* explanations; one might, for example, want to add an important date or name as essential background information. Whatever is inside the brackets should fit smoothly into the syntax of the quotation and should not be a distraction for the reader. Do not, for example, use brackets as a means of carrying on a running dialogue with the author you are quoting:

> Sophie Tucker suggests that up to the age of eighteen "a girl needs good parents. [This is true for men, too.] From eighteen to thirty-five, she needs good looks. [Good looks aren't that essential anymore.] From thirty-five to fifty-five, she needs a good personality. [I disagree because personality is important at any age.] From fifty-five on, she needs good cash."

Because brackets are used primarily for the purpose of insertion into quotation and are therefore a relatively unusual kind of punctuation, they may not appear on your typewriter or computer keyboard. If so, leave a space before and after the material to be bracketed, and insert the brackets in ink when you proofread your completed essay.

EXERCISE 11

A. Choose one of the quotations below. By using ellipses, incorporate a portion of the quotation into a sentence of your own; remember to include the author's name in the citation.

B. Choose a second quotation. Incorporate a portion of the quotation into another sentence of your own; use the insertion of words in brackets to clarify one or more of the quoted words.

    1. Until you have become really, in actual fact, a brother to every one, brotherhood will not come to pass. No sort of scientific teaching, no

kind of common interest, will ever teach men to share property and privileges with equal consideration for all. Every one will think his share too small and they will always be envying, complaining, and attacking one another. (Fyodor Dostoyevsky)

2. Man, biologically considered, and whatever else he may be in the bargain, is simply the most formidable of all the beasts of prey, and, indeed, the only one that preys systematically on its own species. (William James)

3. All propaganda has to be popular and has to adapt its spiritual level to the perception of the least intelligent of those towards whom it intends to direct itself. (Adolf Hitler)

4. I not only "don't choose to run" but I don't even want to leave a loophole in case I am drafted, so I won't "choose." I will say "won't run" no matter how bad the country will need a comedian by that time. (Will Rogers)

5. The whole machinery of our intelligence, our general ideas and flaws, fixed and external objects, principles, persons, and gods are so many symbolic, algebraic expressions. They stand for experience; experience which we are incapable of retaining and surveying in its multitudinous immediacy. We should flounder helplessly, like the animals, did we not keep ourselves afloat and direct our course by these intellectual devices. (George Santayana)

6. To waste, to destroy, our natural resources, to skin and exhaust the land instead of using it so as to increase its usefulness, will result in undermining in the days of our children the very prosperity which we ought by right to hand down to them amplified and developed. (Theodore Roosevelt)

7. Unconditional war can no longer lead to unconditional victory. It can no longer serve to settle disputes. It can no longer be of concern to great powers alone. For a nuclear disaster, spread by winds and waters and fear, could well engulf the great and the small, the rich and the poor, the committed and the uncommitted alike. (John F. Kennedy)

8. I do not mean that there is any lack of wealthy individuals in the United States; I know of no country, indeed, where the love of money has taken stronger hold on the affections of men and where a profounder contempt is expressed for the theory of the permanent equality of property. But wealth circulates with inconceivable rapidity, and experience shows that it is rare to find two succeeding generations in the full enjoyment of it. (Alexis de Tocqueville)

Citing the Author's Name

At the time of *first* reference, refer to the author by using his or her full name—without Mr. or Miss or Mrs. After that, should you need to cite the author again, use the last name only. If there is a sizable gap between references to the same author, or if the names of several other authors intervene, you may wish to repeat the full name and remind your reader of the earlier citation(s).

First reference:

John Stuart Mill writes, "The opinion which it is attempted to suppress by authority may possibly be true."

Second reference:

Mill continues to point out that "all silencing of discussion is an assumption of infallibility."

By citing the last name only, you are conforming to conventional usage, which discourages overly familiar and distracting references like "John thinks," "JSM thinks," or "Mr. Mill thinks."

At first reference, you may want to include the title of the work from which the quotation was taken:

In <u>On Liberty</u>, John Stuart Mill writes . . .

Avoid the habit of referring to the author twice in the same citation, once by name and once by pronoun:

In John Stuart Mill's <u>On Liberty</u>, he writes . . .

Finally, unless you genuinely do not know the author's name, use it! There is no point in being coy, even for the sake of variety:

A famous man once made an ironic observation about child-rearing: "If you strike a child, take care that you strike it in anger. . . . A blow in cold blood neither can nor should be forgiven."

Your guessing game will only irritate readers who are not aware that this famous man was George Bernard Shaw.

Choosing the Introductory Verb

The citation leading up to the quotation represents an important link between your thoughts and those of your source. The introductory verb can tell your reader something about your reasons for presenting the quotation and its context in the work that you are quoting. Will you choose "J. S. Mill says," or "J. S. Mill writes," or "J. S. Mill thinks," or "J. S. Mill feels"? Those are the most common introductory verbs—so common that they have become boring. Try to get away from these stereotyped verbs, at least occasionally. Since the senses are not directly involved in writing, avoid "feels" entirely. And, unless you are quoting someone's spoken words, substitute a more accurate verb for "says."

Here is a list of possibilities:

insists	declares	suggests
argues	adds	proposes
concludes	explains	finds
states	agrees	continues
establishes	compares	disagrees
maintains	observes	notes

Of course, once you get away from the all-purpose category of "says" or "writes," you have to remember that verbs do not have interchangeable meanings; you must choose the verb that best suits your purpose. The citation should suggest the relationship between your own ideas (in the previous sentence) and the statement that you are about to cite. You must examine the quotation before writing the citation and define for yourself the way in which the author is making this point: is it being asserted forcefully? Use "argues" or "declares" or "insists." Is the statement being offered only as a possibility? Use "suggests" or "proposes" or "finds." Does the statement immediately follow a previous reference? Use "continues" or "adds." For the sake of clarity, the introductory verb may be expanded into a slightly longer phrase:

    X is aware that . . .
    X stresses the opposite view:
    X provides one answer to the question:
    X makes the same point as Y:

But make sure that the antecedent for the "view" or the "question" or the "point" is clearly expressed in the previous sentences. Finally, observe that all the examples of introductory verbs are given in the present tense, which is the conventionally accepted way to introduce a quotation.

Varying Your Sentence Patterns

Even if you carefully choose a different verb for each quotation, the combination of the author's name, introductory verb, and quotation can become repetitious and tiresome after a while. One way to achieve some variety is to place the name of the source in a less prominent position, tucked into the quotation instead of calling attention to itself at the beginning. You can interrupt the quotation by *placing the citation in the middle*.

    "Knowledge is of two kinds," points out Dr. Johnson; "we know a sub-
    ject ourselves, or we know where we can find information on it."

Notice that the verb and the name may be placed in reverse order (instead of "Dr. Johnson points out") when the citation follows the beginning of the quotation.

One citation is quite enough. There is no need to inform your reader twice, back to back, as does this repetitive example:

> "The only prize much cared for by the powerful is power," states Oliver Wendell Holmes. He concludes, "The prize of the general . . . is command."

Nor can you interrupt the quotation at any point. The citation in the following sentence should be placed at a more logical break in the sentence:

> "The only prize much cared for," states Oliver Wendell Holmes, "by the powerful is power."

Another way to avoid the monotonous "X says that . . ." pattern is by *phrasing the citation as a subordinate clause or a phrase.*

> According to Henry Kissinger, "power is 'the great aphrodisiac.'"

> In Richard Nixon's opinion, "I made my mistakes, but in all my years of public service, I have never profited from public service. I have earned every cent."

> As John F. Kennedy argues, "mankind must put an end to war or war will put an end to mankind."

In your quest for variety, however, avoid placing the citation *after* the quotation; the author's name at the end generally detracts from the force of the statement, especially if the citation is pretentiously or awkwardly phrased:

> "I am the inferior of any man whose rights I trample underfoot," as quoted from the writings of Robert Ingersoll.

Two rules, then, should govern your choice of citation: don't be too fancy, but be both precise and varied in your phrasing.

Presenting An Extended Quotation

Occasionally, you may have reason to present an extended quotation, a single extract from the same source which runs four typewritten lines or more. For extended quotations, set off the quoted passage by indenting the entire quotation on the left. Introduce an extended quotation with a colon.

1. Start each line of the quotation ten spaces from the left-hand margin; stop each line at your normal right-hand margin.
2. Triple-space before and after the quotation. Double-space *within* the quotation. (Some instructors prefer single-spacing for extended quotations, so consult your instructor about the style appropriate for your course or discipline.)
3. Omit quotation marks at the beginning and end of the quoted passage; the indented margin (and the introductory citation) will tell your readers that you are quoting.

Here is an example of an extended quotation:

Although he worked "hard as hell" all winter, Fitzgerald had difficulty finishing The Great Gatsby. In a letter to Maxwell Perkins, his editor at Scribner's, he wrote on April 10, 1924:

> While I have every hope & plan of finishing my novel in June . . . even [if] it takes me 10 times that long I cannot let it go unless it has the very best I'm capable of in it or even as I feel sometimes better than I'm capable of. It is only in the last four months that I've realized how much I've--well, almost deteriorated. . . . What I'm trying to say is just that . . . at last, or at least for the first time in years, I'm doing the best I can.

INTEGRATING QUOTATIONS
INTO YOUR PARAGRAPHS

Now that you understand how to present the words of others with accuracy and appropriate acknowledgment, you must also learn to subordinate what you are quoting to the larger purpose of your paragraph or essay. Here are some suggestions for keeping quotations in their proper place.

1. *Use quotation sparingly.* If quotation seems to be your primary purpose in writing, your reader will assume that you have nothing of your own to say. Quote only when you have a clear reason for doing so, when you are intending to analyze a quotation, when you are sure that the wording of the quotation is essential to your argument, or when you simply cannot say it in your own words. In any case, do not quote repeatedly within a single paragraph.

2. *Use quotations in the body of your paragraph, not at the very beginning as a replacement for the topic sentence.* The topic sentence should establish—in your own words—what you are about to explain or prove. The quotation will normally appear later in the paragraph as supporting evidence.

3. *Let the quotation make its point; don't follow it with a word-for-word translation of its meaning.* Once you have presented a quotation, it is usually not necessary to provide another version of the same idea in your own words and make the same point twice. By all means, follow up a quotation with an *explanation* of its relevance to your paragraph or an *interpretation* of its meaning; but make sure that your commentary does more than echo the quotation.

In the following example, the quotation used in the development of the paragraph assumes a position that is no more or less important than any of the other supporting sentences. Notice that the inclusion of the quotation adds interest to the paragraph because of the shift in tone and the shift to a sharper, narrower focus.

> Some parents insist on allowing their children to learn through experience. Once a child has actually performed a dangerous action and realized its consequences, he will always remember the circumstances and the possible ill effects. Yvonne Realle illustrates the adage that experience is the best teacher by describing a boy who was slapped just as he reached for a hot iron. The child, not realizing that he might have been burned, had no idea why he had been slapped. An observer noted that "if he had learned by experience, if he'd suffered some discomfort in the process, then he'd know enough to avoid the iron next time." In the view of parents like Yvonne Realle, letting a child experiment with his environment will result in a stronger lesson than slapping or scolding the child for trying to explore his surroundings.

EXERCISE 12

1. The first paragraph below is taken from a student essay entitled "Adolescents and Alcohol." The second passage comes from "Changing Habits in American Drinking," an article in *Fortune* magazine.

   Choose one appropriate supporting quotation from the article; decide where to place it in the student paragraph; and insert the quotation correctly and smoothly into the paragraph. Remember to lead into the quotation by mentioning the source.

Student paragraph:

To a great extent, teenagers acquire their attitudes about drinking from observation of their own families. Being brought up in a household where drinking is accepted can have good or bad consequences. An impressionable adolescent can learn to take alcohol for granted and end up consuming too much at the wrong time or place. On the other hand, acquiring a casual attitude towards having a beer or a glass of wine can take a lot of the mystery out of drinking. It's hard to regard alcohol as a desirable symbol of adulthood if you've been allowed to drink it--in reasonable amounts--from childhood on.

Source:

How [teenagers] will eventually handle alcohol depends to a great extent upon what they learn about the culturally accepted drinking style. Children will tend to drink according to the examples their parents and peers set. Some cultures have historically had low rates of problem drinkers—most notably, Jews, Chinese, and Italians. It's not that all of these groups have great numbers of abstainers, or are light drinkers; the Italians, in fact, are among the world's heaviest drinkers. But children are exposed from their earliest years to a temperate drinking practice—the Italians drink much of their wine with meals, for example, and Jews accord it a special place in family religious celebrations. Alcohol does not acquire the "forbidden fruit" image that tempts the young drinker to assert his or her independence through excess.

2. The first paragraph below is taken from a student essay titled "Anorexia and Bulimia: The Danger for Teenage Girls." The second passage comes from "Cinderella's Stepsisters: A Feminist Perspective on Anorexia Nervosa and Bulimia," by Marlene Boskind-Lodahl.

Choose one appropriate supporting quotation from the article; decide where to place it in the paragraph; and insert the quotation correctly and smoothly into the paragraph. Remember to lead into the quotation by mentioning the source.

Student paragraph:

Bulimia is a disease which tends to affect young girls who are determined to be as thin as possible. Losing a great deal of weight and then maintaining that loss is, of course, extremely difficult and forces them to an abstinence from food that is really unnatural. With bulimia, the teenager engages in what is called the "binge and purge" syndrome. What happens is that she suddenly decides to eat and eat and eat. Then, after stuffing herself, she feels guilty and determines to rid herself of all the food that she has consumed, so she induces vomiting or uses laxatives, and the food disappears. Through the whole process, the girl is really indulging and then punishing herself for having allowed herself to have a good time.

Source:

The cycle the bulimiarexic endures can be physically damaging. The women report fasting, habitual forced vomiting, and amphetamine and laxative abuse as a means to counteract a binge. However, for these young women who have been "good" girls, and who are afraid of parental disapproval and the rejection that might result from sexual activity, food is one of the few elements in their tightly regulated lives that they can choose to indulge in excessively. For the person who is struggling to meet unrealistic goals by imposing severe and ascetic control over herself, the binge is a release.

ASSIGNMENT 2

1. Choose one of the following topics. Each is a specific question that can be answered adequately in a single paragraph.

   A. question: Should children be spanked?
   B. question: Is there such a thing as a "bad" child?
   C. question: How can the gap between parents and children be bridged?

2. Ask someone you know to comment briefly on the question you have chosen, offering a suggestion or an example. Write down any part of the comment that you think might be worth quoting; transcribe the words accurately; and then show the statement to your source for confirmation of its accuracy. Make sure that you have the name properly spelled. If the first person you ask does not provide you with a suitable quotation, try someone else.
3. Answer your own question in a single paragraph of four to eight sentences, limiting the paragraph to ideas that can be clearly developed in such a brief space. The paragraph as a whole should express *your* views, not those of your source. Choose a *single* quotation from your source and integrate it into the development of your paragraph, using proper punctuation and citation and (if necessary) ellipses and brackets. If your source agrees with you, use the quotation as support. If your source disagrees, answer the objection in your own way. Try not to quote in the first or second sentence of your paragraph. With

your paragraph, hand in the sheet on which you originally wrote down the quotation.

Avoiding Plagiarism

Quoting without quotation marks is called *plagiarism*. Even if you were to cite the source's name somewhere on your page, a word-for-word quotation without marks would still be considered a plagiarism. *Plagiarism is the unacknowledged use of another writer's words or ideas. The only way to acknowledge that you are using someone else's actual words is with citation and quotation marks.* Chapter 9 discusses plagiarism in detail. At this point, what is important is that you understand that literate people consider plagiarism to be equivalent to theft; that, if you plagiarize, you will never learn to write; and that plagiarists eventually get caught.

It is easy for an experienced reader to detect plagiarism. Every writer, professional or amateur, has a characteristic style or voice, which readers quickly learn to recognize. With time, the writer's voice becomes familiar, so that the reader only notices that there *is* a voice when the style changes and, suddenly, there is a new, unfamiliar voice. When there are frequent acknowledged quotations, the reader has to adjust to a series of changes in tone and a series of new voices. The mixture of several distinctive voices, without quotation marks, usually suggests to an experienced reader that the work is flawed, poorly integrated, and probably plagiarized. Plagiarized essays are often identified in this way. Teachers have a well-developed awareness of style and are trained to recognize inconsistencies and awkward transitions. The revealing clue is the patched-together, mosaic effect. The next exercise should help to improve your own perception of shifting voices and should encourage you to rely on your own characteristic style as the dominant voice in everything that you write.

EXERCISE 13

The following paragraphs contain several plagiarized sentences. Examine the language and tone of each sentence, as well as the continuity of the entire paragraph. Then underline the plagiarized sentences.

The Beatles' music in the early years was just plain melodic. It had a nice beat to it. The Beatles were simple lads, writing simple songs simply to play to screaming fans on one-night stands. There was no deep, inner meaning to the lyrics. Their songs included many words like I, and me, and you. As the years went by, the Beatles' music became more poetic. Sergeant Pepper is a stupefying collage of music, words, background noises, cryptic utterances, orchestral effects, hallucinogenic bells, farmyard sounds, dream sequences, social observations, and apocalyptic vision, all masterfully blended together on a four-track tape machine over nine agonizing and expensive months. Their music was beginning to be more philosophical, with a deep, inner, more secret meaning. After it was known that they took drugs, references to drugs were seen in many songs. The "help" in Ringo's "A Little Help From My Friends" was said to have meant pot. The songs were poetic, mystical; they emerged from a self-contained world of bizarre carnival colors; they spoke in a language and a musical idiom all their own.

*　*　*

Before the Civil War, minstrelsy spread quickly across America. Americans all over the country enjoyed minstrelsy because it reflected something of their own point of view. For instance, Negro plantation hands, played usually by white actors in blackface, were portrayed as devil-may-care outcasts and minstrelmen played them with an air of comic triumph, irreverent wisdom, and an underlying note of rebellion, which had a special appeal to citizens of a young country. Minstrelsy was ironically the beginning of black involvement in the American theater. The American people learned to identify with certain aspects of the black people. The Negro became a sympathetic symbol for a pioneer people who required resilience as a prime trait.

PARAPHRASING

Some passages are worth quoting for the sake of their precise or elegant style or their distinguished author. But many of the sources that you will use in your college essays are written in more ordinary language. Indeed, some sources whose *contents* should be included in your essay may be written in the jargon of an academic discipline or the bureaucratic prose of a government agency. You will not be doing your readers a favor by quoting this material. Rather, you have a positive duty *not* to quote, but to help your readers by providing them with a clear paraphrase.

Paraphrase is the point-by-point recapitulation of another person's ideas, expressed in your own words. By using paraphrase, you are proving to your reader that you understand what you are writing about. Paraphrase is like summary in that both report your understanding to a reader; but, unlike a summary, a paraphrase covers a relatively short passage and reports *everything* in the passage, accurately, completely, and consecutively. When you paraphrase, you do not select, condense, interpret, or reorder the ideas; you retain everything about the original writing but the words.

Using Paraphrase in Your Essays

Your readers depend upon your paraphrased explanations to gain a fairly detailed understanding of sources that they may never have read and, indirectly, to become convinced that your own thesis is valid. There are two major reasons for using paraphrase in your essays, which correspond to the major reasons for using quotation.

1. Use paraphrase to present ideas or evidence whenever there is no special reason for using a direct quotation.

Many of your sources will not have a sufficiently authoritative reputation or distinctive style to justify your quoting their words. The following illustration, taken from a *New York Times* article, paraphrases a report written by an anonymous group of "municipal auditors" whose writing merits paraphrase rather than quotation:

> A city warehouse in Middle Village, Queens, stocked with such things as snow shovels, light bulbs, sponges, waxed paper, laundry soap and tinned herring, has been found to be vastly overstocked with some items and lacking in others. Municipal auditors, in a report issued yesterday, said that security was fine and that the warehouse was quicker in delivering goods to city agencies than it was when the auditors made their last check, in August, 1976. But in one corner of the warehouse, they said, nearly 59,000 paper binders, the 8½-by-11 size, are gathering dust, enough to meet the city's needs for nearly seven years. Nearby, there is a 10½-year supply of cotton coveralls.
>
> Both the overstock and shortages cost the city money, the auditors said. They estimated that by reducing warehouse inventories, the city could save $1.4 million, plus $112,000 in interest. . . .

2. Use paraphrase to give your readers an accurate and comprehensive account of ideas taken from a source—ideas that you intend to explain, interpret, or disagree with in your essay.

The first illustration comes from a *Times* article on the work of the behavioral psychologist B. F. Skinner, pointing out the increasing pessimism of his thought. As evidence, the writer of the article uses a paraphrase of material from Skinner's essay "A Matter of Consequence." Notice the limited use of carefully selected quotations within the paraphrase.

"Why do we not act to save our world?" [Dr. Skinner] says at the start of "A Matter of Consequence." The answers he offers are complex and bound up in the behavioral theory, which says that people do not initiate action on their own, but act in ways that have been successful in the past. But today's problems of overpopulation, pollution, energy depletion and other environmental hazards cast a pall over the future that promises to make it more unlike the present than perhaps at any other point in modern history, Dr. Skinner suggests. Therefore, solving such potential life-and-death problems through strategies that worked before is little more than a pipedream, according to Dr. Skinner.

The only hope, he says, would be to get people to act on *predictions* of future conditions and thus alter institutions and practices. But a basic tenet of behavioral theory states that the environment shapes people's actions; and since, as Dr. Skinner notes, "the future does not exist, how can it affect contemporary human behavior?" The solution might be somehow to persuade people, through behavioral techniques, that their very survival might depend on their actions right now.

The next example shows how paraphrase can be used more briefly, to present another writer's point of view as the basis for discussion. Again, notice that the writer of this description of a conference on nuclear deterrence has reserved quotation to express the precise point of potential dispute:

Scientists engaged in research on the effects of nuclear war may be "wasting their time" studying a phenomenon that is far less dangerous than the natural explosions that have periodically produced widespread extinctions of plant and animal life in the past, a University of Chicago scientist said last week. Joseph V. Smith, a professor of geophysical sciences, told a conference on nuclear deterrence here that such natural catastrophes as exploding volcanoes, violent earthquakes, and collisions with comets or asteroids could produce more immediate and destructive explosions than any nuclear war.

Using Paraphrase as Preparation for Reading and Writing Essays

Paraphrase is sometimes undertaken as an end in itself. When you are reading a complex essay or chapter, writing a paraphrase of the difficult passages can help you to improve your understanding. When you easily grasp an essay at first reading, when its ideas are clearly stated in familiar vocabulary, then you can be satisfied with annotating it or writing a brief outline or summary. But when you find an essay hard to understand, writing down each sentence in your own words forces you to stop and review what you have read, so that you succeed in working out ideas that at first seem beyond your comprehension.

Paraphrase can also be a means to an end, a preparation for writing an essay of your own. Let's assume that you are taking notes for an essay based on one or more sources. If you write down nothing but exact quotations, you will not only be doing a good deal of unnecessary transcription, but you will also be encouraging yourself to quote excessively in your essay. Instead, when you take notes, paraphrase; quote only when recording phrases or sentences that, in your opinion, merit quotation. These phrases and sentences should be transcribed accurately in your notes, with quotation marks clearly separating the paraphrase from the quotation.

Writing a Good Paraphrase

All academic writers are expected to be scrupulously accurate in their presentation of material taken from their sources. The ideas in the paraphrase should be presented in the same order as the original, and no one point should be emphasized more than another (unless the original writer chose to do so). In this respect, a paraphrase resembles an outline. But when you write down the main points of a chapter or an essay in outline form—leaving them in roughly the same order—you are merely writing a list, a memorandum for future reference. You are not attempting to present all the reasoning leading up to these ideas; you are only pulling out the key points, nothing more. The paraphrase, however, must suggest the scope and reasoning of the original as well as specify the main ideas. Moreover, an outline can be very short and condensed, but a paraphrase may be as long as the original text (or even longer if there are complex ideas that need to be explained). On the whole, though, passages to be paraphrased are usually brief excerpts; you are providing a full account of a single idea or piece of information rather than presenting the entire work in which it is found.

The paraphraser is really like a translator. As if the text were in a foreign language, you are trying to recreate its meaning in your own voice. Like the translator, you use your own idiom, and within the scope of that idiom, you often have to rewrite the text. In a good paraphrase, the sentences and the vocabulary do not echo those of the original. Nor can you merely substitute synonyms for key words and leave the passage otherwise unchanged; that is plagiarism in spirit, if not in fact, for word-by-word substitution does not demonstrate that you have really understood the ideas.

The level of abstraction within your paraphrase should resemble that of the original: neither more general nor more specific. If you do not understand a sentence, do not try to guess or cover it up with a vague phrase that slides over the idea. Instead, look up all the words; think of what they mean and how they are used together; consider how the sentences are formed and how they will fit into the context of your entire paraphrase; and then, to test your understanding, write it all out. Remember that a good paraphrase makes sense by itself; it is coherent and readable, without requiring reference to the original essay.

Here is a summary of the requirements for a successful paraphrase:

1. a paraphrase must be accurate;
2. a paraphrase must be complete;
3. a paraphrase must speak in the voice of the person writing the paraphrase;
4. a paraphrase must make sense by itself.

Free Paraphrase

When a paraphrase moves far away from the words and sentence structure of the original text and presents ideas in the paraphraser's own style and idiom, then it is said to be "free." A free paraphrase can be more challenging to write and interesting to read than the original— provided that the substance of the source has not been altered, disguised, or substantially condensed. A free paraphrase can summarize if the original text is repetitive, and so it will probably be somewhat shorter than the original.

Here, side-by-side with the original, is a free paraphrase of an excerpt from Machiavelli's *The Prince*. This passage exemplifies the kind of text, very famous, very difficult, which really benefits from a comprehensive paraphrase. *The Prince* was written in 1513. Even though the translation from the Italian used here was revised in this century, the paraphraser has to bridge a tremendous gap in time and in style in order to present Machiavelli in an idiom suitable for modern readers.

Original version	*Paraphrase*
It is not, therefore, necessary for a prince to have [good faith and integrity], but it is very necessary to seem to have them. I would even be bold to say that to possess them and always to observe them is dangerous, but to appear to possess them is useful. Thus it is well to seem merciful, faithful, humane, sincere, religious, and also to be so; but you must have the mind so disposed that when it is needful to be	It is more important for a ruler to give the impression of goodness than to be good. In fact, real goodness can be a liability, but the pretense is always very effective. It is all very well to be virtuous, but it is vital to be able to shift in the other direction whenever circumstances require it. After all, rulers, especially recently elevated ones, have a duty to perform which may absolutely

Original version

Paraphrase

otherwise you may be able to change to the opposite qualities. And it must be understood that a prince, and especially a new prince, cannot observe all those things which are considered good in men, being often obliged, in order to maintain the state, to act against faith, against charity, against humanity, and against religion. And therefore, he must have a mind disposed to adapt itself according to the wind, and as the variations of fortune dictate, and . . . not deviate from what is good, if possible, but be able to do evil if constrained.

A prince must take great care that nothing goes out of his mouth which is not full of the above-mentioned five qualities, and to see and hear him, he should seem to be all mercy, faith, integrity, humanity, and religion. . . . Everyone sees what you appear to be, few feel what you are, and those few will not dare to oppose themselves to the many, who have the majesty of the state to defend them; and in the actions of men, and especially of princes, from which there is no appeal, the end justifies the means. Let a prince therefore aim at conquering and maintaining the state, and the means will always be judged honorable and praised by every one, for the vulgar are always taken by appearances and the issue of the event; and the world consists only of the vulgar, and the few who are not vulgar are isolated when the many have a rallying point in the prince.

require them to act against the dictates of faith and compassion and kindness. One must act as circumstances require and, while it's good to be virtuous if you can, it's better to be bad if you must.

In public, however, the ruler should appear to be entirely virtuous, and if his pretense is successful with the majority of people, then those who do see through the act will be outnumbered and impotent, especially since the ruler has the authority of government on his side. In the case of rulers, even more than for most men, "the end justifies the means." If the ruler is able to assume power and administer it successfully, his methods will always be judged proper and satisfactory; for the common people will accept the pretense of virtue and the reality of success, and the astute will find no one is listening to their warnings.

Paraphrase and Summary

To clarify the difference between paraphrase and summary, here is a paragraph which *summmarizes* this same excerpt from *The Prince*.

> According to Machiavelli, perpetuating power is a more important goal for a ruler than achieving personal goodness or integrity. Although he should act virtuously if he can, and always appear to do so, it is more important for him to adapt quickly to changing circumstances. The masses will be so swayed by his pretended virtue and by his success that any opposition will be ineffective. The wise ruler's maxim is that "the end justifies the means."

It may be useful to review the four characteristics of the brief summary:

1. A summary is comprehensive. Notice that this one says more than "the end justifies the means." Although that may be the most important idea in the passage, it does not convey enough of its contents. (For one thing, it contains no reference at all to princes and how they should rule—and that, after all, is Machiavelli's subject.)
2. A summary is concise. It should say exactly as much as you need—and no more. Sometimes you cannot summarize complex material in a single sentence; nor is there any reason why a summary should not take up a short paragraph. And, while this summary is four sentences long, it is still much shorter than the paraphrase.
3. A summary is coherent. As you can see, the ideas are not presented in the same sequence as that of the original passage; nor are the language and tone at all reminiscent of the original. Rather, the summary includes only the passage's most important points, linking them together in a unified paragraph.
4. A summary is independent. What is most striking about the summary, compared with the paraphrase, is the writer's attitude toward the original text. While the paraphraser has to follow closely Machiavelli's ideas and point of view, the summarizer does not. Characteristically, Machiavelli's name is cited, calling attention to the fact that the summary is of *another person's ideas*.

Both the summary and paraphrase provide the raw materials for easy reference to this passage in an essay. Which you would choose to use would depend on your topic, on the way you are developing your essay, and on the extent to which you wish to discuss Machiavelli. Thus, an essay citing Machiavelli as only one among many political theorists might use the brief four-sentence summary; you might then briefly comment upon Machiavelli's ideas before going on to summarize (and perhaps compare them with) another writer's theories. If, however, you were writing an essay about a contemporary politician, and if you planned to analyze the way in which your subject does or does not carry out Machiavelli's strategies, then you probably would want to familiarize your readers with *The Prince* through a fairly lengthy paraphrase. The paraphrase could then be included at length, interspersed, perhaps, with your discussion of your present-day "prince."

Writing an Accurate Paraphrase

The minimal objective of paraphrase is to present the main ideas contained in the original reading. Without this basic coverage, a paraphrase is worthless. When an attempt at paraphrase fails to convey the substance of the source, there are three possible explanations:

1. *misreading*: The writer genuinely misunderstood what she was reading.
2. *projecting*: The writer insisted on reading her own ideas into the text.
3. *guessing*: The writer had a spark of understanding and constructed a paraphrase that roughly develops that spark, but ignores much of the original text.

Read Christopher Lasch's analysis of the changing role of the child in family life. Then examine each of the three paraphrases that follow, deciding whether it conveys Lasch's principal ideas and, if not, why it has gone astray. Compare your reactions with the analysis that follows each paraphrase.

Original

The family by its very nature is a means of raising children, but this fact should not blind us to the important change that occurred when child-rearing ceased to be simply one of many activities and became the central concern—one is tempted to say the cental obsession—of family life. This development had to wait for the recognition of the child as a distinctive kind of person, more impressionable and hence more vulnerable than adults, to be treated in a special manner befitting his peculiar requirements. Again, we take these things for granted and find it hard to imagine anything else. Earlier, children had been clothed, fed, spoken to, and educated as little adults; more specifically, as servants, the difference between childhood and servitude having been remarkably obscure throughout much of Western history. . . . It was only in the seventeenth century in certain classes that childhood came to be seen as a special category of experience. When that happened, people recognized the enormous formative influence of family life, and the family became above all an agency for building character, for consciously and deliberately forming the child from birth to adulthood.

"Divorce and the Family in America,"
Atlantic Monthly, November 1966

Paraphrase A

The average family wants to raise children with a good education, and to encourage for example, the ability to read and write well. They must be taught to practice and learn on their own. Children can be treated well without being pampered. They must be treated as adults as they get older and experience more of life. A parent must build character and the feeling of independence in a child. No longer should the children be treated as kids or servants, for that can cause conflict in a family relationship.

This paraphrase has very little in common with the original passage. True, it is about child-rearing, but the writer chooses to give advice to parents, rather than to present the contrast between early and modern attitudes towards children, as Lasch does. Since the only clear connection between Lasch and this paragraph is the reference to servants, one might safely conclude that the writer was confused by the passage, and (instead of slowing down the process and paraphrasing it sentence by sentence) guessed—mistakenly—at its meaning. There is also some projection of the writer's ideas about family life. Notice how assertive the tone is; the writer seems to be admonishing parents rather than presenting Lasch's detached analysis.

Paraphrase B

When two people get married, they usually produce a child. They get married because they want a family. Raising a family is now different from the way it used to be. The child is looked upon as a human being, with feelings and thoughts of his own. Centuries ago, children were treated like robots, little more than hired help. Now, children are seen as people who need a strong, dependable family background to grow into persons of good character. Parents are needed to get children ready to be the adults of tomorrow.

This paragraph might be regarded as a combination of guessing (beginning) and projection (end). The middle sentences present Lasch's basic point, but the beginning and the end both go off on tangents, so that the paraphrase as a whole does not bear much resemblance to the original text. There is also an exaggeration: are the servants "robots"?

Paraphrase C

> Though the family has always been an important institution, its child-rearing function has only in recent centuries become its most important activity. This change has resulted from the relatively new idea that children have a special, unique personality. In the past, there was little difference seen between childhood and adulthood. But today people realize the importance of family life, especially the family unit as a means of molding the personalities of children from childhood to adulthood.

Although this paraphrase is certainly the most accurate of the three, it is not really long enough to be a complete paraphrase. In fact, the writer seems to have succumbed to the temptation to summarize, rather than paraphrase. Lasch's main idea is undoubtedly there, but the following points are missing:

1. there is a tremendous gulf between pre–seventeenth-century and twentieth-century perceptions of childhood;
2. before the seventeenth century, it was difficult to distinguish between the status and treatment of children and that of servants;
3. child-rearing has now become of overriding ("obsessive") importance to the family;
4. children are different from adults in that they are less hardened and experienced.

The omission of point 2 is particularly important. The author has done a thorough job of the beginning and the end of Lasch's passage, and evidently left the middle to take care of itself. But a paraphrase cannot be considered a reliable "translation" of the original text unless all the supporting ideas are given appropriate emphasis.

Here is a more comprehensive paraphrase of the passage:

> Though the family has always been the institution responsible for bringing up children, only in recent times has its child-raising function become the family's overriding purpose and its reason for being. This striking shift to the child-centered family has resulted from the gradual realization that children have a special, unique personality, easy to influence and easy to hurt, and that they must be treated accordingly. Special treatment for children is the norm in our time; but hundreds of years ago, people saw little or no difference between childhood and adulthood, and, in fact, the child's role

in the family resembled that of a servant. It was not until the 17th
century that people began to regard childhood as a distinctive stage
of growth. That recognition led them to understand what a powerful
influence the family environment must have on the child and to define
"family" as the chief instrument for molding the child's personality
and moral attitudes.

EXERCISE 14

The passage below is followed by a group of paraphrases. Examine each
paraphrase and identify those which conform to the guidelines for paraphrasing. Ask yourself whether the paraphrase contains any point that is
not in the original passage and whether the key points of the original are
all clearly presented in the paraphrase.

> Underlying the entire issue [of the insanity defense] is a basic conflict
> between the legal and psychiatric understandings of insanity. Essen-
> tially, the law is concerned with establishing fault; it focuses on indi-
> vidual responsibility as a way of controlling behavior and articulating
> public morality. Psychiatry, by contrast, is interested in identifying, di-
> agnosing and treating mental disorders and in understanding the atti-
> tudes, actions and environmental causes behind such disorders. The
> current debate over the insanity defense will not be settled quickly or
> easily. It touches on deeply felt American attitudes toward crime, pun-
> ishment and personal responsibility, and raises some of the most com-
> plex questions in criminal jurisprudence. But whatever changes are
> made should not be the result of an urge to punish a particular man.
> The principle behind the insanity defense—that individuals may take
> actions for which they cannot justly be held criminally responsible—
> should not be abandoned thoughtlessly.
>
> Irving R. Kaufman, from "The Insanity Plea on Trial"

1. When considering the concept of the insanity defense, there is a
   basic issue that divides the medical view from the legal view. It is
   the approach to what insanity really involves. Legally, we want to
   make people accountable and help to keep the crime rate down. Medi-
   cally, we desire a means of treatment and prevention. There are no
   easy answers to an issue that concerns many of our most deeply held
   values. Answers should evolve over time, because there is value in
   the underlying tenets of the insanity defense.

2. At the heart of the problem of the insanity defense are two fundamentally different perceptions of insanity--one for lawyers, and

one for psychiatrists. The lawyer's mission is to figure out who is responsible for a crime. The purpose of the law is to protect the public by ensuring that people behave appropriately according to socially acceptable guidelines. However, the psychiatrist's mission is to try to cure mental illness and to learn more about the reasons why people act abnormally. Given these contradictory concerns--public vs. private--the controversy over the insanity defense will remain an unresolved issue for a long time to come. Americans have very strong beliefs about law and order, penalties for committing crimes, and individual accountability, all of which make it difficult to solve the problem easily. In any case, the ultimate solution should not resemble a public vendetta against a specific person. Unless there is strong reason to do otherwise, we should retain the basic idea that people cannot always control what they do and that it would be unfair to hold them responsible for their actions under all circumstances.

3. Lawyers and psychiatrists disagree about the insanity defense. People who commit crimes frequently don't get punished because they claim that they are insane. The law wants to make sure that the person responsible is given an appropriate punishment. The courts are there to uphold law and order. But the psychiatric profession is not interested in morality and only wants to understand the reasons why the crime took place. Psychiatrists are interested in the supposedly insane person who committed the crime, not the victim or the danger to the public. This issue is vital for the future of America since we have strong beliefs about law and order. While we shouldn't be vindictive, we ought to support the idea that individuals are responsible for their actions.

PARAPHRASING IN TWO STAGES

Since "translating" another writer's idiom into your own can be difficult, a paraphrase is often written in two stages. In your first version, you work out a word-for-word substitution, staying close to the sentence structure of the original, as if, indeed, you are writing a translation. This is the literal paraphrase. Then, once you have substituted your own words for those of the original, you work from your own literal paraphrase, turning it into a free paraphrase by reconstructing and rephrasing the sentences to make them more natural and more characteristic of your own writing style.

Writing a Literal Paraphrase

To write a paraphrase that is faithful to the original text is impossible if you are uncertain of the meaning of any of the words. You will need to use a dictionary as you paraphrase a difficult passage, especially if there is obsolete or archaic language. Try writing down a few possible synonyms for each difficult word, to make sure that you are aware of all the connotations and can choose the most precise substitute when you start writing your own version. Too often, the writer of a paraphrase forgets that there *is* a choice and quickly substitutes the first synonym to be found in the dictionary. Even when appropriate synonyms have been carefully chosen, the first version of a paraphrase can look peculiar and sound dreadful. While the old sentence structure has been retained, the key words have been yanked out and new ones plugged in. Still, at the beginning your only object is to work out the exact meaning of each sentence.

To illustrate the pitfalls of this process, here is a short excerpt from Francis Bacon's essay "Of Marriage and Single Life," written around 1600. Some of the phrasing and word combinations sound archaic and even unnatural; but, in fact, there is nothing in the passage that is inaccessible to modern understanding, if the sentences are read slowly and carefully.

> He that hath wife and children hath given hostages to fortune; for they are impediments to great enterprises, either of virtue or mischief. Certainly the best works and of greatest merit for the public have proceeded from the unmarried or childless men: which both in affection and means have endowed the public.

The passage's main idea is not too difficult to find: unmarried men, without the burden of a family, can afford to contribute to the public good. But by now you must realize that such a brief summary is not the same as a paraphrase; Bacon's reasoning is not fully presented, and it would not be fair to pass off this sentence as the equivalent of the original. In contrast, look at these two very different *literal paraphrases* of Bacon's first sentence. (The key words have been underlined.)

> He who has a wife and children has <u>bestowed prisoners</u> to <u>riches</u>; for they are <u>defects</u> in huge <u>business organizations</u>, either for <u>morality</u> or <u>damage</u>.

> He who has a wife and children has <u>given</u> a <u>pledge</u> to <u>destiny</u>; for they are <u>hindrances</u> to large <u>endeavor</u>, either for <u>good</u> or for <u>ill</u>.

Neither sentence sounds very normal or very clear; but the second has potential, while the first makes no sense. Yet, in both cases, the inserted words *are* synonyms for the original vocabulary. In the first sentence, the words do not fit Bacon's context; in the second sentence, they do. For example, it is misleading to choose "business organization" as a synonym for "enterprises," since the passage doesn't actually concern business, but refers to any sort of undertaking requiring freedom from responsibility. "Impediment" can mean either "defect" (as in speech impediment) or "hindrance" (as an impediment to learning); but—again, given the context—it is the latter meaning that Bacon has in mind. Choosing the correct connotation or nuance is possible only if you think carefully about the synonyms and use your judgment: the process cannot be hurried.

A phrase like "hostage to fortune" offers special difficulty, since it is a powerful image expressing a highly abstract idea. No paraphraser can improve upon the original wording or even find an equivalent phrase. However, expressing the idea is important: a bargain made with life—the renunciation of future independent action in exchange for a family. Wife and children serve as a kind of bond ("hostage") to ensure one's future conformity. The aptness and singularity of Bacon's original phrase are measured by the difficulty of producing a paraphrase of three words in less than two sentences!

Writing a "Free" Version of the Literal Paraphrase

Correct though the synonyms may be, Bacon's sentence cannot be left as it is in the second paraphrase, for no reader would readily be able to understand the meaning of this stilted, artificial sentence. It is necessary to rephrase the paraphrase, making sure that the meaning of the words is retained, but making the sentence pattern sound more natural. The first attempt at "loosening" the paraphrase remains as close as possible to the original sentence, leaving everything in the same sequence, but using a more modern idiom:

> Married men with children are hindered from embarking on any important undertaking, good or bad. Indeed, unmarried and childless men are the ones who have done the most for society and have dedicated their love and their money to the public good.

The second sentence (which is simpler to paraphrase than the first) has been inverted here, but the paraphrase is still a point-by-point recapitulation of Bacon. This version is acceptable, but can be improved, both to clarify Bacon's meaning and to introduce a more personal voice. What exactly *are* these unmarried men dedicating to the public good? "Affection and means.'' And what is the modern equivalent of means? Money? Effort? Time? Energy?

> A man with a family has obligations which prevent him from devoting himself to any activity that pleases him. On the other hand, a single man or a man without children has a greater opportunity to be a philanthropist. That's why most great contributions of energy and resources to the good of society are made by single men.

The writer of this paraphrase has not supplied a synonym for ''affection,'' assuming perhaps that the expenditure of energy and resources presupposes a certain amount of interest and concern; affection is almost too weak a motivation for the philanthropist as he is described here.

> The responsibility of a wife and children prevents a man from taking risks with his money, time, and energy. The greatest social benefactors have been men who have adopted the public as their family.

The second sentence here is the only in all five versions that has come close to Bacon's economy of style. ''Adopted the public'' is not quite the same as ''endowed the public'' with one's ''affection and means''; but nevertheless, this is a successful paraphrase because it speaks for itself. It has a life and an importance of its own, independent of Bacon's original passage; yet it makes the same point that Bacon does.

EXERCISE 15

The following brief passage is followed by a *literal* paraphrase. The literal paraphrase is a distortion of the original; some inappropriate synonyms have been inserted, and no attempt has been made to understand and express the meaning of the passage as a whole. Consult the original text, and try to salvage the paraphrase.

> Every blessing hath somewhat to disparage and distaste it: children bring cares; single life is wild and solitary; eminence is envious; retiredness obscure; fasting painful; satiety unwieldy; religion nicely severe; liberty is lawless; wealth burdensome; mediocrity contemptible: everything has faults either in too much or too little.
>
> Joseph Hall, from ''The Malcontent''

> Every stroke of good fortune has some amount to belittle and offend it: children bring disturbing thoughts; being alone is untamed and

isolated; being well known is wrongly desired; reserve incomprehensible; self-denial masochism; gluttony awkward; belief in God benignly harsh; independence is disorderly; affluence oppressive; average proficiency scornful: everything has flaws, excessive or not enough.

ASSIGNMENT 3

Paraphrase the following passages, using this procedure:

1. Look up in a dictionary the meanings of all the vocabulary of which you are uncertain. Pay special attention to the italicized words.
2. Write a literal paraphrase of each passage by substituting appropriate synonyms within the original sentence structure. (Don't restrict yourself to changing the italicized words; use your own vocabulary throughout the passage.)
3. Revise your literal paraphrase, keeping roughly to the same length and number of sentences as the original, but using your own sentence style and phrasing throughout. (It may be helpful to put the original passage aside at this point, and work entirely from your own version.)
4. Read your "free" paraphrase aloud and make sure that it makes sense.

A. This, then, is held to be the duty of the man of wealth: To set an example of *modest, unostentatious* living, *shunning display* or extravagance; to provide moderately for all of the *legitimate wants* of those dependent upon him; and after doing so, to consider all *surplus revenues* which come to him simply as trust funds, which he is called upon to *administer*, and strictly bound as a matter of duty to administer in the manner which, in his judgment, is best calculated to produce the most beneficial results for the community—the man of wealth thus becoming the mere trustee and *agent* for his poorer brethren.

Andrew Carnegie, from *The Gospel of Wealth* (1899)

B. In the second century of the Christian era, the empire of Rome *comprehended* the fairest part of the earth, and the most *civilized* portion of mankind. The frontiers of that extensive monarchy were guarded by ancient *renown* and *disciplined valor*. The gentle but powerful *influence* of laws and manners had gradually cemented the union of the provinces. Their peaceful inhabitants enjoyed and *abused* the advantages of wealth and luxury. The image of a free *constitution* was preserved with *decent* reverence: the Roman senate appeared to possess the *sovereign* authority, and *devolved* on the emperors all the executive powers of government.

Edward Gibbon, from *The Decline and Fall
of the Roman Empire* (1776)

C. These are the times that try men's souls. The summer soldier and the sunshine patriot will, in this crisis, shrink from the service of his country: but he that stands it *now*, deserves the love and thanks of men and women. *Tyranny*, like hell, is not easily conquered: yet we have this *consolation* with us, that the harder the conflict, the more glorious the triumph. What we obtain too cheap, we *esteem* too lightly: 'tis *dearness* only that gives everything its value. Heaven knows how to set a proper price upon its goods and it would be strange, indeed, if so celestial an article as freedom should not be highly *rated*.

Thomas Paine, from *The Crisis* (1776)

D. The underlying aim of industrial psychology is to secure the maximum will to work and to create the impression of harmony of interest between the workers and the management. The implication of the term psychology, with its *psychoanalytic* and *psychiatric* overtones, is that most workers—*slackers*, absentees, and worst of all, agitators and strikers, any, indeed, who rebel against *exploitation*; in fact all but the model—are sick people requiring diagnosis and treatment to adjust them to their conditions of work. Their home lives need to be looked into, their wrong ideas about the owners corrected, their uncooperativeness *modified* by group exercises. Everything needs to be done for them except the one thing from which they would really benefit—the end of exploitation. As long as exploitation of workers for profit remains, the only result of successful industrial psychology can be to hinder the worker from pressing his demands for better wages and conditions, and thus to diminish his share in the product of his labour. To use science for this purpose is to make it *accessory to deception*, even when the scientist himself is not aware that he is doing so.

J. D. Bernal, from *The Social Sciences* (1965)

E. From the Russian Revolution onwards, education has served a special function in communist societies, one radically different from the role of education in the democratic world. While practically every society develops educational policies with an eye towards the *inculcation* of attitudes of responsible citizenship and respect for the national culture, communist regimes teach children to become productive and patriotic citizens in ways that vary sharply from the methods that a free society would find acceptable. Communist and democratic educational systems represent two fundamentally opposed *philosophies*, not simply different techniques for achieving similar goals, a fact that educational authorities in communist societies readily admit. In coun-

tries ruled by a single *monolithic* communist party, the schools are expected to instill "socialist" values in children, promote unquestioning
devotion towards the motherland and the communist system, encourage contempt for other non-communist societies (the United States
above all) and convince the younger generation that there is but one
correct interpretation of history, that set down by the state. In other
words, *indoctrination*—pure and simple—is perceived as a *legitimate*
job of the schools.

Arch Puddington, from "Compelling Belief" (1985)

F. In early times, music often served as an accompaniment to other
activities—dancing, socializing, religious worship. Only in the nineteenth century did music come to be segregated from ordinary life and
surrounded with an *aura* of *sanctity*. This development coincided
with the elevation of the performing artist and, above all, the composer to heroic status. Formerly, composers, like other musicians, had
been regarded as craftsmen, as staff members of educational or religious institutions, even as superior household servants. In the nineteenth century, the artistic genius came to be seen as a heroic rebel,
iconoclast, and pathbreaker. . . . The flowering of music in the century should not obscure the possibility that, in the long run, this *deifi-
cation* of artistic genius had very bad effects, leading to the dead end
of experimentation, the struggle for novelty and originality, and the
defiance of established forms and constraints, or their *reimposition* in
the most *stifling* manner, that characterize the music scene today.

Christopher Lasch, from "The Degradation of Work
and the Apotheosis of Art" (1982)

G. The propaganda for *abolition* [of capital punishment] speaks in
hushed tones of the *sanctity* of human life, as if the mere statement of
it as an *absolute* should silence all opponents who have any moral
sense. But most of the abolitionists belong to nations that spend half
their annual income on weapons of war and that honor research to
perfect means of killing.

Jacques Barzun, from "In Favor
of Capital Punishment"

H. Once the idea is imported into sport that a man's *subsistence* depends
upon it, then the pleasantness of sport as a recreation ceases, and we
import into it the bitterness of the world's struggle for existence.
There are things which a man will do when his back is against the wall,
and he feels that his own livelihood or that of his wife and children are
dependent upon him, which he would not dream of doing if this feeling were removed. A man who is hard pushed to keep up his home,
and sees his way to make money out of sport, is under a terrible temptation to sin against the *gospel of sportsmanship*. How, for instance, if
the builder of boats or cycles offers assistance in return for advertise-

ment, the sports promoter in return for the gate which he hopes to attract by a well-known name, or the bookmaker in return for the money of deluded backers betting on a race sold in advance? Is not the man whom I have described likely to yield to their *solicitations*?

H. Graves, from "A Philosophy of Sport" (1900)

I. Freedom of expression, in all its forms, can be justified on two fundamental grounds. For the individual, the right to speak and write as one chooses is a form of liberty that contributes in important ways to a rich and stimulating life. To be deprived of such liberty is to lose the chance to participate fully in an *intellectual* exchange that helps to develop one's values, to make one's meaning of the world, to exercise those qualities of mind and imagination that are most distinctively human. Beyond its significance to the individual, freedom of speech has traditionally been regarded in this country as important to the welfare of society. Throughout history, much progress has occurred through growth in our understanding of ourselves, our institutions, and the environment in which we live. But experience teaches us that major discoveries and advances in knowledge are often highly unsettling and distasteful to the existing order. Only rarely do individuals have the intelligence and imagination to conceive such ideas and the courage to express them openly. If we wish to stimulate progress, we cannot afford to *inhibit* such persons by imposing *orthodoxies*, censorship, and other artificial barriers to creative thought.

Derek Bok, from *Beyond the Ivory Tower* (1982)

J. It is somewhat ironic to note that grading *systems* evolved in part because of [problems in evaluating performance]. In situations where *reward* and *recognition* often depended more on who you knew than on what you knew, and *lineage* was more important than ability, the cause of justice seemed to demand a method whereby the individual could demonstrate specific abilities on the basis of *objective criteria*. This led to the establishment of specific standards and public criteria as ways of reducing *prejudicial* treatment and, in cases where *appropriate* standards could not be specified in advance, to the normal curve system of establishing levels on the basis of group performance. The *imperfect achievement* of the goals of such systems in no way negates the importance of the underlying purposes.

Wayne Moellenberg, from "To Grade or Not to Grade—Is That the Question?" (1973)

INCORPORATING PARAPHRASE INTO YOUR ESSAY

The paraphrased ideas of other writers should never take control of your essay, but should always be subordinate to the points that *you* are making. Brief paraphrasing prevents the source-material from dominating your writing and enables the paraphrased sentence to be tucked into a paragraph in your essay. However, the paraphrase of the original text, whether short or long, must still contain an accurate and fair representation of its ideas.

Most academic writers rely on a combination of quotation, paraphrase, and summary to present their sources. To illustrate the way in which these three techniques of presentation can be successfully combined, here is an extract from an article by Connor Cruise O'Brien that depends on a judicious mixture of paraphrase, summary, and quotation. In "Violence—And Two Schools of Thought," O'Brien gives an account of a medical conference concerned with the origins of violence. Specifically, he undertakes to present and (at the end) comment on the ideas of two speakers at the conference.

VIOLENCE—AND TWO SCHOOLS OF THOUGHT*

Summary   The opening speakers were fairly representative of the   1
two main schools of thought which almost always declare themselves when violence is discussed. The first school sees a propensity to aggression as biological but capable of being socially conditioned into patterns of acceptable behavior. The second sees it as essentially created by social conditions and therefore capable of being removed by benign social change.

Quotation   The first speaker held that violence was "a bio-social   2
phenomenon." He rejected the notion that human beings were blank paper "on which the environment can write whatever it likes." He described how a puppy
Paraphrase   could be conditioned to choose a dog food it did not like and to reject one it did like. This was the creation of conscience in the puppy. It was done by mild punishment. If human beings were acting more aggressively and antisocially, despite the advent of better social conditions and better housing, this might be because permissiveness, in school and home, had checked the process of social conditioning, and therefore of conscience-building. He favored the reinstatement of conscience-building, through the use of mild punishment and token rewards.
Quotation   "We cannot eliminate violence," he said, "but we can do a great deal to reduce it."

Summary   The second speaker thought that violence was the   3
result of stress; in almost all the examples he cited it was

*In its original format in *The Observer*, the article's paragraphing, in accordance with usual journalistic practice, occurs with distracting frequency; the number of paragraphs has been reduced here, without any alteration of the text.

Paraphrase and Quotation stress from overcrowding. The behavior of apes and monkeys in zoos was "totally different" from the way they behaved in "the completely relaxed condi- *Paraphrase* tions in the wild." In crowded zoos the most aggressive males became leaders and a general reign of terror set in; in the relaxed wild, on the other hand, the least ag- *Quotation* gressive males ruled benevolently. Space was all: "If we could eliminate population pressures, violence would vanish."

Summary The student [reacting to the arguments of the two 4 speakers] preferred the second speaker. He [the second speaker] spoke with ebullient confidence, fast but clear, and at one point ran across the vast platform, in a lively imitation of the behavior of a charging ape. Also, his message was simple and hopeful. Speaker one, in contrast, looked sad, and his message sounded faintly sinister. *Author's comment* Such impressions, rather than the weight of argument, determine the reception of papers read in such circumstances.

Paraphrase Nonetheless, a student queried speaker two's "relaxed 5 wild." He seemed to recall a case in which a troop of chimpanzees had completely wiped out another troop. The speaker was glad the student had raised that question because it proved the point. You see, where that had occurred, there had been an overcrowding in the jungle, just as happens in zoos, and this was a response to overcrowding. Conditions in the wild, it seems, are not al- *Author's comment* ways "completely relaxed." And when they attain that attributed condition—through the absence of overcrowding—this surely has to be due to the "natural controls," including the predators, whose attentions can hardly be all that relaxing, or, indeed, all that demonstrative of the validity of the proposition that violence is not a part of nature. Speaker two did not allude to predators. Nonetheless, they are still around, on two legs as well as on four.

The Observer, 11 February 1979

Selecting Quotations

Although we do not have the texts of the original papers to compare with O'Brien's description, this article seems to present a clear and comprehensive account of a complex discussion. O'Brien provides guidelines for understanding in the brief summaries of the first paragraph, followed by two separate, noncommital treatments of the two main points of view.

The ratio of quotation to paraphrase to summary works very effectively. O'Brien offers quotations for two reasons: aptness of expression and the desire to disassociate himself from the statement. For example, he chooses to quote the vivid image of the blank paper "on which the environment can write whatever it likes." And he also selects points for quotation that he regards as open to dispute—"totally different"; "completely relaxed"; "violence would vanish." Such strong or sweeping statements are often quoted so that the writer can disassociate himself from their implications and so that he cannot be accused of either toning down or exaggerating the meaning in his own paraphrase. In short, quote when:

1. there are no words at your disposal to represent the original's economy and aptness of phrasing;
2. a paraphrase would possibly alter the statement's meaning;
3. a paraphrase would not clearly distinguish between your views and the author's.

Don't quote merely because of:

1. lack of understanding;
2. awe for the authority of the source;
3. feelings of inadequacy;
4. laziness.

Avoiding Plagiarism by Giving Credit to Your Paraphrased Sources

There is one possible source of confusion in O'Brien's article, occuring at the point when he turns to his own commentary. In the last two paragraphs, it is not always easy to determine where his paraphrase of the speakers' ideas ends and his own opinions begin. His description (in the fourth paragraph) of the student's reactions to the two speakers appears objective. (We learn afterwards that O'Brien is scornful of the criteria that the student is using to evaluate these ideas.) But it takes a while for the reader to realize that O'Brien is describing the student's observation, and not giving his own account of the speaker's platform maneuvers. It would be clearer to us if the sentence began: "According to the responding student, the second speaker spoke with ebullient confidence. . . ." Similarly, in the last sentence of the same paragraph, there is no transition from the student to O'Brien as the source of commentary; yet the sentence is undoubtedly O'Brien's opinion.

This confusion of point of view is especially deceptive in the last paragraph when O'Brien moves from his paraphrased and neutral account of the dialogue between student and speaker to his own opinion: that certain predators influence behavior in civilization as well as in the wilds. It requires two readings to notice the point at which the author is no longer paraphrasing but beginning to speak in his own voice. Such confusions can be clarified by the insertion of citations in the appropriate places: the name of the source or an appropriate pronoun or reference label.

As you know by now, in academic writing the clear acknowledgment of the source is not merely a matter of courtesy or clarity, but an assurance of the writer's honesty:

When you paraphrase another person's ideas, you must cite his name, as you do when you quote, or else you are subject to a charge of plagiarism.

Borrowing ideas is just as much theft as borrowing words. You leave off the quotation marks when you paraphrase, but you must not omit the citation. Of course, the insertion of the name should be smoothly integrated into your sentence, and you should follow the guidelines used for citation of quotations.

The source's name need not appear at the beginning of the sentence, but it should signal the beginning of the paraphrase:

> Not everyone enjoys working, but most people would agree with Jones's belief that work is an essential experience of life.

This sentence depends on two sources: the writer of the essay is responsible for the declaration that "not everyone enjoys working" and that most people would agree with Jones's views; but the belief that "work is an essential experience of life" is attributed to Jones. The citation is unobtrusively placed; and there are no quotation marks, so presumably Jones used a different wording.

The proper citation of paraphrases requires one additional precaution. When you quote, there can never be any doubt about where the borrowed material begins and where it ends: the quotation marks provide a clear indication of the boundaries. But when you paraphrase, though the citation may signal the *beginning* of the source material, your reader may not be sure exactly where the paraphrase *ends*. There is no easy method of indicating termination. (As you will see in Chapter 9, the author's name in parentheses can serve as a useful signal.) Of course, it is possible to indicate the end of a paraphrase simply by starting a new paragraph. However, unity and coherence often require you to incorporate more than one person's ideas into a single paragraph.

When you are presenting several points of view in fairly rapid succession, be careful to acknowledge the change of source by citing names. You can easily signal the shift from paraphrased material to *your own* opinions by using the first person. Whatever you may have been told to the contrary, it is quite acceptable to use "I" in your essays, as long as you do not insert it unnecessarily or monotonously. A carefully placed "I" can leave your reader in no doubt as to whose voice he is hearing.

EXERCISE 16

1. Read "Sports Violence Seen as Ritual Amid the Chaos," by Douglas Martin.
2. In the margin, indicate where the author uses quotation (Q), paraphrase (P), summary (S), and commentary (C).
3. Evaluate the use of quotation, paraphrase, and summary. Be prepared to indicate those places in the article where, in your opinion, one of the techniques is inappropriately or unnecessarily used, or where the transition from one technique to the other is not clearly identified.

SPORTS VIOLENCE SEEN AS RITUAL AMID THE CHAOS

Violence in professional ice hockey, a scholar at the University of Maine suggests, has become as formal and ritualized as a medieval duel. "Although fist fights are spontaneous and sometimes vicious," James Herlan, the scholar, said here last weekend, "they are nevertheless subject to certain ceremonial prescriptions to determine the nature of the battle. The first important element is the throwing down on the ice of the protective gloves, an act that provides a marvelous connection with the medieval ritual of throwing down the gauntlet." Ushers show patrons to their seats; games begin with the solemn playing of the national anthems; the spectacle is divided into three acts, and players attired in stylized costumes zip about in a sort of speeded-up theater-in-the-round.   1

Mr. Herlan presented this view of hockey to a conference on "War and Violence in North America" held at the University of Toronto. He was on a panel entitled "Sacks, Strikes and Slapshots," which endeavored to address the overall issue of violence in sports. The seminar, part of the first joint meeting of the Canadian Association for Canadian Studies in the United States, was one of 16 on topics ranging from sexual violence in "Uncle Tom's Cabin" to a look at suicide and myth in 19th-century America to an examination of Canadian minerals and their meaning to the United States military.   2

The choice of violence as a topic for one of the first such meetings of intellectuals from the two countries might have seemed surprising to some, given the overwhelmingly pacific nature of their bilateral relationship. Yet the sports discussion alone provided enough blood and guts to satisfy a caveman's tastes—the broken neck of a football star, the chewed-off ear of a professional wrestler, the damaged eye of a hockey player. And the participants at the conference regarded the potential social implications as ominous, indeed.   3

"The consequences of the mania for winning success can range 4
from destroyed egos in children to dirty tricks by a committee to re-
elect the President," Arnold Talentino of the State University of New
York at Cortland said in a paper linking the darker features of American history to present-day violence in sports. "Or, simply to violence."

Despite the level of the violence that often manifests itself in sports, 5
the academics gathered here say there has been little systematic investigation of the phenomenon. What initial work has been done tends to
suggest two intertwining causes: a heightened need on the part of
Modern Man to let out pentup frustrations, and a general acculturation
to violence in "advanced" societies.

Jeffrey H. Goldstein, for instance, convincingly presented several 6
years ago in the journal "Sociometry" that observing hostility on the
athletic field significantly increased spectators' hostility. In fact, there
is the possibility that contact sports, by their very nature, breed socially aggressive behavior. "The sportsman is more than an occasional
visitor to the psychiatrist's couch," said Dr. J. A. Harrington in a 1975
address to Britain's Institute of Sport Medicine. The notion that sports
necessarily enhance mental equilibrium, Dr. Harrington said, was
"tripe of the first order."

The Toronto discussion limited itself for the most part to the reac- 7
tion of North American fans to violence on the field, rather than fan-
generated violence like Europe's persistent soccer riots and Central
American wars sparked by the passions of that sport.

Mr. Talentino, who like Mr. Herlan, the other chief participant on 8
the sports panel, teaches literature and developed his interest in sport
violence through reading, offered American history as a prism through
which to view the cheap shot of a linebacker. From the time Columbus
captured a group of Arawak Indians to present to the King and Queen
of Spain, he suggested, the American dream and reality amounted to
success through violent conquest. This served two purposes. "Mani-
fest destiny had become an ego trip for the cocksure new Americans;
they became accustomed to winning and winners never quit," Mr. Talentino said in his paper. "Secondly, the bigger the territory the more
wealth."

With the conquest of Indians, Mexicans and the land, America's out- 9
ward push was stemmed by the Pacific Ocean. So it's a good thing, the
theory goes, that baseball came along when it did. Developed in the
Eastern industrial cities in the mid-19th century, by 1893 it had spread
throughout the nation. After baseball, football soon sprouted from its
Ivy League nest, and a tamer, no-longer-pioneer America was learning
the joys of voyeuristic sport.

Mr. Talentino sketches numerous examples of athletes eager to 10
make their skills into an ego trip for any paying customer, while subju-
gating their own egos to the imperatives of today's sports conglomer-

ates, particularly if the price is right. To underline this point, he quotes Larry Zeidel, a member of the 1975 Philadelphia Flyers hockey team:

"I needed every bit of toughness at my command," Mr. Zeidel said. 11 "Toughness with the fist and toughness with the stick because my opponents were ruthless. They'd put their stick right through me if they were given a chance. So I had to be sure and hit first."

And the fans? "Nonathletes practice the aggressive ethic while on 12 the job, and in their free time they reinforce their belief in the ethic by watching athletes play violent games and identifying closely with some of the best players as well," Mr. Talentino writes. In the end, he says, sports violence thus comes down to money and ego satisfaction.

In professional hockey, Mr. Herlan maintains, there is also what 13 amounts to a code of chivalry. Players go just so far with their violence and no further, he suggests, pointing as evidence to the fact [that] stick-swinging incidents are relatively rare and that players seldom use their razor-sharp skates in fights. But they resent outside interference. He points to an incident last summer when a Detroit Federal court awarded $850,000 to a former Detroit Red Wing, Dennis Polonich, who suffered facial injuries when he was struck by Wilf Paiement's stick in a 1978 game. The judgment elicited sharp criticism from the hockey establishment.

Pat Quinn, former coach of the Philadelphia Flyers, observed, "Most 14 of the public doesn't know the code in hockey." He continued, "Polonich is a guy who lived by the sword and should have expected to die by it."

Participants in the panel suggested that television, with its capacity 15 to convey violence more vividly than many other occurrences, makes eliminating displays of over-aggression problematic. Mr. Talentino told of watching a women's arm wrestling tournament on television, and seeing one participant break another's arm. The snap, he said, was audible. "I watched both instant replays with fascination," he said. "And you know my views on violence."

Hopes for any improvement appear to lie in enough players and 16 owners reaching the conclusion that pure sport can attract customers without designated "goons" beating one another on the head. The Philadelphia Flyers, for years considered one of hockey's dirtiest teams, have deliberately set out to cut the time players spend in the penalty box this season and have been successful.

Mr. Herlan is lyrical, if realistic, in his hopes for a more peaceful 17 breed of hockey. "The odds are that such a transformation will not occur easily, but if it should come about, the sport may again be the joyous game originally played on boreal ponds, a unique metaphor evoking the triumph of the human spirit over the rigors of winter."

Douglas Martin, *New York Times*, 26 October 1982

EXERCISE 17

All of the quotations in the following paragraph come from a single source: "Grading Students: A Failure to Communicate," by Reed G. Williams and Harry G. Miller. The student quoting from this article has carefully put opening and closing quotation marks around all the sentences, but has made no effort to write a continuous paragraph. Make the paragraph coherent by reducing the number of quotations through paraphrase (the finished paragraph should contain only one quotation, if any). Remember to acknowledge the authors, making clear how much of the paragraph is taken from their essay.

A minority of faculty members in colleges would prefer to solve the problem of grades by eliminating them. "A strategy sometimes adopted by those who wish to abolish grades, but who are unable to muster enough support among colleagues to obtain the necessary changes in policy, is that of blanket grading or the awarding of very high grades." "Such strategies sometimes are adopted with the deliberate intent of sabotaging the grading system, while others use them to avoid the unpleasant task of giving low grades." "Whatever the purpose, however, high grades which are not based on superior achievement have negative consequences for both students and institutions." "In many ways the awarding of unjustified high grades has consequences for the academic system which are comparable to the effects of counterfeit currency on a monetary system." "In both cases, the ones who suffer most are those who struggle hard under non-inflationary conditions to accumulate the legitimate currency, which then loses its value because of the inflation caused by the bogus issues which have no real meaning in the standard system." "Finally, in both cases, the breakdown of the standardized medium of exchange leaves a vacuum which permits frauds to flourish and makes legitimate transactions difficult."

PRESENTING SOURCES: A SUMMARY
OF PRELIMINARY WRITING SKILLS

1. *Annotation*: underlining the text and inserting marginal comments on the page.

   The notes can explain points that are unclear, define difficult words, emphasize key ideas, point out connections to previous or subsequent paragraphs, or suggest the reader's own reactions to what is being discussed. Since writing down marginal comments assumes the presence of a text, annotation can never serve as a substitute for or a complete reference to another person's ideas.

2. *Outlining*: constructing a systematic list of ideas that reflects the basic structure of an essay or book, with major and minor points distributed on different levels.

Outlining is a reductive skill that suggests the bones of a work, but little of its flesh or outward appearance. Outlining is especially useful for covering a long sequence of material containing ideas whose relationship is easy to grasp. Densely written passages that rely on frequent and subtle distinctions and dexterous use of language are not easily condensed into an outline.

3. *Summary*: condensing a paragraph or an essay or a chapter into a relatively brief presentation of the main ideas.

Unlike annotation, a summary should make sense as an independent, coherent piece of writing. Unlike paraphrase, a summary does not try to include everything. However, the summary should be complete in the sense that it provides a fair representation of the work and its parts. Summary is the all-purpose skill; it is neither crude nor overly detailed.

4. *Quotation*: including another person's exact words within your own writing.

Although quotation requires the least amount of invention, it is the most technical of all these skills, demanding an understanding of conventional and complex punctuation. In your notes and in your essays, quotation should be a last resort. If the phrasing is unique, if the presentation is subtle, if the point at issue is easily misunderstood or hotly debated, quotation may be appropriate. When in doubt, paraphrase.

5. *Paraphrasing*: recapitulating, point-by-point, using your own words.

A paraphrase is a faithful and complete rendition of the original, following much the same order of ideas. Although full-length paraphrase is practical only with relatively brief passages, it is the most reliable way to make sense out of a difficult text. Paraphrasing a sentence or two, together with a citation of the author's name, is the best method of presenting another person's ideas within your own essay.

EXERCISE 18

Consider each of the following situations, and decide which of the five skills summarized would be an appropriate method of preparation.

(More than one skill may be applicable to each situation, but try to write them down in order of probable usefulness.)

1. You are about to take a closed-book exam based on materials from six different sources—about a hundred pages in all.
2. You are a social worker who has had a client transferred to her; you have a lengthy case history to absorb before the next staff meeting.
3. You are preparing to participate in a debate on foreign policy, for which you have read two books; you will be given twenty-five minutes to present your point of view.
4. You are preparing to participate in a roundtable discussion that will be debating a controversial book; the format will be conversational.
5. You have been given access to archives containing irreplaceable historic letters, too fragile to be photocopied.
6. You are about to take an open-book exam based on a single text.
7. You are a law student looking up a crucial court decision that will be a precedent for a mock trial in which you are the prosecutor.
8. You are taking notes at a one-hour lecture in your field of specialization.
9. You are interviewing an important official who has suddenly begun to talk about his political intentions.
10. You are being given verbal instructions in the working of complex scientific apparatus which, if misused, may blow up.

Part II
WRITING FROM SOURCES

The previous two chapters have described the most basic methods of understanding another writer's ideas, and presenting them accurately and naturally, as part of your own writing. However, the units of writing with which you have been working have been extremely brief and limited: the sentence and the paragraph. Now you can use the skills that you practiced in Part I to develop your own ideas in a full-length essay that is based on other people's work.

When you write at length from sources, you must deal with two points of view—your own and those of your sources. As the writer you have a dual responsibility: you must do justice to yourself by developing your own ideas, and you must do justice to each source by providing a fair representation of its author's ideas. But blending the ideas of two or more people within the same essay can create confusion: Who should dominate? How much of yourself should you include? How much of your source? Moreover, in academic and professional writing you may have to respond to a third voice—that of your teacher or supervisor, who may assign a topic or otherwise set limits and goals for your essay.

Chapter 3 discusses three approaches to writing based on a single source. Each represents a method of reconciling the competing influences on your writing and blending the voices that your reader ought to hear:

1. You can distinguish between your source and yourself by writing about the two separately, first the source and then yourself.
2. You can help your reader to understand a difficult and confusing source by presenting your own interpretation of the author's ideas.
3. You can use your source as evidence for the development of your own ideas by writing an essay on a similar or related topic.

In the end, yours must be the dominant voice. It is you who will choose the thesis and control the essay's shape and direction; it is your understanding and judgment that will interpret your source materials for your reader. When you and your classmates are asked to write about the same reading, your teacher hopes to receive, not an identical set of essays, but rather a series of individual interpretations with a common starting point in the same source.

Combining your own ideas with those of your source inevitably becomes more difficult when you begin to work with a group of sources and thus have several authors to be represented. This is the subject of Chapter 4. It is more than ever vital that your own voice dominate your essay and that you do not simply summarize first one source and then the next, without any perspective of your own. Blending together a variety of sources is usually called *synthesis*. You try to look beyond the claims of any one author's assertions and develop a broader generalization into which all of the source material may be subordinated. Your own generalized conclusions become the basis for your essay's thesis and organization, while the ideas of your sources serve as the evidence that supports those conclusions.

Chapter 4 will emphasize the standard methods of marshaling your sources: the analysis of each source in a search for common themes, the establishment of common denominators or categories that cut across the separate sources and provide the structure for your essay, the evaluation of each source's relative significance as you decide which to emphasize, and the citation of a group of references from several different sources in support of a single point. These skills are closely related to some of the most common and useful strategies for constructing an essay: definition, classification, and comparison. The chapter also includes some specialized practice in the selection, arrangement, and presentation of sources.

3.
The Single-Source Essay

Writing from a source requires that you understand another writer's ideas as thoroughly as you understand your own. The first step in carrying out each of the strategies described in this chapter is to read carefully through the source essay, using the skills for comprehension that you learned about in Chapter 1: annotation, outlining, and summary. Once you are able to explain to your reader what the source is all about, then you can begin to plan your rebuttal, interpretation, or analysis of the author's ideas, or you can write your own essay on a similar topic.

STRATEGY ONE: SEPARATING
SOURCE AND SELF

The simplest way to write about someone else's ideas is complete separation: the structure of your essay breaks into two parts, with the source's views presented first and your own reactions given equal or greater space immediately afterwards. This approach works best when you are writing about an author with whom you totally or partially disagree. Instead of treating the reading as evidence in support of your point of view and blending it with your own ideas, you write an essay that first analyzes and then refutes your source's basic themes. Look, for example, at Roger Sipher's "So That Nobody Has to Go to School if They Don't Want To."

SO THAT NOBODY HAS TO GO TO SCHOOL IF THEY DON'T WANT TO

A decline in standardized test scores is but the most recent indicator that American education is in trouble.

One reason for the crisis is that present mandatory-attendance laws force many to attend school who have no wish to be there. Such children have little desire to learn and are so antagonistic to school that neither they nor more highly motivated students receive the quality education that is the birthright of every American.

The solution to this problem is simple: Abolish compulsory-attendance laws and allow only those who are committed to getting an education to attend.

This will not end public education. Contrary to conventional belief, legislators enacted compulsory-attendance laws to legalize what already existed. William Landes and Lewis Solomon, economists, found little evidence that mandatory-attendance laws increased the number of children in school. They found, too, that school systems have never effectively enforced such laws, usually because of the expense involved.

There is no contradiction between the assertion that compulsory attendance has had little effect on the number of children attending school and the argument that repeal would be a positive step toward improving education. Most parents want a high school education for their children. Unfortunately, compulsory attendance hampers the ability of public school officials to enforce legitimate educational and disciplinary policies and thereby make the education a good one.

Private schools have no such problem. They can fail or dismiss students, knowing such students can attend public school. Without compulsory attendance, public schools would be freer to oust students whose academic or personal behavior undermines the educational mission of the institution.

Has not the noble experiment of a formal education for everyone failed? While we pay homage to the homily, "You can lead a horse to water but you can't make him drink," we have pretended it is not true in education.

Ask high school teachers if recalcitrant students learn anything of value. Ask teachers if these students do any homework. Quite the contrary, these students know they will be passed from grade to grade until they are old enough to quit or until, as is more likely, they receive a high school diploma. At the point when students could legally quit, most choose to remain since they know they are likely to be allowed to graduate whether they do acceptable work or not.

Abolition of archaic attendance laws would produce enormous dividends.

First, it would alert everyone that school is a serious place where one goes to learn. Schools are neither day-care centers nor indoor street corners. Young people who resist learning should stay away; indeed, an end to compulsory schooling would require them to stay away.

Second, students opposed to learning would not be able to pollute the educational atmosphere for those who want to learn. Teachers could stop policing recalcitrant students and start educating.

Third, grades would show what they are supposed to: how well a student is learning. Parents could again read report cards and know if their children were making progress.

Fourth, public esteem for schools would increase. People would stop regarding them as way stations for adolescents and start thinking of them as institutions for educating America's youth.

Fifth, elementary schools would change because students would find out early that they had better learn something or risk flunking out later. Elementary teachers would no longer have to pass their failures on to junior high and high school.

Sixth, the cost of enforcing compulsory education would be eliminated. Despite enforcement efforts, nearly 15 percent of the school-age children in our largest cities are almost permanently absent from school.

Communities could use these savings to support institutions to deal with young people not in school. If, in the long run, these institutions prove more costly, at least we would not confuse their mission with that of schools.

Schools should be for education. At present, they are only tangentially so. They have attempted to serve an all-encompassing social function, trying to be all things to all people. In the process they have failed miserably at what they were originally formed to accomplish.

Roger Sipher, *New York Times*, 19 December 1977

Presenting Your Source's Point of View

Sipher opposes compulsory attendance laws. Let us suppose that you, on the other hand, can see strong advantages in imposing a very strict rule for attendance. In order for you to challenge Sipher convincingly, you will have to incorporate both his point of view and yours within a single short essay.

Since your objective is to *respond* to Sipher, you begin by presenting his ideas to your readers. State them as fairly as you can, without pausing to argue with him or to offer your own point of view about mandatory attendance. Even though you seem to be giving the first round to your opponent, his ideas need not dominate your essay. In fact, Sipher is more likely to dominate if you simply copy the structure of his essay, presenting and answering each of his points one by one. While at first it may seem easiest to follow Sipher's sequence of ideas (especially since his points are so clearly numbered), if you do so, you will be arguing on his terms, according to his conception of the issue rather than yours. Instead, make sure that your reader understands what Sipher is actually saying before you begin your rebuttal. To do so, carry out *both* of the following steps:

1. **Briefly summarize the issue and the reasons that prompted the author to write the essay.** You do this by writing a brief summary, as explained in Chapter 1. Here is a summary of Sipher's article:

> Roger Sipher argues that the presence of the classroom of unwilling students who are indifferent to learning can explain why public school students as a whole are learning less and less. Sipher therefore recommends that public schools discontinue the policy of mandatory attendance. Instead, students would be allowed to drop out if they wished, and faculty would be able to expel students whose behavior made it difficult for serious students to do their work. Once unwilling students were no longer forced to attend, schools would once again be able to maintain high standards of achievement; they could devote money and energy to education, rather than custodial care.

You can make a summary like this one more detailed by adding paraphrased accounts of some of the author's arguments, as well as a quotation or two.

2. **Analyze and present some of the basic principles that underlie the author's position on this issue.** In debating the issue with the author, you will need to do more than just contradicting some of his main ideas: Sipher says mandatory attendance is bad, and you say it is good; Sipher says difficult students don't learn anything, and you say all students learn something useful; and so on. This point-by-point rebuttal shows that you disagree, but it provides no context in which readers can decide who is right and who is wrong. You have no starting point for your counterarguments and no choice but to sound arbitrary.

Instead, ask yourself why the author has taken this position, one which you find so easy to reject. What are the foundations of his arguments? What larger principles do they suggest? In the case of Sipher, what policies is he objecting to? Why? What values is he determined to defend? Can these values or principles be applied to issues other than attendance? You are now examining Sipher's specific responses to the practical problem of attendance in order to infer some broad generalizations about his philosophy of education.

While Sipher does not state these generalizations in this article, you would be safe in concluding that Sipher's views on attendance derive from a conflict of two principles: the belief that education is a right that may not be denied under any circumstances, and the belief that education is a privilege to be earned. Sipher would advocate the latter. Thus, immediately after you summarize the article, you analyze Sipher's implicit position in a paragraph.

> Sipher's argument implies that there is no such thing as the right to an education. A successful education can only depend on the student's willing presence and active participation. Passive or rebellious students cannot be educated and should not be forced to stay in school. Although everyone has the right to an opportunity for education, its acquisition is actually the privilege of those who choose to work for it.

By analyzing Sipher's position, you have not only found out more about the issue being argued, but you have also established a common context—eligibility for education—within which you and he disagree. Provided with a clear understanding of the differences between you, your reader will have a real basis for choosing between your opposing views. At the same time, your reader is being assured that *this* and no other is the essential point for debate; thus, you will be fighting on ground that *you* have chosen.

Presenting Your Point of View

3. **Present your reasons for disagreeing with your source.** Once you have established your opponent's position, you may then plan your own counterarguments by writing down your reactions and pinpointing the exact reasons for your disagreement. (All the statements analyzed in this section are taken from such preliminary responses; they are not excerpts from finished essays.) Your reasons for disagreeing with Sipher might fit into one of three categories:

1. you believe that his basic principle is not valid (Student B);
2. you decide that his principle, although valid, cannot be strictly applied to the practical situation under discussion (Student C);
3. you accept Sipher's principle, but you are aware of other, stronger influences which diminish its importance (Student E).

Whichever line of argument you choose, it is impossible to present your case successfully if you wholly ignore Sipher's basic principle, as Student A does:

Student A:

> Sipher's isn't a constructive solution. Without strict attendance laws, many students wouldn't come to school at all.

Nonattendance is exactly what Sipher wants: he argues that indifferent students should be permitted to stay away, that their absence would benefit everyone. Student A makes no effort to refute Sipher's point; he is, in effect, saying to his source, "You're wrong!" without explaining why.

Student B, on the other hand, tries to establish a basis for disagreement:

Student B:

If mandatory attendance were to be abolished, how would children acquire the skills to survive in an educated society such as ours?

According to Student B, the practical uses of education have become so important that a student's very survival may one day depend on having been well educated. Implied here is the principle, in opposition to Sipher's, that receiving an education cannot be a matter of choice or a privilege to be earned. What children learn in school is so important to their future lives that they should be forced to attend classes, even against their will, for their own good. But this response is still superficial. Student B is confusing the desired object—getting an education—with one of the means of achieving that object—being present in the classroom; attendance, the means, has become an end in itself. Since students who attend, but do not participate, will not learn, mandatory attendance cannot create an educated population.

On the other hand, although attendance may not be the *only* condition for getting an education, the student's physical presence in the classroom is certainly important. In that case, should the decision about attendance, a decision likely to affect much of their future lives, be placed in the hands of those too young to understand the consequences?

Student C:

The absence of attendance laws would be too tempting for students and might create a generation of semi-illiterates. Consider the marginal student who, despite general indifference and occasional bad behavior, shows some promise and capacity for learning. Without a policy of mandatory attendance, he might choose the easy way out instead of trying to develop his abilities. As a society, we owe these students, at whatever cost, a chance at a good and sound education.

Notice that Student C specifies a "chance" at education. In a sense, there is no basic conflict between his views and Sipher's. Both agree in principle that society can provide the opportunity, but not the certainty, of being educated. The distinction here lies in the way in which the principle is applied. Sipher feels no need to make allowances or exceptions: there are limits to the opportunities that society is obliged to provide. Student C, however, believes that society must act in the best interests of those too young to make such decisions; for their sake, the principle of education as a privilege should be less rigorously applied. Students should be exposed to the conditions for (if not the fact of) education, whether they like it or not, until they become adults, capable of choice.

Student D goes even further, suggesting that not only is society obliged to provide the student with educational opportunities, but schools are responsible for making the experience as attractive as possible:

Student D:

Maybe the reason for a decrease in attendance and an unwillingness to learn is not that students do not want an education, but that the whole system of discipline and learning is ineffective. If schools concentrated on making classes more appealing, the result would be better attendance.

In Student D's analysis of the problem, the passive students are like consumers who need to be encouraged to take advantage of an excellent product that is not selling well. To encourage good attendance, the schools ought to consider using more attractive marketing methods. Implicit in this view is a transferral of blame from the student to the school. Other arguments of this sort might blame the parents, rather than the schools, for not teaching their children to understand that it is in their own best interests to get an education.

Finally, Student E accepts the validity of Sipher's view of education, but finds that the whole issue has become subordinate to a more important problem.

Student E:

We already have a problem with youths roaming the street, getting into serious trouble. Just multiply the current number of unruly kids by five or ten, and you will come up with the number of potential delinquents that will be hanging around the streets if we do away with the attendance laws that keep them in school. Sipher may be right when he argues that the quality of education would improve if unwilling students were permitted to drop out, but he would be wise to remember that those remaining inside school will have to deal with those on the outside sooner or later.

In this perspective, security becomes more important than education. Student E implicitly accepts and gives some social value to the image (rejected by Sipher) of school as a prison, with students sentenced to mandatory confinement.

A reasonably full response, like those of Student C and Student E, can provide the material for a series of paragraphs that argue against Sipher's position. Here, for example, is Student E's statement after it was broken down into the basic topics for a four-paragraph sequence. The numbers in parentheses suggest a reordering of the topics, using the student's basic agreement with Sipher as the starting point.

<table>
<tr><td>danger from dropouts if Sipher's plan is adopted (3)

custodial function of school (2)
concession that Sipher is right about education (1)

interests of law and order outweigh interests of education (4)</td><td>We already have a problem with youths roaming the street, getting into serious trouble. Just multiply the current number of unruly kids by five or ten, and you will come up with the number of potential delinquents that will be hanging around the streets if we do away with the attendance laws that keep them in school. Sipher may be right when he argues that the quality of education would improve if unwilling students were allowed to drop out, but he would be wise to remember that those remaining on the inside of the school will have to deal with those on the outside sooner or later.</td></tr>
</table>

Student E can now develop four full-length paragraphs by explaining each point and offering supporting evidence and illustrative examples.

ASSIGNMENT 4

Read "Smokers Have Rights, Too" and "What Our Educational System Needs is more F's," and choose, as the starting point for a summary-and-response, the essay with which you disagree most. Alternatively, bring in an essay which you are certain that you disagree with, and have your instructor approve your choice. First write a two-part summary of the essay, the first part describing the author's position and explicitly stated arguments, the second analyzing the principles underlying that position. Then present your own rebuttal of the author's point of view. The length of your essay will depend on the number and complexity of the ideas that you find in the source and the number of counterarguments that you can assemble. The minimum acceptable length for the entire assignment is two typewritten pages (approximately 500–600 words).

SMOKERS HAVE RIGHTS, TOO

Enough is enough, and we have seen enough of the harassment and intimidation of smokers.

True, smoking is bad for the smoker's health, and when he finally suffers his heart attack, or gets lung cancer, abstinent taxpayers have to pay for his hospitalization. As a result, many nonsmokers favor laws prohibiting smoking, at least in public and semipublic places. This may seem logical, but it puts us, as a society, on a dangerous, slippery slope, raising the prospect that we will soon be preventing all kinds of other people from doing what they want because of hazards to their health and our pocketbooks.

After all, taxpayers are also compelled to help pay for the hospitalization of drinkers, obese overeaters and those too lazy to exercise. Should we, then, have legal regulation of eating, drinking and exercising? How much liberty—the liberty to enjoy one's own habits and even vices—are we willing to sacrifice?

People smoke, or drink, or eat the wrong things, despite bad physical effects, because of the psychological gratification they obtain. In his 60's, Sigmund Freud underwent the first of more than 30 painful operations for oral cancer. He was told that it was caused by cigar smoking, but he continued nevertheless. In his 72d year he wrote: "I owe to the cigar a great intensification of my capacity to work and . . . of my self-control." By then, he had an artificial jaw and palate. He smoked till he died, in his 80's.

Most nonsmokers simply cannot understand this, and they scornfully label it "addiction." I prefer to call it a dependence, like reliance on a lover. Such a reliance may be enjoyable and productive; and it may have bad, even tragic, effects as well. But even when the bad effects become clear, one may want to continue because of the gratifications: the habit, once formed, is usually hard to shake. If one is deprived of the lover, or of the cigars, one suffers withdrawal symptoms, be they physical or psychological. Love is seldom called an addiction. Why should smoking be?

The nonsmoking taxpayer is right about one thing: he should not have to pay for hospitalizations caused by smoking. Instead, we should impose a Federal tax on tobacco sufficient to pay all the extra costs that smoking causes. Insurance companies, too, might charge higher rates to smokers and drinkers.

But what about the health effects of "passive smoking" and the annoyance that smoking may cause?

Some people are indeed allergic to smoke, and any civilized person will avoid smoking when they are around. Allergic people should, in turn, avoid places and occasions known to be smoky—discothèques, bars or dinner with Winston Churchill. But allergies to smoking have increased amazingly in recent years—a sudden increase that suggests that many of them are hysterical, or faked, to justify the imposition of the nonsmoker's preference on smokers.

In fact, dubious statistics to the contrary and except in instances of rare genuine allergies, smoking does not ordinarily endanger the health of nonsmokers unless they are exposed to smoke for a long time in an unventilated space.

As for annoyance, life is full of annoyances, some hazardous to health, that we must tolerate for the sake of other people, who want, or need, to do what annoys us. We all have to breathe polluted air, even if we never ride in a car or bus, simply because others want to.

Far more people refrain from smoking now than in the past—which is fine. But harassment will not increase their number. Nor will the prohibition of cigarette advertising. Marijuana does quite well without such promotion. People learn to smoke, or drink, from others, not from advertisements.

Is there nothing to be done? Certainly, wherever possible we should separate nonsmokers from smokers and provide ventilation. We do so now on big airplanes. But in most other places, in offices and restaurants, for instance, smokers and nonsmokers will have to reply on mutual tolerance. Courtesy cannot be replaced by one-sided and unenforceable regulations which, even if temporarily effective, will in the long run simply discredit the law.

Ernest van den Haag, New York Times, 9 April 1985

WHAT OUR EDUCATION SYSTEM NEEDS IS MORE F's

I suggest that instituting merit raises, getting back to basics, marrying the university to industry, and the other recommendations will not achieve measurable success [in restoring quality to American education] until something even more basic is returned to practice. The immediate need for our educational system from prekindergarten through post-Ph.D. is not more money or better teaching but simply a widespread giving of F's.

Before hastily dismissing the idea as banal and simplistic, think for a moment about the implications of a massive dispensing of failing grades. It would dramatically, emphatically, and immediately force into the open every major issue related to the inadequacies of American education.

Let me make it clear that I recommend giving those F's—by the dozens, hundreds, thousands, even millions—only to students who haven't learned the required material. The basic problem of our educational system is the common practice of giving credit where none has been earned, a practice that has resulted in the sundry faults delineated by all the reports and studies over recent years. Illiteracy among high-school graduates is growing because those students have been passed rather than flunked; we have low-quality teaching because of low-quality teachers who never should have been certified in the first place; college students have to take basic reading, writing, and mathematics courses because they never learned those skills in classrooms from which they never should have been granted egress.

School systems have contributed to massive ignorance by issuing unearned passing grades over a period of some 20 years. At first there was tolerance of students who did not fully measure up (giving D's to students who should have received firm F's); then our grading system continued to deteriorate (D's became C's, and B became the average grade); finally we arrived at total accommodation (come to class and get your C's, laugh at my jokes and take home B's).

Higher salaries, more stringent certification procedures, getting back to basics will have little or no effect on the problem of quality education unless and until we insist, as a profession, on giving F's whenever students fail to master the material.

Sending students home with final grades of F would force most parents to deal with the realities of their children's failure while it is happening and when it is yet possible to do something about it (less time on TV, and more time on homework, perhaps?). As long as it is the practice of teachers to pass students who should not be passed, the responsibility will not go home to the parents, where, I hope, it belongs. (I am tempted to make an analogy to then Gov. Lester Maddox's statement some years ago about prison conditions in Georgia—"We'll get a better grade of prisons when we get a better grade of prisoners"—but I shall refrain.)

Giving an F where it is deserved would force concerned parents to get themselves away from the TV set, too, and take an active part in their children's education. I realize, of course, that some parents would not help; some cannot help. However, Johnny does not deserve to pass just because Daddy doesn't care or is ignorant. Johnny should pass only when and if he knows the required material.

Giving an F whenever and wherever it is the only appropriate grade would force principals, school boards, and voters to come to terms with cost as a factor in improving our educational system. As the numbers of students at various levels were increased by those not being passed, more money would have to be spent to accommodate them. We could not be accommodating them in the old sense of passing them on, but by keeping them at one level until they did in time, one way or another, learn the material.

Insisting on respecting the line between passing and failing would also require us to demand as much of ourselves as of our students. As every teacher knows, a failed student can be the product of a failed teacher.

Teaching methods, classroom presentations, and testing procedures would have to be of a very high standard—we could not, after all, conscionably give F's if we have to go home at night thinking it might somehow be our own fault.

The results of giving an F where it is deserved would be immediately evident. There would be no illiterate college graduates next spring—none. The same would be true of high-school graduates, and consequently next year's college freshmen—*all* of them—would be able to read.

I don't claim that giving F's will solve all of the problems, but I do argue that unless and until we start failing those students who should be failed, other suggested solutions will make little progress toward improving education. Students in our schools and colleges should be permitted to pass only after they have fully met established standards; borderline cases should be retained.

The single most important requirement for solving the problems of education in America today is the big fat F, written decisively in red ink millions of times in schools and colleges across the country.

Carl Singleton, *Chronicle of Higher Education,*
1 February 1984

STRATEGY TWO: INTERPRETING WHAT YOU SUMMARIZE

Interpretation means the explanation or clarification of something that has been read, seen, or heard; the interpreter serves as a link between the author and the reader or audience. At the United Nations, interpreters translate speeches into other languages so that all the delegates can understand them. A writer interprets a source by "translating" the author's ideas into terms that readers may find more understandable and more meaningful.

In daily life, you interpret ideas and information for yourself and for others whenever you try to explain an action or event or situation. Suppose that a friend has asked you to explain the reasons for the recent bankruptcy of the drugstore on the next corner. The easiest way to do so might be to provide a full account of the reasons in chronological order, year by year, month by month: two years ago, the owner of the Best Pharmacy fell ill and was unable to supervise the store; shortly afterward, the zoning laws changed and the neighborhood became less residential; next, the chief pharmacist decided to move to the south; meanwhile, an outbreak of vandalism and petty thefts had begun; then a discount store opened a block away; only two months ago, the overworked owner had his second heart attack; and so on. Without stressing any one event, you could elaborate upon each step, providing exact dates and details to form a chronological summary of the store's gradual decline.

But if your friend only wanted a brief account of the long story, you would need to emphasize one (or more) of the reasons, probably removing it from its place in the chronological order. As soon as you make that choice and decide which piece of information to take out of the original time-sequence, you have begun to interpret the event. Of course, you must be familiar with all the stages in order to pull out one fact and confidently state that *this* was the primary reason for the pharmacy's decline. But, after weighing each fact against the others, you might finally assert that the drugstore failed because of a shift in residential patterns in that area of the city. Then (you might choose to add) this shift led to outbreaks of crime, the pharmacist's move to Florida, and the worries that brought about the owner's heart attack.

The chronological summary was a factual list, with no attempt made to stress one idea more than the next; therefore, there was little possibility of dispute. But as soon as you emphasize certain reasons for the drugstore's bankruptcy, another informed observer might refuse to accept your interpretation of events. Instead, she might claim that, in *her* view, the success of a neighborhood store always depends on the diligence of the owner and the quality of service; therefore the illness of the owner and, to a lesser extent, the departure of the pharmacist were chiefly responsible for the loss of business. Given the conflict between these two interpretations—declining residential population versus declining service—each of you might wish to expand your summary and supply some supporting evidence to reinforce your main point. The second observer might offer personal experience to back up her interpretation: after several of the substitute employees had been rude and neglectful, she and her neighbors began to shop at the discount store up the street. You, on the other hand, might cite statistics about the effect of the new zoning laws on all small businesses in the neighborhood.

The point is that both interpretations may be equally valid. Each is based on personal judgment as well as factual evidence. Each person has employed particular values and preconceptions in interpreting the actual events, which are common knowledge. (There is not always as much opportunity for speculation and disagreement when one is interpreting a *written* source.) In fact, another interpretation of the same event might emphasize a quite different idea. A stranger to the city, who has listened to both versions, might later conclude that "there are *two* main reasons why that drugstore failed. . . . " Or, by now quite familiar with all the events (and more objective than either of the first two interpreters), he might try to incorporate *all* the reasons into a new interpretive summary: "Conditions of modern urban life do not favor the small, owner-operated business." Notice that, in order to encompass everything that has come before, this final summary is more general than the first two.

EXERCISE 19

Reviews of films, plays, television programs, and books generally serve a dual purpose: they explain what the work is about (summary and interpretation) and they assess its value for an audience (evaluation). It is important to be able to distinguish between *interpretation* (which does not explicitly pass judgment on the worth of a work) and *evaluation* (which contains the reviewer's opinion of the work as well as the standards which, according to the reviewer, the work should meet).

Read the following review, and use different symbols to mark:

A. passages and phrases where the author *summarizes* the plot (include and identify quotation and paraphase);
B. passages and phrases where he *interprets* (or provides additional background for) the ideas and themes of the program;
C. passages and phrases where he *evaluates* the program.

Are there any passages that do not fall into one of the three categories above? What is their function in the review?

"PAPER DOLLS" IS A GLOSSY POP FANTASY

This evening's two-hour premiere of "Paper Dolls," on ABC at 9 o'clock, does have the distinction of being a television rarity. Most of the film is simply a remake not of some Hollywood classic but of a made-for-TV movie that racked up some impressive ratings a little over two years ago. The subject is New York's modeling industry. One of the chief characters is a tall young lady who bears at least a passing resemblance to Brooke Shields, complete with protective mother. And the entire production is a glossy testimonial to popular fantasies of the chic life in New York, with its posh stores, beautiful people and seductive promises of easy sex and accessible drugs. Add a thumpingly contemporary music track, along the lines of Michael Jackson's "Billie Jean," and you have a fairly accurate idea about where the producer's exploration-exploitation tactics are headed.

At the outset, we meet the 16-year-old but already jaded Taryn Blake (Nicolette Sheridan) having a temper tantrum outside the Plaza Hotel about being overworked and cold. Wesley Harper (Dack Rambo), the head of Harper Cosmetics, is not amused as he watches his ad campaign for a new perfume being jeopardized by the young model's behavior. Meanwhile, cheerfully sauntering up Fifth Avenue are Dinah Caswell (Jennifer Warren), a former model, and her 16-year-old daughter Laurie (Terry Farrell). Stopping to see what is going on, they are spotted by old friends on the production's crew and are persuaded to do a couple of horseplay poses for old times' sake. Needless to say, when the pictures are being developed, the man in the darkroom takes one look at Laurie and sighs, "Little girl, get ready, because you are something else."

At the upper echelons of real power, there are Grant Harper (Lloyd Bridges) and Racine (Morgan Fairchild). He is Wesley's father and the chairman of Harper World Wide, an international cosmetics conglomerate. She runs a top modeling agency and, when not being cynical and conniving, dines on white wine, slivers of cheese and grapes (she loathes Chinese food because "you're never quite sure what you've eaten"). Mr. Harper is not terribly fond of Wesley, but he dotes on his daughter Blair (Mimi Rogers), also a model and now reaching the dangerous age of 30. And although a neglectful and occasionally philandering husband, he enables his adoring wife to live in style on a lavish Long Island estate that includes stables and real horses, this year's status symbol among television's affluent classes. Racine, on the other hand, is devoted only to the fees she collects on the photogenic talents of her clients.

Leonard Goldberg, the producer of this glitzy effort, has revealed that he was originally drawn to the subject when he noticed the youthfulness of many of the models being used in some of the more sophisticated television and magazine advertisements. He wondered, Mr. Goldberg says, what happened to these children after they finished playing the suggestive roles of grown-ups. Mr. Goldberg's concern has now been translated into a television package that is described this way by the network: "The glamorous world of fashion and beauty—where the stakes are profits, power and passion, and top models are discovered or destroyed with the snap of the shutter. . . . In a youth-oriented business, the emphasis is on cutthroat competition." Watch Taryn, "a tempestuous teen superstar on the verge of burnout." Or Racine, "the modeling agent whose business is built on relentless ambition and cold calculation." And so on.

Any moral or social concerns that can be detected in "Paper Dolls" are minimal. There are, admittedly, passing moments. Laurie's mom, who, after all, should know the business, is a bit wary about letting her daughter get into an industry that "has all the wrong values." It will mean, Mom warns, being treated like a piece of meat and never eating ice cream again. But Laurie's nice-guy stepfather argues that "it's not as if we're selling her into white slavery." That's before he knows anything about the business practices of Wesley Harper. And then poor Taryn, being pushed mercilessly by her money-hungry mother, would gladly give up her cocaine and sexual games to be a normal kid with nice friends. When Taryn attempts suicide, Harper Grant, assuming his most statesmanlike manner, reminds her mother: "She's a child! She doesn't need agents and movie producers—she needs a mother!"

"Paper Dolls" is not without its bits of humor. When Blair turns 30, Daddy's birthday party for her includes a fabulous diamond-and-emerald necklace as a gift and Bobby Short, the cabaret singer, as the entertainment for the guests gathered at his sumptuous mansion. "We should all be grateful," someone murmurs, "that Venice isn't for sale."

And Racine's chronic bitchiness can be amusing. Comforting Blair, who has already lost some major modeling jobs to "younger and fresher" faces, Racine purrs, "Darling, you're going to adore being 30." Once in a great while, the script threatens to get rather serious. When a noted television interviewer begins broadcasting "exclusives" about troubles within the Harper empire, Grant invites her to lunch where they discuss how he, as a businessman, exploits his employees, and how she, as a journalist, "exploits the exploited." They agree that "we're both feeding the public's tastes" and then smilingly conclude that "it's all their fault."

Overall, the new "Paper Dolls" is not as good, not as much trashy fun as the two-year-old "Paper Dolls." The original had more flashbulb-popping glitter, not to mention a better cast. Joan Collins was her inimitable self as the modeling-agency owner. Taryn was played by Daryl Hannah ("Splash") and her mother by the late Joan Hackett. The whole production flitted by entertainingly, tying up all the loose plot ends unconvincingly but with a kind of dizzily grand aplomb. This evening's series premiere fades out with at least three major story developments unresolved and dangling. Viewers could decide to stick with "Paper Dolls" when it settles into its regular weekly slot Tuesday evenings at 9. That is, if they have nothing better to do.

John J. O'Connor, *New York Times*,
23 September 1984

Interpreting an Essay

When you decide to write about a long and complex essay, one with many ideas woven together, you may sometimes have to interpret and recast its contents. In such cases, you present your interpretation of the source through a lengthy summary—through the ideas and information that you choose to emphasize, through your explanations of ambiguous or contradictory ideas, through the connections that you make between apparently unrelated ideas, and through the gaps or deficiencies in the author's argument that you may decide to point out. While giving credit to the source and remaining faithful to its ideas, you will be presenting those ideas in a new and clearer light, enabling your reader to understand them more easily.

Since your purpose is summary as well as interpretation, you should condense the original material, using selection and emphasis to convey to the reader what is important and what is not. Nevertheless, your version may run almost as long as the original essay. Its contents will be organized according to *your* interpretation of the source's ideas, and, because it is a summary, the readers will be hearing *your* characteristic voice, not the author's. For these reasons, the interpretive summary may be regarded as a separate essay in its own right.

An interpretive summary would probably be the appropriate strategy in any or all of the following circumstances:

1. An essay contains a great many major ideas interwoven together.
2. An essay presents a lengthy argument whose step-by-step sequence is so complex that, if any stage is omitted, the reader will be missing something vital.
3. An essay is very disorganized and would benefit from reordering.
4. An essay is ambiguous and needs to have certain contradictions pointed out, if not resolved.

All four of these conditions could exist in a single essay, and then the summarizer would indeed be performing a service by clarifying what is obscure.

Guidelines for Writing an Interpretive Summary

After reading "The Corruption of Sports," study the five guidelines for writing an interpretive essay, together with the explanation of each rule as it could be applied to Christopher Lasch's essay.

THE CORRUPTION OF SPORTS

Among the activities through which men seek release from everyday life, games offer in many ways the purest form of escape. Like sex, drugs, and drink, they obliterate awareness of everyday reality, not by dimming that awareness but by raising it to a new intensity of concentration. Moreover, games have no side-effects, produce no hangovers or emotional complications. Games satisfy the need for free fantasy and the search for gratuitous difficulty simultaneously; they combine childlike exuberance with deliberately created complications.   1

By establishing conditions of equality among the players, Roger Caillois says, games attempt to substitute ideal conditions for "the normal confusion of everyday life." They re-create the freedom, the remembered perfection of childhood and mark it off from ordinary life with artificial boundaries, within which the only constraints are the rules to which the players freely submit. Games enlist skill and intelligence, the utmost concentration of purpose, on behalf of utterly useless activities, which make no contribution to the struggle of man against nature, to the wealth or comfort of the community, or to its physical survival.   2

In communist and fascist countries sports have been organized and promoted by the state. In capitalist countries the uselessness of games makes them offensive to social reformers, improvers of public morals, or functionalist critics of society like Veblen, who saw in the futility of upper-class sports anachronistic survivals of militarism and tests of prowess. Yet the "futility" of play, and nothing else, explains its   3 appeal—its artificiality, the arbitrary obstacles it sets up for no other purpose than to challenge the players to surmount them, the absence of any utilitarian or uplifting object. Games quickly lose part of their charm when pressed into the service of education, character development, or social improvement.

Modern industry having reduced most jobs to a routine, games in   4
our society take on added meaning. Men seek in play the difficulties and demands—both intellectual and physical—which they no longer find in work. The history of culture, as Huizinga showed in his classic study of play, *Homo Ludens*, appears from one perspective to consist of the gradual eradication of the elements of play from all cultural forms—from religion, from the law, from warfare, above all from productive labor. The rationalization of these activities leaves little room for the spirit of arbitrary invention or the disposition to leave things to chance. Risk, daring, and uncertainty, important components of play, have little place in industry or in activities infiltrated by industrial methods, which are intended precisely to predict and control the future and to eliminate risk. Games accordingly have assumed an importance unprecedented even in ancient Greece, where so much of social life revolved around contests. Sports, which satisfy also the starved need for physical exertion—for a renewal of the sense of the physical basis of life—have become an obsession not just of the masses but of those who set themselves up as a cultural elite.

The rise of spectator sports to their present importance coincides   5
historically with the rise of mass production, which intensifies the needs sport satisfies while at the same time creating the technical capacity to promote and market athletic contests to a vast audience. But according to a common criticism of modern sport, these same developments have destroyed the value of athletics. Commercialized play has turned into work, subordinated the athlete's pleasure to the spectator's, and reduced the spectator himself to a state of passivity—the very antithesis of the health and vigor sport ideally promotes. The mania for winning has encouraged an exaggerated emphasis on the competitive side of sport, to the exclusion of the more modest but more satisfying experiences of cooperation and competence. The cult of victory, loudly proclaimed by such football coaches as Vince Lombardi and George Allen, has made savages of the players and rabid chauvinists of their followers. The violence and partisanship of modern sports lead some critics to insist that athletics impart militaristic values to the young, irrationally inculcate local and national pride in the spectator, and serve as one of the strongest bastions of male chauvinism.

Huizinga himself, who anticipated some of these arguments and   6
stated them far more persuasively, argued that modern games and sports had been ruined by a "fatal shift toward over-seriousness." At the same time, he maintained that play had lost its element of ritual,

had become "profane," and consequently had ceased to have any "organic connection whatever with the structure of society." The masses now crave "trivial recreation and crude sensationalism" and throw themselves into these pursuits with an intensity far beyond their intrinsic merit. Instead of playing with the freedom and intensity of children, they play with the "blend of adolescence and barbarity" that Huizinga calls puerilism, investing games with patriotic and martial fervor while treating serious pursuits as if they were games. "A far-reaching contamination of play and serious activity has taken place," according to Huizinga:

> The two spheres are getting mixed. In the activities of an outwardly serious nature hides an element of play. Recognized play, on the other hand, is no longer able to maintain its true play-character as a result of being taken too seriously and being technically over-organised. The indispensable qualities of detachment, artlessness, and gladness are thus lost.

An analysis of the criticism of modern sport, in its vulgar form as well as in Huizinga's more refined version, brings to light a number of common misconceptions about modern society. A large amount of writing on sports has accumulated in recent years, and the sociology of sport has even entrenched itself as a minor branch of social science. Much of this commentary has no higher purpose than to promote athletics or to exploit the journalistic market they have created, but some of it aspires to social criticism. Those who have formulated the now familiar indictment of organized sport include the sociologist Harry Edwards; the psychologist and former tennis player Dorcas Susan Butt, who thinks sport should promote "competence" instead of competition; disillusioned professional athletes like Dave Meggyesy and Chip Oliver; and radical critics of culture and society, notably Paul Hoch and Jack Scott. **7**

Critics of sport, in their eagerness to uncover evidence of corruption and decline, attack intrinsic elements of athletics, elements essential to their appeal in all periods and places, on the erroneous assumption that spectatorship, violence, and competition reflect conditions peculiar to modern times. On the other hand, they overlook the distinctive contribution of contemporary society to the degradation of sport and therefore misconceive the nature of that degradation. They concentrate on issues, such as "over-seriousness," that are fundamental to an understanding of sports, indeed to the very definition of play, but that are peripheral or irrelevant to the ways they have changed in recent history. **8**

Take the common complaint that modern sports are "spectator-oriented rather than participant-oriented." Spectators, in this view, are irrelevant to the success of the game. What a naïve theory of **9** human motivation this implies! The attainment of certain skills unavoidably gives rise to an urge to show them off. At a higher level of mastery, the performer no longer wishes merely to display his virtuosity—for the true connoisseur can easily distinguish between the performer who plays to the crowd and the superior artist who matches himself against the full rigor of his art itself—but to ratify a supremely difficult accomplishment; to give pleasure; to forge a bond between himself and his audience, a shared appreciation of a ritual executed not only flawlessly but with much feeling and with a sense of style and proportion.

In all games, particularly in athletic contests, the central importance   10 of display and representation serves as a reminder of the ancient connections between play, ritual, and drama. The players not only compete, they enact a familiar ceremony that reaffirms common values. Ceremony requires witnesses: enthusiastic spectators conversant with the rules of the performance and its underlying meaning. Far from destroying the value of sports, the attendance of spectators is often necessary to them. Indeed one of the virtues of contemporary sports lies in their resistance to the erosion of standards and their capacity to appeal to a knowledgeable audience. Norman Podhoretz has argued that the sports public remains more discriminating than the public for the arts and that in sports "excellence is relatively uncontroversial as a judgment of performance." The public for sports still consists largely of men who took part in sports during boyhood and thus acquired a sense of the game and a capacity to make discriminating judgments.

The same can hardly be said for the audience of an artistic perform-   11 ance, even though amateur musicians, dancers, actors, and painters may still comprise a small nucleus of the audience. Constant experimentation in the arts, in any case, has created so much confusion about standards that the only surviving measure of excellence, for many, is novelty and shock-value, which in a jaded time often resides in a work's sheer ugliness or banality. In sport, on the other hand, novelty and rapid shifts of fashion play only a small part in its appeal to a discriminating audience.

Yet even here, the contamination of standards has already begun.   12 Faced with rising costs, owners seek to increase attendance at sporting events by installing exploding scoreboards, broadcasting recorded cavalry charges, giving away helmets and bats, and surrounding the spectator with cheerleaders, usherettes, and ball girls. Television has enlarged the audience for sports while lowering the quality of that audience's understanding; at least this is the assumption of sports commentators, who direct at the audience an interminable stream of tutelage in the basics of the game, and of the promoters, who reshape one game after another to conform to the tastes of an audience supposedly incapable of grasping their finer points.

The American League's adoption of the designated hitter rule, which   13
relieves pitchers of the need to bat and diminishes the importance of
managerial strategy, provides an especially blatant example of the dilu-
tion of sports by the requirements of mass promotion. Another example is the "Devil-Take-the-Hindmost Mile," a track event invented by
the San Francisco *Examiner*, in which the last runner in the early
stages of the race has to drop out—a rule that encourages an early
scramble to avoid disqualification but lowers the general quality of the
event. When the television networks discovered surfing, they insisted
that events be held according to a prearranged schedule, without regard to weather conditions. A surfer complained, "Television is destroying our sport. The TV producers are turning a sport and an art
form into a circus." The same practices produce the same effects on
other sports, forcing baseball players, for example, to play World Series games on freezing October evenings. Substituting artificial sur-
faces for grass in tennis, which has slowed the pace of the game,
placed a premium on reliability and patience, and reduced the element
of tactical brillance and overpowering speed, commends itself to television producers because it makes tennis an all-weather game and even
permits it to be played indoors, in sanctuaries of sport like Caesar's Palace in Las Vegas.

As spectators become less knowledgeable about the games they   14
watch, they become more sensation-minded and bloodthirsty. The
rise of violence in ice hockey, far beyond the point where it plays any
functional part in the game, coincided with the expansion of professional hockey into cities without any traditional attachment to the
sport—cities in which weather conditions, indeed, had always pre-
cluded any such tradition of local play. But the significance of such
changes is not, as such critics as Jack Scott and Paul Hoch imagine, that
sports ought to be organized solely for the edification of the players
and that corruption sets in when sports begin to be played to spectators for a profit. It is often true that sport at this point ceases to be enjoyable and becomes a business. Recent critics go astray, however, in
supposing that organized athletics ever serve the interests of the players alone or that "professionalization" inevitably corrupts all who take
part in it.

In glorifying amateurism, equating spectatorship with passivity, and   15
deploring competition, recent criticism of sport echoes the fake radicalism of the counterculture, from which so much of it derives. It
shows its contempt for excellence by proposing to break down the
"elitist" distinction between players and spectators. It proposes to replace competitive professional sports, which notwithstanding their
shortcomings uphold standards of competence and bravery that might
otherwise become extinct, with a bland regimen of cooperative diver-
sions in which everyone can join in, regardless of age or ability—"new

sports for the noncompetitive," having "no object, really," according to a typical effusion, except to bring "people together to enjoy each other." In its eagerness to strip from sport the elements that have always explained its imaginative appeal, the staged rivalry of superior ability, this "radicalism" proposes merely to complete the degradation already begun by the very society the cultural radicals profess to criticize and subvert.

What corrupts an athletic performance, as it does any other performance, is not professionalism or competition but the presence of an unappreciative, ignorant audience and the need to divert it with sensations extrinsic to the performance. It is at this point that ritual, drama, and sports all degenerate into spectacle. Huizinga's analysis of the secularization of sport helps to clarify this issue. In the degree to which athletic events lose the element of ritual and public festivity, according to Huizinga, they deteriorate into "trivial recreation and crude sensationalism." But even Huizinga misunderstands the cause of this development. It hardly lies in the "fatal shift toward over-seriousness." Huizinga himself, when he is writing about the theory of play rather than the collapse of "genuine play" in our own time, understands very well that play at its best is always serious; indeed that the essence of play lies in taking seriously activities that have no purpose, serve no utilitarian ends. He reminds us that "the majority of Greek contests were fought out in deadly earnest" and discusses, under the category of play, duels in which contestants fight to the death, water sports in which the goal is to drown your opponent, and tournaments for which the training and preparation consume the athletes' entire existence.   16

The degradation of sport, then, consists not in its being taken too seriously but in its subjection to some ulterior purpose, such as profit-making, patriotism, moral training, or the pursuit of health. Sport may give rise to these things in abundance, but ideally it produces them only as by-products having no essential connection with the game. When the game itself, on the other hand, comes to be regarded as incidental to the benefits it supposedly confers on participants, spectators, or promoters, it loses it peculiar capacity to transport both participant and spectator beyond everyday experience—to provide a glimpse of perfect order uncontaminated by commonplace calculations of advantage or even by ordinary considerations of survival.   17

Christopher Lasch, New York Review of Books, 28 April 1977

Step one.   After reading the essay once, go through it again slowly, making a list of each separate idea; as you read each sentence and paragraph, ask yourself whether the new point is individual enough, im-

*portant enough, and pertinent enough to the essay's main themes to be
an entry on your list.*

Since "The Corruption of Sports" is a very complex essay, the listing
of ideas becomes an especially crucial and illuminating step. A preliminary reading suggests that Christopher Lasch is chiefly concerned with
the contrast between the original life-enhancing function of sports and
the commercialization and sensationalism that characterize sports today.
To write a list with a narrow focus, you must exclude (or list separately)
any points, interesting in themselves, that are only loosely connected to
Lasch's central themes. The numerous references to Huizinga are a good
example: while Huizinga's classic work certainly provides an excellent
background for understanding Lasch, he cites Huizinga only in order to
provide evidence in support of his own points; the excerpts from Huizinga are not intended to be central ideas in their own right.

As you write the list of ideas, try to make each entry a complete sentence *in your own words.* When you retain the original wording, you
may be including on your lists phrases that sound good but do not actually stand for coherent ideas. Remember also that you will not necessarily find a new idea in every paragraph, and some paragraphs will contain
more than one idea worth listing. Here is one student's summary-list
(with the relevant paragraph number cited):

A. One of the functions of sports is to provide escape. (1)
B. Sports heighten the mind and the senses; they are activities that
   require concentration, yet are relaxing. (1)
C. Sports provide an opportunity to live out one's fantasies. (1)
D. It is a characteristic of games that they should be played in artifi-
   cial, almost ideal circumstances, in which the players are theoreti-
   cally equal. (2)
E. Games should be essentially purposeless, lacking reality and with
   no connection to the real world or usefulness to society. (2) (3)
F. Games provide an artificial challenge not found in modern working life, a sense of controlled risk and danger. (4)
G. Sports give people an opportunity to exercise, to regain contact
   with their physical selves. (4)
H. Sports have been commercialized and are now more like work
   than play. (5)
I. The need to make sports profitable has made it vital to gather together the largest possible audience; spectators now tend to be
   passive, rather than interested participants. (5)
J. Sports now emphasize victory at all costs, which encourages violence and unsportsmanlike tactics, and competition at the expense of teamwork and skill. (5)
K. Spectators now tend to be partisans and regard players and teams

as "my side" and "the other side," something that can have un-pleasant militaristic overtones. (5) (6)

L. Spectators have always been essential to the success of sport, as audiences appreciate the players' skill and artistry. (9)

M. Sports have a social function as the ritual enactment of shared beliefs and values, which is why audience participation is so important. (10)

N. A knowledgeable audience can be used to maintain high standards of playing. (10)

O. To attract the largest possible audience, organizers need to satisfy people in the quickest, easiest way; audiences these days are very unsophisticated and have not been encouraged to expect a high standard of play. (12)

P. The present emphasis on victory and lethal competition results from the belief that only an appeal to primitive emotions will ensure spectator interest. (13) (14)

Q. Some people suggest that a return to amateur sports would solve the problem, since there would be less commercialization and less need for violent competition, but the loss of the competitive spirit would be just as corrupting to sports as commercialization has been. (15)

R. The importance of sports in our lives is related to its ability to be played as an end in itself, apart from the everyday concerns of the world; when it is used to fulfill a social, political, or economic function, then it gets corrupted. (17)

Step two.   Rearrange your list of points into an outline of the essay, following the author's basic strategy.

Step three.   Using your outline of the essay, designate each major entry as a separate paragraph in your summary.

The outlining of the source-essay and the paragraphing of your own essay are actually part of the same process. (To review the procedure for outlining a complex essay, see Chapter 1. pp. 39–43.) After reviewing your list of central ideas, you should realize that the essay breaks into two overlapping parts: the first six paragraphs contain a description of the original purposes of sports, emphasizing the degree to which games provide a safe and relaxing means of escaping from the realities of daily life; the next eight paragraphs contain an analysis of the ways in which these purposes have been commercialized and corrupted. Towards the end, in paragraphs 15 and 17, Lasch considers ways by which sports might be restored to their original wholesome and therapeutic functions.

Essentially, Lasch is working with two strategies. First of all, he is presenting a contrast between sports in the past and sports in the present, a before-and-after comparison. So, as an experiment, you might try to organize an interpretation around this strategy by selecting and rearranging certain items on your list:

Sports: Original Function

A. One of the functions of sports is to provide escape.

B. Sports heighten the mind and the senses; they are activities that require concentration, yet are relaxing.

G. Sports give people an opportunity to exercise, to regain contact with their physical selves.

C. Sports provide an opportunity to live out one's fantasies.

E. Games should be essentially purposeless, lacking in reality and with no connection to the real world or usefulness to society.

F. Games provide an artificial challenge not found in modern working life, a sense of controlled risk and danger.

D. It is characteristic of games that they should be played in artificial, almost ideal circumstances, in which the players are theoretically equal.

M. Sports have a social function as the ritual enactment of shared beliefs and values.

Sports: Present Function

H. Sports have been commercialized and are now more like work than play.

J. Sports now emphasize victory at all costs, which encourages violence and unsportsmanlike tactics.

K. Spectators now tend to be partisans.

I. Spectators now tend to be passive.

What you immediately notice when you look at this list is that the comparison is not well-balanced: you have many more items on the "original function" side than you have on the "present function" side. This imbalance does not result from lack of interest, for Lasch devotes more than half his essay (and the title) to describing how corrupt sports have become. Indeed, what really occurs halfway through the essay is that Lasch switches his strategy. After starting with a straightforward description of the purposes of sport—focusing on the players—he begins to analyze the reasons why these purposes can no longer be carried out;

and that shift requires a parallel change of focus from the players to the spectators. In Lasch's view, a major problem has been the corruption of the spectators, primarily for economic reasons; that has really brought about the corruption of the players and of the various sports themselves. At the end of the essay, a solution that he suggests requires a more active and knowledgeable audience, one composed of participants rather than just spectators.

To present this larger strategy in your essay, it is necessary to rearrange your list, selecting only those items that contribute to an understanding of the *problem and its possible solution*. Again, the numbers in parentheses represent paragraphs in the original essay.

I. Ideal: Sports as they should be
   A. One of the functions of sports is to provide escape. (1)
      Sports provide an opportunity to live out one's fantasies. (1)
   B. Games should be essentially purposeless, lacking reality and with no connection to the real world or usefulness to society. (2)(3)
      Games provide an artificial challenge not found in modern working life, a sense of controlled risk and danger. (4)
      It is a characteristic of games that they should be played in artificial, almost ideal circumstances, in which the players are theoretically equal. (2)
   C. Sports have a social function as the ritual enactment of shared beliefs and values, which is why audience participation is so important. (10)
      Spectators have always been essential to the success of sports, as audiences appreciate the players' skill and artistry. (9)

II. Problem: Sports as they are today
   A. The need to make sports profitable has made it vital to gather together the largest possible audience; spectators now tend to be passive, rather than interested participants. (5)
   B. To attract the largest possible audience, organizers need to satisfy people in the quickest, easiest way; audiences these days are very unsophisticated and have not been encouraged to expect a high standard of play. (12)
      The present emphasis on victory and lethal competition results from the belief that only an appeal to primitive emotions will ensure spectator interest. (13)(14)
      Sports now emphasize victory at all costs, which encourages violence and unsportsmanlike tactics, and competition at the expense of teamwork and skill. (5)
   C. Spectators now tend to be partisans and regard players and teams as "my side" and "the other side," something that can have unpleasant militaristic overtones. (5)(6)

III. Solution: Making sports "free" again
   A. Some people suggest that a return to amateur sports would solve the problem, since there would be less commercialization and less need for violent competition, but the loss of the competitive spirit would be just as corrupting to sport as commercialization has been. (15)
   B. A knowledgeable audience can be used to maintain high standards of playing. (10)
   C. The importance of sports in our lives is related to their ability to be played as ends in themselves, apart from everyday concerns of the world; when they are used to fulfill a social, political, or economic function, then sports get corrupted. (17)

You will observe that two of the points on the original list (B and G) have been omitted from this outline; physical relaxation as a reason for participating in sports does not really belong in an interpretation that emphasizes spectators as well as players. Notice also that this revised list has already been converted into a rough outline; related points are grouped together for inclusion in individual paragraphs.

Step four. Plan an introductory paragraph that contains a clear statement of the author's thesis and scope; if you can, include some suggestions of the author's strategy.

Make sure that your introduction provides a fair account of Lasch's intentions. Some summarizers go beyond their legitimate function as interpreters of the original essay and wander off into digressions that the author did not include or intend. Here is the beginning of an introduction in which the summarizer's own views are attributed to Christopher Lasch:

> According to Christopher Lasch, it is no longer worthwhile for a spectator to attend sports events because the players and teams are interested only in profit. The average baseball, football or tennis star is eager to become a millionaire as quickly as possible. Lasch thinks that these greedy individuals are corrupting sports and providing audiences with a poor show.

This writer is manipulating Lasch's ideas in order to write an argumentative essay of her own. She starts out by changing Lasch's emphasis and attributing the problem to the players rather than the organizers. Later in the essay, it might be appropriate to disagree with the author, provided that it is made clear who is responsible for which point of view; but, as an introduction, the first point that the reader will encounter, such a statement can only create a false impression. Here is an introduction in which the scope, purpose, and strategy of Lasch's essay are described more objectively:

> In "The Corruption of Sports," Christopher Lasch sets out to explore the reasons why so many sports and games have become unpleasant, even violent confrontations, with bloodthirsty spectators cheering on players and teams that try to pulverize the opposition, not just win the game. After describing the traditional spirit of sports, with participants appreciating skill as well as power, Lasch analyzes the ways in which the emphasis on profits has resulted in a new kind of audience and a new kind of player. This problem of corruption in sports can be solved, he concludes, only if games are once again played purely for their own sake, rather than to serve an economic or social function.

Step five. As you write each paragraph, include related minor points and a few key details from the original essay, which are to be subordinated to the paragraph's central topic.

You need to convey to your reader some sense of the supporting materials that were provided in the original text. Although the actual writing of the summary's paragraphs ought to be relatively easy once the strategy and outline have been established, there are a few pitfalls to avoid. For example, you may pull a minor point out of the context of accompanying ideas and misinterpret it. One summarizer chose to cite the rising incidence of violence in ice hockey, which Lasch discusses in paragraph 14:

> Lasch thinks that ice hockey should be played only in the cold-weather cities where it originated; in other places, more violent kinds of playing are encouraged.

In fact, Lasch is not in favor of restricting the locations for playing ice hockey; he is merely making a comment on the higher quality of play that occurs in places where the audiences are more knowledgeable. By all means make use of the examples that Lasch provides, but be careful to interpret them correctly. And do not hesitate to include illustrations of your own. You might, for example, raise the issue of the Olympics and the way in which television coverage tends to encourage support for national teams rather than admiration for fine athletes of all nations.

Other equally serious problems can arise from a confusion between the author and his sources. Since Lasch generally agrees with Huizinga and frequently cites the latter's theories as evidence for his own ideas, you might be tempted to attribute to Lasch Huizinga's argument (in paragraph 6) that sports have become excessively serious and are no longer sufficiently linked to the fabric of society. However, Lasch recognizes this as a point of disagreement between himself and Huizinga—and says so later in the essay, in paragraph 16. It is important to be aware that, while they may not all be equally important, there are three points of view represented in your essay—Lasch's, Huizinga's, and your own. The reader must be made aware of the boundary lines dividing these three points of view. The writer of a successful interpretive summary will integrate but not confuse his own opinions, those of the original author, and those of the original author's sources.

ASSIGNMENT 5

Write an interpretive summary for Charles Silberman's "The Insufficiency of Human Institutions," an excerpt from *Criminal Violence, Criminal Justice*. Before taking the first step and writing a list of ideas, consider why this essay needs and deserves to be interpreted at length.

THE INSUFFICIENCY OF HUMAN INSTITUTIONS

We punish criminals for a variety of sometimes conflicting ends. The first and most important is to establish and maintain a sense of fairness and balance in society; failure to punish criminal offenders would mean that those who comply with the law voluntarily would be penalized, while those who break the law would gain an unfair advantage.

We punish criminals, in short, because justice, i.e., fairness, requires it; punishment is a way of restoring the equilibrium that is broken when someone commits a crime. Hence punishment must be guided by the notion of desert, a less emotionally charged designation than the more familiar concept of retribution. This means focusing on the past—on what the offender has already done—rather than on what he may do in the future. It also means linking the nature and severity of the punishment meted out to the nature and severity of the crime that has been committed; if justice requires that criminals be punished, the notion of desert requires that punishment be commensurate with the severity of the crime.

But justice is not the only goal. Punishment is also designed to reduce crime—to deter people from breaking the law, or to prevent those who have already committed a crime from doing so again. Future crime may be prevented by executing criminals, by incapacitating them in prison, by maintaining some form of surveillance or supervision over them, or by rehabilitating them, i.e., changing them so that they no longer want (or need) to break the law.

The debate over deterrence has been misleading, on both sides, because the wrong issues have been addressed. What is at stake is not whether punishment deters crime (or, put another way, whether punishment affects behavior); of course it does. The relevant question is whether *more* punishment (or speedier, or more severe, or more certain punishment) would deter crime more effectively than the punishment now being administered. As I will elaborate in the chapters that follow, there is reason to doubt that it would, except, perhaps, in juvenile court, where the wrong youngsters tend to be punished.

Those opposed to harsher punishment have weakened their case by attacking the usefulness of deterrence itself. Yet even the most adamant admit that the threat of punishment deters at least *some* crime; to argue otherwise would be to insist that crime would not increase at all if the police and the courts were to disappear. Something of the sort happened in Denmark during World War II. In September, 1944, the occupying German army arrested the entire Danish police force, substituting an unarmed and improvised corps in its place. In Copenhagen, there was an almost immediate tenfold increase in robbery and burglary, and the number of robberies continued to grow until the end of the war. There was little increase, on the other hand, in crimes such as embezzlement and fraud, where the perpetrator was more likely to be known to others, and where informal social controls thus continued to operate.

In assessing the role of punishment, we need to distinguish between *individual* and *general* deterrence, a distinction critics often fail to make. Unless a deterrent is 100 percent effective, there will always be some people who are not deterred. The fact that they are not tells us only that, for them, the threat of punishment was ineffective; it tells us nothing about the number of people who *might* have committed a crime in the absence of the threat. In any case, punishing a few violators makes the threat of punishment credible to the many; the sight of but one or two police cars handing out tickets is enough to persuade most motorists to slow down. Failure to punish offenders, on the other hand, may weaken the rest of the population's willingness to conform to the law. Johannes Andenaes, a Norwegian criminologist and legal scholar who helped revive the serious study of deterrence, points out that "The unthinkable is not unthinkable any longer when one sees one's comrades doing it. Why should one be honest when others are not? The risk seems less real, and, at the same time, moral inhibitions are broken down."

A desire to avoid punishment is not unique to the middle class, or to law-abiding members of the lower class. To be sure, some lower-class criminals seem to arrange their own capture; . . . it is hard to avoid the conclusion that they *want* to be punished. For them, the threat of punishment may encourage rather than deter crime. But most criminals, even the disorganized lower-class youths who do not plan their crimes, would rather avoid a prison term if they could. Their lack of planning reflects their general incompetence, an exaggerated (and often liquor- or drug-heightened) faith in their own omnipotence, or a belief in "fate," rather than indifference to punishment. Indeed, one cannot spend time with criminals and ex-criminals, as I have done, without being impressed by the importance they attach to the threat—and reality—of punishment. In explaining why they went straight, most ex-offenders I talked to emphasized their desire to avoid a prison term (or to avoid another such term). As young offenders approach adulthood, they attach a heavier weight to the threat of punishment—in part because adults are more likely to be incarcerated than juveniles, and in part because a prison term appears more painful as they begin to think about, or take on, the responsibilities of a job, marriage, and parenthood.

This is not to suggest that juvenile or adult offenders are Benthamite creatures, carefully calculating and weighing the relative costs and benefits of every act before proceeding. The threat of punishment affects behavior on the unconscious as well as conscious level; in Freudian terms, guilt and punishment are what the superego is all about. Freud aside, the fear of punishment affects attitudes and behavior in a variety of ways. Fear of punishment is an attention-getting device, opening people's eyes to the immoral nature of an act they otherwise might consider harmless or acceptable. Some people avoid crime out of fear of being punished. Others refrain from criminal activity because they consider such activity wrong. One reason they consider it wrong is that those who commit crimes are punished. Hardly a day goes by for any of us, in fact, in which the opportunity to break the criminal law is not present. Sometimes we are well aware of the opportunity and accept or reject it on a conscious level. Most of the time, we do not think about what we do; we simply act—or so it seems to us. But how we act—which alternative we choose—is affected by the fear of punishment and sense of guilt to which we have become conditioned.

The fact that punishment deters crime does not mean that we can guarantee a reduction in criminal violence simply by cranking up the amount of punishment meted out to offenders. For one thing, we already are punishing a large proportion of those found guilty of serious crimes—a far larger proportion than most law-and-order advocates assume—and punishment appears to be subject to the law of diminishing returns. If no one is being punished, introducing even a modest penalty is likely to have a significant impact on behavior. But if a majority of offenders are being punished, many of them severely, it is not at all certain that increasing either the number who are punished or the severity of their punishment will have any noticeable effect.

On the contrary, recent research on deterrence suggests that increasing the *certainty* of punishment has considerably more impact on crime than does increasing its *severity*. This appears to be true regardless of the level of punishment; in other words, whether penalties are moderate or severe, an increase in certainty will reduce crime more than a comparable change in severity. But the relationship is not symmetrical. The less certain punishment is, the smaller the impact that comes from a change in severity; the threat of punishment is not likely to loom very large if potential offenders feel confident that they will not get caught. And ours is a system in which certainty of punishment is low and severity high; for any one crime, although not for a criminal career, the chances of being caught are small. (. . . getting away with so many crimes is what helps persuade criminals that they are omnipotent, but sooner or later they *do* get caught.) Catching more criminals, therefore, would reduce the crime rate; so would convicting more of those who are caught. But . . . we do not know how to do either.

To decide whether a particular punishment is an effective deterrent, we need to ask, As compared to what? Whether or not the death penalty deters murder in some absolute sense is beside the point, for convicted murderers do not go unpunished. The relevant question is whether the death penalty would deter murder more effectively than does life imprisonment or imprisonment for some other long term. To be sure, scholars have written impressive-looking papers on the subject, filled with mathematical equations unintelligible to anyone save mathematicians and econometricians. Some purport to prove that the death penalty does deter murder more effectively than existing penalties; others, that it does not. The National Research Council's Panel on Research on Deterrent and Incapacitative Effects took a long and searching look at these papers. After analyzing each scholar's assumptions and methodology, the panel concluded that the results "provide no useful evidence" on which a conclusion can be drawn. Indeed, the panel pronounced itself "skeptical that the death penalty . . . can ever be subjected to the kind of statistical analyses" needed to draw conclusions with confidence.

> . . . the Panel considers that research on this topic is not likely to produce findings that will or should have much influence on policy makers.

Thus the debate over the death penalty must be resolved on other grounds, as must disagreements over the punishments to be meted out for other crimes. The margin of error in research on deterrence is simply too large for it to be the basis on which important decisions are made. Because of the small number of cases (and perhaps because passions run so high), the margin is particularly large for research on the death penalty. Isaac Ehrlich's paper "proving" that capital punishment deters murder more effectively than other sanctions provides a case in point. Ehrlich's analysis covers the period 1933–69; when his equations are applied to data for 1933–61, they indicate that there was no deterrent effect whatsoever connected with the death penalty. By picking other terminal years, critics have been able to use Ehrlich's equations to "prove" that the death penalty actually encourages crime. Be that as it may, Ehrlich's conclusion that each execution deters between one and eight murders rests entirely on what happened during the eight years 1962–69. But robbery, burglary, larceny-theft, and aggravated assault—crimes *not* punishable by the death penalty anywhere in the United States—increased even more dramatically than murder during that period. . . . Since Ehrlich's data indicate that the death penalty did not deter homicide during the preceding twenty-nine years, it is reasonable to assume that the 1962–69 increase was due not to the rapidly declining use of the death penalty, but to an independent set of factors causing a rapid increase in all kinds of criminal violence.

I am not proposing that the debate over the death penalty be stilled; I suggest only that we recognize that the case for and against it is based on moral and political, rather than empirical, considerations. Those who favor the death penalty do so on retributive grounds. In their view, murder is so heinous a crime that only the most extreme punishment we possess can uphold the moral code; as Ernest van den Haag puts it, justice requires that murderers be executed.

Perhaps it does; but justice can be purchased at too high a price. According to rabbinic legend, Abraham remonstrated with God over His unquestionably just decision to destroy every inhabitant of Sodom and Gomorrah.

> If it is the world you seek,
>> there can be no strict justice;
> and if it is strict justice you seek,
>> there can be no world.
> Why do you grasp the rope by both ends,
> seeking both the world and strict justice?
> Let one of them go,
> for if you do not relent a little,
>> the world cannot endure.

The world may not be at stake, but our sense of decency is. It is not some bloodless abstraction called "society" or "the state" that carries out the death sentence; human beings have to kill other human beings. When he was warden of Sing Sing, Lewis Lawes invited prosecutors and judges to witness the executions they recommended or imposed; no one ever accepted.

Capital punishment is wrong, too, because it is human beings, with all the imperfections to which humans are subject, who make the decision to take a condemned man's life. "Though the justice of God may indeed ordain that some should die," Charles Black of Yale Law School has written, paraphrasing a passage in the Talmud, "the justice of man is altogether and always insufficient for saying whose these may be." We may reduce the margin for error by erecting more and better rules and procedural safeguards, but there is no way to eliminate human error altogether. As John T. Noonan, Jr., points out, "it is no accident that in those trials which have been celebrated in literature and in the history of our consciousness—the trial of Socrates, the trial of Thomas More, the trial of Jesus—the rules were followed and yet the human judgment has been that injustice was done. . . ."

The death penalty aside, decisions about punishment ultimately are moral judgments, to which the literature on deterrence has little to contribute. We simply do not know enough to predict with confidence how much crime will be deterred by any given change in punishment, or even whether stepped-up punishment will have any effect at all. There are too many other factors affecting the crime rate, in both directions, and the statistical techniques for estimating the separate influence of each of them are too crude. If, say, we find that the crime rate is higher in states that impose mild punishments than in those that impose severe ones, this does not, by itself, prove that the stricter penalties are responsible for the lower rate of crime. The causal relationship could run the other way: states with a low crime rate may have a lower tolerance for crime, hence impose stricter penalties, than states with a great deal of crime. Looking at the complexity of the process of deterrence and the crudity of the techniques for measuring it, the criminologist Jack Gibbs has written, "Only an incorrigible ideologue would regard such evidence as conclusive one way or another." Unfortunately, most of the literature on deterrence seems to have been written by incorrigible ideologues.

We also know very little about the effects of incapacitation. To be sure, separating offenders from society is bound to have *some* impact on crime; while they are in prison, criminals are effectively prevented from committing any additional crimes, except against prison guards and inmates. Incapacitation need not be permanent. As we have seen, crime is a young man's occupation; like professional athletes, criminals lose the necessary physical stamina and coordination, as well as nerve, at a relatively early age. Thus criminal activity drops off sharply when offenders reach their mid-twenties, and again in their mid-thirties. If hardened criminals spend their most productive years in prison, the chances are that they will commit fewer crimes over the course of their careers.

How large a reduction in crime might be produced by incarcerating more offenders, or by keeping them in prison longer, is another question. To answer it with any confidence, we would need to know far more than we do. Some criminologists, among them David Greenberg and Stephan van Dine, Simon Dinitz, and John Conrad, have tried to show that even large increases would produce only a modest decline in crime. Others, notably Reuel and Shlomo Shinnar, have tried to show that "substantial, but not extreme" increases in the prison population would produce dramatic reductions in crime, especially street crime. These different conclusions can be traced directly to different assumptions the various scholars make about the frequency with which those now being caught and convicted break the law, the kinds of crimes they commit (e.g., are they specialists or generalists), and the way their criminal activity changes as they age.

There is another kind of uncertainty as well. The Panel on Research on Deterrent and Incapacitative Effects observed that we do not know "the extent to which offenders' criminal activity persists in the community even after they are incapacitated." If the people locked up were members of criminal gangs, there may be no diminution in the crime rate; the gangs may simply continue to operate without their missing members. More important in the long run, as the panel points out, a reduction in criminal activity that comes from incapacitation may be offset if new people are recruited into the criminal labor market. This appears to happen with organized crime; when operations are hampered by incarceration of old members, crime syndicates apparently "open their books" and recruit new members.

Much the same process may occur with street crime, though in a less systematic fashion. The case for deterrence, after all, rests on the assumption that behavior is affected by incentives—that increasing the cost of crime will reduce its supply. The other side of the coin is that criminal activity must also be affected by the return. If the supply of criminals is reduced through incapacitation while the number of criminal opportunities remains the same, economic theory tells us that the return from crime should increase, thereby attracting new people into the criminal labor market. How many would be attracted would depend on whether the return from crime increased more or less than the cost.

Incapacitation may backfire, moreover, if people perceive punishment as unduly harsh. This is a subjective judgment, of course; what the Shinnars call a "substantial, but not extreme" increase in the New York State prison population (needed to bring about a major reduction in violent crime) turns out to be a growth from 9,000 inmates to 40,000 to 60,000. I would call a 350 to 550 percent increase quite extreme; others may not. When people feel that the criminal justice system is too harsh, they become reluctant to cooperate with the police or the courts—and as we shall see in the next two chapters, both institutions are heavily dependent on citizen cooperation to catch and convict criminals.

Equally important, draconian sentences tend not to be imposed at all. Juries may acquit guilty defendants if the jurors feel the sentence would be too harsh, or they may find defendants guilty of some lesser charge; and the longer the minimum sentence, the larger the proportion of offenders who demand a jury trial. Moreover, prosecutors and the police are likely to charge offenders with crimes that carry lesser penalties if they feel the crime that was committed carries too harsh a penalty; and parole boards are likely to release offenders at the first opportunity if they feel that sentences are too long. Discretion is so central to the institutions of the criminal justice system, and there are so many points where it can be (and usually is) exercised, that any change imposed from the outside is likely to be neutralized.

If we are to reduce crime, we will have to recognize that more punishment is not the answer. The law is an educating institution, shaping behavior through its pedagogical or moral influence, as well as through fear. From the law, as Johannes Andenaes has put it, "there emanates a flow of propaganda" that reinforces people's willingness to conform to social norms. The criminal law, in particular, may strengthen moral inhibitions against crime and make law-abiding behavior a matter of habit. "The achievement of inhibition and habit is of greater value than mere deterrence," Andenaes has written, since habit keeps people law-abiding even in situations in which they need not fear detection or punishment. When this is the case, the law-abiding majority is likely to exert social pressure toward conformity on those who may not, themselves, accept the moral code.

Behavior that emanates from respect for law is different from behavior that reflects a fear of punishment; to ignore the distinction is to confuse authority with coercion. To be sure, coercion may reinforce respect for law. But in the last analysis, respect for authority depends on acceptance of its legitimacy—on people's willingness to obey the law because it is the law. Acceptance of the legitimacy of law is a far more effective instrument of social control than is fear of punishment. Thus the moral-pedagogical role of the law is central to the functioning of any society.

Charles Silberman, from Criminal Violence,
Criminal Justice

STRATEGY THREE: USING A SOURCE AS THE STARTING POINT FOR YOUR OWN ESSAY

This third strategy gives you the freedom to develop your own ideas and present your own point of view in an essay that is only loosely linked to the source. Reading an assigned essay helps you to generate ideas and topics and provides you with evidence or information to cite in your own essay; but the thesis, scope, and organization of your essay are entirely your own.

As always, you begin by studying the assigned essay carefully, establishing its thesis and main ideas. As you read, start noting ideas of your own that might be worth developing. The essay that you are planning need not cover exactly the same material as the source essay. What you want is a spinoff from the original reading, rather than a recapitulation. If you read the essay a few times without thinking of a topic, test out some of the standard strategies for developing an essay by applying them to the source essay in ways that might not have occurred to the original author. Here, for example, are some strategies that helped to generate topics for an essay based on Blanche Blank's "A Question of Degree." You will notice that the proposed topics and the source become less and less closely connected and that some of the final suggestions will result in essays almost entirely independent of Blanche Blank's.

Argumentation

You can argue for Blanche Blank's assertions or against them. If you disagree with her conclusions, if you do not believe that the role of college has been overemphasized, then you can follow the first strategy described in this chapter and refute her arguments, disproving her evidence or casting doubt on her interpretation of the evidence. On the other hand, it is also possible to agree with Blanche Blank and to support and confirm her thesis by suggesting new lines of argument or citing new sources of evidence. The resulting essay would be an amalgamation of her basic ideas and yours.

You cannot always argue for or against an author's thesis; not all source essays provide clearcut assertions for you to support or refute. Several readings in this book explain and analyze a topic rather than attempting to convince the reader of a specific point of view. To understand the difference, compare "A Question of Degree" with "Values and Violence in Sports Today." Both essays are concerned with the ways in which our institutions may have lost their original purpose; but the authors of the latter are trying to inform their readers and examine the evidence rather than persuade them to accept a point of view.

Process

You might examine in detail one of the processes that Blank only describes generally. For example, you could cite your own experience to explain the ways in which teenagers are encouraged to believe that a college degree is essential, citing high school counseling and college catalogues and analyzing the unrealistic expectations created by what young students see and read. Or, if you have sufficient knowledge, you might describe the unjust manipulation of hiring procedures or the process by which a college's Liberal Arts curriculum gradually becomes "practical."

Illustration

If you focused on a single discouraged employee, showing in what ways ambitions for better status and salary have been frustrated, or a single disillusioned college graduate, showing how career prospects have failed to measure up to training and expectations, your strategy would be an illustration proving one of Blank's themes.

Definition

Definition can sometimes result from a discussion of the background of an issue. What should the work experience be like? What is the function of a university? What is a good education? By attempting to define one of the components of Blank's theme in terms of the ideal, you are helping your reader to understand her arguments and evaluate her conclusions more rationally.

Cause and Effect

You can examine one or more of the reasons why a college degree has become a necessary credential for employment. You can also suggest a wider context for discussing Blank's views by describing the kind of society that encourages this set of values. In either case, you will be accounting for, but not necessarily justifying, the nation's obsession with degrees. Or you can predict the consequences, good or bad, that might result if Blank's suggested legislation were passed. Or you might explore some hypothetical possibilities and focus on the circumstances and causes of a situation different from the one that Blank describes. What if everyone in the United States earned a college degree? What if education after the eighth grade were abolished? By taking this approach, you are radically changing the circumstances that Blank depicts, but still sharing her concerns and exploring the principles discussed in her essay.

Comparison

You can alter the reader's perspective by moving the theme of Blank's essay to another time or place. Did our present obsession with education exist a hundred years ago? Is it at this moment a problem outside the United States? Will it probably continue into the twenty-first century? Or, focusing on late twentieth-century America, you might want to contrast contemporary trends in education and employment with comparable trends in other areas of life—housing, finance, recreation, child-rearing, and communications. All of these approaches ask you to begin with a description of Blank's issue and contrast it with another set of circumstances, past or present, real or hypothetical. But before choosing one of these speculative topics, you must first decide whether it is practical, whether it requires research, and whether, when fully developed, it will retain some connection with the source essay. For example, there may be some value in comparing the current emphasis on higher education with monastic education in the Middle Ages. Can you write such an essay? How much research will it require? Will a discussion of monastic education help your reader better to understand Blank's ideas? Or will you immediately move away from your starting point—and find no opportunity to return to it? Have you a serious objective, or are you simply indulging in the comparison "because it's there"?

PLANNING THE SINGLE-SOURCE ESSAY

1. Taking Notes and Writing a Thesis

Consider how you might develop an essay based on one of the topics suggested above. Notice that the chosen topic is expressed as a question.

Topic: What is the function of a university in the 1980s?

After thinking about your topic, start your list of notes *before* you re-read the essay, to make sure that you are not overly influenced by the author's point of view and to enable you to include some ideas of your own in your notes. Then, review the essay and add any relevant ideas to your list, remembering to indicate when an idea originated with the source and not with you.

Here is the complete list of notes for an essay defining the function of a university. The paragraph references, added later, indicate which points were made by Blank and where in her essay they can be found. The thesis, which follows the notes, was written after the list was complete.

What the university ought to do
A. to increase a student's understanding of the world around him,
   e.g., to become more observant and aware of natural phenomena
   (weather, for example) and social systems (like family relationships)
B. to help a student to live a more fulfilling life
   to enable him to test his powers and know more and become more
   versatile; to speak with authority on topics that he didn't
   understand before
C. to help a student to live a more productive life
   to increase his working credentials and qualify for more interesting and well-paying jobs (B.B., ¶ 3-9)

D. to serve society by creating a better informed, more rational group of citizens

not only through college courses (like political science) but through the increased ability to observe and analyze and argue (B.B., ¶3, 14)

E. to contribute to research that will help to solve scientific and social problems

(not a teaching function) (B.B., ¶3, 14)

F. to serve as a center for debate to clarify the issues of the day

people should regard the university as a source of unbiased information and counsel; notable people should come to lecture (B.B., ¶3, 14)

G. to serve as a gathering place for great teachers

students should be able to regard their teachers as worth emulating

H. to allow the student to examine the opportunities for personal change and growth

this includes vocational goals, e.g., career changes (B.B., ¶4)

What the university should not do

I. it should not divide the haves from the have-nots

college should not be considered essential; it should be possible to be successful without a college degree (B.B., ¶8, 10)

J. it should not use marketing techniques to appeal to the greatest number

what the university teaches should be determined primarily by the faculty and to a lesser extent by the students; standards of achievement should not be determined by students who haven't learned anything yet

K. it should not ignore the needs of its students and its community by clinging to outdated courses and programs

L. it should not cooperate with business and government to the extent that it loses its autonomy (B.B., ¶6, 9)

M. it should not be an employment agency and vocational center to the exclusion of its more important functions (B.B., ¶6, 9, 16)

Thesis: As Blanche Blank points out, a university education is not a commodity to be marketed and sold; a university should be a resource center for those who want the opportunity to develop their intellectual powers and lead more productive, useful, and fulfilling lives.

2. Deciding on a Strategy

As a rule, you would consider strategies for your essay as soon as you have established your thesis. In this case, however, the choice of strategy—definition—was made at an earlier point, when you chose your topic and considered several possible strategies. The notes, divided into what a university should and should not do, already follow a definition strategy, with its emphasis on differentiation.

3. Constructing an Outline

Having made all the preliminary decisions, you are ready to plan the structure of your essay. But before doing so, return once more to the reading and single out those portions which you will need to use in support of your thesis: your essay is going to be based on both your own ideas and the ideas of your source, yet, since writing your thesis, you have not actually checked the text of the essay. Now, you need to know whether your notes accurately paraphrase the source, and also how many source references you intend to make so that you can write a balanced outline. You should also double-check to make sure that you are giving the source credit for all paraphrased ideas.

You are now ready to organize your notes in groups, each of which will be developed as a separate paragraph or sequence of related paragraphs. Then, after you have set up these categories and decided on their order, incorporate in your outline some of the points from Blanche Blank's essay that you intend to use as support (or possibly to argue against). Cite the paragraph number of the relevant material with your outline entry. If the paragraph from "A Question of Degree" contains several references that you expect to place in different parts of your outline, use a sentence number or a set of symbols or a brief quotation for differentiation. Here is what one section of the completed outline would look like, incorporating notes C, M, I, and H from the original list, respectively:

I. The university should help a student to live a more productive life, to increase his working credentials and qualify for more interesting and well-paying jobs. (¶ 6--last sentence)
   A. But it should not be an employment agency and vocational center to the exclusion of its more important functions. (¶ 9-- "servicing agents," ¶ 12-- "joylessness in our university life," ¶ 16)
   B. It should not divide the haves from the have-nots; success without a college degree should be possible. (¶ 2-- "two kinds of work," ¶ 17)
II. The university should allow the student to examine the opportunities for personal growth and change; this includes vocational goals, e.g., career changes. (¶ 4-- "an optional and continuing experience later in life")

WRITING A SINGLE-SOURCE ESSAY

When you write from sources, you are engaged in a kind of partner-ship. You must strive to strike an appropriate balance between your own ideas and those of your source. By reading your source carefully and using annotation, outlining, and paraphrase, you familiarize your-self with the source's main ideas and reasoning and prepare to put those ideas in your essay. But it is your voice that should dominate the essay. You, after all, are writing it; you are responsible for its contents and its effect on the reader. For this reason, all the important "positions" in the structure of your essay should be filled by you; the topic sentences, as well as the introduction, should be written in your own words and, if possible, should stress your views, not those of your author. On the other hand, your reader should not be allowed to lose sight of the source essay; it should be treated as a form of evidence and cited whenever it is relevant, but always as a context in which to develop your own strategy and assert your own thesis.

Here are the steps to follow when you write a one-source essay:

Step one: Identify the source essay's thesis; analyze its underlying themes, if any, and its strategy; and construct a rough outline of its main ideas.

Step two: Decide on two or three possible essay topics based on your work in step 1, and narrow down one of them. (Be prepared to sub-mit your topics for your teacher's approval and, in conference, to choose the most suitable one.)

Step three: Write down a list of notes about your own ideas on the topic, being careful to distinguish in your notes between points that are yours and points that are derived from the source.

Step four: Write a thesis of your own that fairly represents your list of ideas. Mention the source in your thesis if appropriate.

Step five: If you have not done so already, choose a strategy that will best carry out your thesis; it need not be the same strategy as that of the source essay.

Step six: Mark (by brackets or underlining) those paragraphs or sen-tences in the source that will help to develop your topic.

Step seven: Draw up an outline for your essay. Combine repetitious points; bring together similar and related points. Decide on the best sequence for your paragraphs.

Step eight: Decide which parts of the reading should be cited as evi-dence or refuted; place paragraph or page references to the source in the appropriate sections of your outline. Then decide which sen-tences of the reading should be quoted and which should be para-phrased.

Step nine: Write the rough draft, making sure that, whenever possible, your topic sentences express your views, introduce the material that you intend to present in that paragraph, and are written in your voice. Later in the paragraph, incorporate references to the source as smoothly as you can, and link your paragraphs together with transitions.

Step ten: Write an introduction that contains a clear statement of your thesis, as well as a reference to the source essay and its role in the development of your ideas. You may also decide to draft a conclusion.

Step eleven: Proofread your first draft very carefully to correct errors of grammar, style, reference, and spelling.

Step twelve: Using standard-size paper and leaving adequate margins and spacing, type or neatly write the final draft. Proofread once again to catch careless errors in copying.

ASSIGNMENT 6

A. One of the three essays that follow will serve as the starting point for an essay of your own. Assume that the essay you are planning will be about three or four pages long, or 500–1,000 words. Using steps one and two, think of three possible topics for such an essay, and submit the most promising (or, if your teacher suggests it, all three) for approval.

B. Plan your essay by working from notes to an outline. Be prepared to submit your thesis and outline of paragraphs (with indications of relevant references to the source) to your teacher for approval.

C. Write a rough draft after deciding which parts of the essay should be cited as evidence or refuted, distributing references to the source among appropriate sections of your outline, and determining which parts of the reading should be quoted and which should be paraphrased.

D. Write a final draft of your essay.

BLOODBATHS DEBASE MOVIES AND AUDIENCES

Most moviegoers know them only as names on marquees, and the names are ugly and interchangeable. Whether the title is "The Burning" or "Maniac," "The Slumber Party Massacre" or "Humongous," it's the same old story. There is a killer on the loose. He is mean, mysterious and apparently unstoppable. Murdering pretty young women excites him most, but he's really not particular. He'll gladly butcher anyone who gets in his way.

As with hard-core sexual pornography, these very systematic, very violent movies remain outside the realm of most audiences' experience. Even for someone who sees the occasional horror hit—in this genre, films not better than "Friday the 13th" and "Halloween" really are the top of the line—the very sleaziest exploitation films must be difficult to imagine. Everyone knows they've gotten more clinical in recent years, thanks to technical innovations that make it possible to show an ax entering a forehead, a drill puncturing a stomach, or anything else once better left to the imagination. But I wonder if the other changes in these films are as widely recognized.

At no time in horror movie history has the violence been as literal as it is today, or as numbing. The metaphorical aspects of an old-fashioned monster, mad scientist or vampire film have no counterpart in the 15-dead-babysitters format. There is no opportunity to view the monster as the embodiment of a community's fears, or as the darker side of man's nature, or as anything other than a cryptic, single-minded creep. There's no time to identify with the characters, since they are killed off so quickly that they don't have time to impress themselves upon an audience. There isn't even much use of the "Towering Inferno" morality, whereby the adulterers, sneaking off to a different floor from everyone else at the party, are the first characters to fry. In a movie like "The Burning," the arbitrary murders have nothing to do with morality. There is no notion of sin here, and hence no possibility of redemption.

What's left? The spectacle of pure killing, isolated from the context of everyday life. Campers, stewardesses or sorority girls with no distinguishing characteristics are slaughtered one after another, by a killer whose motives are explained only in the most laughably cursory manner. He's identified either as an escaped lunatic, or perhaps as someone who has been horribly injured and now wants revenge. Since no one in any of these films ever has the brains to lock a door, to stay near the campfire, to head *away* from the direction from which those funny sounds are emanating, there is absolutely no hope that the killer will be outwitted. At the end of the film, he will simply run out of steam and be stopped—only temporarily—by the lone survivor. That way they're both around for a sequel, should anyone want to see one.

These films are disturbing for plenty of reasons, but I don't think they're as scary as they used to be; the format has become too familiar. The ordeal of watching one amounts to a war of nerves—hence, perhaps the genre's popularity with teen-agers, eager to test their mettle—but it's a war that can be won. These movies have by now become so crude and so imitative that the violence occurs on cue, and it's easy enough to make one's mind wander just as the hatchet is being raised. Even the obligatory "Carrie"-style ending—that final frisson from the ghoul who hasn't fully been vanquished—isn't very startling any more. The genre has grown so derivative that it seldom comes up with anything surprising.

To say that these films aren't very frightening is not to say that they don't have a profound effect on those who watch them. Go see one, and you'll have empirical proof that a film like this makes audiences mean. You will leave the theater convinced that the world is an ugly, violent place in which aggression is frequent and routine. Lurid headlines in the tabloids will seem positively realistic; after watching a dozen young vacationers being garotted, the news of, say, a gunman on the loose in a hospital ward will sound comparatively harmless. Violence in the real world becomes much more acceptable after you've seen infinitely greater violence on the screen.

And this kind of horror film, in addition to inuring its audience to genuine violence, has a debasing effect as well. In this respect it harkens back to hard-core sexual pornography, the tactics of which it carries to the most extreme degree. Years ago, when sexual explicitness on screen seemed to have advanced as far as it possibly could go, it was often remarked that only by actually penetrating the body could the camera go farther. That, in a sense, is what the camera does now.

The carnage is usually preceded by some sort of erotic prelude: footage of pretty young bodies in the shower, or teens changing into nighties for the slumber party, or anything that otherwise lulls the audience into a mildly sensual mood. When the killing begins, the eroticism is abruptly abandoned, for it has served its purpose, that of lowering the viewer's defenses and heightening the film's physical effectiveness. The speed and ease with which one's feelings can be transformed from sensuality into viciousness may surprise even those quite conversant with the links between sexual and violent urges.

It goes without saying that these films exploit and brutalize women; that doesn't mean women are not blithely involved in making them. Debra Hill, co-producer of "Halloween III" and other horror films, recently told a television interviewer that she couldn't understand why no one would take her seriously as a would-be maker of comedies and love stories—if you've proven yourself in one branch of filmmaking, she asked rhetorically, haven't you proven yourself in others? Certainly not, when most of what you've shown is an ability to simulate impersonal, unmotivated killing. And Amy Jones and Rita Mae Brown, a woman director and a feminist novelist, lately collaborated on "The Slumber Party Massacre." This supposed spoof is no less bloody, sexist or ugly than comparable films made by men. But it's a little more reprehensible, because its creators ought to know better.

The oldest argument on behalf of the horror genre is that it produces catharsis: By putting us in contact with our deepest fears, it provides some relief. That, after all, is why people slow down to look at traffic accidents or watch television films about tragic illness—because the knowledge that these things have befallen others provides a grim relief for those who have been spared. Horror films used to fulfill this function, and the best of them still do. But the stripped-down, impersonal bloodbath movies to which I've been referring do nothing of the kind, any more than sexual pornography fulfills a viewer's romantic longings.

This latest kind of pornography—violent pornography—doesn't even begin to allow its audience the catharsis of the traditional horror story. Such catharsis isn't what these films are after, and truly cathartic horror needn't be as explicit or literal as this. And in fact, the extreme gore works against any possibility of release, since it deadens the audience and creates a feeling of utter hopelessness. These films aim simply at shocking and numbing their audiences, and perhaps the only good thing to be said about them is that their future isn't bright. Like sexual pornography, violent pornography has its implicit limitations, and it's gone about as far as it can go.

Janet Maslin, *New York Times,* 21 November 1982

SELF-ESTEEM AND EXCELLENCE:
THE CHOICE AND THE PARADOX

The 1985–86 school year is likely to be a tense one for teachers. The Excellence Commission has spoken. The states have responded. Intellectual accountability is the order of the day. Mandated tests are mushrooming, and results are being demanded. Standards must be raised, and test scores with them. The pressure is on. Everyone must know more, learn faster, be smarter. And teachers must make it all happen.

Most teachers would like to do just that—there is no conspiracy against excellence—but it is one thing to say it, another to do it. How, after all, does a child's intelligence develop? How can teachers help each child to stretch and grow, and reach for excellence?

Today's teachers have been taught that self-esteem is the answer, and many believe that it is. Others, who don't, often face great pressure to conform to the prevailing view. Some have been effectively silenced, or driven out of the profession altogether. The result is that the role of self-esteem in learning has a special status. On a host of other pedagogical questions, teachers have varying viewpoints, and express them freely. On this one, the settled answer goes largely unchallenged. Teachers generally seem to accept the modern dogma that self-esteem is the critical variable for intellectual development—the master key to learning. According to this view, children with high self-esteem forge ahead, academically, easily and naturally; children with low self-esteem fall behind. They cannot achieve excellence, or even competence, in many cases, until their self-esteem is raised. That, at any rate, is assumption one in what I call the self-esteem theory of intellectual development.

Assumption two is that many children are in this boat because low self-esteem is common in childhood. It prevents many youngsters from learning and achieving and striving for excellence.

Two main implications follow from these assumptions. First, teachers must give priority to the task of raising children's self-esteem. To do this, they must accept each child just as he is, and provide him with constant praise and encouragement, seeing to it that he experiences a feeling of success in school, as often and as immediately as possible. This is assumed to be helpful for all children and especially critical for children who are doing badly in school. If they can be taught to think better of themselves, their classroom work and behavior will improve, the theory tells us.

Implication two—that teachers must always act to protect children's self-esteem from injury—is the flip side of the coin, and just as important as promoting self-esteem. After all, if high self-esteem is the essential ingredient in superior intellectual performance, then anything and everything that could damage a child's self-esteem, however slight and transient the injury, is educationally counterproductive and should be eliminated from the classroom. Criticism always hurts self-esteem and should be avoided at all costs, and the same is true for academic and disciplinary standards. After all, children who fail to meet them are likely to feel badly about it, and about themselves as a result of it. That will lower their self-esteem, and increase the odds on future failures, the theory tells us.

Is it a good theory? Will it really help today's teachers to develop excellence in their students? There are two main ways for teachers to judge. One way is to compare it to some contrasting theory to see which is more helpful in making sense of their own experiences with students in today's classrooms. The other way is to look at what has happened to American education as a whole over the last few decades, and then assess both theories in light of it.

Many teachers will be hard-pressed to think of a contrasting theory. The self-esteem theory of educational development has been the reigning orthodoxy for so long—a quarter of a century, now—that they were never taught anything else. Let me, then, offer two contrasts: the views of Alfred Binet, the father of intelligence testing, on the development of intelligence; and the views of Sigmund Freud, the father of psychoanalysis, on self-esteem in childhood.

Writing in the first decade of this century, Alfred Binet gave a very different answer to questions about what intelligence is and how it develops. He thought that a self-critical stance was at the very core of intelligence, its sine qua non and seminal essence. Not just a critical stance, which is quite compatible with the highest possible levels of self-esteem, but a *self*-critical stance, which is not.

He did not see self-criticism as an inborn trait, either. He thought children needed to be taught to engage in it, and to use it, habitually, to monitor and appraise their own performance, constantly looking for ways to improve it. He thought that was worth teaching, because children who learned to do it learned more about everything else as a result, and developed their intellectual powers more fully than children who didn't. That is why he saw self-criticism as the essence of intelligence, the master key that unlocked the doors to competence and excellence alike.

Binet thought self-criticism had to be taught precisely because it did not come naturally. Teachers, and the standards and discipline they imposed, were vital in his formulation. Without them, he thought children were likely to approach intellectual problems by accepting the first response that occurred to them, applauding their own performance quite uncritically, and then moving restlessly on, looking for more quick responses, more applause.

Binet's views on intelligence and its development were novel—he was a pioneer, there—but his views on the natural inclinations of children were not novel at all. They reflected a long-standing consensus among thoughtful adults who worked with children—teachers and others—that egotism is the natural state of childhood, high self-esteem the natural gift that accompanies it. Teachers who took this view saw it as their job to help children overcome their egotism, widening their view of the world, deepening their awareness of it, and learning to see themselves and their accomplishments in realistic perspective in order to take realistic steps towards excellence.

They thought that standards—and criticism of academic work and classroom behavior that did not meet them—were essential elements in this learning process, and they did not worry too much about their impact on a child's self-esteem because they saw it as naturally robust, not fragile and in imminent danger of collapse without constant reinforcement. Like all compassionate adults, they recognized exceptions when they saw them and treated them accordingly, but they saw them as just that—exceptions—not a disproof of the general rule that self-esteem comes naturally, self-criticism does not.

Binet's contemporary, Sigmund Freud, provided powerful reinforcement for his view of childhood, and gave it new depth and resonance with his vivid descriptions of the long struggle of each human individual to move beyond the exclusive self-love of childhood and develop into a fully functioning adult, capable of loving others and of doing productive work. The heart of the struggle, as Freud described it, was to get out from under the seductive domination of the pleasure principle, accepting the reality principle instead, and acting in accord with it. The point of the struggle was to learn to make good things happen in reality, instead of just wishing they would and fantasizing about them, or trying to coerce or manipulate others into doing it for you.

Learning to reject the impulse to seek immediate gratification—focusing only on what feels good now—is one key step in this process. What feels good now is success, instant and effortless, in a fantasy world where the self is omnipotent, and all things exist to serve it. It is pleasant to live in this fantasy world, and very enhancing to self-esteem, but Freud believed that children who did not move out of it could not be successful, in love or in work. To be successful in either, in the real world, Freud thought that each of us had to struggle to break out of the shell of self-absorption into which we were born. We had to learn to focus our attention, at least part of the time, on the world beyond the self, and to tolerate the frustration and delay that is an inevitable part of learning to deal with it—learning to care for others, to work hard, and to persevere in the face of obstacles.

Breaking out of that shell and learning all of these things is not easy. It is not immediately enhancing to self-esteem of the infantile variety that Freud called narcissism, and I call *feel-good-now* self-esteem, either. Often, the immediate effect is deflating, particularly to highly inflated narcissistic egos, but the ultimate results—caring relationships with others, the development of competence, and a shot at excellence—do tend to build self-esteem of another, more durable sort. I call it *earned* self-esteem.

Earned self-esteem is based on success in meeting the tests of reality—measuring up to standards—at home and in school. It is necessarily hard-won, and develops slowly, but it is stable and long-lasting, and provides a secure foundation for further growth and development. It is not a precondition for learning but a product of it. In this, and in a host of other ways, it is the polar opposite of feel-good-now self-esteem. Standards, and demands on students to keep working until they really succeed in meeting them, are critical steps forward on the road to earned self-esteem. They are, simultaneously, steps back from feel-good-now self-esteem.

Teachers who believed in the old theories did not mind. They were comfortable, in earlier decades, emphasizing earned self-esteem at the expense of feel-good-now self-esteem, especially for older children. They were comfortable, in part, because they were convinced that that was the right thing to do, to help their students stretch and grow, and reach for excellence. In addition, it helped a lot that they could generally count on the support of their professional and administrative colleagues, and of the wider community, too. Today's consensus is very different, and today's teachers get a very different—indeed an opposite—message. Feel-good-now self-esteem is the only kind of self-esteem that the modern self-esteem theory of educational development recognizes for children of all ages, and schools of education have been telling teachers for a quarter of a century now that their prime job is to maximize it, assuring them that if they succeeded, their students would not only have high self-esteem, but would also stretch and grow, and reach for excellence.

Which theory is closest to the truth? Which one will best help today's teachers in their struggle to develop excellence in their students, this year, and in the years ahead? As we noted at the outset, one good way for teachers to re-examine these questions is to go back over their own past experiences—with students, classrooms, and schools—to see which theory is most helpful in making sense of them. Teachers whose past experience is short might also want to consult with fellow teachers who have been at it longer.

One useful way to start is to think first about the ways in which the self-esteem theory has been implemented in your school, because it is being implemented in most American schools today, in one way or another. The implementation process has been in motion for about a quarter of a century now, and it has made today's schools strikingly different from the schools of the 1950s, and of earlier decades. A recent book, *The Shopping Mall High School*, may be helpful here. In it, Arthur Powell, the senior author, provides as vivid, intimate and detailed a picture as I have yet seen in print, of what some American schools have come to look like under the domination of the Self-Esteem-Now theory of educational development. As such, it provides a useful reference point, a kind of academic photo album with which to compare your own school, and the classrooms in it. These comparisons are easiest for high school teachers to make, because all of the schools Powell and his colleagues studied were high schools. Still, I think his snapshots are candid enough to be evocative for grade school teachers too, and, with appropriate modifications, almost as relevant.

The Shopping Mall High School describes a system in which the concept of mastering an essential body of knowledge and skills gives way to the need to protect student self-esteem and to avoid discipline problems and dropouts. The vast array of courses—one school's catalog featured over 400— "is seen as a way for students to avoid failure." The schools push "nobody beyond his or her preferences." Indeed, they are remarkably neutral about those preferences, about whether "Tall Flags" is as valid a course choice as "Beginning French," "Apartment and Income Properties Management" as essential as "Chemistry." What *is* seen as essential is "for teenagers 'to plug into something that gives them support,'" or as one student put it, "a curriculum that everybody can do."

Complementing the broad horizontal curriculum is a steep vertical one: courses with virtually identical titles but so staggeringly different in content, seriousness, and difficulty as to render their common name all but meaningless. Again, the purpose of this—and of similar latitude within as well as between classrooms in smaller schools, less able to specialize—is to avoid failure, to make sure no student is pushed to go any faster than he wishes to go.

> Failure is anathema because success—*feeling* success—is so deeply cherished as both a goal and a means to other goals. Many teachers seem preoccupied by the psychological costs of failure and the therapeutic benefits of success. That was what one teacher was talking about when she said, "If you don't get it done, you don't fail. You don't get credit, but you don't experience failure." "The most important thing to me is to make them feel they are human beings, that they are worthwhile," another teacher emphasized. Still another's primary goals were to "build confidence, to build trust . . . I try to affirm them as people." A math teacher prescribed "a daily dose of self-respect." And a social studies teacher explained why he didn't stress thinking skills: "I just encourage them to make the most of their ability to have pride in themselves." In all these instances, the need for students to feel success is disconnected from the idea of students mastering something taught. . . . Mastery and success are like ships that pass in the night.

In the schools examined by Powell and his colleagues, students who choose to work hard and to reach for excellence are accommodated, and praised and encouraged; students who choose to do little or no hard work, reaching only for what feels good now, are also accommodated, and praised and encouraged even more. The assumption, in the modern Shopping Mall School, is that they need more praise and encouragement because their self-esteem is lower—that is why they do not work as hard.

Will more praise and encouragement help them to work harder, eventually, and to learn more? The Self-Esteem-Now theory tells us that it will, and that the extraordinary accommodations many modern schools make to give all students a feeling of immediate success are fully justified—necessary steps on the road to self-esteem and excellence. The old theories—the ones that it replaced—make opposite assumptions, and opposite predictions. They assume that most students have high self-esteem to begin with, and they predict that in contemporary classrooms like those described by Powell and his cohorts, grandiosity will be more common than excessive modesty. They assume that in those classrooms, many students will be preoccupied with fantasies and dreams of excellence—the warm flow of constant positive feedback is thought to be conducive to that, particularly in an atmosphere where few demands are made—but they predict that under these circumstances, few students will actually undertake the self-critical struggle necessary to achieve excellence in reality. Only their egos will swell and grow; their intellectual skills and abilities will atrophy, or fail to develop in the first place.

Teachers who are rethinking their own experiences in contemporary classrooms are left, then, with a series of professional judgment calls to ponder. First, what kind of a school do I teach in? Is the Self-Esteem-Now theory as fully implemented in my school as it is in the Shopping Mall High School? Is it as fully implemented but in a different way? Or do I teach in a different kind of a school altogether?

Second, which theory best describes the students who have passed through my classrooms? Was low self-esteem and excessive modesty really a common problem? Or were inflated egos more prevalent? How did students of each type fare, intellectually? Did the more modest and self-critical ones always learn less than those whose self-esteem was at peak levels? Or did the ones with the highest self-esteem often seem to exhibit a childish arrogance and impatience that actually stunted their intellectual growth and development?

Thoughtful teachers will want to start with their own experience, but they will not want to stop there. They will also want to take a look at what has happened to American education as a whole over the last few decades, and then reassess both theories in light of it. The Excellence Commission Report can help here. It provides a generally accurate summary of one-half of the story—the intellectual half. It tells us that on norm-referenced tests—the kinds of tests that make it possible to compare students from different decades and countries—American students fared very badly in the 1960s and 1970s. Few achieved excellence. Many did not even achieve competence.

It tells us, too, that this sad situation was a new one. In the 1950s, before the Self-Esteem-Now theory was widely implemented in American schools, competence was widespread, and excellence was common enough to make American students equal to those of any nation. In the 1970s, that was no longer so. Only our youngest students—those in grades K through 4—were still doing well. All of our other students were learning less, much less. That is an important half of the story, but it is only half.

The other half of the story has to do with self-esteem and happiness, and it, too, is important, but you will not find it in the Excellence Commission Report, or in any of the other recent education reports that I know of. Much of the evidence is in, though, collected and presented in a variety of ways by a wide array of scholars, using very different approaches and techniques, but arriving at very similar conclusions. Look, for example, at the clinical literature, and at the literature on psychopathology in particular. Narcissism is to the 1960s and the

1970s what neuroticism was to earlier decades. Historians as diverse as Oscar Handlin and Christopher Lasch see it as a major contemporary social problem, too. Excessive self-esteem, it seems, can cause as much trouble as inadequate self-esteem, for individuals and for whole societies, too.

Low self-esteem is not as common in childhood as the self-esteem theorists assume it is, either, and it is no more common among black children than it is among white ones. These findings came as a great surprise to many of the self-esteem researchers who found them, staring back at them from their data, but the findings were no flukes: They turned up again and again, in study after study. Public opinion poll data suggest the same thing, indicating, as they do, that the self-esteem of young Americans of all races and classes was generally high and rising—sometimes to dizzying new heights—throughout most of the last two decades.

For American education as a whole, then, it seems fair to conclude that while the Self-Esteem-Now theory of educational development failed to produce excellence and may even have retarded its development, it did succeed in raising the self-esteem of American students to a marked degree. What we are left with, it seems, is a choice, a forced choice. We cannot really maximize intellectual development and self-esteem of the feel-good-now type at the same time. We must choose between them, giving one priority over the other.

For some teachers, and some parents, too, the choice will seem easy. They would prefer to have both simultaneously but, if forced to choose, they will opt for self-esteem on the grounds that students are whole human beings, not disembodied intellects, and their happiness is more important than their test scores. Alas, the choice is not as simple and straightforward as it looks, because we are confronted with a paradox as well as a choice.

The paradox is that by focusing only on children's happiness, we may end up with heart-breakingly high numbers of unhappy children. That, at any rate, is what happened in America in the 1960s and the 1970s. The evidence is in on that score, too, and it all points in the same paradoxical direction. High self-esteem notwithstanding, those were not happy decades for American youth. They were decades of trouble and tragedy.

Look, for example, at statistics on drug and alcohol abuse among young Americans. Addiction rates soared in the 1960s and the 1970s with tragic consequences for hundreds of thousands of young lives. Look, too, at teenage crime and venereal disease and suicide rates. They climbed, steeply, during those decades. And look, especially, at the number of out-of-wedlock births to teenaged girls. Those rates skyrocketed, and have not levelled off yet. Looking at all these statistics, it is hard to avoid the conclusion that high self-esteem of the feel-good-now type works no better as a guarantor of happiness than it does as a master key to intellectual development.

These statistics have been pulled together from multiple sources and meticulously reassembled in a single, slim volume that teachers who want to go beyond the Excellence Report will find useful. Its title is *Losing Ground*, its author is Charles Murray, and it was published by Basic Books in 1984. The statistics in it prove that the paradox exists, but they do not explain why.

The old theories of child development do. They tell us that despite all the momentary pleasures it provides, an exclusive focus on feel-good-now self-esteem, at home and at school, will not produce happiness. It will produce restlessness and dissatisfaction, a constant hunger to get more for less, and a life organized in search of it. In such a life, relationships with others will tend to be superficial and unstable, and the lure of drugs, alcohol, irresponsible sexuality, and crime will be powerful, and hard to resist. They promise the satisfactions that self-esteem seekers are looking for, and they promise them *now*. Instant pleasure. Instant relief. Instant success. They feel good now, the old theories tell us, but they will produce unhappiness as well as incompetence.

That could well be what happened to us in the 1960s and the 1970s. American parents, like American teachers, went to great lengths to ensure the happiness of American children in those decades, nurturing their self-esteem and protecting it from injury, discarding standards and discipline, at home and at school. They did it because establishment experts in schools of education and psychology convinced them that feel-good-now self-esteem was the master key that unlocked both doors, the one to intellectual development and the one to happiness, too. In truth, it seems to have unlocked neither, but many American parents and teachers are still its captives.

There was one great rebellion, though, in the late 1970s. It was called the minimum competence testing movement, and it gives us the best evidence we have about what parents and teachers can accomplish when they join together to insist that a standard must be met. The standard they chose was literacy, and they proved they were serious about it, in most states, by decreeing that no student could graduate from high school without passing a test designed to measure it.

Experts in the Self-Esteem-Now establishment were appalled. They were sure that the movement would damage students' self-esteem without helping them to learn, and that it would have especially devastating effects on black students. At first, it looked as if they might be right. In Florida, 80 to 90 percent of the black students who took that state's minimum competence test failed it on their first try, and a federal judge declared the whole program unconstitutional, issuing an injunction against it in 1979.

In 1983, he lifted it, permanently, and no wonder. The program's results were spectacular. The students who failed the test on their first try may have suffered a blow to their self-esteem, but they were not crushed, and they did not quit. They kept trying, bouncing back after each failure, and redoubling their efforts, By the fifth try, more than 90 percent of them passed the test, and got their diplomas, along with a healthy dose of *earned* self-esteem.

Could the same thing happen again, if parents and teachers throw off the yoke of the Self-Esteem-Now theory once more, embracing excellence in the 1980s as they embraced competence in the late 1970s? All the evidence we have indicates that it could, and that it would be a great decade for American education if they did.

Barbara Lerner, American Educator, Winter 1985

VALUES AND VIOLENCE IN SPORTS TODAY: THE MORAL REASONING ATHLETES USE IN THEIR GAMES AND IN THEIR LIVES

To be good in sports, you have to be bad. Or so many athletes, coaches and sports fans believe. Heavyweight champion Larry Holmes, for example, revealed a key to his success during a *60 Minutes* interview with Morley Safer: Before he enters the ring, he said, "I have to change, I have to leave the goodness out and bring all the bad in, like Dr. Jekyll and Mr. Hyde."

Even sports fan Ronald Reagan suggested that normally inappropriate ways of thinking and acting are acceptable in sports. When he was governor of California, he reportedly told a college team during a pep talk that in football, "you can feel a clean hatred for your opponent. It is a clean hatred since it's only symbolic in a jersey."

Does success today really depend on how well an athlete or team has mastered the art of aggression? The question is usually answered more by ideology than by evidence. But there is a more fundamental question that needs to be asked: Is it really OK to be bad in sports? In particular, is aggression an acceptable tactic on the playing field? If it is morally unacceptable, the debate about its utility misses the mark.

It seems odd to ask whether being bad is all right. But in contact sports particularly, acts of aggreession are seldom condemned, usually condoned and often praised. Sport is a "world within a world" with its own unique conventions and moral understandings.

Lyle and Glenn Blackwood of the Miami Dolphins are nicknamed "the bruise brothers." Their motto—"We don't want to hurt you, just make you hurt"—aptly expresses the ambiguity many people feel about sport aggression. To reduce such ambiguity, many athletes appeal to game rules, informal agreements or personal convictions to decide the legitimacy of aggressive acts. As one collegiate basketball player told us in an interview: "It's OK to try to hurt somebody if it is legal and during the game. If the guy doesn't expect it, it's a cheap shot. That's no good. You can be aggressive and do minor damage without really hurting him and still accomplish your goal."

As social scientists, we are interested in the moral meaning athletes and fans attach to aggression. Do sport participants think about aggression in moral terms? Does the maturity of athletes' moral reasoning influence their aggressive behavior? What are the unique characteristics of sport morality and how does this "game reasoning" influence the perceived legitimacy of aggression?

Most recommendations for reducing sport aggression have focused on rules and penalties against fighting, beanballs, slugging and other forms of violence. We believe, however, that reducing athletic aggression requires the transformation of both external sports structures such as rules and penalties and internal reasoning structures. To reduce aggression, we must first understand the meaning athletes attach to it.

By aggression, we mean acts that are intended to inflict pain or injury. Robust, physically forceful play not meant to harm another player is better termed assertion. Unfortunately, this distinction is often blurred on the mat, the ice and the Astroturf.

We believe that aggression is more than a convention; it is a moral issue and can be investigated as such. If this is true, there should be an inverse relationship between the maturity of athletes' moral reasoning and their acceptance of aggression. Our research . . . suggests that this relationship exists. The higher their level of moral reasoning, the less aggression athletes practice and condone.

Establishing a link between moral reasoning and sport aggression is only the first step in understanding it. It is still not clear why many people find everyday aggression objectionable but have few moral qualms when they or others hurl a beanball at a batter. We can develop a more complete portrait of athletic aggression by exploring the unique patterns of moral reasoning that sport encourages.

Some social scientists have noted a curious fact that athletes and fans take for granted: Sport is set apart both cognitively and emotionally from the everyday world. Anthropologist Don Handelman, for example, has observed that play "requires a radical transformation in cognition and perception." Sociologist Erving Goffman has described play activities as enclosed within a unique "social membrane" or conceptual "frame."

In a 1983 interview, Ron Rivera, then a linebacker with the University of California at Berkeley and now with the Chicago Bears, described the personality transformation he undergoes on the field. The off-field Ron, he said, is soft-spoken, considerate and friendly. When asked to describe the on-field Ron, he replied, "He's totally opposite from me. . . . He's a madman. . . . No matter what happens, he hits people. He's a guy with no regard for the human body." Elaborating further, Rivera revealed, "I'm mean and nasty then. . . . I'm so rotten. I have a total disrespect for the guy I'm going to hit."

Does this personality transformation include a fundamental change in moral reasoning? To explore this possibility, we designed a study to see whether the same people would use similar levels of moral reasoning in response to hypothetical dilemmas set in sport-specific and daily life contexts. One "sport dilemma," for example, centered on Tom, a football player who is told by his coach to injure an opponent to help Tom's team win. One of the "daily life" dilemmas hinged on whether a person should keep his promise to deliver some money to a rich man or use it to help his hungry kin.

We presented four dilemmas to 120 high school and college athletes and nonathletes and asked them to reason about the best way to resolve each dilemma. Most of the students clearly perceived a difference between morality in sport and in everyday life. One comment by a high school female basketball player exemplified this perspective: "In sports, it's hard to tell right from wrong sometimes; you have to use game sense." Both athletes and nonathletes used lower-level egocentric moral reasoning when thinking about dilemmas in sport than when addressing moral issues in other contexts.

These and other findings suggest that moral norms which prescribe equal consideration of all people are often suspended during competition in favor of a more egocentric moral perspective. One male college basketball player explained the difference this way. "In sports you can do what you want. In life it's more restricted. It's harder to make decisions in life because there are so many people to think about, different people to worry about. In sports you're free to think about yourself."

This theme was echoed by many others who referred to sport as a field where each person or team seeks personal triumph and where opponents need not be given equal consideration.

There are several reasons sports may elicit an egocentric style of game reasoning. The very nature of competition requires that self-interest be temporarily adopted while the athlete strives to win. In everyday life, such preoccupation with self almost inevitably leads to moral failings. But in sport, participants are freed to concentrate on self-interest by a carefully balanced rule structure that equalizes opportunity. Players are guarded against the moral defaults of others by protective rules and by officials who impose sanctions for violations. Moral responsibility is thus transferred from the shoulders of players to those of officials, the enforcers of the rules, and to coaches, whom the players learn to see as responsible for all decisions.

If the nature of competition encourages egocentricity, the "set aside" character of sport helps to justify it. Sport consists of artificial goals that are achieved through arbitrarily defined skills and procedures. Although running across a line or shooting a ball through a hoop is all-important in the immediate game context, neither has significant consequences outside sports. This lack of any "real world" meaning to sport actions helps make egocentric reasoning seem legitimate.

Not all sport goals, of course, lack real-world implications. In boxing, for example, where the goal involves damage to another person, serious injury or even death is possible. Another exception is professional sports, and even some collegiate and high school sports, where winners may receive prizes, bigger paychecks, more perks or expanded educational and professional opportunities. The moral implications of harm as a sport goal (boxing) and extrinsic rewards contingent on sport performance (in professional and quasiprofessional sports) still need to be investigated.

The dynamic of competition, the structural protection provided by officials and rules and the relatively inconsequential implications of sport intentions combine to release sport participants from the usual demands of morality. But game-specific moral understandings do not completely replace everyday morality. Just as sport exists in a unique space and time within the everyday world, so game reasoning is a form of "bracketed morality." The transformed morality that occurs in sport does not take the place of everyday morality; rather, it is embedded in the broader, more encompassing morality of daily life.

Because of this, most athletes limit the degree of sport aggression they accept as legitimate in line with their general understanding of the rights of others. Coordinating these two sets of standards is not easy. Consider, for example, how one athlete reasoned about the football dilemma in which Tom is told to injure his opponent:

"If Tom looks at it as a game, it's OK to hurt the guy—to try to take him out of the game. But if he looks at the halfback as a person, and tries to hurt him, it's not OK." Asked, "How do you decide which to go by?" the athlete explained, "When you're on the field, then the game is football. Before and after, you deal with people morally."

This man recognized that aggression can be viewed from two contrasting viewpoints but eliminated his ambivalence by subordinating everyday morality to game reasoning. For him, an opponent is a player, not a person. This objectification of opponents reduces an athlete's sense of personal responsibility for competitors.

Among some of the other athletes we interviewed, accountability was alleviated by simply "not thinking about it." As one athlete stated succinctly, "In sports you don't think about those things [hurting others]; mostly you don't think about other people, you just think about winning."

Most athletes, however, tried to coordinate game and everyday morality by distinguishing between legitimate and illegitimate aggression. As one man explained: "Some [aggressive acts] are not acceptable. The game is a game. You go out to win, but there's a line—limitations— there are rules. . . . You try to dominate the other player, but you don't want to make him leave the game."

Another athlete put it this way: "Tom shouldn't try to hurt him. He should just hit him real hard, stun him, make him lose his wind, make sure he's too scared to run the ball again."

Players use a complex moral logic in attempts to coordinate the goal of winning with the need to respect limits to egocentricity. Some athletes identify the rules as the final arbiter of legitimacy, but most appeal to less formal criteria. Themes such as intimidation, domination, fairness and retribution are continuously woven into participants' fabric of thought, providing a changing picture of what constitutes legitimate action.

Shifting expectations, created by the fast-paced and emotionally charged action, can readily lead to perceived violations or "cheap shots." Cheap shots, of course, are in the eye, or ribs, of the beholder. As a college basketball player explained, physical contact may be interpreted by athletes as either assertive or aggressive, depending on their perception of intent: "I've played with guys who try to hurt you. They use all kinds of cheap shots, especially elbows in the face and neck. But that's different than trying to maintain position or letting a guy know you're there. An elbow can be for intimidation or it can be for hurting. I just use elbows in the regular course of the game."

Given the complex and variable conditions of sport, it is not surprising that among the athletes we interviewed there was not a clear consensus about the line between legitimate and illegitimate aggression. Generally, we found that the more mature the athletes' moral reasoning, the less aggression they accepted as legitimate—both for the fictitious character Tom in the hypothetical football dilemma and for themselves as they reasoned about personal aggression.

Yet even the more morally mature athletes often accepted minor forms of aggression as legitimate game strategy. In fact, such minor aggression was sometimes viewed as a positive, enhancing aspect of the game. As a high school player explained: "Football is a rough game and if it weren't for rules people would get hurt real bad—even killed. Some people just want to hurt other people real bad." Asked, "Should the present rules be changed to reduce football injuries?" he replied, "No. Nobody will want to play if the rules get so uptight that you can't hit hard."

Moral research inevitably leads beyond descriptions about what people do to questions about what people ought to do. Perhaps most athletes accept some aggression as "part of the game," but should they? Should any degree of aggression be considered legitimate?

Based on what we have learned about game reasoning, we believe two criteria can be employed to distinguish morally mature athletes' judgments of aggression which they may perceive as legitimate from aggression which certainly is not. First, any act intended to inflict an injury that is likely to have negative consequences for the recipient once the game has ended is illegitimate. The legitimacy of game reasoning depends partly on the irrelevance of sport action to everyday life. Consequently, inflicting such "game-transcending" injuries as a broken leg or a concussion cannot be morally justified.

Second, game reasoning is also legitimated because it occurs within a situation that is defined by a set of rules that limit the relevant procedures and skills which can be used during the game. Therefore, any act is illegitimate if it occurs apart from the strategic employment of game-relevant skills, even if such an act is intended to cause only minor injury or mild discomfort. Such behavior impinges upon the protective structure that releases participants from their normal moral obligations.

The implications of our research on athletes' game reasoning may extend to other spheres of life. If game reasoning is distinct from the morality of general life, are there other context-specific moralities, such as business reasoning or political reasoning? Perhaps the list could be extended indefinitely. While every context raises unique moral issues, however, we agree with most moral-development theorists that the fundamental structure of moral reasoning remains relatively stable in nearly all situations.

Sport is employed frequently as a metaphor for other endeavors, and game language is often utilized in discussions of such diverse topics as business, politics and war. A recent book by Thomas Whisler of the University of Chicago, *Rules of the Game*, has little to do with sport and everything to do with corporate boardrooms.

The borrowing of sport images and language may reflect a tendency to transplant game morality from its native soil to foreign gardens. If this is the case, game reasoning has social implications that extend far beyond the limited world of sport. Game morality is legitimated by protections within the sport structure, but most other contexts lack such safeguards. If game reasoning leads to manipulation to gain job advancement, for example, are adequate laws available and enforced to guarantee equal opportunity? Can the dirty tricks of politics be legitimated as if they were just a game? Does game reasoning encourage a view that nuclear war is winnable, propelling us toward the "game to end all games"? And if it does, who consents to play these games?

Brenda Jo Bredemeier and David L. Shields,
Psychology Today, October 1985

4.
The Multiple-Source Essay

Until now, most of your writing assignments have been based on information that has been derived from a single source. You have learned to paraphrase, summarize, rearrange, and unify your evidence without sacrificing accuracy or completeness.

Now, as you begin to work with a wider range of sources, you will have to understand and organize much more diverse material. Your goal is to present the ideas of your sources in all their variety, while, at the same time, maintaining your own single perspective, which encompasses all the shades of opinion. How can you describe each author's ideas without taking up a large amount of space for each one? How can you fit all your sources smoothly into your essay without allowing one to dominate? How can you convert a group of disparate ideas into an essay that is yours?

To make it easier for you to learn to work with multiple sources, most of the examples, exercises, and writing assignments in this chapter will use materials that are brief and easy to experiment with. Most of these materials are notes taken by students during informal interviews or short, written responses to a topic or an article. In the writing assignments, you may be asked to collect your own materials by doing a series of interviews or by joining your classmates in writing down your reactions to a general question. The statements that you will work with in this chapter not only provide useful practice, but also have their equivalents in professional writing such as case notes, case studies, legal testimony, and market research.

SELECTING INFORMATION
FOR A MULTIPLE-SOURCE ESSAY

In academic writing, you do not usually find the materials for an essay in a neatly assembled package. On the contrary, before beginning to organize an essay, you will often be faced with the preliminary problem of finding and selecting your materials. The first stage of a research project is traditionally the trip to the library with a topic to explore, a search for information that will later be interpreted, sifted, and synthesized into a finished piece of writing.

To demonstrate this process in miniature, assume that you have been assigned the following project, which calls for a narrow range of research:

> Read an entire newspaper published on a day of your choosing during this century, and write a summary describing what life was like on that day. Your sources are the assorted articles and advertisements in the day's paper.

Given the amount and variety of information contained in the average newspaper, your greatest difficulty would be to decide what and how much to include. You would hope to provide a balance of two kinds of evidence—major events that altered the fabric of most people's lives, and more ordinary happenings that could tell a good deal about how people typically spent their days. While these events may have taken place before your birth, your not having been there at the time would actually be an advantage: as an outsider, you would be able to distinguish more easily between stories of historic importance and those that simply reflect their era.

To begin this project, you would follow these steps:

1. Read rapidly through the entire newspaper. Then read the same issue again more slowly, jotting down your impressions of important *kinds* of events or *characteristics* of daily life. Search for a pattern, a thesis that sums up what you have read.

2. Review your notes, and isolate a few main ideas that seem worth developing. Then read the issue a third time, making sure that there really is sufficient evidence for all the points that you wish to make. Make notes of any additional information that you expect to use, and write down the page number next to each reference in your notes. Remember that you are not trying to "use up" all the available information.

3. Plan a series of paragraphs, each focusing on a somewhat different theme that is either significant in itself or typical of the day that you are describing. Spend some time choosing a strategy for a se-

quence of paragraphs that will not only introduce your reader to the world that you are describing, but also make apparent the pattern of events (or thesis) that you have discovered through your reading.

Drawing Conclusions from Your Information

Through your essay, you should help your readers to form conclusions about the significance of the information that you are providing for them. The evidence should not be expected to speak for itself. Consider the following paragraph:

> Some popular books in the first week of 1945 were Brave Men by Ernie Pyle, Forever Amber by Kathleen Windsor, and The Time for Decision by Sumner Welles. The average price of these new, hard-cover books was about three dollars each. The price of the daily Times was three cents, and Life magazine was ten cents.

What is probably most interesting to the person who reads this account today is how little the reading material cost. However, nothing is said about the books. Can you tell what they were about? Why were they popular? Do they seem typical of 1945's best seller list? Unexplained information is of no value to your reader, who cannot be assumed to know more than—or even as much as—you do.

In contrast, another student, writing about a day shortly after the end of World War II, built a paragraph around a casualty list in the *New York Times.* What seemed significant about the list was the fact that by the end of the war, casualties had become routine and had assumed almost a minor place in daily life. Notice that the paragraph begins with a topic sentence that establishes the context and draws its conclusion at the end.

> For much of the civilian population, the worst part of the war had been the separation from their loved ones, who had gone off to fight in Europe, Africa, and the Pacific. Even after the end of the war, they still had to wait for the safe arrival home of the troops. In order to inform the public, the New York Times ran a daily list of troop arrivals. However, not everyone was destined to return, and the Times also ran a list of casualties, which, on September 4, was to be found on the bottom of page 2.

Another paragraph about May 6, 1946, forms the conclusion that the postwar mid-forties were a transitional period:

> The process of switching over from a wartime to a peacetime economy was not without its pains. Then, as now, there was a high rate of

unemployment. The Times featured a story about the million women
production workers who had recently lost their jobs in war industries. Returning male and female veterans were also flooding the job
market. Some working wives were waiting to see how their husbands
readjusted to postwar jobs. If their ex-GI husbands could bring home
enough money to support the family, they could return to their roles
as housewives. If their husbands chose to continue their education or
vocational training under the GI Bill, they would expect to stay on
the job as long as they could.

The bulk of this paragraph appears to be a straightforward account of
circumstances in support of the writer's conclusion, which is contained
in the topic sentence; but she is, in fact, summarizing information taken
from *several* articles in that day's newspaper. (Notice that, while the
source of the information—the *Times*—is being cited, the identity of the
reporters is not considered significant in this case, and no names are included.) The suggestion of a personal comment—unemployment, one
gathers, is a recurring problem—adds immediacy and significance to a
topic that might otherwise be remote from present concerns.

Finally, it is not always necessary to present your conclusion in a topic
sentence at the *beginning* of your paragraph. Here is one in which the
evidence is presented first:

The July 30, 1945 issue of Newsweek lists three bills that were
going before Congress. The first, the Burton-Ball-Hatch Bill, proposed that all industries institute a labor management mediation
system. The second, the Kilgore Bill, proposed providing $25 a week in
unemployment for a period of 26 weeks. And the third, the Mead bill,
proposed raising the minimum wage from 40 cents to 65 cents. It is
obvious from these three bills that a great deal of attention was
being focused on employment, or the lack of it. Here we have another
clue about the life-style of 1945. The majority of the working class
must have been dissatisfied with conditions for their congressmen to
have proposed these improvements. These bills were also in keeping
with the late President Roosevelt's New Deal policy, which was primarily directed toward the improvement of economic conditions. From
these bills, it is safe to assume that the cost of living may have been
rising, that unemployment was still something of a problem, and that
strikes by workers were becoming so prevalent that a mediation system
seemed necessary.

This paragraph explicitly links together three related points, suggests
their possible significance, and provides a historical context (the New
Deal) in which to understand them.

EXERCISE 20

Read the following student essay, a description of life in New York City on September 21, 1967. Analyze each paragraph and be prepared to discuss the following:

1. The writer's reasons for building a paragraph around that piece of information. (Use your own knowledge of the contents of the average newspaper today to estimate the range of choices that the writer might have had.)
2. The clarity and completeness with which the information is presented.
3. The inclusion of topic sentences that interpret the information and suggest its significance for the reader.
4. The organization of the essay: the relationship between paragraphs; the sequence of paragraphs; the unity within each paragraph.
5. The establishment of a thesis and the success of the author's attempt to characterize September 21, 1967, as typical of its era and as a contrast to her own era.

According to the New York Times, on September 21, 1967 there was considerable violence and unrest in the United States, much of it in response to the United States' involvement in the Vietnam War. The United States had increased its bombing of Vietnam in an attempt to cut off the port of Haiphong from contact with the rest of the world. As a result, a group opposed to President Johnson's Vietnam policy began an "anti-Johnson" campaign. They were a coalition of Democrats who hoped to block his reelection. Meanwhile, seventy female antiwar demonstrators were arrested outside the White House. Later, to protest their arrest, 500 members of Women Strike for Peace marched to the White House and clashed with police.

There was not only civil unrest on this day, but also a conflict between President Johnson and the House Ways and Means Committee over the President's proposed tax increase. The committee would not approve the increase without a five billion dollar cut in spending. The Senate proposed the following cuts: a two billion dollar decrease in defense spending; a one billion dollar decrease in "long-range research"; and a two billion dollar decrease in other civilian services. However, aid to the poor and to cities was not to be cut. In defense of the President's request, Secretary of Commerce Trowbridge said that a tax increase would be necessary because of inflation.

Throughout the rest of the country, there was much racial tension and violence. There had been days of fighting in Dayton, Ohio's West Side, which had a large black population. A rally took place there to protest the killing of a black Social Security Administration field-worker. There was also a supermarket fire in Dayton, which resulted in $20,000 of damage. In the end, twenty teenagers were arrested. In the Casa Central Outpost, a Puerto Rican neighborhood in Chicago, Governor Romney of Michigan, a would-be presidential candidate, was given a hostile welcome. His visit to the Outpost was blocked by its director, Luis Cuza, who handed him a two-page press release claiming that the Governor was only touring these poor neighborhoods for political gain. Governor Romney expressed outrage at the accusation and the fact that the Outpost had not informed him earlier that he would not be welcome. In the meantime, the streets of Hartford, Connecticut's North End were quiet after three days of racial violence. Civil rights demonstrators were marching against housing discrimination in the South End, a predominantly middle class, Italian neighborhood. There were 66 arrests, mainly of young blacks. To control the violence, five to ten policemen were posted at every intersection, and the mayor asked for a voluntary curfew.

On the local level, a protest against traffic conditions took place in the Bronx, at 149th Street and Courtlandt Avenue. The protestors, four clergymen and dozens of neighbors, wanted Courtlandt Avenue to be one-way. Two men refused to leave after police tried to disperse the crowd.

There was not only racial unrest in the country on this day, but also many labor disputes and strikes. Seventeen thousand Prudential Insurance Company of America agents threatened to strike if no contract was agreed on in four days. They could not accept any of the proposals previously given to them. Also, the steelhaulers' strike in Chicago was spreading east, and had already resulted in a violent confrontation in Pittsburgh. Finally, on strike were the 59,500 New York public school teachers, whose refusal to enter the classrooms had kept more than one million students out of school for eight days. The teachers' slogan was "no contract, no work."

Even the weather was in turmoil. Hurricane Beulah, in Texas, had winds estimated at 80 miles per hour at the center of the storm and 120-150 miles per hour at its peak. Eighty-five percent of Port Isabel, a town at the southern tip of Texas, was destroyed, and four people were killed by the record number of 27 tornadoes spawned by Beulah. All the gulf states experienced heavy rain in Beulah's aftermath. Meanwhile, rain and thunderstorms also battered the east coast.

GENERALIZING FROM EXAMPLES

Summarizing the contents of a newspaper can cause problems for the writer because newspaper stories describe specific incidents which often have nothing in common except that they all happened on the same day. Academic writing is usually not so arbitrary: a distinct, common theme often links apparently dissimilar ideas or facts. The writer has to take advantage of this common theme and construct a few generalizations that cover several items in the sources.

Assume that you have been asked to consider and react to seven different but related situations, and then formulate two generalizations:

A. In a sentence or two, write down your probable reaction if you found yourself in each of the following situations.* Write quickly; this exercise calls for an immediate, instinctive response.

1. You are walking behind someone. You see him take out a cigarette pack, pull out the last cigarette, put the cigarette in his mouth, crumple the package, and nonchalantly toss it over his shoulder onto the sidewalk. What would you do?

2. You are sitting on a train and you notice a person (same age, sex, and type as yourself) lighting up a cigarette, despite the no-smoking sign. No one in authority is around. What would you do?

3. You are pushing a shopping cart in a supermarket and you hear the thunderous crash of cans. As you round the corner, you see a two-year-old child being beaten, quite severely, by his mother, apparently for pulling out the bottom can of the pile. What would you do?

4. You see a kid that you recognize shoplifting at the local discount store. You're concerned that he'll get into serious trouble if the store detective catches him. What would you do?

5. You're driving on a two-lane road behind another car. You notice that one of its wheels is wobbling more and more. It looks as if the lugs are coming off one by one. There's no way to pass, because cars are coming from the other direction in a steady stream. What would you do?

6. You've been waiting in line (at a supermarket or gas station) for longer than you expected and you're irritated at the delay. Sud-

*Adapted from "Strategy 24" in Sidney B. Simon et al., *Values Clarification* (New York: Hart, 1972).

denly, you notice that someone very much like yourself has sneaked in ahead of you in the line. There are a couple of people before you. What would you do?

7. You've raised your son not to play with guns. Your rich uncle comes for a long-awaited visit and he brings your son a .22 rifle with lots of ammunition. What would you do?

B. Read over your responses to the seven situations and try to form two general statements (in one or two sentences) about *the circumstances in which you would take action* as opposed to *the circumstances in which you would choose to do nothing.* Do not simply list the incidents, one after the other, in two groups.

You can work out an answer to this problem only by examining the group of situations in which taking action seems desirable and determining what they have in common. (It is also important to examine the "leftovers," too, and to understand why these incidents did *not* warrant your interference.) As a first step, you might try looking at each situation in terms of either its *causes* or its *consequences.* For example, in each case there is someone to blame, someone who is responsible for creating the problem—except for number five, where fate (or poor auto maintenance) threatens to cause an accident. As for consequences, in some of the situations (littering, for example) there is little potential danger, either to oneself or to the public. Do these circumstances discourage action? In others, however, the possible victim is oneself or a member of one's family. Does self-interest alone drive one to act? Do adults tend to intervene in defense of children—even someone else's child—since they cannot stand up for themselves? Or, instead of calculating the consequences of *not* intervening, perhaps one should imagine the possible consequences of interference. In which situations can one expect to receive abuse for failing to mind one's own business? As always, only by examining the evidence can one discover the basis for a generalization.

The list of examples has two characteristics worth noting:

1. Each item on the list is intended to illustrate a specific and a very different situation. Thus, although it does not include every possible example, the list as a whole constitutes a *set* of public occasions for interfering with and regulating a stranger's conduct.

2. Since you probably would not choose to act in every situation, you cannot use the entire list as the basis for your generalization. Rather, you must establish a boundary line, dividing those occasions when you would intervene from those times when you would decide not to act. The exact boundary between interven-

tion and nonintervention will differ from person to person, as will the exact composition of the smaller list of occasions justifying intervention. Thus, there is no one correct generalization.

The product of this exercise is a set of guidelines for justifiably minding other people's business. You formulate the guidelines by applying your own standards to a sampling of possible examples.

Broad concepts offer a great deal of room for disagreement and ambiguity and therefore allow a great many interpretations. You may wish to clarify your ideas and opinions about any important abstract issue by setting up such a set of illustrations, marking off a subgroup, and then consructing a generalization that describes what is *inside* the boundary: the common characteristics of the contents of the subgroup. Thus, in the previous problem, one person might consider the set of seven examples and then decide to intervene only in situations 3 (the child beaten in a supermarket), 5 (the wobbly wheel), and 7 (the gift of a gun). What makes these three cases different from the others? They and they alone involve protecting some person from physical harm. This process of differentiation, followed by generalized description, is usually called *definition,* and it can serve as an essay strategy in its own right or as the basis for a *comparison, classification, argumentation,* or *evaluation essay.*

ANALYZING MULTIPLE SOURCES

When you write from sources, your object is not to establish a single "right" conclusion but, rather, to present a general thesis statement of your own that is based on your examination of a variety of views. Some of these views may even conflict with your own and with each other. Because of this diversity, organizing multiple sources is more difficult than working with a series of examples, with the contents of a newspaper, or with even a highly complex single essay.

The writing process for multiple sources begins with the *analysis of ideas*: breaking a mass of information down into individual pieces and inspecting the pieces. As you underline and annotate your sources, you look for similarities and distinctions in meaning, as well as the basic principle underlying each statement. Only when you have taken apart the evidence of each source and seen how it works can you then begin to find ways of putting everything back together again in your own essay.

To illustrate the analysis of sources, assume that you have asked five people what the word "foreign" means. You want to provide a reasonably complete definition of the word by exploring all the shades of meaning or connotations that the five sources suggest. If each one of the five gives you a completely different answer, then you will not have much choice in the organization of your comprehensive definition. In that case, you would probably present each separate definition of "foreign" in a separate paragraph, citing a different person as the source for each paragraph. But responses from multiple sources almost always overlap, as these do. Notice the common meanings in this condensed list of the five sources' responses:

John Brown: "Foreign" means unfamiliar and exotic.

Lynn Williams: "Foreign" means strange and unusual.

Bill White: "Foreign" means strange and alien (as in "foreign body").

Mary Green: "Foreign" means exciting and exotic.

Bob Friedman: "Foreign" means difficult and incomprehensible (as in "foreign language").

The common meanings are what is crucial to the planning of your essay, not the names of the five sources. That is why the one-source-per-paragraph method should hardly ever be used (except on those rare occasions when the sources completely disagree). When you organize ideas taken from multiple sources, you should reject the idea of devoting one paragraph to each page of your notes, simply because all the ideas on that page happen to have come from the same person. If you did so, each paragraph would have a topic sentence that might read, "Then I asked John Brown for his definition," as if John Brown were the topic for discussion, instead of his views on "foreign." And if John Brown and Mary Green each gets a full paragraph, there will be some repetition because both think that one of the meanings of "foreign" is "exotic." "Exotic" should dominate one of your paragraphs, not the person (or the people) who suggested that meaning.

Analyzing Shades of Meaning

Here is a set of notes, summarizing the ideas of four different people about the meaning of the word "individualist." How would you analyze these notes?

Richard Becker: an "individualist is a person who is unique and does not "fall into the common mode of doing things"; would not follow a pattern set by society. "A youngster who is not involved in the drug scene just because his friends are." A good word; it would be insulting only if it referred to a troublemaker.

Simon Jackson: doing things on your own, by yourself. "She's such an individualist that she insisted on answering the question in her own way." Sometimes the word is good, but mostly it has a bad connotation: someone who rebels against society or authority.

Lois Asher: one who doesn't "follow the flock." The word refers to someone who is very independent. "I respect Jane because she is an individualist and her own person." Usually very complimentary.

Vera Lewis: an extremely independent person. "An individualist is a person who does not want to contribute to society." Bad meaning: usually antisocial. She first heard the word in psych. class, describing the characteristics of the individualist and "how he reacts to society."

At first glance, all the sources seem to say much the same thing: the individualist is different and "independent." However, it is worthwhile to examine the context in which the four sources are defining this word. First, all the responses define the individualist in terms of other people, either the "group," or the "flock," or "society." Oddly enough, it is not easy to describe the individualist as an individual, even though it is his isolation that each person is emphasizing. Whatever is "unique" about the individualist—the quality that makes him "independent"—is defined by the gap between him and everyone else. (Notice that both "unique" and "independent" are words that also suggest a larger group in the background; after all, one has to be independent *of* something!)

Having found a meaning that is coming to all four sources and, just as important, having established the context for a definition, you must now look for differences. Obviously, Lois Asher thinks that to be an individualist is a good thing; Vera Lewis believes that individualism is bad; and the other two suggest that both connotations are possible. But simply describing the reactions of the four sources stops short of defining the word according to those reactions.

Richard Becker and Lois Asher, two people who suggest a favorable connotation, characterize the group from which the individual is set apart in similar and somewhat disapproving terms: "common"; "pattern set by society"; "follow the flock." Becker and Asher both seem to be suggesting a degree of conformity or sameness which the individualist is right to reject, as Becker's youngster rejects his friends' drugs. But Vera Lewis, who thinks that the word's connotation is a bad one, places the individualist in the context of a more benign society, with which the individual ought to identify himself and to which he ought to contribute. To be antisocial is to be an undesirable person—from the point of view of Lewis and society. Simon Jackson (who is ambivalent about the word) uses the phrases "by yourself" and "on your own," which suggest the isolation and the lack of support, as well as the admirable independence, of the individualist. In Jackson's view, the individualist's self-assertion becomes threatening to all of us in society ("antisocial") only when he begins to rebel against authority. Probably for Jackson, and certainly for Vera Lewis, the ultimate authority should rest with society as a whole, not with the individualist. Even Richard Becker, who admires the individualist, draws the line at allowing him complete independence: when the individualist's reliance on his own authority leads to "troublemaking," the term becomes an insult.

EXERCISE 21

Analyze the following set of notes for a definition of the word "discipline." Then explore some ways to organize these notes by following these steps:

A. Find the important terms or concepts that can lead to a context for defining "discipline."
B. Write two generalizations that might serve as topic sentences for a two-paragraph essay. (Do not use "favorable" and "unfavorable" as your two topics.)

Sabrina Bryant: to make someone behave or obey, often by threat of punishment; to chastise or correct someone; often relates to teaching. "The class had been taught discipline and always stood up when the principal entered the room."

Cynthia Martin: having or maintaining control or order; efficiently run, well organized; no disruption. "In a well-disciplined household, everyone is assigned a group of chores."

John St. Clair: following a right standard; conforming to the rules; accepting authority. "Jack was disciplined enough to refuse to go to a party the night before final exams."

Regina Torres: well educated, well brought up, or well trained; good manners; usually refers to children; results in self-control and self-reliance. "Because he was well disciplined, my little cousin knew how to behave when he was visiting other people's homes."

Margaret Williams: punishment; used to make people obey; often involves physical punishment or deprivation; a symbol that the person is unsatisfactory or has not behaved well. "The army recruit had been disciplined so often that he no longer cared what happened to him.''

MAKING A CHART OF COMMON IDEAS

Once you have analyzed each of your sources and discovered their similarities and differences, you then reassemble these parts into a more coherent whole. This process is called *synthesis*. Although at first you may regard analysis and synthesis as contradictory operations, they are actually overlapping stages of a single, larger process.

To illustrate the way in which analysis and synthesis work together, let us work with a set of answers to the question: *Would you buy a lottery ticket? Why?* First, read through these summaries of all seven responses.

Mary Smith: She thinks that lottery tickets were made for people to enjoy and win. It's fun to try your luck. She looks forward to buying her ticket, because she feels that, for one dollar, you have a chance to win a lot more. It's also fun scratching off the numbers to see what you've won. Some people don't buy tickets because they think the lottery is a big rip-off; but ''a dollar can't buy that much today, so why not spend it and have a good time?''

John Jones: He would buy a lottery ticket for three reasons. The first reason is that he would love to win. The odds are like a challenge, and he likes to take a chance. The second reason is just for fun. When he has two matching tickets, he really feels happy, especially when he thinks that dollars can be multiplied into hundreds or thousands. ''It's like Russian Roulette.'' The third reason is that part of the money from the lottery goes towards his education. The only problem, he says, is that they are always sold out!

Michael Green: He has never bought a lottery ticket in his life because he doesn't want to lose money. He wants to be sure of winning. Also, he says that he isn't patient enough. The buyer of a lottery ticket has to be very patient to wait for his chance to win. He thinks that people who buy tickets all the time must enjoy ''living dangerously.''

Anne White: Buying a lottery ticket gives her a sense of excitement. She regards herself as a gambler. ''When you win two dollars or five dollars you get a thrill of victory, and when you see that you haven't, you feel the agony of defeat.'' She thinks that people who don't buy tickets must be very cautious and non-competitive, since the lottery brings "a sense of competition with you against millions of other people.'' She also knows that the money she spends on tickets goes towards education.

Margaret Brown: She feels that people who buy tickets are wasting their money. The dollars spent on the lottery could be in the bank, getting interest. Those people who buy tickets should expect to have thrown out their money, and should take their losses philosophically, instead of jumping up and down and screaming about their disappointment. Finally, even if she could afford the risk, the laws of her religion forbid her to participate in "any sort of game that is a form of gambling.''

William Black: He would buy a lottery ticket, because he thinks it can be fun, but he wouldn't buy too many, because he thinks it's easy for people to get carried away and obsessed by the lottery. He enjoys the anticipation of wanting to win and maybe winning. "I think that you should participate, but in proportion to your budget; after all, one day you might just be a winner.''

Elizabeth Watson: She wouldn't buy a lottery ticket because she considers them a rip-off. The odds are too much against you, 240,000 to 1. Also, it is much too expensive, "and I don't have the money to be throwing away on such foolishness.'' She thinks that people who indulge themselves with lottery tickets become gamblers, and she's against all kinds of gambling. Such people have no sense or self-control. Finally, "I'm a sore loser, so buying lottery tickets just isn't for me.''

Since you are working with seven sources with varying opinions, you need a way to record the process of analysis. One effective way is to make a chart of commonly held views. To do so, follow these two steps, which should be carried out simultaneously:

1. Read each statement carefully, and identify each separate reason that is being cited for and against playing the lottery by writing a number above or right next to the relevant comment. When a similar comment is made by another person, use the same number to provide a key to the final list of common reasons. *In this step, you are analyzing your sources.*

Here is what the first two sets of notes might look like once the topic numbers have been inserted:

Mary Smith: She thinks that lottery tickets were made for people to enjoy and win. It's fun to try your luck. She looks forward to buying her ticket, because she feels that, for one dollar, you have a chance to win a lot more. It's also fun scratching off the numbers to see what you've won. Some people don't buy tickets because they think the lottery is a big rip-off; but "a dollar can't buy that much today, so why not spend it and have a good time?"

John Jones: He would buy a lottery ticket for three reasons. The first reason is that he would love to win. The odds are like a challenge, and he likes to take a chance. The second reason is just for fun. When he has two matching tickets, he really feels happy, especially when he thinks that dollars can be multiplied into hundreds or thousands. "It's like Russian Roulette." The third reason is that part of the money from the lottery goes towards his education. The only problem, he says, is that they are always sold out!

2. At the same time as you number each of your reasons, also write a chart or list of reasons on a separate sheet of paper. Each reason should be assigned the same number you wrote next to it in the original statement. Don't make a new entry when the same reason is repeated by a second source. Next to each entry on your chart, put the names of the people who have mentioned that reason. *You are now beginning to synthesize your sources.*

Here's what your completed chart of reasons might look like:

Reason	Sources
1. People play the lottery because it's fun.	Smith; Jones
2. People play the lottery because they like the excitement of taking a chance and winning.	Smith; Jones; Green; White; Black

Reason	*Sources*
3. People don't play the lottery because they think it's a rip-off.	Smith; Watson
4. People play the lottery because they are contributing to education.	Jones; White
5. People don't play the lottery because they have better things to do with their money.	Green; Brown; Watson
6. People play the lottery because they like to gamble.	White; Brown; Watson
7. People who play the lottery and those who refuse to play worry about the emotional reactions of the players.	Green; White; Brown; Black; Watson

The process of synthesis starts as soon as you start to make your chart. This list of common reasons represents the reworking of seven separate sources into a single new pattern that can serve as the basis for a single new essay.

Distinguishing between Reasons

One of the biggest problems in making a list of topics is deciding, in cases of overlapping, whether you actually have one reason or two. Since overlapping reasons were deliberately not combined, the list above may be longer than one that you might have made.

For example, reasons one and two reflect the difference between the experiences of having fun and feeling the thrill of excitement—a difference in sensation that most people would understand. You might ask yourself, "Would someone play the lottery *just for fun* without the anticipation of winning? Or would someone experience a *thrill of excitement* without any sense of fun at all?" If one sensation can exist without the other, you have sufficient reason for putting both items on your chart. Later on, the similarities, not the differences, might make you want to combine the two; but, at the beginning, it is important to note down exactly what ideas and information are available to you.

The distinction between the thrill of excitement (2) and the pleasure of gambling (6) is more difficult to perceive. The former is, perhaps, more innocent than the latter and does not carry with it any of the obsessive overtones of gambling.

Resenting the lottery because it is a rip-off (3) and resenting the lottery because the players are wasting their money (5) appear at first glance to be similar reactions. However, references to the rip-off tend to emphasize the "injured victim" whose money is being whisked away by a public agency. In other words, reason three emphasizes self-protection from robbery; reason five emphasizes the personal virtue of thrift.

Reason seven is not really a reason at all. Some of the comments in the notes do not fit into a tidy list of reasons for playing; yet they provide a valuable insight into human motivation and behavior as expressed in lottery-playing. An exploration of the emotions that characterize the player and the nonplayer (always allowing for the lottery preference of the source) might be an interesting way to conclude an essay.

Deciding on a Sequence of Topics

The topics in your chart appear in the same random order of your notes. Once the chart is completed, you have to try to decide on a more logical sequence of topics by rearranging the entries in the list. Here are two possible ways to arrange the "lottery" reasons. Which sequence do you prefer? Why?

1. fun	1. fun
2. excitement	2. rip-off
3. gambling	3. excitement and gambling
4. education	4. misuse of money
5. rip-off	5. education
6. misuse of money	6. personality of the gambler
7. personality of the gambler	

You can make an indirect impact on your reader by choosing a sequence that supports the pattern that you discovered in analyzing your sources. The right-hand sequence contrasts the advantages and disadvantages of playing the lottery. Moving back and forth between paired reasons calls attention to the relation between opposites and, through constant contrast, makes the material interesting for the reader. The left-hand sequence places all the "advantages" and "disadvantages" together, providing an opportunity to explore positive and negative reactions to the lottery without interruption and therefore encourages a more complex development. Both sequences are acceptable.

EXERCISE 22

This exercise is based on a set of interview notes, answering the question: Do you think children should have to wear school uniforms?

A. Read through the notes. 1) Identify distinct and separate reasons by placing numbers next to the relevant sentences. 2) As you number each new reason, add an entry to the chart. (The first reason is already filled in.)

Reason   *Source*

  1. Uniforms look neat.
  2.
  3.
  4.
  5.
  6.
  7.
  8.
  9.
10.

B. Arrange the numbered points in a logical sequence. If it makes sense to you, combine those that belong together. Be prepared to explain the reasoning behind your sequence of points. If you can find two possible sequences, include both, explaining the advantages of each.

Notes

Peter Mays: One advantage of attending a school where children have to wear uniforms is that they all look neat in their appearance. No one child stands out more than the rest. It is very easy to keep their clothes tidy and clean. If you walk into the classroom, you will not find that some child is looking out of place because he does not have a tie on or she is wearing an unsuitable dress. The children themselves won't feel out of place because no one will look different from the rest. Sometimes, children look more like they are going to a party than attending a class. That won't happen if everyone wears the same uniform. Finally, parents save money because they don't have to buy clothes all year long. Children's clothes are very expensive.

Ada Montanez: If children wear uniforms, parents won't have to spend incredible amounts of money every few months getting their children new clothes to go to school. Each child needs two or three sets of uniforms at the beginning of the school year, and there will be very little additional cost after that. Uniforms also give children a sense of unity with their fellow students, and some regimentation, that might bring back some of the respect for schools that has disappeared from our society. The uniforms should be brightly colored, but not gaudy, and different for each school. In that way, the children would not only identify with their school but also be ready to compete with other schools. The bright colors would enable them to travel at night and avoid car accidents. Uniforms would also lower the absentee rate as well as the accident rate. A child could no longer hang out freely after being sent to school by his or her parents. Finally, parents would have to show more interest in what their child wears; no longer could they take just anything out of the closet and send the child to school in it.

David Brown: Grade school children should not have to wear school uniforms because too many parents would be forced to spend a large portion of their income on buying special clothes. This is a burden to low-income families. Children whose parents couldn't afford the uniform and who had to wear their regular clothes to school would suffer a cruel embarrassment. In addition, buying the child the school's uniform won't make the child any smarter. Outward appearance doesn't really have anything to do with intelligence or academic ability. Schools should be more concerned with training the minds than making the bodies look all alike.

Sandra Fusilli: When different schools require different kinds of uniforms, the way the students dress acts as a mark of identification for the school and gives children a sense of belonging to a community. The children will feel equal, because they are all dressed the same way. Sometimes, kids who are wearing the latest fashions look down on those who have cheap sneakers or the wrong kind of jeans. Those kids will refuse to make friends with the ones who don't meet their standards in fashions. Both groups of children suffer: the shabby kids feel inferior, and the others are clothes-crazy. With uniforms, they'd have no excuse to avoid thinking about their work. Finally, uniforms are easy to spot and would enable policemen to identify truants and make sure that their parents and schools are notified.

Ann Ducek: Uniforms leave no room for individuality. In school, children are supposed to learn how to develop their own talents and abilities and to be themselves. If you make them all wear the same uniform, then the message they will get is that it is important to be just like everyone else and to conform. Kids already have a tendency to want to fit in with the crowd; uniforms will just make that tendency worse. Also, not all parents can afford to buy uniforms. And, even if they can, some children may not like the color or look well in the style. Being uncomfortable in your clothes can have a bad psychological effect and prevent you from learning easily. It's important for children to learn to be independent, and making the decision to wear this dress or that shirt each day is a necessary part of their education.

Jim Scott: Children should not be compelled to wear uniforms in the public schools because that would interfere with the individual freedom of choice that is part of our democratic society. If children are forced to wear uniforms, then the system would no longer be public, that is, free, but would be more like a private, closed system. Children will have to conform soon enough when then are holding down jobs and have to please whatever organization they are working for. We don't want to have an army- or prison-like atmosphere in our schools, with all the inmates looking alike. In addition, many parents will simply not be able to afford payments for these unnecessary uniforms and will keep their children home on that account, thus depriving them of the education which is their right.

ORGANIZING MULTIPLE SOURCES

Playing the lottery is not a subject that lends itself to lengthy or abstract discussion; therefore, charting reasons for and against playing the lottery is not difficult. The article that follows defines a social, political, and humanitarian problem and suggests two methods of dealing with it, without favoring either "solution" or the values on which each is based. The reporter's sources, quoted in the article, simply cite aspects of the problem and the hope that the courts will deal with it.

Fifteen students were asked to read the article and to voice their opinions, which are listed following the article. Assume as you read the article and the student opinions that you plan to address the issue and synthesize the opinions in an essay of your own.

CITY LAYOFFS HURT MINORITIES MOST

City officials reported yesterday that layoffs resulting from the fiscal crisis were having "devastating" effects on minority employment in government.

In the last 18 months, they disclosed, the city lost half of its Spanish-speaking workers, 40 percent of the black males on the payroll and almost a third of its female workers.

"You are close to wiping out the minority work force in the City of New York," said Eleanor Holmes Norton, the chairman of the Commission on Human Rights, after releasing the data in response to a request.

The dwindling employment, in turn, has put the city in "serious jeopardy" of losing various kinds of Federal aid, according to Deputy Mayor Paul Gibson, Jr.

The city's fiscal failure and the resultant layoffs have worsened the situation in such predominantly male, white agencies as the Police Department, where, after some limited gains in recent years, the ranks of women police officers have been reduced by 55 percent because of the budget crisis, according to the city's latest data.

Meanwhile, a Federal appeals court declared that Civil Service seniority was not immune from legal challenge by women police officers who were dismissed because of the city's fiscal crisis.

Scores of complaints alleging discrimination have been filed by laid-off workers, both as class members and individuals, squeezing the city between the pressures of the traditional primacy of union seniority protections and Federal equal-employment requirements.

Federal officials said yesterday they were processing the complaints, which could result in a cut-off of funds. They added that they were hoping for guidance from the United States Supreme Court this year on the clash between the seniority principle, which tends to protect male white workers, and the Federal minority employment guidelines of Federal law.

The data on dismissals, which had been quietly compiled by city officials in recent weeks, were a further indication of the price the city is paying in the campaign to balance the budget and come to grips with its huge legacy of excessive debt.

Inevitably, the requirements of the austerity drive interfere, too, with attempts to soften the layoff effects on minority-group workers and women.

For example, Commissioner Norton emphasized that the levying of budget cuts on an even percentage basis in city agencies was the best way to protect equal opportunity. But various fiscal experts intent on improving the city's management say across-the-board cutting is the worst way of economizing because it ignores the relative quality of programs.

"We had begun to make an effort," Commissioner Norton said. "But one recession takes it all out in an instant."

Since the budget crisis surfaced in the summer of 1974, the city payroll has been reduced by 40,000 jobs—two-thirds of them reported as layoffs. This was a total cut of 13 percent to the current level of about 255,000 workers, according to city records.

A maxim of the seniority system that the last hired should be the first dismissed is the chief factor preventing an even 13 percent sharing of the layoff burden without regard to race or sex, city officials say.

The austerity drive, in which the city must try to cut its spending by $1 billion in less than three years, is forcing the conflict between what

Commissioner Norton describes as "two competing and legitimate interests"—seniority and equal opportunity.

Federal and city civil rights officials were reluctant to discuss the scope of the complaints that have been filed. Werner H. Kramarsky, the state's Commissioner of Human Rights, described the issues raised as "very thorny" and extending to such questions as whether provisional, or temporary, employees should be created with time on the job in determining relative seniority.

The available public records indicate that the state commission is handling at least 35 cases, some of them class complaints, and has sent 98 cases involving former city welfare workers to Federal officials of the Equal Employment Opportunity Commission, which already has received about 160 complaints from welfare workers alone.

The complaints are being pressed not only by women and minority group members, but also by a group of a half dozen disabled persons who contend that they were unfairly victimized in the layoff drive, according to state records.

There have been various court challenges in recent years of the seniority protections, which generally have been unsuccessful. One recent ruling threw out a racial quota program for city school principals. Federal civil rights officials emphasize that the Supreme Court is considering the issue at present and the hope is that some definitive standard will be set.

According to Deputy Mayor Gibson, minorities represented 31 percent of the payroll, but suffered 44 percent of the cuts. Males, he said, were 70 percent of the payroll and were affected by 63 percent of the cuts.

Commissioner Norton said that even before the layoffs, Federal officials had warned the city from time to time that financing for various programs would be cut off because of noncompliance with equal opportunity standards. She said that Mayor Beame had signed an executive order in 1974 committing city agencies to specific improvement programs.

Thus far there have been no Federal threats of cutoffs during the fiscal crisis, she said, apparently because the city is on record as pledging to seek a more equitable system in the event it ever resumes full-scale hiring.

But Deputy Mayor Gibson feels the situation is becoming critical. "We're losing ground," he said.

Francis X. Clines, New York Times, 20 February 1976

Student Opinions

Lydia Allen: The performance of a job must be the primary focus in deciding layoffs. I feel that as a whole people with more seniority in a job would perform that job best. Therefore, seniority, not minority, rights must be the deciding vote.

Grace Burrows: I believe that both sides have validity. I do feel that because minorities have been held back for so long *some* concessions should be made in their favor. Minorities were just beginning to make progress and now they will be set back once again. A person who's been on a job for a number of years shouldn't be made to suffer either.

Marion J. Buskin: I believe that an individual should be dismissed according to his ability to produce. A person with more seniority should not be allowed to keep his job if someone with less time on the job is capable of performing it better.

Robert Fuhst: I believe in seniority for job protection. If seniority doesn't prevail, then your job is based on how well you are liked and your freedom to express yourself is hampered.

John Giannini: Minorities should have a say in matters of layoffs, especially when a large percentage of the minority is affected. Minorities and senior personnel should share layoffs equally.

Dorothy Humphrey: I think there should be equal employment in this country. If an individual is senior in a field and satisfactorily functioning, he should remain employed. On the other hand, if a member of a minority can function even better, why not employ him instead? Production of work is what counts, not who performs it.

Rosemary McAleer: I favor seniority in employment because it is a system which does not permit discrimination. Regardless of race, color, or creed, if you have acquired more time than another employee, your job should be secure.

Marc Page: The longer a man is yoked to a job and its connected financial position, the more severe are the effects of being sundered from it. Seniority is the overriding consideration.

Megan Phillips: I feel seniority of employment is important in the job crisis because it is the only way of ensuring good and efficient services. Secondly, I feel the more mature one is in a job, the more the job becomes a part of one's welfare, as opposed to a younger person or a novice in the job, who only performs the job for the money.

Alice Reich: I think seniority in employment is an important consideration for the major reason that the benefits of seniority are hard-earned over the years. It seems unjust for a person who has given perhaps seven-eighths of his working lifetime to a job to find himself "out in the cold." Worse yet, the time of life when seniority would count is the time, very often, when other employment is unobtainable.

Robert Rivera: I feel that minority groups should be protected from job cutbacks. The reason is that the minorities that were hired were hired to fulfill the employment clauses set up through government laws. This law deals with equal opportunity for sexes and minorities to hold jobs and offices. Since this law has been recently enforced (in the last five or six years), why should minorities then hired be affected so tremendously by unemployment?

Jesse Rogers: I feel that minority workers for the city government should be protected, because it does not seem fair that, after waiting so long to get "in," they are so easily kicked out by the unions.

Peter Rossi: I believe the federal government should compensate the minority people who were fired because of budget cuts and lack of seniority. The compensation should be the creation of new jobs and not unemployment insurance.

John Seeback: Most jobs run on the idea that the last hired are the first fired, even if the jobs held by senior workers are costing the business millions of dollars. Also, the white majority of senior workers feels superior to the minority workers on a racial basis rather than on a performance basis. Many employers also feel the minority workers are expendable: they had to hire them because of the law; now they have a good reason to fire them.

Nancy Vitale: Men and women, after putting their time and effort (not to mention their skills) into a job for a great number of years, deserve the protection of their jobs in accordance with seniority. It is unfair to dismiss a person from his longstanding position to make a position for a minority member.

When you prepare to explore a variety of opinions about a complex and perhaps controversial subject, follow these steps:

1. **Summarize the facts of the issue:** Write a brief, objective summary of the issue under discussion (in this case, the problem described in the article). Your summary of this article would convey

both the situation and the two key ideas that are stressed. Try structuring your paragraph to contrast the conflicting opinions.

2. **Establish your own point of view:** Write a brief statement of your own point of view to suggest a possible direction for your essay.

The second step is more important than it might at first seem. Once you begin to analyze a mass of contradictory opinion, you may find yourself being wholly convinced by first one source and then another, or you may try so hard to stay neutral that you end up with no point of view of your own at all. You need to find a vantage point for yourself from which to judge the validity of the statements that you read. Of course, you can (and probably will) adjust your point of view as you become more familiar with all the arguments and evidence that your sources raise. Do not regard your initial statement of opinion as a thesis to be proven, but rather as a hypothesis to be tested, modified, or even abandoned.

3. **Categorize your evidence:** Label your set of opinions and establish categories. The statements following the article are all personal reactions to job layoffs and the issue of seniority protection versus equal employment opportunity. For each statement do the following:

   A. *Read each statement carefully and think about its exact meaning.* First, get a rough idea of what each statement says— do a mental paraphrase, if you like. You will naturally notice which "side" the author of each statement is on. There is a tendency to want to stop there, as if the authors' positions are all that one needs to know. But your object is not only to find out which side of an issue each person is on, but also to understand *why* that side was chosen.
   B. *Try to pick out the chief reason put forth by each person, or, even better, the principle that lies behind each argument.* Sum up the reasoning of each person in a word or two, a phrase— inventing a distinguishing label, as if for a scientific specimen.
   C. When you have labeled most of the statements, the next step becomes easier. *Look through all your summarizing phrases to see if there is an abstract idea, used to describe several statements, which might possibly serve as a category title.* (Some change in the wording may be necessary.) Once two or three larger group titles become obvious, you should consider their relationship to each other: are they parallel? are they con-

trasting? Then attempt to see how the smaller groups fit into the pattern that is beginning to form.

How the Three Steps Work

Following is one student's exploration of the New York City layoffs article and the fifteen opinions.

Step one: summary. Here the student identifies the article to which he and his sources are responding, summarizing the issue and the nature of the conflict.

> In a February 20, 1976, article in the New York Times, Francis X. Clines reported that the budget crisis had substantially reduced the number of minorities--blacks, women, and Hispanics--on New York City's payroll. The minority members laid off were the employees most recently hired by the city to meet federal minority employment requirements. Eleanor Holmes Norton, chairman of the Commission on Human Rights, described the situation as a conflict between "two competing and legitimate interests"--the traditional principle of union seniority protection and equal opportunity employment.

Step two: stating your own point of view (hypothesizing). Here the student ventures an opinion that suggests the possible direction of his essay. At this point he has not studied the group of opinions that accompanies the article.

> Both the competing interests are right in their claims, but there is a third principle that goes beyond both: in the name of fairness, the city should take the trouble to evaluate the performance of all its employees and dismiss those whose performance is inferior. Where a senior employee and a minority employee share the same performance rating but are competing for a single position, the city should help both employees and wait for retirements to make room for both.

Step three: labeling your set of opinions and establishing categories. In this step, the student moves away from the article to examine the opinions of others who have read the article, determining first the position of each respondent and then the reasoning behind the position.

Lydia Allen: The performance of a job must be the primary focus in deciding layoffs. I feel that as a whole people with more seniority in a job would perform that job best. Therefore, seniority, not minority, rights must be the deciding vote.

Allen: seniority ensures performance

Grace Burrows: I believe that both sides have validity. I do feel that because minorities have been held back for so long *some* concessions should be made in their favor. Minorities were just beginning to make progress and now they will be set back once again. A person who's been on a job for a number of years shouldn't be made to suffer either.

Burrows: evades the issue--both approaches unfortunate

Marion J. Buskin: I believe that an individual should be dismissed according to his ability to produce. A person with more seniority should not be allowed to keep his job if someone with less time on the job is capable of performing it better.

Buskin: performance should be the only criterion

Robert Fuhst: I believe in seniority for job protection. If seniority doesn't prevail, then your job is based on how well you are liked and your freedom to express yourself is hampered.

Fuhst: seniority deserves protection (without it employment becomes a popularity contest)

John Giannini: Minorities should have a say in matters of layoffs, especially when a large percentage of the minority is affected. Minorities and senior personnel should share layoffs equally.

Giannini: minorities and senior personnel should share burden equally

Dorothy Humphrey: I think there should be equal employment in this country. If an individual is senior in a field and satisfactorily functioning, he should remain employed. On the other hand, if a member of a minority can function even better, why not employ him instead? Production of work is what counts, not who performs it.

Humphrey: performance should be the prevailing criterion

Rosemary McAleer: I favor seniority in employment because it is a system which does not permit discrimination. Regardless of race, color, or creed, if you have acquired more time than another employee, your job should be secure.

McAleer: seniority protection is fundamentally the only nondiscriminatory criterion

Marc Page: The longer a man is yoked to a job and its connected financial position, the more severe are the effects of being sundered from it. Seniority is the overriding consideration.

Page: seniority protection is the more humane policy

Megan Phillips: I feel seniority of employment is important in the job crisis because it is the only way of ensuring good and efficient services. Secondly, I feel the more mature one is in a job, the more the job becomes a part of one's welfare, as opposed to a younger person or a novice in the job, who only performs the job for the money.

Phillips: seniority protection leads to greater efficiency, i.e., performance

Alice Reich: I think seniority in employment is an important consideration for the major reason that the benefits of seniority are hard-earned over the years. It seems unjust for a person who has given perhaps seven-eights of his working lifetime to a job to find himself "out in the cold." Worse yet, the time of life when seniority would count is the time, very often, when other employment is unobtainable.

Reich: seniority protection is the more humane policy (other employment often impossible for those laid off)

Robert Rivera: I feel that minority groups should be protected from job cutbacks. The reason is that the minorities that were hired were hired to fulfill the employment clauses set up through government laws. This law deals with equal opportunity for sexes and minorities to hold jobs and offices. Since this law has been recently enforced (in the last five or six years), why should minorities then hired be affected so tremendously by unemployment?

Rivera: the law requires that minorities be protected

Jesse Rogers: I feel that minority workers for the city government should be protected, because it does not seem fair that, after waiting so long to get "in," they are so easily kicked out by the unions.

> Rogers: minority protection is the more humane policy in the light of history

Peter Rossi: I believe the federal government should compensate the minority people who were fired because of budget cuts and lack of seniority. The compensation should be the creation of new jobs and not unemployment insurance.

> Rossi: federal government should compensate laid-off minority employees with new jobs (implication that city should not lay off senior employees in order to accommodate minority employees in their present jobs)

John Seeback: Most jobs run on the idea that the last hired are the first fired, even if the jobs held by senior workers are costing the business millions of dollars. Also, the white majority of senior workers feels superior to the minority workers on a racial basis rather than on a performance basis. Many employers also feel the minority workers are expendable: they had to hire them because of the law; now they have a good reason to fire them.

> Seeback: (implies that) minorities, as victims of union and employer prejudice, deserve protection

Nancy Vitale: Men and women, after putting their time and effort (not to mention their skills) into a job for a great number of years, deserve the protection of their jobs in accordance with seniority. It is unfair to dismiss a person from his longstanding position to make a position for a minority member.

> Vitale: seniority protection is the more humane policy

From this list, the student can establish five categories that cover the range of answers. His categorical chart follows:

Category	Source	Note
seniority ensures good performance	Allen Phillips	

Category	Source	Note
performance should be the prevailing criterion	Buskin Humphrey	
seniority protection should be the prevailing criterion	Page	(financial and emotional hardship greatest for laid-off senior employees)
	Reich Vitale	
	Fuhst	(employment would be popularity contest without it)
	McAleer	(truly nondiscriminatory policy)
minority protection should be the prevailing criterion	Rivera	(legally)
	Seeback	(compensation for past and present injustices)
	Rogers	
each group should share the burden	(Burrows) Giannini Rossi	(federal government should hire laid-off minorities; senior employees should retain city jobs)

EVALUATING SOURCES

Although you are obliged to give each of your sources serious and objective consideration and a fair presentation, synthesis also necessitates a certain amount of selection. No one's statement should be immediately dismissed as trivial or crazy; include them all in your chart, but do not assume that all statements are equally convincing and deserve equal representation in your essay.

The weight of a group of similar opinions can add authority to an idea. If most of your sources suggest the same reason, you will probably give that reason a proportionate prominence in your essay. However, the structure of your essay should not be governed entirely by majority rule. Your own perspective is the framework for your essay, and you must use your understanding of the topic—which is more thorough and detached than that of any of your sources—to evaluate your materials.

Review the hypothesis that you formulated before you begin to analyze the sources. Decide whether that hypothesis is still valid or whether you wish to change it or abandon it entirely in the light of your more complex understanding of the subject. Then, having reaffirmed your hypothesis or chosen another, sift through all the statements and decide which ones are thoughtful and well-balanced, supported by convincing reasons and examples, and which are thoughtless assertions that rely on stereotypes, catch phrases, and unsupported references. Your evaluation of the sources will differ from someone else's, but you must assert your own point of view and assess each source in the context of your background, knowledge, and experience. You owe it to your reader to evaluate the evidence that you are presenting, partly through what you choose to emphasize and partly through your explicit comments about flawed and unconvincing statements.

Your basic task is to present the range of opinion on a complex subject. You need not draw firm conclusions in your essay or provide definitive answers to the questions that have been raised. But you must have a valid thesis, an overall view of the competing arguments to present to your reader. Your original hypothesis, either confirmed or altered in the light of your increased understanding, becomes the thesis of your essay.

WRITING THE SYNTHESIS ESSAY

Although constructing a chart of categories certainly is the most difficult part of the synthesis process, don't neglect the actual writing of the essay. Spend some time planning your sequence of ideas and considering possible arrangements and strategies. Do your topic and materials lend themselves to a cause-and-effect structure, or definition, or problem and solution, or comparison?

Next, before starting to write each paragraph, look back over the relevant parts of your sources' statements. You may be fully aware of the reasoning underlying each point of view and the pattern connecting them all. But you may forget that your reader does not know as much as you do, and you may neglect to explain your main ideas in sufficient detail to make all the complex points clear. Remember that your reader has neither made a chart nor even read the original sources. It is therefore important to include some explanation in your own voice, in addition to quoting and paraphrasing specific statements.

If possible, you should present your sources by using all three methods of reference: summary, paraphrase, and quotation. Remember that, as a rule, paraphrase is a far more useful device than quoting. When you paraphrase someone's reaction in your own voice, you are underlining the fact that *you* are in charge, that the opinion you are citing is only one of a larger group, and that a full exploration of the topic will emerge from your presentation of all the evidence, not from any one source's quoted opinion. That is why the first sentence presenting any new idea (whether the topic sentence of a new paragraph or a shift of thought within a paragraph) should be written entirely in your own voice, as a generalization, without any reference to your sources.

To summarize, each paragraph of your essay should make use of several or all of the following elements:

1. *Topic sentence:* Introduce the category or theme, and state the idea that is the common element tying this group together.

2. *Explanation:* Support or explain the topic sentence. Later in the paragraph, if you are dealing with a complex group of statements, you may need a connecting sentence or two, showing your reader how one reason is connected to the next. For example, an explanation might be needed in the middle of the "seniority protects the worker" paragraph, as the writer moves from financial and emotional hardship for laid-off senior employees to the prevention of discriminatory job conditions.

3. *Paraphrase or summary:* Present specific ideas from your sources in your own words. In these cases, you must of course *acknowledge your sources* by inserting names into your sentence.

4. *Quotation:* Quote from your sources when the content or phrasing of the original statement justifies word-for-word inclusion. In some groups there may be several possible candidates for quotation; in others there may be only one; often you may find no source worth quoting. For example, read the statements made by Page, Reich, and Vitale once again. Could you reasonably quote any of them? Although Reich and Vitale both take strong positions well worth presenting, there is no reason to quote them and every reason to use paraphrase. On the other hand, Page's briefer statement might be quoted, since the contrast between "yoked" and "sundered" is effective and difficult to paraphrase.

EXERCISE 23

Read the following paragraph and decide which sentences (or parts of sentences) belong to each of the categories in the list above. Insert the appropriate category name in the left margin, and bracket the sentence or phrase illustrating the term. Be prepared to explain the components of the paragraph in class discussion.

Those who emphasize the upgrading of minority employment have pointed out that, since the hiring of minorities has been encouraged by governmental legislation only for the last few years, the seniority system will of necessity operate against those minorities. Thus, in the opinion of Robert Rivera, it is only fair that, during the present budget crisis, workers from minority groups be protected from cutbacks. One statement, by John Seeback, even suggests the possibility of a return to racial discrimination by white workers who have seniority and by employers, if equal opportunity laws are not enforced: "Many employers feel the minority workers are expendable: they had to hire them because of the law; now they have a good reason to fire them." In a related argument, Jesse Rogers points out that, since minorities have waited such a long time for decent job opportunities, a certain amount of preferential treatment might serve as a concrete measure of compensation. Neither Seeback nor Rogers emphasizes the abstract principle of equal opportunity implemented by law. Peter Rossi advocates a practical solution: the federal government should undertake "the creation of new jobs," so that, presumably, there would be enough to satisfy both groups.

Citing Sources

Throughout your essay, it is essential that you refer to your sources by name, for they are to serve as authorities for your explanations and conclusions. Although you should cite the source's full name, whether you are quoting or not, try not to *begin* every sentence with a name, nor should you introduce every paraphrase or quotation with "says." Each sentence should do more than name a person; don't include "empty" sentences: "Mary Smith agrees with this point." If possible, support your general points with references from several different sources, so that you will have more than one person's opinion or authority to cite.

When you have several relevant comments to include within a single paragraph, consider carefully which one should get cited first—and why. While it is not essential to name every person who has mentioned the point (especially if you have several almost identical statements), you may find it useful to sum up two people's views at the same time, citing two sources for a single paraphrased statement: "Mary Smith and John Jones agree that playing the lottery can be very enjoyable. She finds a particular pleasure in scratching off the numbers to see if she has won," (Notice that the first sentence would not be possible if you *quoted* "very enjoyable." Only one source can be cited for a quotation, unless both have used exactly the same wording.) If the idea under discussion was frequently mentioned in your sources, you might convey the relative weight of support by citing "five people" or "several commentators.'' Then, after summarizing the common response, cite one or two specific opinions, with names. (But try not to *begin* a paragraph with "several people"; remember that, whenever possible, the topic sentence should be a generalization of your own, without reference to the supporting evidence.) Opposing views can be discussed within a single paragraph as long as the two points of view have something in common. Radically different ideas should, of course, be explained separately. Use transitions to indicate the relationship between contrasting opinions.

Here is an example of a paragraph that follows these guidelines. Notice that it is based on contrasting views, with a turn of thought at the word "but."

> Most people would agree that children need money to buy the things that they want: candy, small toys, games, ice cream. A regular allowance will prevent children from having to go to their parents whenever they need money for small purchases. Edward Andrews thinks that a child needs money when he goes out to buy things with his friends; otherwise, he'll feel left out. Similarly, Edna Rogers believes in giving an allowance because the child will always have money when she needs it. But those who oppose giving allowances argue that parents usually start such a routine to keep children from bothering them all the time. According to Barbara Lewis, an allowance can easily become a means for the neglectful parent to avoid responsibility.

THE LIMITS OF SYNTHESIS

In synthesis, you begin with several separate sources of information—a group of statements, a collection of essays—and you proceed to analyze each individual point of view and each way of looking at the topic. In the long run, however, your object is not to present individual summaries of every source, but rather to incorporate them all in a new essay that is designed to represent a variety of opinion as well as your own point of view. Your thorough presentation of the topic counts more than the contribution of any single author. If the process of synthesis has been complete, coherent, and impartial, readers of a single synthesis essay can learn just as much about the overall topic and learn it more quickly than they would by reading each of the source materials.

The danger is that the sources may lose much of their distinctiveness and individuality. Synthesis depends not so much on distinguishing between your materials as on recognizing their similarities. The terminology of synthesis includes such instructions as "break down" and "reduce to common denominators." "Reduction," however, has a double implication: it suggests distillation through the elimination of impurities, but it also leads to a loss of substance. You should not be so intent on making your material conform to your synthesis chart that you ignore the awkward but interesting bits of information—the impurities—which are being eliminated from your notes. Synthesis is a method, not an end in itself.

The academic writer should be able to distinguish between material that is appropriate for synthesis and material whose individuality should be recognized and preserved. One example of the latter is fiction; another is autobiography. Assume that three writers are reminiscing about their first jobs: one was a clerk in a drugstore, the second a telephone operator, and the third plowed his father's fields. In their recollections, the reader can find several similar themes: accepting increased responsibility; sticking to the job; learning appropriate behavior; living up to the boss's or customers' or father's expectations. But, just as important, the three autobiographical accounts are sharply different in their context and circumstances, in their point of view and style. You cannot lump them together in the same way that you might categorize statements about the lottery or opinions about school uniforms, for they cannot be reduced to a single common experience. The three are not interchangeable; rather, they are comparable.

SYNTHESIS AND COMPARISON

Since synthesis cannot always do justice to the individual source materials, comparison might be a more effective strategy for writing about several full-length essays with a common theme. In many ways, comparison resembles synthesis. In both, there is an assumption that some fruitful conclusion must result from examining the ideas of several people, and there is also the same search for a single vantage point from which to view these separate sources. However, there is an important difference. While the writer of a synthesis to a large extent constructs a new work out of the materials of the old, the writer of a comparison leaves the sources as intact as possible throughout the organizational process, so that each can retain its individuality.

Moreover, the functions of synthesis and comparison rarely overlap. In academic and professional writing, you will use synthesis to assimilate assorted facts and ideas into a coherent body of information. When you are assigned an essay topic, and when you seek out several sources and make use of their ideas and discoveries, you are not likely to want to *compare* the information that you have recorded in your notes; rather, you will *synthesize* that material into a complete presentation of the topic. One of your sources may be an encyclopedia; another a massive survey of the entire subject; a third may devote several chapters to a scrutiny of that one small topic. In fact, these three sources are really not comparable, nor is your primary purpose to distinguish between them or to understand how they approach the subject differently. You are only interested in the results that you can achieve by using and building on this information. In contrast, the appropriate conditions for comparison are more specific and rare: you must have two or more works of similar length and complexity that deal with the same subject and merit individual examination. Equally important, you should recognize the differences between them; the differences will, in most cases, outnumber and outweigh the similarities.

Point-to-Point and Whole-to-Whole Comparison

Point-to-point comparison is very much like synthesis. The writer selects certain major ideas which are discussed in all the works being compared and then, to support conclusions about these ideas, describes the full range of opinion concerning each point, one at a time. Because point-to-point comparison cuts across the source essays, as synthesis does, the writer must work hard to avoid oversimplification. If you are focusing on one isolated point, trying to relate it to a comparable reaction in another essay, don't forget that the works being compared are separate and whole interpretations of the topic. Otherwise, you may end up emphasizing similarities just for the sake of making your point.

Here is a paragraph taken from a point-to-point comparison of three movie reviews:

> None of the three reviewers regards Lady and the Tramp as a first-rate product of the Walt Disney studio. Their chief object of criticism is the sugary sentimentality, so characteristic of Disney cartoons, which has been injected into Lady in excessive quantities. Both John McCarten in the New Yorker and the Time reviewer point out that, for the first time, the anthropomorphic presentation of animals does not succeed because the "human" situations are far too broadly presented. Lady and Tramp are a "painfully arch pair," says McCarten. He finds the dialogue given to the movie's human characters even more embarrassing than the clichés exchanged by the animals. Even Bosley Crowther of the Times, who seems less dismissive of feature cartoons, finds that Lady and the Tramp lacks Disney's usual "literate originality." Crowther suggests that its oppressive sentimentality is probably made more obvious by the film's use of the wide screen. McCarten also comments on the collision between the winsome characters and the magnified production: "Obviously determined to tug all heartstrings," Disney presents the birth of Lady's puppy "while all the stereophonic loudspeakers let loose with overwhelming barrages of cooings and gurglings." All the reviewers agree that the audience for this film will be restricted to dog lovers, and lap-dog lovers at that.

Whole-to-whole, the other major method of organizing a comparison, is more likely to give the reader a sense of each source's individual qualities. But unless the selections that you are writing about are fairly short and simple, this method can be far more unwieldy than point-to-point. If you discuss a series of long and complex works, and if you complete your entire analysis of one before you move on to the next, the reader may get no sense of a comparison and forget that you are relating several sources to each other. Without careful structuring, whole-to-whole comparison becomes a series of loosely related summaries, in which the reader must make all the connections and discover for himself all the parallels and contrasts.

Writers who choose whole-to-whole comparison have two ways of making sure that the structure of the comparison remains clear to the reader.

1. Although each work is discussed separately and presented as a whole, the writer should nevertheless try to present their common ideas in the same order, an order that will carry out the development of her own thesis about the works being compared.

Thus, whichever topic you choose as the starting point for your discussion of the first work should also be used as the starting point for your treatment of each of the others. The reader should be able to find the same general point discussed in (roughly) the same place in each of the sections of a whole-to-whole comparison.

2. The reader should be reminded that this is a comparison by frequent "cross-cutting" to works already discussed; the writer should make frequent use of the standard transitional phrases to establish such cross-references.

Initially, you have to decide which work to begin with. The best choice is usually a relatively simple work that nonetheless touches on all the major points of comparison and that enables you to establish your own perspective. Beginning with the second work, you should often refer back to what you have said about the first writer's ideas, showing the way in which they differ from those of the second. (This process can become extremely complex when you are analyzing a large number of essays, which is one reason that whole-to-whole comparison is rarely used to compare more than three works.)

Here is the second major paragraph of a whole-to-whole comparison that deals with critical reaction to the film *West Side Story*:

> Like the author of the Time review, Pauline Kael criticizes West Side Story for its lack of realism and its unconvincing portrayal of social tensions. She points out that the distinction between the

ethnic groups is achieved through cosmetics and hair dye, not dialogue and actions. In her view, the characters are like Munchkins, stock figures without individual identities and recognizable motives. Natalie Wood as the heroine, Maria, is unfavorably compared to a mechanical robot and to the Princess telephone. Just as the Time reviewer accuses the film of oversentimentalizing its teenage characters at society's expense, so Kael condemns the movie's division of its characters into stereotypical good guys and bad guys. In fact, Kael finds it hard to account for the popularity of West Side Story's "frenzied hokum." She concludes that many may have been overwhelmed by the film's sheer size and technical achievements. The audience is persuaded to believe that bigger, louder, and faster has to be better. Her disapproval extends even to the widely praised dancing; like the rest of the movie, the choreography tries too hard to be impressive. In short, Pauline Kael agrees with the Time review: West Side Story never rises above its "hyped-up, slam-bang production."

Whether you choose point-to-point or whole-to-whole comparison depends on the nature of your materials. Whichever you choose, begin planning your comparison by establishing a chart of important ideas discussed by several of your sources. If you eventually choose to write a point-to-point essay, then your chart can become the basis for your paragraph outline. If you decide to deal with each of your essays as a whole, your chart can suggest what to emphasize and will help you to decide the order of topics within the discussion of each work. These charts can never be more than primitive guidelines; but unless you establish the primary points of similarity or difference among your sources, your essay will end up as a series of unrelated comments, not a comparison.

SUPPLEMENTARY EXERCISES AND ASSIGNMENTS

This section contains a variety of assignments to give you practice in synthesis.

ASSIGNMENT 7

1. At the library, examine the issue of the *New York Times* that was published on the day that your mother or father was born. Most libraries keep complete microfilms of the *New York Times*. Ask your librarian how to locate and use these microfilms. (Alternatively, lo-

cate an issue of a news magazine that covers that week.) Select the articles that seem to you to be most interesting and typical of the period, and use them as evidence for an account of what it was like to live on that day. This essay should not merely be a collection of facts; you are expected to suggest the overall significance of all the information that you include. Remember that your reader was almost certainly *not* born on that date, and that your job is to arouse that reader's interest. If you like, draw some parallels with the present time, but don't strain the comparison. The essay should not run much more than 1,000 words: select carefully and refer briefly to the evidence.

2. Use a newspaper or magazine published *this* week and try to construct a partial portrait of what it is like to live in America (or in your city or town) right now. Don't rely entirely on news stories, but, instead, draw your evidence as much as possible from advertisements and features (like TV listings, classifieds, announcements of all sorts). Try, if you can, to disregard personal knowledge; pretend you are a Martian if that will enable you to become detached from your familiar environment. Don't offer conclusions that the evidence does not substantiate, and don't try to say *everything* that could possibly be said.

EXERCISE 24

In each of the following situations, would you give money to the person who is begging? Write yes or no.

1. A man is sitting on the sidewalk, dressed in clean-looking rags, with no visible legs and a box of pencils. There is a sign: "There but for the grace of God."
2. A middle-aged businessman approaches you, says that he is renovating the brownstone on the next block and has been locked out, and asks for the fare to get to his home where there is a spare key.
3. A woman, very untidy, but not visibly unclean, is standing quite straight on the sidewalk, entertaining the passersby by singing (very badly) at the top of her voice. It is not possible to determine whether she is drunk.
4. A small, adorable, smudged-looking child is selling small, untidy bunches of dandelions for 50 cents.
5. A man with a cane is tapping his way through a crowded subway car, politely thanking each person who drops change into his cup.
6. A man with a dirty rag is wiping the windshields of cars stopping for red lights. Clearly drunk, he is arguing with some of the drivers and

might prove to be a nuisance if he continues to cling to the car after the light changes.

7. A young boy is wiping the windshields of cars stopping for red lights. He is smiling and polishing carefully.

8. In a coffee shop, a sweet old lady approaches you at the cash register and, saying that she has forgotten her purse, timidly asks if you would lend her the money to pay for her meal.

9. A huge old woman, looking like a rag pile, is crouching on the steps leading to a subway train, monotonously repeating, "Give me a quarter."

10. In a stationery store, a small boy needs an extra quarter to buy a piece of oaktag. He says that the store is closing in five minutes and that, if he doesn't get it, his teacher will kill him.

11. A young woman between twenty and thirty, neatly dressed in ordinary clothes (jeans and sneakers), indistinguishable from the other passengers, walks through a subway train, politely and pleasantly asking for change.

12. Leaving a theatrical performance at the first intermission, you are approached by an ordinary-looking man who asks if he can have your ticket stub to see the remainder of the program.

13. A drunken woman asks for change for a beer.

14. A dirty little boy leads a slumped man, presumably his father, to the bus stop and asks for money to get on the bus.

15. A man dressed in a Santa Claus costume rings a bell at Christmas time; the name of the charitable organization is clearly displayed on a sign next to him.

16. A blind man holds a sign that says "Help me to get a seeing-eye dog."

17. A young woman in religious habit approaches you at the airport, blocks your way, and asks for a contribution.

18. Two young musicians, clean and neatly dressed, play music professionally and pleasantly, with a sign saying: "Help us complete our studies."

19. Your cousin is participating in a walkathon for a local charity and asks you to give money by sponsoring her.

20. A young man in faded army fatigues with a sign "I am a Viet Vet" asks you for money.

21. Chanting, a group of young people with shaven heads, wearing strange orange clothes, dances up to you, hands outstretched.

Consider your motives for giving or refusing charity in each case. Under what circumstances do you give money to beggars? Without mentioning any of the specific situations described above, write—a sentence or two—your personal definition of *charity*.

EXERCISE 25

Make up a set of materials for a definition exercise, like the set used on pp. 225–226. Think of a representative group of examples illustrating one of the following:

A. several possible occasions for parents interfering in the affairs of their children (i.e., *private* intervention);
B. several possible occasions for complaining to authority about another person's conduct (consider the classroom and the office environments);
C. protection *or* cleanliness *or* innocence.

Remember that your list of illustrations should not be restricted to those that would satisfy your own personal definition; try to provide the broadest possible base. For that reason, if your teacher approves, it may be helpful to work on this exercise with a group of students in your class.

EXERCISE 26

Read the following story.

Jack is in his third year of college and doing passing but below-average work. His mother has been insisting that he plan to enroll in law school and become an attorney, like his father. Angry at him for not receiving better grades, she has told him that under no circumstances will he get the car or the trip that he has been promised unless his average goes up one full grade. Although Jack has done slightly better work this term, he has been having trouble with his sociology course, especially with the term paper. Twice he has asked for a conference with his teacher, but Professor Brown has told him that he isn't being paid to run a private tutoring service. So Jack has postponed writing the paper and finally puts it together hastily the night before it is due. Then, Professor Brown calls him in and tells him that the paper is disgraceful and that he has no chance of getting a passing grade or even an incomplete unless he submits a more acceptable essay by 9:00 A.M. the next day. Jack tries to explain his situation and his mother's demands, and he asks for some more time to revise the paper, but his teacher is inflexible and says, "You probably don't belong in college anyway." Since there is no way that Jack is going to be able to produce the revised essay in time, he decides to salvage the car and trip by getting somebody to write it for him. He has heard about Victor, a recent graduate who always needs money. Victor agrees and, after some haggling about the fee, he writes an acceptable paper overnight. A few days after Professor Brown has accepted the paper and given Jack his grade, Jack gets a call from Victor, who says that, unless he gets double the original fee, he will reveal the entire transaction to Professor Brown and the Dean. Jack doesn't have the money and cannot tell his parents.

1. In your opinion, who is the worst person in the story? Write a few sentences explaining your reasons.

2. Here are some statements containing frequently expressed reasons for disliking each of the characters. Consider why each person considers his or her choice the worst person in the story. Then try to generalize about the ethical principles that lie behind each group of responses. The people who consider Jack (for example) worse than Victor are employing a particular set of values. What principles or beliefs are most important to each group? You are being asked to describe a set of *negative* opinions in terms of the underlying *positive* beliefs. Therefore, stress positive values. Try not to say, "The people who condemn Jack's mother strongly believe that she is too ambitious."

Jack's mother

Barbara Bailey: Jack's mother is trying to run his life. He is old enough to decide what he wants to do. But she is trying to make him be just like his father. She hasn't bothered to ask him whether he wants to be a lawyer. He might not even be smart enough to get through law school. She is forcing him to live up to her expectations; she is trying to live through him. Even if Jack eventually becomes successful, he will be unhappy and dissatisfied, like his mother.

Gina Britton: She is forcing her son past his natural abilities. She does not see him as a separate individual with separate needs. She should be happy that Jack is attending college and trying to get an education. But she doesn't seem to care about his feelings or his future. She is too ambitious.

Wallace Humphrey: Jack's mother should have understood that her son was trying hard to pass. If she had shown more patience and sympathy, he might have done well. She hasn't done her part as a mother, so Jack can't be a good son.

Kathy Harris: Jack's mother is threatening to punish him, not because she honestly wants him to succeed, but because she is so angry with him. In a way, she is forcing him into a desperate act. It is her demands which cause Jack eventually to become the victim of blackmail.

Mohammed Taylor: Jack's mother is very unreasonable. She expects her son to be like her husband, but they are two different people, and Jack should be treated as an individual. She is encouraging him to cheat. By bribing him, she is encouraging him to use bribery himself to get his paper written. How can he do well in his studies with a mother like her?

Summary: The people who condemn Jack's mother strongly believe ____

_____

_____

_____

Jack

Chris Bennett: Jack is the worst person because he is not doing the work for its own sake, but for the gain he will receive from his mother. Although his teacher refused to see him, Jack shouldn't have waited to write his paper. He could have sought help from another teacher or from the tutoring center.

Dona Morrow: Jack regards college as a bargaining institution. First he bargains with his mother over his material reward; then he bargains with his teacher as to how much time he'll have for an assignment; last, he bargains with his college acquaintance over money. Jack is too greedy to enjoy life, and he doesn't want to do any work.

Josephine Navarre: Jack allows himself to be placed in this pressure chamber by trying to avoid his responsibilities, by his use of deception, by not standing up for his rights, by his unwillingness to be held accountable for his actions or lack thereof.

Bernice Richards: As a junior in college, Jack should already know how to write a paper. He sought only one source of (unwilling) help—his professor. There's no reason for Jack to get so negative about Professor Brown; he should have realized that his teacher was the inflexible type, and he should have tried to write a good paper the first time. Jack expects everyone to oblige him without making any effort. He just waits around to be bailed out by someone else.

John Suarez: School is a responsibility, just as a job is, and Jack does not live up to his responsibility. He is now in college, not high school, so we have to assume that he chose to take the course that he's failing. What will happen when he gets to law school? Who will do his work when he's defending a client? Jack is just a helpless whiner.

Summary: The people who condemn Jack strongly believe _____
_____
_____
_____

Professor Brown

Jack Dougherty: Professor Brown is the worst character because he could have listened to Jack's complaints and pleas for help. He isn't doing his job. He's not getting paid to tutor, but he is getting paid to teach, and helping students is part of teaching.

Andrea Notare: This story shows that some teachers don't give a damn about their students. Professor Brown is not only offensive to Jack, with no justification, but he makes impossible demands. If he'd helped Jack with his paper in the first place, maybe Jack would have received a passing grade. To expect Jack to hand in an acceptable paper in twenty-four hours is impossible and unjust.

Mary Ann Smith: Professor Brown has placed Jack in a situation which has no reasonable answer. He did not want to help Jack and yet demanded a better paper. Trapped, Jack must resort to cheating. This is ironic, since a teacher is supposed to represent learning.

Raphael Alvarez: Professor Brown appears as a person who doesn't care for his students or his profession and who teaches only for the money. His attitude is as mercenary as Victor's, but since he's a teacher, his attitude is more hypocritical.

Summary: The people who condemn Professor Brown strongly believe
_____
_____
_____

Victor

Margo Droban: Since he had already agreed on a fee, it is not right for Victor to exploit the situation and ask Jack for double the amount. He is using another person's unfortunate position for personal gain. Victor is a greedy blackmailer, and there's nothing worse than that.

Denise Generale: Victor shouldn't have agreed to help Jack with the paper. Though he is not breaking the law by writing the paper, he is helping Jack to violate the rules of the college and, unlike Jack, he has no desperate need to do so. If he's such a good writer, he should turn his talent to a legitimate business and get a decent job.

Chris Pappas: Victor has made a deal with Jack and has reneged on this arrangement in an underhanded way. He is a shake-down artist.

Harry Murphy: Victor makes his final ultimatum to Jack of his own free will; he doesn't have to do it. Unlike the other characters, he has no emotional involvement in the situation. He is intentionally mean and cruel when he asks for that money.

Tom Natoli: Victor is a criminal. He has agreed to do the work for a set fee through a verbal contract with Jack. He goes back on his word in the end, all for money (which, as everyone knows, is the root of all evil anyway), when he blackmails Jack.

Summary: The people who condemn Victor strongly believe _____
_____
_____
_____

ASSIGNMENT 8

All the words in the following list are in common use and have either more than one usual meaning or a meaning that can be interpreted both favorably and unfavorably. Choose one word from the list as the topic for a definition essay, or, if your teacher asks you to do so, select a word from the dictionary or the thesaurus.

shrewd	clever	self-interest
curiosity	ordinary	respectable
capitalism	power	conservative

progress	cautious	small
eccentric	welfare	workman
obedience	solitude	smooth
habit	dominance	experience
politician	culture	cheap
prejudice	sentimental	privilege
ambition	revolution	intrigue
credit	aggression	fashion
genius	glamorous	enthusiast
duty	passive	smart
ladylike	failure	criticize
failure	self-confidence	obligation
poverty	influential	shame
royalty	feminine	freedom
competition	passionate	control
sophisticated	criticism	idealistic
masculine	imagination	artificial
peace	impetuous	luxury
humility	jealousy	perfection

Clarify your own definition of the word by writing down your ideas about its meaning. Then interview five or six people, or as many as you need, to get a variety of reactions. Your purpose is to become aware of several ways of using your word. You are to take careful and complete notes of each reaction that you receive. As you note reactions, consider how the meaning of the word changes and try to identify the different circumstances and usages which cause these variations. Be alert, for example, for a discrepancy between the *ideal* meaning of the word and its *practical* application in daily life. If one person's reaction is merely an echo of something that you already have in your notes, you may summarize the second response more briefly; but keep an accurate record of who (and how many) said what. Although your notes for each source may run only a paragraph or two, plan to use a separate sheet for each person. Your notes should include not only a summary of each reaction, but, if possible, also a few quotations. If someone suggests a good definition or uses the word in an interesting way, try to record the exact words; read the quotation back to the speaker to make sure that what you have quoted is accurate; put quotation marks around the direct quotation. Make sure that the names of all your sources are accurately spelled. *Your notes should be handed in with your completed essay.*

Each person should be asked the following questions:

1. What do you think X means? Has it any other meanings that you know of?

2. How would you use this word in a sentence? (Pay special attention to the way in which the word gets used, and note down the differences. Two people might say that a word means the same thing, and yet use it differently.)

3. Is this a positive word or a negative word to use? In what situation could it possibly have a favorable or unfavorable connotation?

In listening to the answers to these questions, do not hesitate to ask, "What do you mean?" It may be necessary to make people think hard about a word that they use casually.

An analysis of your notes should result in an outline of possible meanings and contexts. First, explain the most common meaning attributed to the word, according to your sources. Be sure to cite different examples of this prevalent usage. Then, in successive paragraphs, review the other connotations, favorable and unfavorable, making sure always to try to trace the relationships and common contexts among the different meanings. With your overview of all the variations of meaning, you are in an excellent position to observe and explain what the worst and the best connotations of the word have in common. There is no set length for this essay. Contents and organization are governed entirely by the kind and extent of the material in your notes.

ASSIGNMENT 9

Choose a topic from the list below; or think of a question that might stimulate a wide range of responses, and submit the question for your teacher's approval. (Try to avoid political issues and very controversial subjects. You want a topic in which everyone you interview can take an interest, without becoming intensely partisan.)

Suggestions for Topics

Should wives get paid for housework?
Is jealousy a healthy sign in a relationship, or is it always destructive?
Should boys play with dolls?
Is "traditional" dating still desirable today?
If you could be reborn, would you change your sex?
Does it matter whether an elementary school child has a male or female teacher?
Is there a right age to get married?
What are the ingredients for a lasting marriage?
Should children be given the same first names as their parents?

Is it better to keep a friend by not speaking your mind or risk losing a friend by honesty?

What should a child of (pick an age) be told about death?

Is it alienating to live in a large city?

How should "citizenship" be taught in the schools?

How should the commandment "honor thy parents" be put into practice today?

What, if anything, is wrong with the nuclear family?

Are students forced to specialize too soon in their college experience?

Should schools stay in session all year round?

Should citizens have to pay a fine for not voting?

Should movies have a rating system?

Should grade-school students be left back?

Should children's TV time be rationed?

Should parents be held legally or financially responsible for damage done by their children?

At what age is it acceptable for children to work (outside the family)?

Should high school students be tested for drug use?

Should hosts who serve alcohol be held responsible if their guests later are involved in auto accidents?

Should students have to maintain passing grades in order to participate in school athletics?

How should society deal with homeless people?

When should parents cease to be financially responsible for their children?

Once your topic is decided (and, if necessary, approved), interview at least six people, or as many as you need to get a variety of reactions. (Some of your sources should be students in your class.) Your purpose is to learn about several ways of looking at the topic, not to argue, but to exchange views. If you wish, use the following format for conducting each interview:

Name: (first and last: check the spelling!)

Do you think . . . . ?

Why do you think so? What are some of your reasons? (later) Are there any other reasons?

Why do you think people who take the opposite view would do so?

Do any examples come to your mind to illustrate . . . . ?

Quotation:

Take careful and complete notes of the comments that you receive. (You will be expected to hand in all your notes, in their original form, with your completed essay.) Keep a separate sheet for each person. If one of your sources says something worth quoting, write down the exact words; read them back to make sure that what you have quoted is what the speaker meant to say; then put quotation marks around the direct quotation. Otherwise use summary or paraphrase. Do not hesitate to ask, "What do you mean?" or "Is this what I heard you say?" or "How does that fit in with what you said just before?"

Make a chart of ideas from your notes and arrange the points in a sequence of your choice. Then write an essay that presents the full range of opinion, paraphrasing and, if desirable, quoting from representative sources.

ASSIGNMENT 10

Read *Hetrick v. Martin,* a case heard before the U.S. Sixth Circuit Court of Appeals in 1973. Write a summary of the point at issue, and then a brief explanation of your own opinion of the case. Next, use the twelve statements that follow as the basis for a synthesis essay. These statements were written by students in response to the question: "Can a university refuse to renew an instructor's contract on the grounds that she deviated from acceptable teaching standards?" Analyze each statement; label each kind of reason; and organize all the categories in a chart. Then write an essay that presents the full range of opinion, paraphrasing and, if desirable, quoting from representative sources.

HETRICK v. MARTIN

480 F.2d 705 (6 Cir. 1973)

McCREE, *Circuit Judge.*

This appeal requires us to decide whether the First Amendment prevents a state university from discharging a teacher whose pedagogical style and philosophy do not conform to the pattern prescribed by the school administration. The district court, sitting without a jury, held that the Constitution did not bar officials of Eastern Kentucky University from refusing to renew plaintiff's teaching contract on the ground of impermissible deviation from the teaching standards thought appropriate by her superiors. We affirm.

Plaintiff Phyllis Hetrick was employed as a nontenured assistant English professor at Eastern Kentucky for the 1969–70 school year, and during her first semester was assigned to teach two sections of freshman composition, one sophomore literature course, and an upper level modern drama course. Her troubles with the school administration apparently began when unnamed students as well as the parents of one student complained about certain of her in-class activities. Specifically, at one point, in an attempt to illustrate the "irony" and "connotative qualities" of the English language, she told her freshman students "I am an unwed mother." At the time, she was a divorced mother of two, but she did not reveal that fact to her class. Also, she apparently on occasion discussed the war in Vietnam and the military draft with one of her freshman classes. The district court found that even though the school administration was concerned about the appropriateness of these occurrences, "it does not appear that any of the faculty members felt that Dr. Hetrick had on those particular occasions exceeded the bounds of her teaching prerogative." The student complaints during October and November 1969 allegedly centered on their inability to comprehend what she was attempting to teach them or what was expected of them, although no students were produced at trial to testify that he or she had complained about or was dissatisfied with plaintiff's teaching methods.

Other conflicts between Dr. Hetrick and her superiors developed. She did not obtain her PhD until late in her second semester, although she agreed that she would do so by the close of the first semester. She covered only 11 plays in her modern drama course, from a textbook that had been ordered by her predecessor, and the head of the English Department, Dr. Thurman, testified that plaintiff had been told that she was expected to cover between 20 and 25 plays and that he thought the work load she assigned was too light.

In February 1970, Dr. Thurman convened a "secret evaluating committee" of four other faculty members of the English Department to meet with him. The committee, according to Dr. Thurman, was to evaluate all the nontenured teachers. Dr. Thurman recommended to the committee that plaintiff not be rehired for the following year because: her freshman class assignments were inconclusive; she was inclined to discuss extraneous matter in class; she lacked "a sense of camaraderie" and did not seem to adjust to the other members of the English Department; and she had not fulfilled her PhD requirements as promised. The committee voted to terminate Dr. Hetrick.

The district court found that these reasons asserted by Dr. Thurman were "supported by fact." However,

> the court finds from the tenor of the evidence, that the nonrenewal of Dr. Hetrick's contract was not based so much on those specific reasons, as it was on the feeling of Dr. Thurmond [sic] and the other faculty members of the English Department that Dr. Hetrick's teaching philosophy and the manner in which she implemented it were not adaptable to the achievement of the academic goals of the University.

The evidence to which the court referred consisted in part of plaintiff's testimony of the defendant's concerning what was expected of teachers at Eastern Kentucky. The school administration considered the students as generally unsophisticated and as having "somewhat restrictive backgrounds," and for this reason apparently expected the teachers to teach on a basic level, to stress fundamentals and to follow conventional teaching patterns—in a word, to "go by the book." Plaintiff's evidence, on the other hand, tended to show that her teaching emphasized student responsibility and freedom to organize class time and out-of-class assignments in terms of student interest, all in an effort, she claims, to teach them how to think rather than merely to accept and to parrot what they had heard.

After her termination by the University, plaintiff brought this action. . . . She asserted that her First and Fourteenth Amendment rights had been violated by her termination without a hearing or written statement of reasons, on an arbitrary basis, for making in-class statements about the war and the draft, and because of her beliefs and ideas. . . .

The district court concluded that the decision not to renew plaintiff's contract was the result of defendants' "concern for her teaching methods and ability," and was not prompted by her exercise of First Amendment rights. In discussing the scope of the protection afforded teachers by the First Amendment, the court stated:

> The First Amendment guarantee of academic freedom provides a teacher with the right to encourage a vigorous exchange of ideas within the confines of the subject matter being taught, but it does not require a University or school to tolerate any manner of teaching method the teacher may choose to employ. A University has a right to require some conformity with whatever teaching methods are acceptable to it. In this case it simply appears that Dr. Hetrick's teaching techniques were not acceptable to the University. The court is not in a position to weigh the merits of Dr. Hetrick's educational philosophy—it may be that her methods of teaching were and are more desirable than those embraced by the other members of the English Department—but the fact that the University decided that they were not and chose not to renew her contract, does not mean that her constitutional rights to academic freedom and freedom of speech were impinged.

In a memorandum opinion filed with the court's findings of fact and conclusions of law, the court elaborated on its findings in this regard:

> It is Dr. Hetrick's position that the non-renewal of her contract resulted from certain statements she made in her classes relating to the Vietnam War and the military draft. Were this contention

adequately corroborated it may be that relief would be proper; however, the evidence produced at the hearing leads only to the conclusion that the University's determination not to rehire was based solely upon concern for her pedagogical attitudes. Although the court is inclined to believe that the classroom inadequacies that Dr. Hetrick was alleged to have displayed—inconclusive assignments, extraneous classroom discussions, and insufficient coverage of suggested materials—were largely superficial and thus easily correctable, it is not the duty of the court to evaluate the wisdom of the University's decision not to renew the contract. It simply seems that Dr. Hetrick's teaching methods were too progressive, or perhaps less orthodox than the other faculty members in her department felt were conducive to the achievement of the academic goals they espoused. The court must conclude that a State University has the authority to refuse to renew a non-tenured professor's contract for the reason that the teaching methods of that professor do not conform with those of the tenured faculty or with those approved of by the University.

On appeal, plaintiff has raised two issues: does it violate the First Amendment for a public university to terminate a teacher because her teaching methods and educational philosophy do not conform with those approved by the university; did the district court err in concluding that the decision to terminate was not based on or influenced by constitutionally protected statements she made in the classroom, i.e., the "unwed mother" remark and statements about the Vietnam war and the draft?

With respect to the latter issue, assuming arguendo that the uttering of these in-class statements would be protected by the First Amendment, we conclude upon examination of the record that the findings of the district court are fully supported by the evidence and that plaintiff was not discharged because of any statements she may have made.

Thus, we are squarely presented with the question whether the administration of a public school may, consistent with the First Amendment, fail to renew a nontenured teacher because of displeasure with her "pedagogical attitudes." We conclude, as did the district court, that it may. . . .

. . . [Plaintiff claims] that what is at issue here is her constitutional right to "teach her students to think" and that the First Amendment protects her from termination for using teaching methods and adhering to a teaching philosophy that are "well-recognized within the profession" (although it does not appear that plaintiff introduced expert testimony on this question [Citation]). Plaintiff would thus have us convert the vague, inclusive term "teaching methods" into a specific, protected form of speech that cannot be considered by a school administration in determining whether a nontenured teacher should be renewed. In effect, plaintiff would have us substitute the First Amendment for tenure, and would thereby succeed in elevating contract law to constitutional status.

We do not accept plaintiff's assertion that the school administration abridged her First Amendment rights when it refused to rehire her because it considered her teaching philosophy to be incompatible with the pedagogical aims of the University. Whatever may be the ultimate scope of the amorphous "academic freedom" guaranteed to our Nation's teachers and students [Citations], it does not encompass the right of a nontenured teacher to have her teaching style insulated from review by her superiors when they determine whether she has merited tenured status just because her methods and philosophy are considered acceptable somewhere within the teaching profession. . . .

For the foregoing reasons, and the reasons advanced by the district court, the judgment of the district court is affirmed.

Stacy Brown: I certainly agree that the University was right to fire Hetrick since she overlooked the orders given to her by the English department. She only taught what was of interest to her and ignored her students' needs. They may have been very uncomfortable being forced to listen to stories and opinions not concerned with the school's curriculum. Professors who expect to teach in universities should be willing to make some sort of adjustment to the expectations of their colleagues in their department and of the school administration.

Robert Gold: It seems to me that Hetrick's competence was very questionable, as illustrated by her completing only half of the assigned number of plays and by the complaints of her students. While it may be true that the school administration used her incompetence as a teacher as an excuse to rid themselves of a radical element in their midst, this is pure speculation. A preponderance of the evidence points to the fact that she was dismissed mostly because she was an unsatisfactory teacher.

Regina Harper: It is troubling that a school administration would summarily dismiss a teacher without first giving her a warning about her shortcomings and then an opportunity to change her methods and conform to the requirements of the administration. It seems as if the court is willing to accept no jurisdiction over academic matters. It would also seem that Hetrick or any other nontenured teacher has few rights under the present system of justice. In the interests of fairness, I would have expected the school administration to have a list of guidelines that their teachers must follow. Hetrick should be reinstated with the understanding that she must follow these guidelines, and dismissed only if she then deviates from the established rules.

Douglas Hayes: There is no doubt that the root of the matter is in the contract, which did not make the University's expectations clear enough. Hetrick could not do what she did not know was expected of her or what she had not agreed to do. Hetrick therefore should have been dismissed only if her attitude and actions were clearly not in accordance with what was explicitly stated in the contract.

Carla Joseph: Hetrick's intention was to teach her students and let them teach themselves. She wanted them to have the chance to develop their abilities outside of a book. However, Eastern Kentucky University is a formal institution. They have rules and regulations that cannot be changed by a teacher. If all teachers taught whatever they thought best, chaos would result. One teacher cannot have the authority to change a system that has been the same for many years. For that reason, I think that the University was justified in dismissing Hetrick.

John Keary: The University has a right to hire teachers who they believe will best represent them and carry out their goals. As long as guidelines for teachers are provided in advance and agreed to by prospective employees, then the University can take action if these standards are not met. Hetrick was, after all, nothing more than an employee of the University. Their action in dismissing her was in no way a violation of her rights as expressed in the First Amendment.

Robin Lee: Each university should present an outline of its goals and expectations for students' progress to any person applying to teach. The qualifications of any prospective teacher should also be carefully examined, and perhaps there should be a brief probation period of a semester or two. After that, however, the teacher should not be forced to educate students using exactly the same pattern as other teachers. As long as the subject is taught effectively, the methods should not be arbitrarily judged.

Gregory Townsell: The traditional style of teaching that the University seems to prefer may have been effective when colleges were populated almost exclusively by traditional students. In recent years, however, more and more nontraditional students have been entering the student population. To encourage them to think analytically about ideas and to freely express their thoughts, teachers have to accept the challenge of discovering new methods. Hetrick recognized that a system designed for traditional students wouldn't effectively serve all her students. Inherent in the University's response is a prejudice against those who are culturally, economically, or socially different from the traditional kind of student.

Laurie Valcarcel: Any educational institution occasionally has to face the possibility that it has made a mistake. The University could have been wrong in its judgment of Hetrick's teaching style and dismissing her for failing to meet its standards. Everyone has an individual way of accomplishing things. Who are these professors to sit and judge so negatively? Since they are probably tenured, it may have been years since anyone has visited their classes and decided how well they can teach. It's quite possible that they resented Hetrick's youth and her interest in her students. She wasn't their clone; that's why they accused her of lack of "camaraderie."

Paul Woltmann: The University is entrusted with the duty of educating and developing the minds of the students who attend their institution. Because of this, they must try to maintain a level of academic standards and a certain serious attitude among both faculty and students that they feel is appropriate for learning. This means that they have the right to dismiss anyone who they feel does not conform to their standards. Hetrick had been at the University long enough to know what these standards were. If she chose to ignore them, then the University should not be blamed.

Grace Young: The University should not have fired Hetrick because they did not succeed in proving that she was an incompetent teacher. Nor did they ever spell out the reasons why they thought her an unsatisfactory colleague. Given this lack of proof, it is possible that she was fired because they disagreed with the statements that she made to her students or because they were concerned about her angering alumni or other potential donors with her controversial statements. Such a reaction is wrong. If faculty are not allowed to talk about controversial matters in the classroom, then the universities will be closing their minds to what is really happening in the world.

Larry Zeltzer: I think that the lack of a jury in the case was significant. A jury might have appreciated the fact that neither party presented enough solid evidence to be convincing. This country is supposed to be a democracy, yet, as this case proves, it is not. The huge institutions and foundations really run the country, and the little people who dare to act as they wish are dispensed with. At the very least, the University should have had the common courtesy and human decency to warn Hetrick (verbally or in writing) that her teaching style was not suitable and to meet with her to help her to understand how to meet their standards.

ASSIGNMENT 11

Read "End of Secrecy in Youth Courts Urged," and write a brief summary of its main idea. Next consider the arguments for and against secrecy for juvenile offenders, as well as any other relevant circumstances that the author of the article has not touched upon. Then write a paragraph of three to five sentences in which you argue for or against keeping a juvenile's court and criminal records secret. Submit your summary and paragraph to your teacher.

Your instructor will make copies of all the statements by members of your class. Label and categorize each person's response, make a chart of the labels, and write a synthesis essay presenting a well-rounded examination of the issue and its implications.

END OF SECRECY IN YOUTH COURTS URGED

1) In New York, a juvenile's criminal and court records are kept secret because state policy and law are based on the premise that confidentiality is essential to a juvenile's rehabilitation.

But now some legislators, as well as law-enforcement officials, legal scholars and judges, say that the secrecy provisions surrounding the criminal life of a juvenile should be repealed.

 State Senator Ralph J. Marino, Republican of Oyster Bay, L.I., a leading expert in juvenile law and the chairman of the State Select Committee on Crime, says the confidentiality statutes for some juvenile delinquency proceedings should be repealed.

In an interview, he said he would submit legislation this session to repeal the confidentiality provisions in cases in which a juvenile had one prior delinquency conviction. He predicted it would be an uphill fight.

From the schoolroom to the police precinct, from the courtroom to the juvenile jail, secrecy so pervades the system that even officials who ought to be informed about a child's criminal conduct are kept in the dark.

"Nobody has ever exchanged information," said Angelo Aponte, director of school safety for the New York City Board of Education. "The trouble is we lose kids in the system. If a kid is arrested and charged with a crime, we aren't told that. He is merely listed with us as truant. Kids can be involved with the cops, the Board of Education and the Family Court and none of these institutions talks to each other.''

At the same time, the schools are reluctant to share information with prosecutors. District Attorney Mario Merola of the Bronx said he was particularly concerned about the number of guns in public schools. Since last September, school officials said, 148 guns have been confiscated, a fraction of the number of guns the police say are in the schools.

''When I try to find out about these kids,'' Mr. Merola said, ''I'm told by the school system that there is a privacy issue.'' A student's education, personnel and health records are confidential. Only parents may waive confidentiality.

Like the schools, the police and the courts, correction officials refuse to identify teen-agers in custody. Officials at the State Division for Youth, which is responsible for the care and treatment of convicted juvenile felons, will not even confirm that a child is in custody.

 Juveniles quickly learn that the state is their best friend when it comes to keeping secret the nature of their crime and the length of their incarceration. The law permits a youth convicted of delinquency to say on a job application he has never been convicted of a crime.

First Juvenile Court

The belief that privacy is essential to a juvenile's rehabilitation goes back to 1899, when Illinois created the first juvenile court. The Illinois policy held that juveniles should not be stigmatized for life because they acted immaturely and unwisely or because they were victimized by adults who forced them to commit crimes. But this theory, critics say, should not apply to the tougher juvenile criminals of today.

The veil of secrecy means that policy makers—in the Legislature, in City Hall, in the schools, in the prosecutors' offices, in the Police Department, in the courts and in institutions for juveniles—usually find themselves without the information needed to shape policy.

Martin Guggenheim, a professor of family and juvenile law at New York University Law School, said in an interview that a revision of the confidentiality statutes was long overdue. ''We should eliminate confidentiality,'' he said. ''It has been a protection of terrible abuses.''

Mr. Marino agreed. ''The public agencies involved in the juvenile justice system,'' he said, ''have become hidden bureaucracies whose problems are beyond public mobilization for reform. Typically, the broad scope accorded to the doctrine of confidentiality has been applied and controlled by the very individuals and agencies which benefit from this secrecy directly.''

Mr. Merola and District Attorney Robert M. Morgenthau of Manhattan also want the confidentiality requirements lifted, particularly when it comes to the first courtroom appearance of youths just turned 16, the age of adulthood in New York courts in most cases.

Judges arraigning juveniles over 16 in adult court often have no information about the juvenile's prior record, even if he has committed such serious crimes as homicide or armed robbery.

"We arraign them in the dark," said Mr. Merola. He said the Bronx Family Court does not turn over juvenile records at the time of arraignment. This is so even though since 1976 the law has required that arraignment judges be informed of a juvenile's prior criminal record at the time the judge sets bail.

Family Court officials in the Bronx said that there was no mechanism to get the records to adult court, but prosecutors could get the records if they walked a couple of blocks to the Family Court.

The Legislature has not been unmindful of the information problem.

In 1976, for example, the Legislature enacted a law creating a city-wide juvenile index of criminal activities. Its purpose, the lawmakers said, was to permit officials to learn if the same youngsters were committing crimes in more than one borough. But although the city's Department of Probation finally created the index last year and updates it daily, its information is not available to the city's five District Attorneys. The Legislature did not specify that the material was to be shared with them.

Marcia Chambers, New York Times, 10 March 1982

ASSIGNMENT 12

Carefully read the following examples of embarrassing situations.

1. One day, I was traveling on a public bus filled with young children on their way home from school. One of the kids, a boy of about eleven years, used an indecent word. I was very embarrassed, mostly because of his age and because of the elderly people who were also riding the bus.

2. When I was a child, my parents used to lie about my age in order to get me into the movies at half-price. I was dreadfully embarrassed every time they did this, since I was sure that we'd be caught.

3. I felt embarrassed when I was in the supermarket and I said to my mother, "See those twins in the doorway; they're Nancy and Lauren. I'm their camp counselor. They're bad children, always tickling me." The woman standing behind us said, "I'm Nancy and Lauren's mother." Although she then joked with my mother over the problems of raising twins, I hid behind my sunglasses, mortified.

4. For the first time in my life, I was offered a lift in a limousine with a chauffeur. As I made what I hoped would be a grand exit, I stuck my foot in the wastebasket and had to have the chauffeur remove it before I could make my getaway.

5. I buy tabloid newspapers like the *National Enquirer* regularly, and try to hide the tabloid inside a regular newspaper in order to read it. If it falls out and anyone sees what I'm reading, I get embarrassed.

6. I was embarrassed when my middle-aged father took a group of friends with him to see his maiden voyage in a kayak. Of course, he fell in before he had even managed to sit down and, of course, he didn't know how to swim. Supported by his life preserver, he clung to the kayak and looked like a drowned rat. He had made a fool of himself.

7. When I was ten years old, I grew so much one summer that all my school clothes were much too short. Instead of buying new ones, my mother crocheted a couple of inches of hem at the bottom of each skirt in a matching or contrasting color. I wore those skirts, but I was embarrassed all the time.

8. I still like to watch kids' cartoons on TV. Once when my roommate caught me doing it, I tried to pretend that I'd fallen asleep.

9. When I'm in a restaurant, and the food or the service is bad, if someone at my table complains or sends back the food, I'm embarrassed.

10. I tend to feel some embarrassment whenever anyone compliments me. Somehow, if a friend comments on my clothes or my general appearance, I get nervous. It's almost as if I'm worried that next time I won't look as good.

11. One of the situations that cause me great embarrassment is forgetting someone else's name. This usually happens in the street, when I hear my name called by someone who clearly expects me to recognize him or her. It's not so bad when it's just the name I forget; but sometimes I don't even recognize the face!

12. I sometimes get embarrassed after a conversation, if the topic under discussion has been quite foreign to me. Because I don't want to seem ignorant, I tend to nod my head in agreement or to acknowledge that I understand. Once launched into this pretense, I find it difficult to retreat. Often I get away with it, but all the while I have felt inwardly that my facade of familiarity was transparent. If I only could say, "I really don't know about that."

13. I have felt acute embarrassment in the supermarket when I have unloaded a brimming shopping cart onto the counter and, after the cashier has checked them all out, I discover that I have less money than groceries. The people behind me on line usually whisper and shuffle their feet and look irritated, and all I want is to disappear into the ground.

Now, think of a few occasions when you have felt truly embarrassed, and be prepared to write a brief paragraph describing an embarrassing situation somewhat different from those already on the list.

Once you have been given a sheet with the additional examples contributed by you and your classmates, analyze all of the situations in both lists, distinguishing each example from previous ones; no two instances will be alike in every respect. Your object is to analyze each situation and explain why it proved so embarrassing. Ask yourself about motives, intentions, and responsibilities. Examine the circumstances in which each incident took place; for example, consider the role of onlookers (or the "audience"). Consider also the basic human qualities that seem to be involved in the causes and the consequences of embarrassing actions. Then label and categorize each anecdote, making a chart of your categories, and prepare to write your essay.

In your essay, support each of your topic sentences by describing some of the anecdotes from your list. Make sure that you explain how each example relates to the main idea being discussed. Also make sure that each illustration is clear to your reader (who, you should assume, has not seen the original list).

Either at the beginning or the end of your essay, try to present a complete definition of embarrassment, incorporating the ideas contained in the categories that you have established.

ASSIGNMENT 13

The sixteen situations briefly described below illustrate different ways in which information can be *censored* or suppressed. Read through them rapidly.

1. An act of censorship that may be justifiable is one which censors the obscenities that people sometimes say on television talk shows. Is it really necessary to have to curse in order to make a joke funny?
2. The friends and relatives of an extremely sick person might wish to remove all medical encyclopedias from the household to prevent the patient from learning about his disease before the doctors are ready to inform him.
3. Preventing jurors from discussing a case that is being tried before them is usually considered justifiable because they might otherwise be influenced by the opinions of others, which might result in prejudgment of the defendant.
4. During World War II, a commonly heard phrase was "a slip of the lip can sink a ship." Letters from sailors overseas were read to elimi-

nate any trace of location or dates. If the enemy had no knowledge of where or when a military ship was going, the chances of the ship arriving at its destination were more certain.

5. Aware that certain stock-market figures (or company reports) do not look promising, one person attempts to suppress that information so that his friend will not dispose of his holdings, and the first person can therefore sell at a profit.

6. The motion-picture ratings of all movies are examples of a kind of censorship designed to protect children from listening to profane and vulgar language and from seeing explicit sex and violence.

7. When the *New York Times* obtained copies of the secret *Pentagon Papers,* an account of the U.S. involvement in Indochina, and began to publish them, the Justice Department obtained a temporary restraining order against further publication, arguing that the interests of the country would suffer "immediate and irreparable harm."

8. In Spain, actors were prevented from putting on a scene from a play called *Equus* in which there is a naked couple. Although no one in the audience would have been forced to see the play, the government nevertheless prohibited that scene because of nudity.

9. A mother thinks it best for her young son to become a doctor, despite the boy's preference for athletics. She prevents her son from reading the sports pages at home and forbids him to play on the school teams. She believes that medicine is a more worthwhile and prestigious career than sports.

10. A cigarette company tries to persuade a magazine not to publish a new survey documenting the ill effects of smoking.

11. Some groups are lobbying to prevent the showing of X-rated films on cable television; they argue that small children might watch these movies without their parents' knowledge.

12. A mother whose husband has been brutally murdered tries to prevent any newspapers from coming into the house so that her small children will think that their father died peacefully.

13. A mother whose husband has been found guilty of tax evasion and required to pay a large fine tries to prevent any newspapers from coming into the house so that her small children will not know that their father has committed a crime.

14. A TV network removes from a news magazine show a story about a former president's alleged sexual affairs.

15. A third world country forbids TV journalists to film incidents of unrest in its capital city, saying the such films give a false view of the attitudes of its citizens.

16. A school board bans the teaching of Mark Twain's *Huckleberry Finn* and Shakespeare's *The Merchant of Venice* on the grounds that racial and religious stereotypes might disturb some of the students.

Write an essay that attempts to establish appropriate limits for the public and private distribution of information. Can certain facts, performances, and programs be "censored" without excessively curtailing the liberties of each citizen? In planning your essay, do not settle for dividing the examples into justifiable and unjustifiable forms of censorship. Instead, ask yourself these questions about each situation on the list: Who will benefit? Who is being protected, and from what? Or you might ask questions about the political consequences of suppressing information: Do we invariably have a right to freedom of choice? Should we ever be deprived of the freedom to form opinions, communicate information, and watch the entertainment that we prefer? When, and why? Choose the questions that you wish to ask, and then ask them consistently as you think about and analyze each example on the list.

As you explore each one, decide whether, in your opinion, suppressing this information or imposing this kind of censorship is justified—and why. Take notes to record your decision and your reasons in each case or to indicate your doubt if you cannot decide. As you analyze each instance, you will be engaging in three overlapping operations:

A. *interpreting* each situation;
B. starting to establish some common denominators for *categorizing* the entire group;
C. *evaluating* the various examples in order to develop your own definition of acceptable censorship and suppression of information.

Before beginning to write, make a chart of your categories. The paragraphs in your essay should form a series of generalizations characterizing acceptable and unacceptable systems of censorship. For your reader's information, briefly paraphrase—not just refer to or quote from—each situation that you discuss. (If necessary, add your own examples to those already on the list.) Use your paraphrased descriptions to support the topic sentences of your paragraphs.

ASSIGNMENT 14

Write a comparison of the following three reviews of *Rocky*.

or

Write a comparison of three reviews of another film. Your first concern should be the reactions of the critics, not your own opinion of the work; you are not expected to write a review yourself, but to analyze and contrast each critic's view of the film. Try to describe the distinctive way in which each reacts to the film; each will have seen a somewhat different film and will have a different understanding of what it signifies.

Use the *Readers' Guide to Periodicial Literature* and the *New York Times Index* to locate possible reviews. For films before 1970, you can consult James Salem's *A Guide to Critical Reviews*. Don't commit yourself to a specific film until you have seen a sampling of reviews; if they are all very similar in their criticisms or all very short, choose a different subject. If you have doubts about the reviews' suitability, let your teacher see a set of copies. Be prepared to hand in a full set of the reviews with your completed essay.

I.

The pop-culture present is exploited to excellent effect in *Rocky,* a delightful human comedy that will undoubtedly wind up as the sleeper of this movie year. Very much a latter-day *Marty* in its romantic story of two "losers," it is a strong, unsentimental, and deeply stirring affirmation of human aspiration, of strength of character, and of simple decency. And it is a very personal film, written out of a picaresque youth by thirty-year-old Sylvester Stallone, a triple-talent who served as star and boxing choreographer as well. It is brought to gritty screen reality by director John Avildsen, whose credits include *Joe, Cry Uncle,* and *Save the Tiger.*

Stallone, whom you may recall as the big, dumb marriage patsy in *The Lords of Flatbush,* portrays, in the title role, a blue-collar Philadelphia slugger, a boxer who's all heart and no steam, a neighborhood loan shark's enforcer with more compassion than muscle, a man very much aware of his own limitations and of the possibilities of others. He is honest about himself—"I'm not graceful, but I can slug," he notes; his pride about his nose, unbroken after sixty-four fights; his acknowledgment that fighting is for morons. He is honest in his choice of a woman, the mousy, introverted sister of a loudmouthed pal—"We're a real couple of coconuts. I'm dumb and you're shy," he remarks, wooing her with awkward gallantry and disarming candor. Then lightning strikes: the Muhammad Ali–like heavyweight champion's scheduled Bicentennial exhibition bout with a coeval white contender falls through, and the "smart" decision is to stage it with not merely a local fighter but, better yet, with "The Italian Stallion," as Rocky bills himself. It's a $150,000 payday for Rocky, and the exploiters gather. But Rocky, with the emergent womanliness of his truelove to sustain him, keeps his unbright wits about him. It is not victory he's after but merely a chance to prove, for the first time in his life, that he isn't "just another bum from the neighborhood." And that chance comes in a tough, unpretty, and ferocious fight sequence that stands with the best of the genre in its intensity of physical force and in its suspenseful staging.

The characters are as penetrating as the Philadelphia street atmosphere, with Talia Shire, hitherto *The Godfather* sister, radiant in her flowering under the warmth of respectful love, a fitting complement to the emerging dignity of Stallone as a self-described "nobody" becoming an individual in his own eyes. Burt Young as the girl's pathetically brutish brother, Carl Weathers as the pragmatic champion, Joe Spinell as the tolerant loan shark, and, above all, Burgess Meredith, simply brilliant as a has-been manager determined to pass on the knowledge he won by losing, all stand out in the excellent cast. Packed with moments of comedy, perception, and sensitivity, *Rocky* is a sincere, rousing little film that raises the spirits and gladdens the heart.

Judith Crist, *Saturday Review,* 27 November 1976

II. KNOCKOUT

"Rocky" could have been a sleeper, but it's been turned into a contender. A barrage of advance publicity has proclaimed this modest, low-budget movie an automatic blockbuster and its leading actor and screenwriter, Sylvester Stallone, a major star—the latest successor to Marlon Brando. Parallels between Stallone's own success story and that of the movie's title character, a persistent, golden-hearted boxer, have been widely noted—how the down-on-his-luck actor held out against proposals that Ryan O'Neal or Burt Reynolds star as Rocky and won the chance to play the role himself. Even the most jaded preview crowds, so the media reports go, have burst into applause at the film's closing credits.

The film is likely to leave a lot of moviegoers cheering—the sort of cheering you hear on a sunny day at a football game when the home team is trouncing its archrival. This is one of the few recent movies ("One Flew Over the Cuckoo's Nest" was another) to approach its subject with such black-and-white moral certitude that viewers know exactly which side they're on and don't mind at all the blatant way in which they've been manipulated. Crisply directed by John Avildsen, "Rocky" so skillfully slaps a modern, street-wise veneer onto one of the half-dozen oldest stories in the world that it can freely traffic in sentimentality while seeming to hang tough.

Rocky is a perennial loser, a two-bit boxer and ineffectual thumb-breaker for the mob in Philadelphia, who gets his big chance when the Muhammad Ali–type world champion (Carl Weathers) decides to fight an unknown as a Bicentennial publicity stunt. Simultaneously, Rocky—or "The Italian Stallion," as he calls himself—gets his shot at true love after he realizes that the shy spinster who works at the neighborhood pet shop (Talia Shire) is in fact gorgeous when she takes off her glasses. Any movie with the ad slogan "His whole life was a million-to-one shot" clearly isn't much concerned with the possibility of failure, and there isn't much suspense in either story line. But the film manages to draw considerable drama out of its gritty fairy tale—

thanks almost entirely to the huge, handsome Stallone and his colossal narcissism.

Stallone's gift for self-dramatization propels the action above and beyond its underlying banality. At heart his Rocky is that stock character—the gentle giant—but Stallone has endowed him with such vivid idiosyncrasies that the cliché takes on new life. Rocky talks to his turtles (Cuff and Link) and bemoans his line of work with the good-natured gruffness that Brando should have used with his pet pigeons in "On the Waterfront": "If you guys could sing or dance, I wouldn't be doin' it." He paternally lectures a tough-talking young tomboy in his grimy neighborhood about the perils of hanging out with "them coconuts on the corner." He goes into training so vigorously that he begins to worry the champ's staff, especially after they see a television report of him working out in a meat locker, earnestly pummeling a side of beef.

Throughout, Stallone is funny, immensely likable, and so consistently monolithic that his acting ability is difficult to assess: at times he seems to be giving not so much a full performance as a brilliant monologue. By the time the heavyweight bout takes place, "Rocky" has become completely engaging. The climactic fight sequence, carefully choreographed by Stallone (who reportedly modeled his stolid boxing style on Rocky Marciano's), is brutal and breathtaking, a series of cinematic body blows guaranteed to reduce even the most skeptical observer to a quivering fan. "Rocky" isn't really a movie about sports, but it works on the visceral level of a good sports event, generating blissfully uncomplicated excitement.

Janet Maslin, *Newsweek*, 29 November 1976

III. POOR FOLK

Rocky (United Artists). How's this for the story of a film? An Italian-American boy grows up in a dreary section of Philadelpha, is thin and spindly, develops muscle and good looks, tries to be an actor, flops, works as an athletic instructor at a girls' school abroad, comes back to be an actor again, has spotty luck, writes a couple of novels he can't get published, finds some small parts in TV and in films, writes a film script, is offered $180,000 for it but turns it down though his wife is pregnant and they are broke because he wants to play the lead, is offered $250,000 but still turns it down though his wife is still pregnant and they are still broke because he still wants to play the lead, finally gets low-budget backing (one million dollars) and the lead, makes the film, and, before its release, stirs up the biggest advance publicity fuss since Jack Nicholson blew in.

Well, that's the story *about* the film—about Sylvester Stallone who wrote it and plays the lead. The plot of Stallone's film itself isn't quite as good. Except for little embroideries of frankness and topical reference, this is just one more picture about a club fighter who "coulda been a contender" and suddenly finds he *is* a contender. There's the tough old gym manager who despises our hero because he had the gift but was lazy and who rallies to help him when the kid gets a title shot. And there's the girl (who takes off her glasses and, say, she's Beautiful) who pushes her way down the aisle after the fight to embrace him in the ring and say "I love you," and through puffy lips he replies "I love you," fadeout.

What must have attracted producers to this script was the fact that it hadn't been made in some time and that this latest version had some fancy touches. But not all those touches are credible. We can believe that Rocky—yep, that's the hero's name—works as a strong-arm collector for a loan shark. It's a little harder to believe that Rocky is picked out of a catalogue of available fighters to replace a disabled contender in a match with the heavyweight champion of the world, and is picked solely because of his nickname, the Italian Stallion; and is picked by the champion himself, a Muhammad Ali type; and that he signs without a manager; and that the whole time he trains for this much-publicized fight he has only one visit from the media.

It's all pure Movieland, with updates. Stallone is chesty and pleasant, has big liquid eyes and a Roman nose—an unrunty Al Pacino. (As author, Stallone had to write in a lot of lines to explain how this knockabout pug still had a high-bridged nose. It gets busted, we're told, in the big fight though we can't see it.) He has some appeal. He's a fair enough actor, though once in a while he slips out of mug tonality into something a bit more cultivated. I congratulate him on his double success although, so far, I'm not knocked out by his abilities in either way. (Most impressive moment: While training, he does a series of alternating one-hand pushups.)

The director is John G. Avildsen, not nearly as imaginative as he was in *Joe* or *Save the Tiger*. For instance, he begins hokily here with a closeup of a mosaic Christ on (I guess) the wall of a church hall, then pulls back to show us a savage prize-fight in the middle of that hall. Occasionally Avildsen finds a nice image, holding back in a long shot to let some action be neatly incised almost in silhouette. He handles the climactic fight well but not exceptionally, and he doesn't mind reminding us of other films. When Rocky and the girl, who is Nice, embrace for the first time, they sink to the floor of a dingy apartment like Brando and Eva Marie Saint.

A big handicap is the cinematography of James Crabe. This picture cries out—screams—for black and white. If that was impossible, then at least the colors should have been muted, not primary-postcard splotches. What we see contradicts what we're supposed to be feeling all through the picture.

What we're supposed to be feeling is grimness. The writing and the acting loll around in naturalism at its most sentimental, naturalism as display. Most of the cast were chosen for their ugliness (except Burgess Meredith, who is unusually restrained as the gym manager) and were encouraged to lay it on. No chance is lost in look or sound to be gross, minatory, repellent. I don't suppose things are any prettier in the poor districts of Philadelphia than in the other poor districts, but contradicted as the grime is by the gooey photography and phony story, this film becomes naturalism as romance.

Stanley Kauffmann, *New Republic,*
27 November 1976

Part III
WRITING THE RESEARCH ESSAY

Most long essays and term papers in college courses are based on library research. Sometimes, an instructor will expect you to develop and present a topic entirely through the synthesis of pre-assigned sources; but for many other assignments, you will be asked first to formulate your own opinion and thesis and then to support that point of view by citing a few authorities. Whether your essay is to be wholly or partly substantiated by your research, you will still have to start your essay by finding readings and choosing sources in the library.

Your research essay, or extended multiple-source essay, will depend on a series of decisions that may present you with new problems and contradictions. On the one hand, you will probably be starting out with no sources, no thesis, and only a broad topic to work with. Yet as soon as you go to the library and start your research, you may find yourself with too many sources—shelf after shelf of books and articles from which you will have to make your own selection of readings. Locating and evaluating sources are complex skills, calling for quick comprehension and rapid decision-making. At the card catalog and indexes, you have to judge which books are worth locating; at the shelves, you have to skim a variety of materials rapidly to choose the ones that may be worth reading at length; at the library table, you have to decide which facts and information should go into your notes and which pages should be duplicated in their entirety. In Chapters 5, 6, and 7, you will be given explicit guidelines for using the library, choosing sources, and taking notes.

As you have learned, in order to write a multiple-source essay, you have to establish a coherent structure that builds on your reading and blends together your ideas and those of your sources. In Chapter 8, you will find a stage-by-stage description of the best ways to organize and write an essay based on complex sources. But here, again, is a contradiction. Even as you gather your materials for your essay and synthesize them into a unified whole, you should also keep in mind the greatest responsibility of the researcher—accountability. From your first visit to the library, you must carefully keep track of the precise origin of each of the ideas and facts that you may use in your essay. You already know how to distinguish between your ideas and those of your sources and to make that distinction clear to your readers. Now, you also have to make clear which source is responsible for which idea and on which page of which book that information can be found—without losing the shape and coherence of your own paragraphs.

To resolve this contradiction between writing a coherent essay and accounting for your sources, there is a system that covers the familiar skills of quotation, paraphrase, and citation of authors, as well as the skills of documentation and compiling a bibliography. This system is explained in Chapter 9. Finally, in Chapter 10, you will be able to examine the product of all these research, writing, and documenting techniques: three essays that demonstrate how to write a successful narrative, persuasive, and analytical research essay.

5.
Gathering Materials at the Library: Bibliography

Knowing exactly what you want to write about is a great advantage when you are beginning your research. Your teacher may provide that advantage by assigning a precise topic. On the other hand, you may be asked to narrow a broad subject or to develop a topic of your own choosing, perhaps an idea that you wrote about in your single- or multiple-source essay, which gives you a head start.

Topic-narrowing should be a practical process. How much time do you have? What resources are available to you? How long an essay are you being asked to write? How complex a project are you ready to undertake? Choosing a good topic requires reasonable familiarity with the subject and with the available resources, which is why topic-narrowing will continue throughout the preliminary stages of your research. But even before you start work at the library, you should invest some time in analyzing your subject and considering your options. Here are some initial approaches to topic-narrowing that have worked well for students starting their first research project.

NARROWING THE TOPIC: BIOGRAPHICAL AND HISTORICAL SUBJECTS

Biographical and historical topics have an immediate advantage: they can be defined and limited by space and time. Events and lives have clear beginnings, middles, and ends, as well as many identifiable intermediate stages. If you are not ready to undertake the full span of a biography or a complete historical event, you may wish to select a specific point in time as the focus for your essay. You can choose to examine as broad or as narrow a period as you wish. At the same time you will be reducing to a manageable size both the scope of the project and the amount of research to be done.

Assume, for example, that by choice or assignment your broad subject is Franklin Delano Roosevelt. Instead of tracing all the incidents and related events in which he participated during his sixty-three years, you might decide to describe FDR at the point when his political career was apparently ruined by polio. Your focus would be the man in 1921, and your essay might develop a thesis that draws upon any or all of the following topics—his personality, his style of life, his experiences, his idea of government—at that point in time. Everything that happened to FDR after 1921 would be irrelevant to your chosen perspective. Another student might choose a different point in time and describe the new president in 1933 against the background of the Depression. Yet another might focus on an intermediate point in FDR's presidency and construct a profile of the man as he was in 1940, when he decided to run for an unprecedented third term in office. Or the topic might be made even more specific by focusing on a single event and its causes: What, for example was FDR's attitude toward atomic research in its earliest stages? Did he anticipate using the bomb?

The writer of such a profile attempts to describe the subject and explore his motives and his experiences. In effect, the writer's overriding impression of character or intention can serve as the *thesis*, the controlling idea of the biographical profile. The writer undertakes to determine (on the basis of the available evidence) which facts and details about the subject relate to the thesis and which are irrelevant and to present the evidence and the resultant conclusions to the reader.

You can also view a historical event from a similar specific vantage point. Your broad subject might be the Civil War, which lasted over four years, or the Berlin Olympics of 1936, which lasted a few weeks, or the Johnstown Flood, which lasted a few days. If the span of time is lengthy, you might focus on an intermediate point or stage, which can serve to illuminate and characterize the entire event. The Battle of Gettysburg, for example, is a broad topic often chosen by those interested in the even broader topic of the Civil War. Since the three-day battle, with its complex maneuvers, hardly lends itself to brief or simple narrative, you would want to narrow the focus even more. You might perhaps describe the battlefield and the disposition of the troops, as a journalist would, at a single moment in the course of the battle; in this case, your thesis might undertake to demonstrate that the disposition of the troops at this point was typical (or atypical) of tactics used throughout the battle or that this moment did (or did not) foreshadow the battle's conclusion. In fact, always assuming that sufficient material is available, you will find that narrowing your focus *too* much is hardly possible.

In writing about history, you may also have to consider your point of view. If, for example, you set out to recount an episode from the Civil

War, you first need to establish your perspective: Are you writing from the Union's point of view? the Confederacy's? the point of view of the politicians of either side? the generals? the civilians? industrialists? hospital workers? slaves in the South? black freedmen in the North? If you tried to deal with *all* their reactions to your chosen event, you might have difficulty in settling on a thesis and, in the long run, would only confuse and misinform your reader.

A similar "day in the life" approach can also be applied to events which had no specific date. When and under what circumstances were primitive guns first used in battle? What was the psychological effect of gunfire on the opposing troops? What was the reaction when the first automobile drove down a village street? Or, rather than describe the effects of a new invention, you might focus on a social institution that has changed radically. What, for example, was it like to shop for food in Paris in 1810? in Chicago in 1870? in any large American city in 1945? Instead of attempting to write a complete history of the circus from Rome to Ringling, try portraying the experience of an equestrian performer in Astley's Circus in eighteenth-century London or that of a chariot racer in Pompey's Circus Maximus in 61 B.C.

Setting a target date enables you to focus your research, giving you a practical way to judge the relevance and the usefulness of each of your sources. As you narrow your topic and begin your reading, watch for your emerging thesis—a single, clear impression of the person or event that you wish your reader to receive. Whether you are writing about a sequence of events, like a battle or a flood, or a single event in the life of a well-known person, you will still need both a thesis and a strategy to shape the direction of your essay. A common strategy for biographical and historical topics is the cause and effect sequence—why a decision was made or an event turned out one way and not another.

Finally, do not allow your historical or biographical portrait to become an exercise in creative writing. Your evidence must be derived from and supported by well-documented sources, not just your imagination. The "Napoleon might have said" or "Stalin must have thought" that you find in some biographies and historical novels is often a theory or an educated guess that is firmly rooted in research—and the author should provide documentation and a bibliography to substantiate it.

NARROWING THE TOPIC: CONTEMPORARY ISSUES

When you write about a historical or biographical topic, you can use the perspective of time to achieve a narrow focus by pinpointing a date and a point of view and by deliberately excluding all other angles. But when you work with a more abstract topic, the multiplicity of possible applications and examples may make it difficult for you to find a focus.

If you chose to write about the early history of the circus, you would find an assortment of books describing many traditional kinds of circus activity, from the Roman arena to the turn-of-the-century Barnum and Bailey big top. But because of the enormous increase in the amount of information published in this half of the twentieth century and because reviews and features are printed—and preserved for the researcher— every time Ringling Brothers opens in a new city, planning your reading for an essay about the circus today might be more difficult. Your research will be endless and the results unmanageable unless, quite early, you decide on a single approach. If your topic cannot be defined and narrowed through the perspective of time, you will have to analyze its component parts and select a single aspect as the tentative focus of your essay. You will find that many of the guides and indexes in the reference room contain not only lists of sources but also a useful breakdown of subtopics, suggesting possibilities for the direction of your essay. As an illustration, turn to the entries on education taken from the *Readers' Guide to Periodical Literature* later in this chapter.

You automatically narrow your perspective as soon as you begin to ask questions and apply strategies. How does this topic actually work? Is there a better way of doing it? What are its benefits? its dangers? Which groups does it especially affect? How is it to be compared with this or that variant?

Suppose that *food* is your broad topic. Your approach might be descriptive, analyzing causes and effects: you could write about some aspect of nutrition, discussing what we ought to eat and the way in which our nutritional needs are best satisfied. Or you could deal with the production and distribution of food—or, more likely, a specific kind of food—and use process descriptions as your approach. Or you could analyze a different set of causes: Why don't we eat what we ought to? Why do so many people have to diet, and why aren't diets effective? Or you could plan a problem-solution essay: What would be the best way to educate the public in proper nutrition? By building your topic on a controversial point, you could argue the virtues or defects of food additives, or junk foods, or convenience cooking. Within the narrower focus of food additives, there are numerous ways to develop the topic: To what degree are they dangerous? What was the original purpose of the Food and Drug Act of 1906? Would individual rights be threatened if additives like Nutrasweet were banned? Can the dangers of food additives be compared with the dangers of alcohol? On the other hand, your starting point could be a concrete object, rather than an abstract idea: you might decide to write about the Big Mac. You could describe its contents and nutritional value; or recount its origins and first appearance on the food scene; or compare it to best-selling foods of past eras; or evaluate its relative popularity in different parts of the world. All of these topics require research.

It is desirable to have at least one narrow topic in mind before you begin intensive reading so that as you start to compile your preliminary bibliography you can begin to distinguish between sources that are potentially useful and sources that will probably be irrelevant. What you *cannot* do at this stage is formulate a definite thesis. Your thesis will probably serve as the answer to the question that you asked at the beginning of your research. Although, from the first, you may have your own theories about the answer, and although it can be helpful to consider a possible thesis as you read, you cannot be sure that your research will confirm your hypotheses. Your theories should remain hypothetical and your thesis tentative until your reading has given your essay content and direction.

EXERCISE 27

The following topic proposals were submitted by students who had already spent two sessions at the library narrowing their topics for an eight- to ten-page research essay. Consider the scope and focus of each proposal, and decide which ones suggest *practical* topics for an essay of this length. If the proposal is too broad, be prepared to offer suggestions for narrowing the focus.

Student A:

Much of the interest in World War II has been focused on the battlefield, but the war years were also a trying period for the public at home. I intend to write about civilian morale during the the war, emphasizing press campaigns to increase the war effort. I will also include a description of the way people coped with brown-outs, shortages, and rationing, with a section on the victory garden.

Student B:

I intend to deal with the role of women in feudal life, especially the legal rights of medieval women. I would also like to discuss the theory of chivalry and its effects on women, as well as the influence of medieval literature on society. My specific focus will be the ideal image of the medieval lady.

Student C:

I have chosen the Lindbergh Kidnapping Case as the subject of my essay. I intend to concentrate on the kidnapping itself, rather than going into details about the lives of the Lindberghs. What interests me is the planning of the crime, including the way in which the house was designed and the kidnapping was carried out. I also hope to include an account of the investigation and courtroom scenes.

Student D:

I would like to explore methods of travel one hundred and fifty years ago, and compare the difficulties of traveling then with the conveniences of traveling now. I intend to stress the economic and social background of the average traveler. My focus will be the Grand Tour that young men used to take.

Student E:

I intend to explore certain kinds of revivalist religions in America today, to describe typical experiences, and to try to explain their interest and attraction for so many young people.

Student F:

I'd like to explore different definitions of quality in television programs. Specifically, I'd like to contrast popular and critically acclaimed TV shows of today with comparable programs ten and twenty years ago, in an effort to determine whether there really has been a decline in popular taste. It may be necessary to restrict my topic to one kind of television show--situation comedies, for example, or coverage of sports events.

Student G:

I would like to do research on several aspects of adolescent peer groups, trying to determine whether the overall effects of peer groups on adolescents are beneficial or destructive. I intend to include the following topics: the need for peer acceptance; conformity; personal and social adjustment; and peer competition. I'm not sure that I can form a conclusive argument, since most of the information available on this subject is purely descriptive; but I'll try to present an informed opinion.

EXERCISE 28

Here are ten different ways of approaching the broad topic of *poverty in America*. Decide which of the questions would make good starting points for an eight-to-ten-page research essay. Take into consideration the practicality and the clarity of each question, the probable availability of research materials, and the likelihood of being able to answer the question in approximately nine pages. Try rewriting two of the questions that seem too broad, narrowing the focus.

1. How should the nation deal with poverty in its communities?
2. What problems does a city or town encounter in its efforts to make sure that its citizens live above the poverty level?
3. What are the primary causes of poverty today?
4. Whose responsibility is it to deal with the poor?
5. What effects does a life of poverty have on a family?
6. What can be done to protect children and the aged, groups that make up the largest proportion of the poor?
7. Does everyone have the right to freedom from fear of poverty?
8. What programs for alleviating poverty have been most successful, and why?
9. Should all those receiving welfare funds be required to work?
10. What nations have effectively solved the problem of poverty, and how?

COMPILING A WORKING BIBLIOGRAPHY: LOCATING SOURCES

Preliminary research in the library usually consists of three overlapping stages:

1. discovering and locating the titles of some possible sources
2. recording basic facts about each source
3. noting each source's potential usefulness—or lack of usefulness— to your topic.

These three steps usually form a continuous cycle. It is not likely that you will be able to locate all your sources at once, and then record all your basic information, and lastly take notes on the usefulness of all your sources. Rather, you will have to move back and forth from card catalog and reference room to stacks or computer screen. Even after you begin to plan and write your essay, you will probably find yourself back at the library, checking a potentially useful source.

Because you may be looking at a great many titles and because, in any one session at the library, you may be at a different stage of research with each of several different books and articles, you should thoroughly familiarize yourself with the three steps.

Even before your research essay is assigned, you should familiarize yourself with your college library. Every library has a different layout, and stacks and catalogs use various kinds of numbering systems. Find out how *your* library is organized. Most libraries provide guided tours for groups of interested students. If such a tour is not available, make your own exploratory visit. Ask yourself some of the following questions: How are the books arranged? Are the collections for the different disciplines housed in separate buildings? Do you have access to all the stacks of books? How are the guides and indexes arranged in the reference room? Is there a list of all the periodicals owned by the library? Is there a map of the reference room on the wall? What are microcards? Where are the microfilm and microcard readers, and how do you locate and sign out the cards and spools of film? Is there a computerized data base, and do you have access to it? Get these questions answered before you start your research; then you will not lose time and impetus because of interruptions later on.

Since all libraries are arranged differently, there is no way that this book can tell you precisely where to find sources in your college library. However, there is a standard procedure for finding titles that you may want to look for. Suppose that you come to the library with a broad topic in mind: you plan to write an essay about Prohibition, the period between 1920 and 1933 when the Eighteenth Amendment prohibited the sale and consumption of all alcoholic beverages in the United States. What sources would be available?

The Card Catalogs

Libraries generally have three card catalogs: one organized by authors, one by titles, and one by subjects. Unless you have had a specific book about Prohibition already recommended to you, your search for sources might start with the subject catalog. The way in which this catalog is organized and the way in which supplementary information is presented on each card can differ from library to library. Some libraries do not even use card catalogs, but instead place all information in a series of bound volumes, with forty or more entries per page. Others have computerized their catalogs, enabling you to sit at a terminal and call up information on the screen. Whatever form a library's catalog takes, it will probably list only the holdings of *that* library; later on, if you need to use another library to trace certain essential sources, you may encounter different methods of cataloging. However, in spite of these variables, certain conventions apply to most catalogs.

Subject cards. Some cataloging systems have already broken down broad subjects into narrower topics by grouping the entries according to subtopics. For example, in one catalogue, "Prohibition" might be divided according to the following heading and subheadings:

Prohibition	three titles (cards) under the main heading
Prohibition—Great Britain	one title
Prohibition—Michigan	one title
Prohibition—Tennessee	one title
Prohibition—Texas	one title
Prohibition—United States	thirteen titles
Prohibition—U.S.—History	seven titles
Prohibition—United States	two biographies of Carrie Nation

This system enables you immediately to eliminate titles that are probably irrelevant (like Great Britain or the biographies of Carrie Nation, the temperance crusader, who died eight-and-a-half years before Prohibition became law) or titles that may be too narrow (like Michigan, Texas, or Tennessee).

Other subject catalogs list all titles relating to a single broad topic alphabetically under the one heading. You have to judge each book's usefulness by considering its title, length, and whether it has a bibliography, and by consulting the "tracings" at the bottom of the entry card. The tracings list other subjects under which the title is listed and in this way suggest the contents of the book. On the following page are three different cards from the "Prohibition" section of a subject catalog. How would you decide which title to locate first?

The first two cards would both have clear relevance to your paper topic. The three topics listed at the bottom of the *Ardent Spirits* card are in order of their importance in the book. Thus, Kobler's main emphasis is on Prohibition and its relation to American history; you would almost certainly find some useful information there. Judging from the bottom of its card, *Repealing National Prohibition* is concerned only with Prohibition, and judging from its title, the book focuses only on the end of the period you would be concerned with; thus, its treatment may be more detailed than the first book's. However, for a better overview of the subject, you might begin with *Ardent Spirits*. If you were interested in the connection between the women's suffrage movement and the temperance movement, you might want to consult the third title. But Prohibition is not Paulson's primary subject; it is highlighted on the card only because the card is filed under that broad topic. Moreover, according to the summary, the book consists largely of case studies; your interest would depend on what cases Paulson chooses to examine at length.

Cross-references and bibliographies. A single book may be useful for research on dozens of different topics. Placing a separate card in the cata-

subject heading
call number,
author
title, publication information
miscellany

tracings

HV
5089
.K67 **Kobler, John.**
Ardent spirits; the rise and fall of prohibition. New York, Putnam ₁1973₁

386 p. illus. 22 cm. $8.95

Bibliography: p. ₁358₁–₁373₁

1. Prohibition—United States—History. 2. Temperance—History. 3. Prohibition Party.   I. Title.

HV5089.K67   322.4′4′0973   73–78586
ISBN 0–399–11200–X   MARC

Library of Congress   73 ₁4₁

PROHIBITION

HV
5089 **Kyvig, David E**
.K95   Repealing national prohibition / David E. Kyvig. — Chicago : University of Chicago Press, 1979.

xix, 274 p. : ill. ; 24 cm.

Bibliography: p. 245-266.
Includes index.
ISBN 0-226-46641-8

1. Prohibition—United States.   I. Title.

HV5089.K95   322.4′4′0973   79-13516
                                                        MARC

Library of Congress   79

PROHIBITION

JF
848 **Paulson, Ross E**
.P3   Women's suffrage and prohibition: a comparative study of equality and social control ₁by₁ Ross Evans Paulson. Glenview, Ill., Scott, Foresman ₁1973₁

212 p.   front.   23 cm.

Includes bibliographical references.

1. Woman—Suffrage—Case studies. 2. Prohibition—Case studies. 3. Equality—Case studies. 4. Social control—Case studies.   I. Title.

JF848.P3   324′.3   72–92341
ISBN 0–673–05982–0   MARC

Library of Congress   73 ₁4₁

PROHIBITION

log under every possible subject heading would result in an overflowing catalog and an unmanageable system. Instead, most libraries use cross-referencing. A card is placed only under the subject heading that is most relevant to the book. In some libraries, either at the beginning or the end of the series of cards under the heading "Prohibition," you will find a card containing a list of cross-references. In other libraries, you will find available a large two-volume set entitled *Library of Congress Subject Headings*, containing a standard set of cross-references found in all libraries using the Library of Congress system. Here, for example, is the listing of topics that you could look up *in addition to* Prohibition:

```
PROHIBITION

    see also

LICENSE SYSTEMS
LIQUOR LAWS
LIQUOR PROBLEMS
LOCAL OPTIONS
PROHIBITIONISTS
TEMPERANCE
```

The information on the catalog cards can help you to expand your list of possible titles and indirectly to narrow down your topic. Look again at the sample subject cards and notice that *Ardent Spirits* contains a sixteen-page bibliography, and *Repealing National Prohibition* a twenty-page bibliography. To use these bibliographies, you would have to locate copies of *Ardent Spirits* and *Repealing National Prohibition* in the stacks. You would first copy the book's call number from the upper left-hand corner of the catalog card. In general, there are two systems by which libraries organize their books: the Dewey Decimal system, which uses numbers followed by letters and numbers, and the Library of Congress system, which uses letters followed by numbers and combinations of letters and numbers. (At the base of each sample subject card, the Library of Congress number, used as the call number, appears on the left; the Dewey Decimal numbers are centered.) If the stacks of your library are open to students, explore them until you find the books that you need. Otherwise, use the procedure for having the library staff find these books for you.

Once you locate *Ardent Spirits* and *Repealing National Prohibition*, you check either book's bibliography for more books relevant to your project. In this way, you can add to your own bibliography some of the titles that these authorities used in researching and developing their own work on Prohibition. Of course, you will have to find and examine these other titles before you can use them. Again, you check the author or title catalog, record their call numbers, and then find them in the stacks. If your library does not own these titles, you will have to decide whether any look interesting enough to warrant a visit to another library. If you are unable to locate a vital source in any of the local libraries, you might consult your college librarian about the possibility of an interlibrary loan.

Indexes

So far, your research has been confined to books, for the subject catalog includes no periodical references. You may have found some articles cited in the bibliographies of the books that you checked; but, if your research requires that you consult a variety of periodicals and newspapers—perhaps because your topic is a contemporary one and has not yet been discussed in book-length works—then you will need to spend some time in your library's reference room, using the *Readers' Guide to Periodical Literature*, the *New York Times Index*, and one or more of the subject indexes that specifically relate to your topic.* (For an essay on Prohibition, you would look in the *Social Sciences Index*.) To find a listing of the articles published in any given year—1984, for example—you locate the correct volume by checking the inclusive dates (1983–85) on the binding.

In the *Readers' Guide*, you can find articles taken from popular magazines with titles like "Why Repeal Will Be Coming Soon." Here's what a *Readers' Guide* entry looks like:

After Prohibition, what? L. Rogers. New Repub. 73:91–99 D7 '32

As you can see, the title of the article comes first; then the author's name; then the title of the periodical (often abbreviated); then the volume number, followed by a colon and the pages on which the article appears; then the month, abbreviated, the day, and the year.

In the *Times Index*, you can find topical news articles, such as "Rise in Gangland Murders Linked to Bootlegging." Here is a typical *Times Index* listing for 1933:

25 Buffalo speakeasies and stills raided, S 24, IV, 6:6

The title of the article is followed by the date (24 September), the section of the newspaper (4, indicated in Roman numerals to avoid confusion), the page (6), and the column (the sixth from left).

---

*See Appendix A for a list of the most commonly used periodical indexes.

Since these indexes have to cram a great deal of information into a relatively small space, they cannot afford to have too many double and triple entries, and they therefore make extensive use of cross-referencing. In the *Readers' Guide* for 1932–33, for example, you would find four columns of articles about Prohibition, first divided into regions and then into a series of headings that include "economic aspects," "enforcement," "political aspects," "repeal," and "results." At the very beginning of the list, the reader is referred to possible headlines elsewhere in the *Guide*:

See also
alcohol
liquor problem
liquor traffic
liquor

It is your job to check any of the other headings that seem relevant to your topic. Occasionally, an index will not provide any "See also" lists. In a recent *Social Sciences Index*, for example, you would have to look under the broad heading of "Alcohol" to find an article about Prohibition, such as "Social Interaction in the Speakeasy of 1930." Figuring out which subjects to look up requires some ingenuity and imagination, but writing a successful research essay depends on your doing your research thoroughly, and checking a reasonable number of reference works, bibliographies, indexes, and other sources. If you wonder how many is a "reasonable" number, report your progress to your instructor or a librarian, and ask for comments.

Summary

After you look in card catalogs, bibliographies, and indexes, and perhaps check your library's computerized data base, as well as consulting a reference librarian, your search will probably lead you to list and locate the following *kinds* of sources for an essay on Prohibition:

economic and social histories for a general background of the period
congressional reports, political analyses, and legal studies of the Eighteenth Amendment
contemporary newspaper accounts, magazine articles, and memoirs describing the everyday effects of the ban on liquor
exposés of bootlegging and other criminal activities associated with Prohibition
biographies of prominent people in the Prohibition Party
philosophy and psychology books and articles dealing with recurring forms of puritanism

At the beginning, uncertain about the precise scope and focus of your essay, you may find it difficult to decide which of these sources will ultimately be useful to you. What are you going to write about? Will you stress the reasons for the movement toward Prohibition? the religious influence? the economic background? Prohibition as a consequence of social changes in the era after World War I? the link between Prohibition and organized crime? the effects of Prohibition on recreation and leisure time? the constitutionality of the Eighteenth Amendment? the rituals of illegal drinking? the relationship between the prohibition of alcohol in the twenties and the prohibition of marijuana decades later? the convivial scene in bars all over the nation on the day Prohibition was repealed?

Unless you know from the very beginning precisely what most interests you about your broad topic, you cannot afford to ignore very many of the titles that you see listed. Nor can you afford to stop the search for titles in order to examine each of the sources in detail. For the Prohibition paper you will at this stage still be trying to form an overall picture of Prohibition, to explore the topic's possibilities, and to estimate the amount of material that is available and the approximate amount of time that you will need to spend on research. At the beginning, then, if you have an hour or two to spend in the library, you should spend that time at the card catalog or in the reference room, rounding out your list of possible sources and narrowing down your topic, rather than reading extensively (and taking notes) in any single work. Later on, after you have compiled a working bibliography, you will begin the "reading" part of your research, starting with the most comprehensive source. Certainly, you will want to check the stacks as soon as possible to find out if the most likely titles are available and, if they are, to check them out and take them home. But, at this point, don't spend too much time with each book. At the most, you will want to look at a book's table of contents, index, and bibliography, or flip through an article in order to gain a rough idea of its scope and relevance.

COMPILING A WORKING BIBLIOGRAPHY: RECORDING BASIC INFORMATION

A bibliography is loosely defined as a complete list of all the works that you use in preparing your essay. In practice, however, there are really two kinds of bibliography, corresponding to the stages of your research. Your *preliminary* or *working bibliography* consists of all the sources that you learn about and perhaps examine as you discover what material is available and as you develop your ideas about the topic. The *final bibliography* consists of the material that you will actually use in the writing of your essay. (For a discussion of the final bibliography, see Chapter 9.)

Very precise information is needed for all the entries in your bibliography. Therefore, from the very beginning of your research, as you use the card catalog and the indexes, you should carefully copy down all facts that you may need later on in order to construct a complete and correct final bibliography. These notes can be written either on index cards or in a separate section of your notebook. The major advantage of index cards is that, with one entry per card, the stack can be easily organized and alphabetized when you are assembling your final bibliography. But it really does not matter which method you use; what is important is that your records be accurate, readable, and reasonably consistent, so that, several weeks later, when you are working on your bibliography for submission with your essay, you will be able to transform your notes into the correct format easily. Even though you are at the beginning of your research and cannot be sure which sources will actually become important, make your notes legible and do not abbreviate unless you are aware of the significance of each symbol. If you cannot read your writing, you will have to return to the library to check your references, probably at a point when you can least spare the time.

As you work from the card catalog or from one of the indexes or from a bibliography, start a fresh card or a fresh place on the page for each new item. It may help to assign a number to each new source. If you are using a notebook page, remember to leave enough space for comments about the work's potential usefulness.

Include the following facts in the notes for your bibliography:

For books:

the author's full name
the exact title, underlined
the name of the editor(s) (for an anthology) or the name of the translator (for a work first written in a foreign language)
the date and place of publication and the name of the publisher
the original date of publication and the date of the new edition or reprint, if the book has been reissued
the inclusive page numbers if you are planning to use only a single chapter or section of the book
the call number, so that you will not need to return to the catalog if you decide to locate the book or periodical

For articles:

the author's full name
the title of the article, in quotation marks
the exact title of the periodical, underlined
the volume number and the date of the issue
the inclusive page numbers of the article

Later, when you locate the book or magazine article itself, remember to check all these facts by examining the front and back of the title page of the book or the first page of the article and the title page of the periodical or newspaper. The *Readers' Guide* does not always include the author's name in its entries, so remember to note it down. Check the spelling of the author's name; find out if the book had an editor; make sure that the place of publication was, for example, Cambridge, Massachusetts, and not Cambridge, England.

Here are two sample note cards, each containing basic information about one of the works about Prohibition mentioned earlier in this chapter.

Ross E. Paulson

JF
848
.P3

Women's Suffrage and Prohibition: a comparative study of equality and social control

Glenview, Illinois / Scott, Foresman

1973

212 pp.

Prohibition = Secondary Subject

L. Rogers

"After Prohibition, what?"

New Republic

pp. 91-9

(Reader's Guide)

Notice that the first card contains a note questioning the book's relevance to the topic, and the second specifies the *Readers' Guide to Periodical Literature* as the source of the article.

To show you what information looks like when it is placed in a conventional format, here is a final bibliography for the Prohibition essay, comprising the five works listed so far:

List of Works Consulted

Kobler, John. Ardent Spirits: The Rise and Fall of Prohibition. New York: Putnam, 1973.

Kyvig, David E. Repealing National Prohibition. Chicago: Univ. of Chicago Press, 1979.

Paulson, Ross E. Women's Suffrage and Prohibition: A Comparative Study of Equality and Social Control. Glenview, Ill.: Scott, Foresman, 1973.

Rogers, L. "After Prohibition, What?" New Republic 7 Dec. 1932:91-99.

"25 Buffalo Speakeasies and Stills Raided." New York Times 24 Sept. 1933, sec. 4:6.

Research is open-ended. You cannot judge in advance how many sources will provide adequate documentation for your topic. You need to include enough sources to support your thesis convincingly, yet not so many that you treat them superficially. Your teacher may stipulate that you consult at least five authorities, or ten, or fifteen; but that recommendation is probably an artificial (though realistic) one, intended to make sure that each student in the class does a reasonable and roughly equal amount of research. Certainly, without guidelines, your preliminary list of sources could conceivably reach and exceed the dozens, even the hundreds. If you wished, you could copy out whole trays of the card catalog, or whole pages of the *Readers' Guide*, or whole rows of titles on the shelves; but you would have little knowledge of the contents or the relevance of your "Works Cited." An endless list of sources does not automatically demonstrate your competence in research.

What is important is not quantity, but usefulness for your purpose. A good grade for a research essay is likely to depend on the inclusion of a few crucial sources, the works of well-known authorities, whose evidence or points of view must be considered if your essay is to be thoroughly documented. As you will learn in the next chapter, distinguishing those useful sources from the irrelevant ones requires skill. Thus, it is not enough to have compiled the suggested number of source materials if the works on your list are minor or trivial or peripheral to the topic. Never settle for the first five sources that come into your hands. Your research must continue until you are satisfied that you have consulted all those worth reading.

TAKING NOTES ABOUT THE USEFULNESS
OF EACH SOURCE

In addition to the factual information that you will need for your bibliography, you should also write down a few preliminary notes about the probable usefulness of each work. This third step takes place *after* you have located and briefly examined a source. These are not notes that you will later use in writing your essay, but, rather, comments that suggest which sources merit more thorough examination and note-taking at a later stage of your research. You simply jot down your initial assessment of the work's scope and contents, strong or weak points, and possible relevance to your topic, as well as any rough impressions about the author's reliability as a source. Often, you can write down such a comment just by examining the table of contents and leafing through the pages. (In such a case, however, the note will probably be negative since you won't be finding anything that makes you want to read further and more thoroughly.) *Don't trust to your memory.* If you neglect to note your reaction, weeks later you may find yourself wondering whether to go over to the library and check what seems to be a likely looking title.

Keeping track of your sources through your preliminary comments also enables you to review the progress of your research. You can glance through your notes after each trip to the library and decide whether your topic and (perhaps) your thesis are taking shape, whether your sources are going to be numerous and thorough enough to support an essay on that topic and thesis, and whether you ought to drop a few titles from your working bibliography or go back to the card catalog and reference room to add a few new authors to your list.

Finally, your preliminary notes will be useful when it comes time to write up your final bibliography, especially if you plan to annotate it. *Annotation* means that you insert a short comment after each item in your bibliography, describing the work's scope and specific focus and suggesting its relevance and usefulness to the development of your topic. The notes are usually only a sentence or two, just enough to help your reader judge whether the source will be useful or not. In the following annotated bibliography for an essay on politics and the Olympics, the notes for each entry were taken, with few changes, from the earlier working bibliography.

An Annotated List of Sources Consulted

Espey, Richard. The Politics of the Olympic Games. Berkeley:
    University of California Press, 1979. Espey spends 8 or so pages
    on each of the modern Olympics up to 1976, with an emphasis on

political motivation and the shift of emphasis from the athlete
to the nation.

Kieran, John, and Arthur Daley. <u>The Story of the Olympic Games 776
B.C. - 1960 A.D.</u> Rev. Ed. Philadelphia: Lippincott, 1961.
Approximately 12 pages on each of the games up to 1960, with
concise and interesting narrative, but little interest in politics. The authors assume that the Olympics will always continue
as they have.

Ludwig, Jack. <u>Five Ring Circus.</u> Toronto: Doubleday Canada, 1976.
A lengthy account of the Montreal 1976 Olympics, with anecdotes. Most interesting on the Canadian commercial and political role in staging the Olympics.

Mandell, Richard D. <u>The First Modern Olympics.</u> Berkeley: University of California Press, 1976. A detailed account of the reasons and preparations for reviving the Olympics in Athens in
1896, with an emphasis on Coubertin's personality and philosophy.

Williams, Roger M. "Moscow '80, Playing for Political Points."
<u>Saturday Review</u> 1 September 1979: 12-16. A detailed analysis of
political and nationalistic interests in the Moscow Olympics,
with emphasis on Soviet motivation.

EXERCISE 29

On the following pages are reproduced some entries from the *Readers'
Guide to Periodical Literature (1984–85)* under the comprehensive
heading "Education." Select one article that appears to relate directly to
the topic "How can the nation begin to reform its public school system?" Locate and examine the article. Then prepare an index card containing all the information necessary for a bibliographical entry. (Remember that, although the information is the same, the form used for
entries in the *Readers' Guide* is *not* the form used in the standard bibliography of a research essay; do not simply copy out the entry from the
Guide, but make a list of the facts, indicating what each number or abbreviation signifies. See p. 272 for a sample note card.) Add a few sentences describing the article's scope, focus, difficulty, and usefulness for
this topic.

America's schools: a panorama of excellence [special section] il *Todays
Educ* p3–35 '84/'85

Education [school reform; address, August 8, 1984] M. Lawrence, *Vital
Speeches Day* 51:37–8 N 1 '84

Education. D. Kaercher. See occasional issues of Better Homes and
Gardens

Education and the Sony war [school reform for political and economic needs] J. H. Spring. bibl f il *Phi Delta Kappan* 65:534–7 Ap '84

The education boom. L. Solorzano. il *U S News World Rep* 96:50–1 Mr 19 '84

Education in America [special issue] il *Sch Update* 116:cover + F 3 '84

Educational partnership and the dilemmas of school reform [adaptation of address, October 1983] D. S. Seeley. bibl f il *Phi Delta Kappan* 65:383–8 F '84

Educators' quiz. M. Rosenberg. See issues of The Education Digest

Feeding our myths. D. Meier. *Commonweal* 111:536–8 O 5 '84

The future of public education. L. J. Chamberlin. il *USA Today* 113:64–6 Jl '84

Good news from a study of school improvement. S. F. Loucks. *Educ Dig* 49:14–15 My '84

The great school reform hoax. G. E. Leonard. il *Esquire* 101:47–52 + Ap '84

Improving our schools [address, December 7, 1983] R. Graham. *Vital Speeches Day* 50:198–9 Ja 15 '84

Improving public education: where the crisis really is [address, January 10, 1984] W. Scheider. *Educ Dig* 49:10–11 Ap '84

Improving school quality. U. V. Spiva. *Educ Dig* 49:46–7 F '84

The key to improving education. J. W. Stewig. *Educ Dig* 49:10–13 My '84

Knowledge is power [need for reform] D. P. Gardner. *Science* 224:1383 Je 29 '84

Linking the effective-schools and high school reform movements. J. J. D'Amico. *Educ Dig* 49:42–5 Ja '84

Maintaining a forward course for American education. F. M. Hechinger. *Educ Dig* 49:2–5 Ja '84

National service for all [school reform] C. Parsons. *Phi Delta Kappan* 65:688–9 Je '84

A new design for public education. A. W. Dodd. il *Phi Delta Kappan* 65:685–7 Je '84

Nine proposals to improve our schools. L. Botstein. *Educ Dig* 49:2–5 Mr '84

Nineteen eighty-four: the latest educational reform proposal. G. D. Fenstermacher. il *Phi Delta Kappan* 65:323–6 Ja '84

Notes and quotes on school reform. J. W. Donohue. *America* 151:241–6 O 27 '84

Our public schools: up from C minus. E. McGrath. *Read Dig* 124:91–5 F '84

The principal background of education [address, July 25, 1984] T. R. Brown, *Vital Speeches Day* 50:755–7 O 1 '84

Quality education: on the cutting edge [special section] il *Today's Educ* p37–75 '84/'85

Reflections on the great debate of '83. E. L. Boyer. il *Phi Delta Kappan* 65:525–30 Ap '84

Some hope for the schools. M. A. Scully. *Natl Rev* 36:47 Mr 9 '84

Some practical points about achieving excellence. B. Dollar. *Educ Dig* 50:2–5 S '84

The success of our education system [address, December 12, 1983] P. S. Du Pont, IV. *Vital Speeches Day* 50:272–5 F 15 '84

Teacher isolation and school reform [findings from John Goodlad's Study of schooling] K. A. Tye and B. B. Tye, bibl f il *Phi Delta Kappan* 65:319–22 Ja '84

They're playing our song. B. C. Denny. *Science* 224:447 My 4 '84

Toward strategic independence: nine commandments for enhancing school effectiveness. C. E. Finn. bibl f il *Phi Delta Kappan* 65:518–24 Ap '84

Why teachers fail. J. C. Holt. *Educ Dig* 50:58–60 D '84

Why teachers fail, J. C. Holt il *Progressive* 48:32–3 Ap '84

Aims and objectives

See also

College education—Aims and objectives

Educational sociology

Are schools for learning? H. T. Shapiro. *Educ Dig* 49:13–15 D '83

Autonomy: the aim of education envisioned by Piaget. C. Kamii. bibl f il *Phi Delta Kappan* 65:410–15 F '84

Clarifying the purpose of education. C. A. Tesconi. *Educ Dig* 50:24–5 D '84

Educating for the new order [reprint from November 1935 article] C. A. Dykstra. *Educ Dig* 50:37–9 N '84

Looking ahead in education [reprint from November 1935 issue] H. L. Smith. *Educ Dig* 50:37–9 D '84

Problems with educational comparisons. C. J. Hurn. *Educ Dig* 49:20–1 Mr '84

Suggested priorities and goals for American education. T. H. Bell, *Am Educ* 20 Sp Issue:30–2 Mr '84

What can schools become? S. Wassermann. bibl f il *Phi Delta Kappan* 65:690–3 Je '84

What is the purpose of education? The worthless debate continues. D. W. Rossides. il *Change* 16:14–21+ Ap '84

Evaluation

See also

National Assessment of Educational Progress

National Commission on Excellence in Education (U.S.)

Are American schools working? Disturbing cost and quality trends. E. G. West, bibl f il *Am Educ* 20:11–21 Ja/F '84

Assessing local school strengths in viewing national reports. W. Shreeve and others. *Educ Dig* 50:7–9 D '84

Coercion in the classroom will not work. B. Spock. *Educ Dig* 50:28–31 O '84

Coercion in the classroom won't work. B. Spock. il *Atlantic* 253:28–30+ Ap '84

The commission reports: identifying their possible harm and moving to protect higher education. K. H. Ashworth. *Change* 16:6–7+ Jl/Ag '84

Consumer reports on schools [report entitled Education and work issued by Center for Educational Research and Innovation] J. W. Donohue. il *America* 150:89–92 F 11 '84

The continuing crisis: fashions in education. D. Ravitch. *Am Sch* 53:183–93 Spr '84

Grading time for U.S. schools. D. Goddy. il *Sch Update* 116:2–4 F 3 '84

Gummibears instead of sour grapes: a positive response to the national reports on school reform [Glendale, Ariz.] C. Metzger. il *Phi Delta Kappan* 66:177–80 N '84

Is this any way to build a better school? S. Ohanian. *Educ Dig* 50:2–5 N '84

Making schools work again. R. A. Blume. il por *Humanist* 44:9–12+ Ja/F '84

Monitoring and tailoring to improve educational systems. W. W. Cooley. *Educ Dig* 49:6–9 Ap '84

Public and private schools: the need for competition. P. Brimelow. *Educ Dig* 49:14–17 Ap '84

A report card for the states [Dept. of Education report] D. A. Williams. il *Newsweek* 103:47 Ja 16 '84

The rising tide of school reform reports. K. P. Cross bibl f il *Phi Delta Kappan* 66:167–72 N '84

School programs are changing in response to reform reports: ERS [opinion poll] il *Phi Delta Kappan* 66:301 D '84

The schools and their critics: did the education commissions say anything? P. E. Peterson. *Current* 263:29–37 Je '84

Schools at risk. F. Roberts. il *Parents* 59:104–6+ D '84

Students think schools are making the grade. L. Solorzano. il *U S News World Rep* 97:49–51 Ag 27 '84

Tackling the reform reports of the 1980s. A. H. Passow. bibl f il *Phi Delta Kappan* 65:674–83 Je '84

Teachers' Union president says Bell's report might lead to educational cuts [Mary Futrell, speaker] il *Jet* 65:33 Ja 30 '84

The unattended issues of recent educational studies. H. Howe, II. *Educ Dig* 49:2–6 My '84

What to do about America's schools. P. Brimelow. *Current* 258:7–14 D '83

Why the schools may not improve, J. Adelson. *Commentary* 78:40-5 O
'84

EXERCISE 30

Below, you will find a list of four different topics for a research essay
dealing with the broad subject of advertising, followed by a bibliography
of twenty articles, arranged in order of their publication dates. Each
item in the bibliography is followed by a note giving a brief description
of its contents.

Examine the bibliography carefully and *choose a set of appropriate
sources for each of the four essay topics.* You are not expected to locate
and read these articles; use the notes to help you make your decisions.
The bibliography is numbered to make the distribution process easier.
List the numbers of the articles that you select for each topic. You will
notice that many of the articles can be used for more than one topic.

Topics:

    A. What is an appropriate role for advertising in our society? What
        are the advertiser's responsibilities?
    B. Feminists have argued that the image of women created by the ad-
        vertising industry remains a false and objectionable one: is that a
        valid claim?
    C. How do advertising agencies go about manipulating the reactions
        of consumers? To what extent is this practice unavoidable and
        even acceptable?
    D. How much progress has the movement to protect the consumer
        made since 1970? What has been the response of the advertising
        agencies?

1. "Liberating Women," *Time* 15 June 1970: 93. In a slightly surprised tone,
the author notes that ordinary American women are beginning to support
feminist attacks against ads that show unwelcome stereotypes of women.

2. "TV Ads: Shorter Pitches at Better Prospects," *Business Week* 23 Jan. 1971:
88–89. From the ad agency's point of view, this article describes tactics that
can be used to influence the buying habits of various age groups. Specifically, it's concerned with the right time to show ads that appeal to either the
old or the young.

3. "Advertisers Fight Back," *America* 8 April 1972: 368. This is a brief, abstract
discussion of morality in advertising and pressures from consumerist organizations. It concludes that advertising is only a symptom of a more serious
cultural illness.

4. Woods, Crawford. "American Pie," *New Republic* 168 (2 June 1973): 25. This article explores the basic psychological reasons for audience gullibility; it is very hostile toward the advertising industry for daring to prey upon television viewers. There is a favorable review of a television program that provided an exposé of deceptive commercials.

5. Greenland, Leo. "Advertisers Must Stop Conning Consumers," *Harvard Business Review* 52 (July 1974): 18–20. The consumerist point of view should be accepted by the advertising industry, which should be policing itself. Ad agencies should place more trust in the average person's common sense.

6. Field, Roger. "The Great Paper Towel Deception," *Science Digest* 77 (May 1975): 86–88. This offers a single illustration, in great detail, of the false claims and trickery presented in the commercial for Bounty towels.

7. "The FTC's Ad Rules Anger Industry," *Business Week* 1 Nov. 1976: 30. This article seems very objective. It presents the ad industry's point of view and also the consumer's. The topic is the new guidelines for food and drug advertisement.

8. "Really Socking It to Women," *Time* 7 Feb. 1977: 57–59. According to ad agencies, ads and commercials that abuse women stimulate sales. This article cites examples and tries to explore the reasons for this trend.

9. "Buy the Product, Not the Package," *Changing Times* 31 (April 1977): 21–23. This is a discussion of impulse buying, describing deceptive and manipulative packaging and the consumer's gullibility. It contains advice on how to prevent being fooled by false advertising.

10. Seldin, Joseph J. "A Long Way to Go, Baby," *The Nation* 16 April 1977: 464–466. This article discusses stereotyped images of women presented in ads and commercials, using guidelines from NOW as a frame of reference. The author suggests that such ads are unavoidable since they are merely reflecting generally accepted social values. The author is president of an ad agency.

11. Bush, S. "The Art of Implying More than You Say," *Psychology Today* 10 (May 1977): 36. This describes the way in which the wording of an ad can protect or mislead the consumer. Such ads feature "implied claims." The article stresses public gullibility.

12. Hurst, Lynda. "Modifying Media Imagery," *Atlas World Press Review* April 1978: 36–37. The author describes an increasing reaction against TV commercials that contain degrading depictions of women. The article is useful for its description of the stereotypes of women contained in many ads.

13. Coleman, Daniel. "Braintapping on Madison Avenue," *Psychology Today* 12 (April 1979): 120. This short, useful article, written without technical jargon, describes the way in which ad agencies are using scientific studies (like measuring beta waves for alertness) to judge viewers' reactions to commercials.

14. Ney, Edward. "Beyond the Bottom Line," *Saturday Review* 29 September 1979: 30. Written very much from the point of view of business, this article

justifies the corporation's right to express its philosophy through advertising.

15. "Fuzzy Thinking on Madison Avenue," *Fortune* 16 June 1980: 73. According to this article, which is full of jargon, certain consumer organizations are monitoring toy advertisements to prevent advertisers from making some children feel superior to others.

16. Doan, Michael. "Business Shifts its Sales Pitch for Women," *U.S. News and World Report* 6 July 1981: 46. Concerned with advertisements aimed at working women as well as housewives, this is a superficial article that cites very broad statistics.

17. "Watch Out for the Ads that Trick the Trusting," *Changing Times* December 1982: 68–69. This easy-to-read article describes various swindles resulting from fraudulent advertising appearing in reputable newspapers that fail to check on their advertisers.

18. Bagdikian, Ben. "The Wrong Kind of Readers," *Progressive* 47 (May 1983): 52–54. This focuses on *The New Yorker's* efforts to regain its affluent readership and expand its advertising after its liberal editorial policies during the Vietnam War caused older readers to stop subscribing.

19. Schudson, Michael. "Capitalist Realism," *Harper's* 269 (November 1984): 24–25. In this excerpt from *Advertising, The Uneasy Persuasion*, the author argues that advertising exists in its own reality, containing representative, rather than specific, people and places.

20. "Policing the Health Ads," *Newsweek* 26 November 1984: 75. The specific examples in this short but detailed article describe how the Food and Drug Administration is cracking down on ads that falsely claim therapeutic value for nonmedical products like Kellogg's cereal.

ASSIGNMENT 15

I. Choose a broad topic that, for the next few weeks, you will research and develop into an extended essay of eight or more pages.
   A. If you have a *person or an event* in mind, but do not have sufficiently detailed knowledge to decide on a focus and target date, wait until you have done some preliminary reading. Start with an encyclopedia article or an entry in a biographical dictionary; then use the card catalog and any bibliographies that you find along the way. Decide whether your topic is recent enough to have been featured in available newspapers and periodicals, and consult the appropriate indexes.
   B. If you want to write about a *contemporary issue*, examine some of the entries dealing with that topic in recent volumes of the *Readers' Guide* or the *New York Times Index*; then formulate a few questions that you might undertake to answer.

II. Compile a preliminary bibliography, consulting the relevant card catalogues, indexes, and data bases. At this point, you need not examine all the sources, take notes, or plan the organization of your essay. Your purpose is to assess the *amount* and, as much as possible, the *quality* of the material that is available. Whether or not your teacher asks you to hand in your preliminary bibliography, make sure that the publication information that you record is accurate and legible. Indicate which sources your library has available and which may be difficult to obtain.

III. Submit a topic proposal to your teacher, describing the probable scope and focus of your essay. (If you are considering more than one topic, suggest a few possibilities.) Be prepared to alter the specifics of your proposal as you learn more about the number and availability of your sources.

6.
Gathering Materials at the Library: Evaluating Sources

While compiling a preliminary bibliography, a student has located a promising group of sources. The topic is high school dropouts: specifically, she wants to discuss the age at which adolescents should be allowed to leave school. At the library, the student has consulted indexes and bibliographies, and has found several books and articles, all of which, judging by their titles, may be relevant. Some of these authors will have a better claim to being cited as authorities than others. Since all the names are unfamiliar to her, which should she read first? How can she weigh one source of evidence against another and decide whose ideas should receive prominence in her essay?

First of all, the student can try to find out something about each author's credentials for writing about high school students. Is the writer a teacher? an administrator? an educator? a journalist, presenting second-hand information? Are the source's qualifications consistent with the subject? Someone who specializes in the kindergarten years may not be the best person to offer opinions about sixteen-year-olds. On the other hand, one might not think that an economist would be worth consulting about high school dropouts; yet, if he has made a study of the job market and the career prospects of workers without high school certificates, then an economist's evidence and recommendations should be included in a research essay. Would a social psychologist be a useful source? The answer would depend on the nature of the work: a study of abnormal social behavior in adolescents might be rather remote from the everyday problem of determining the minimum age for leaving high school, but a study of juvenile delinquency might suggest connections between teenage crime and teenage dropouts. Consider the article in Chapter 3 about strict attendance policies in grade school. What *were* Roger Sipher's qualifications for making such tough recommendations? Consider also "A Question of Degree" in Chapter 1. Who *is* Blanche Blank, and why should we believe her claim that we have grossly inflated the value of a college degree? When she wrote "A Question of Degree," was she an employee denied promotion because she lacked a B.A.? a college graduate seeking a more interesting job? a homemaker, eager to return to college? or a college teacher who specialized in education (as, in fact, she is)? What difference would this information make to your understanding of her essay?

On the other hand, you may be asked to write about a writer or a group of writers (in an anthology, perhaps) whose names are all familiar to you. Would you need to find out more about these authors? Would they have been chosen for inclusion in an anthology if their authority were questionable? Once again, how can knowledge of the source help in the writing of your research essay?

LEARNING MORE ABOUT YOUR SOURCES

The mind, the personality, and the experience of the authors that you cite (as well as the times in which they lived) are generally well worth knowing something about, if only to provide a context for understanding their meaning. There may be some significant connection between an author's background—education, previous writings, professional interests, political leanings, life experience—and the ideas in the book or article that you may write about. Finding out about an author's credentials and background not only helps you to decide whether the source is trustworthy, but also enables you to make allowances for an individual approach to the subject and, occasionally, for bias.

In this sense, "bias" is not a bad word, nor is it quite the same thing as "prejudice." Bias means special interest or personal angle: the line of thought that this person would be expected to pursue, which might affect his opinion about the subject that interests you. Few knowledgeable people are entirely detached or objective, whether about their pet interests or about the area of learning which has been their life's work. To some extent, the awareness of bias can weaken your belief in the author's credibility. It is the person who is both knowledgeable and without bias whose opinions tend to carry the most weight. Nevertheless, it is a mistake to discount a good idea automatically just because you believe that the writer's ideas may reflect her special interests. Once you have identified a possible bias, then you can either disregard it as harmless or adjust your judgment to allow for its influence.

Learning the facts about an author's background does not always permit you to make assumptions about his probable point of view. Jumping to conclusions can be dangerous. For example, according to their biographies, several of the authors whose writings are included in this book were active in the antiwar movement of the 1960s. Yet, on the basis of that information, it would be foolish to try to trace a cause-and-effect connection between these activities and the ideas presented in their essays. What is important is not their common experience, but the use that they made of this experience in the development of their ideas. In general, the purpose of inquiring about the author's life and work is to understand more about the wider context of the work that you are reading so that the small area on which you are focusing—a single essay, a chapter in a book, even a brief quotation—will open up, expand, and become that much more revealing and interesting.

Authors

Where do you go to find out about a writer's background? Possibly to the book itself. The preface may contain biographical information, and the "blurb" on the paper cover will probably describe the author (but frequently in such laudatory terms that much of the information may have to be discounted). Periodicals may provide a thumbnail biography of an article's author at the bottom of its first page, or at the end of the article, or in a group of authors' biographies at the beginning or end of an issue. What you should look for are details about the author's education, professional experience, and published works. These facts can tell you quite a bit about the writer's probable approach to the subject of your research. Look out for vague descriptions: "a freelance writer who frequently writes about this topic" can describe a recognized authority or an ignorant amateur. You can also consult one of the many biographical dictionaries, encyclopedias, and indexes. Some of them, however, are not very informative. *Who's Who*, for example, will give you some basic facts about positions held and works published; but you may need to know a good deal about the academic world to interpret this information, and you may not find out very much about the author's characteristic beliefs, activities, or enthusiasms. Good indexes to consult are *Biographical Index* and *Current Biography*.

As an illustration of this evaluating process, let us look more closely at the author of one of the paragraphs in Exercise 8 in Chapter 1. Margaret Mead is a very famous name, yet you may have often read and heard that name without really knowing what she is famous for. Thus, to find out something about her achievements and her credentials for writing about family relationships, you stop in the library and check one of the biographical reference works. (If you know where these books are shelved, this can take less than ten minutes.) In the index to *Current Biography*, you find a listing for Margaret Mead's obituary in the 1978 volume; to supplement that brief paragraph, you can also look up the complete article on Mead in an earlier volume. Here is the obituary, followed by a few excerpts from the much longer 1951 article (which ends with references to twelve other sources of information about Margaret Mead).

MEAD, MARGARET Dec. 16, 1901–Nov. 15, 1978. One of world's foremost anthropologists; pioneered in research methods that helped to turn social anthropology into a major science; curator emeritus (from 1969) of American Museum of Natural History, with which she had been associated since 1926; taught at Fordham, Columbia, and other universities; made many expeditions, to Samoa, New Guinea, Bali, and other parts of South Pacific; author of hundreds of articles and more than a score of books, including all-time best-seller *Coming of Age in Samoa* (1928); commented on American institutions in such books as *And Keep Your Powder Dry* (1942) and *Male and Female* (1949); promoted environmentalism, women's rights, racial harmony, and other causes; died in New York City. See *Current Biography* (May) 1951.

Obituary
NY Times A p1 + N 16 '78

Before leaving [on her second field trip to the West Pacific], Miss Mead completed her now well-known book *Coming of Age in Samoa* (1928). The work was praised in the New York *Times* as "sympathetic throughout . . . but never sentimental" and as "a remarkable contribution to our knowledge of humanity;" it went into five printings within two years and has been twice reissued. . . .

. . . [Mead] published *And Keep Your Powder Dry* (1942), subtitled *An Anthropologist Looks at America* and described in the *Library Journal* as "American character outlined against the background of the seven other cultures" the author had studied.

Dr. Mead during World War II "wrote OWI pamphlets and interpreted GI's to the British" (*Saturday Review of Literature*) and also served (1942–5) as executive secretary of the committee on food habits, the National Research Council. She was a visiting lecturer at Teacher's College (1945–51) and has further served as consultant on mental health, as a member of the committee on research of the mental health division of the National Advisory Mental Health Council of the United States Public Health Service and as a member of the interim governing board of the International Mental Health Congress. . . .

What do you learn from this information? Margaret Mead was a scientist, thoroughly familiar with the rigorous methods, the complexities, and the delays of scientific research; therefore, she is unlikely to be casual in her analysis of the sources of neurosis in children. Moreover, Margaret Mead was a *social* scientist, specifically, an anthropologist; she was accustomed to studying the whole of a community or society, assessing its customs, its stability, its morale, its probable responses to challenges and emergencies; therefore, her training would make her both comprehensive and objective in her description of dynamics within the American family. Nor did Margaret Mead restrict her writing to anthropological studies of remote tribes; this article is by no means her first comment on the American scene, and so her analysis and predictions gain the credibility that comes with repeated observation. Family relationships were among Margaret Mead's special concerns; thus, one can understand and place in context her analysis of the neurotic child. And, finally, the popularity of her best-selling scientific work suggests that her readers would be more likely to accept her conclusions than they would the ideas of an author who was less well-known and whose background had been exclusively academic.

On the other hand, the fact that Mead was a popularizer—one who takes dry and difficult ideas and makes them understandable to a wide public—helps to explain why her presentation may seem facile, with many of its assertions unsupported. (It was written for *Redbook*, not for a scholarly journal.) There is clearly a difference between the writings of Margaret Mead, the anthropologist, and those of Margaret Mead, the social commentator.

Although finding out about your sources may enhance your understanding of what you read, this information should not dominate the research process. Certainly, if your preliminary bibliography contains twenty books, and you are writing an essay in which no single source will be emphasized, don't waste your time looking up each author at length in the reference room. If, however, you are building a paper around a subject for which there are clearly going to be only one or two highly important sources, and if you feel uneasy about your ignorance of their qualifications and characteristic opinions, invest some time in reading a few articles *about* these authors and their writings. Check *Book Review Index* and read reviews of the books that you intend to cite, or look at articles cited in *Biographical Index*. In the end, however, you may have to rely upon your research instincts, which can become remarkably accurate if you spend some time comparing the content and style of the sources that you find.

Dates of Publication

One indication of a work's usefulness for your purpose is its date. If your essay on high school dropouts is intended to survey past and present policy, you would deliberately want to choose some representative works published over the last few decades. However, if you are focusing only on present-day conditions, drawing heavily on material published in the forties or fifties would be pointless (unless you wanted to include some predictions that might or might not have come true). An article that takes for granted outdated school attendance laws or social conditions (like the draft) that have changed would be of little value in preparing an essay about contemporary dropouts. However, you may find older sources with theoretical content that is not dated, such as discussions of the role of education in the formation of personality.

Primary and Secondary Sources

Judging the usefulness of a work may depend on your knowing the difference between primary and secondary sources. A *primary source* is a work that is itself the subject of your essay or (if you are writing a historical research essay) a work written during the period that you are focusing on that gives you direct or "primary" knowledge of that period. The term is frequently used to describe an original document—like the Constitution, for example—or memoirs and diaries of historical interest, or a work of literature that, over the years, has been the subject of much written commentary. Any commentary written both *after* and *about* the primary source can, in turn, be called a *secondary source*. Thus, a history textbook is a secondary source.

While you generally study a primary source for its own sake, the secondary source is important—often, it only exists—because of its primary source. If you are asked to write an essay about *Huckleberry Finn* and your instructor tells you not to use any secondary sources, you are to read *only* Mark Twain's novel and not consult anyone else's commentary. Carl Sandburg's biography of Abraham Lincoln is a secondary source if you are interested in Lincoln, but a primary source if you are studying Sandburg. And if you read the *Times* in order to acquire information about life in America on a certain date, you are using the newspaper as a primary source, since it is your direct object of study; but when you look up a *Times* review of a book or a movie you want to write about, then you are locating a secondary source in order to acquire more information about your primary subject.

In the sciences and social sciences, the most recent secondary sources usually replace earlier ones. However, that rule does not always apply to secondary sources written about historical and biographical subjects. For example, Forster's biography of Charles Dickens, written in the nineteenth century, is still considered a valuable and interesting work, in part because Forster knew Dickens and could provide much firsthand information. However, research is always unearthing new facts about people's lives. Thus, in many ways, Forster's work has been superseded by new biographies which feature the latest information. In fact, for a biographical or historical essay, you would do well to consult some primary sources, a few secondary sources written at the time of the event or during the subject's lifetime, and the most recent and reliable secondary sources. It is the works in the middle—written a few years after your target date, without the perspective of distance—that often lack authenticity or objectivity.

If you are in doubt about using a source, check to see whether the author has included documentation and a bibliography; well-documented works tend to be the most reliable. But the absence of documentation is not the only reason for distrusting a source. You can also suspect that a book should not be taken seriously just by glancing through it. If it is written in a superficial or frivolous or overly dramatic style, then you would be wise to suspect its claim to authority.

Finally, try dividing the available sources into three groups: those you are sure that you will want to use; those you rejected on sight; and those you are doubtful about. Be aware of the reasons for your doubts, and indicate those reasons in the notes for your bibliography. Then, at some point in your research, you can check the qualifications of those sources with your instructor or in reference works; or you can simply annotate your bibliography so that your reader is made aware of your judgments and your reasons for proceeding with caution.

SELECTING SOURCES
THAT WORK WELL TOGETHER

In Chapter 4, when you learned how to work with a group of sources, the process was simplified to make your assignments easier: the sources were all of the same kind, homogeneous, and therefore relatively easy to synthesize. The statements in each group all came from students who had roughly the same skills and experience, and whose opinions were therefore comparable. But in real research at the library, the sources that you find may have nothing at all in common but their subject.

Periodicals provide a clear-cut example, for they are published for a variety of specific audiences with well-defined interests and reading habits and (in some cases) social and political views. Since the readership varies so greatly, articles on the same subject in two different periodicals are likely to be very different in their point of view and development. An article on dropouts in one of the well-known women's magazines is likely to be reassuring and helpful, filled with concrete advice to parents. It will not have the same purpose nor cite the same kinds of evidence nor be expressed in the same kind of vocabulary as an article of comparable length published the same year in *Psychology Today*, which, in turn, will probably not resemble a scholarly essay on dropouts in the *Journal of the American Psychological Association* or the *American Journal of Sociology*. An equivalent article in *Newsweek* or *Time* will be shorter and more lively, filled with vivid, concrete illustrations.

Because of these differences, these periodicals are not considered equally valuable as evidence for your essay. While the news magazine provides some factual information, and *Psychology Today* is an important popularizer of ideas in the social sciences, presenting them in a readable form for a wide audience, the more scholarly journals generally contain a depth of analysis and a breadth of research that makes them more comprehensive and convincing. On the other hand, articles in scholarly journals are often written in a dense style, with a vocabulary characteristic of the discipline; someone writing a freshman essay on a general topic may find these articles difficult to read and understand. Never force yourself to write about a source that, after reasonable effort, you cannot understand.

Books are potentially even more difficult to synthesize since they vary so greatly in length, purpose, and presentation. Suppose that in researching your paper on high school dropouts you have found three very different books, all published recently. One contains 285 pages exclusively about dropouts; chapter after chapter is filled with statistical studies and case histories presented in dense detail and in an abstract language that requires concentration to absorb. The second book is a comprehensive study of the high school curriculum and present levels of achievement; there is one thirty-page chapter about dropouts and student morale in general. The third source is an educational handbook, directed at future teachers, with a page and a half devoted to the importance of making students stay in school; the issue is presented broadly and rhetorically, as if part of a stirring speech.

Can these three sources be integrated into the same essay? All three are relevant to the topic, and each may be interesting and useful in itself. But the difference in depth among them is so great that it is hard to see how the three can be used together in a single essay. And, indeed, the one thing that you should not do is to plunk down excerpts from these three sources side by side, in adjoining sentences. If they are to be integrated at all, you must first recognize and then communicate to your reader that the three sources are not equivalent or even similar.

This does not mean that all of your sources should cover the same range of ideas, should be roughly the same length, and should employ much the same vocabulary and depth of evidence. Working with materials of the same order of difficulty may be convenient, but developing a balanced bibliography that offers a variety of approaches to the topic is more important. You must remain sensitive to the *kinds* of sources that you are using. This awareness begins when you begin your research. As you glance through an article or a chapter in a book, ask yourself whether the content is primarily theoretical or practical. How often does the author offer evidence to support his conclusions? What kind of evidence? Or does the book's thesis depend on a series of broad propositions, linked together into an argument? What is the scope of the book? Is the focus narrow, with the entire work centered around one person's experience? Or does it sum up the work of others? Finally, be alert to the kind of language and rhetoric that the author is using, and make mental or written notes about its difficulty.

Your awareness of the differences between your sources will help you to determine your research priorities. You would not begin your research by taking notes from the 285-page book on dropouts; not everything in it would relate to your eventual thesis. Instead, you would begin with the single comprehensive chapter from the second source, which would give you an overview of the subject and help you to establish your own approach to the topic and your thesis. Once you have a working list of specific points to develop, it might not be necessary for you to work through all 285 pages of the first source. And don't forget the third work, the handbook, which might give you a broader understanding of your topic, as well as provide you with an excellent quotation or two.

INTEGRATING YOUR SELECTED SOURCES

Once you have become familiar with your main sources, their differences and their relative usefulness, how do you integrate them into your essay? Unless the structure is large enough to incorporate them all smoothly, you may simply decide to exclude those that do not mesh easily with the others. You may not want to distract your reader by moving back and forth abruptly from extremely broad statements of policy to minute citations of case studies or statistical evidence, especially if the different segments are expressed in a completely different vocabulary and style. Even if you attempt the difficult task of paraphrasing your sources and using your own style to integrate them, you will still need to insert transitions to prepare your reader for the shift from one approach to the next. In a short essay of only five or six pages, you would probably be wise to restrict your sources to those that blend well together because they are of the same order of difficulty. The writers you cite do not have to agree with each other; rather, their scope and methods should be roughly similar.

For a short essay you would have to decide in the early stages of your research which kind of source would best suit the development of your thesis. How complex will your essay be? How sophisticated is your argument? Does it require support from complex case studies? If you intend to prove that dropouts come from a clearly specified kind of family environment, you will probably need to cite scholarly sources, like the 285-page dropout book. On the other hand, you might want to argue that the dropout rate could be linked to a general decline in standards of education, drawing to some extent on your own high school experience. This thesis would be "popular" in its approach to the subject and would require less rigorous sources. Remember that a popularization is a simplification of a difficult subject; popular essays could not exist without the evidence to be found in longer and more complex works. In a sense, a college research essay has to be "popular" since it is valuable as evidence of the student's understanding of the subject, rather than as a contribution to scholarly knowledge.

In deciding whether or not to use the popular approach, remember to consider the level of the course that you are taking. An introductory course is intended to help you grasp the broad concepts that are basic to the discipline; your instructor will probably not expect you to go out of your depth in hunting scholarly sources for your essay. On the other hand, in an advanced course, you are preparing to do your own research, and so you have to demonstrate your understanding of the work of others as well as the methods that are commonly used in that field. In an advanced course, the popular approach can be regarded as superficial.

In a longer essay of ten pages or more, you should have much less trouble blending ill-assorted sources. With fairly leisurely development, you can position each source in the place where it is most appropriate and where it will have the most convincing effect. Thus, for the dropout essay the quotations that you select from the brief handbook might be placed in the introduction or conclusion of your essay; the theories relating curriculum to student morale could be included in your preliminary presentation of your argument; and you would cite the detailed evidence of the longest source in support of your own ideas or as part of your survey of the work already done in this field. In short, these very different sources could be used together successfully, provided that you did not give your reader the impression that they were interchangeable in their usefulness.

Finally, in your search for a well-balanced bibliography, include only what you yourself understand. If you find yourself consulting and citing sources whose writing makes no sense to you, no matter how eminent and qualified these authorities may be, your essay will be a failure; for you will be pretending a mastery of the subject that you do not actually have.

EXERCISE 31

Examine the following preliminary bibliography of articles for a research essay on the broad topic of education.

A. Make up two *narrow* topics, one focused on a recent issue in education, the other suggesting a retrospective approach and including the last few decades.

B. Carefully read the bibliography, and consider the probable contents of each article, as suggested by the title; the kind of periodical it appears in; the length; and the date of publication. What can you conclude about each article?

C. Determine your research priorities for each of your two topics by choosing a list of five articles that you believe ought to be located and consulted first. Record your two lists.

"Are High-School Standards Too Low?" *Ladies Home Journal* Sept. 1956: 86–88.

"Are Schools Changing Too Much Too Fast?" *Changing Times* Sept. 1966: 6–10.

"Back to Basics in the Schoolhouse." *Readers Digest* Feb. 1975: 149–52.

Bailey, S. K. "Educational Planning: Purposes and Promise." *Public Administration Review* May 1971: 345–52.

Boyle, M. C., and B. Boyle. "Nourish the Love of Learning." *Parents Magazine* Sept. 1959: 45.

Broudy, H. S. "Demand for Accountability: Can Society Exercise Control over Education?" *Education and Urban Society* Feb. 1977: 235–50.

Burris, V. "Social and Political Consequences of Overeducation." *American Sociology Review* Aug. 1983: 454–67.

Clarke, B. C. "America's Power for Good." *PTA Magazine* Feb. 1962: 20–22.

Cobb, J. E. "Educated Citizenry." *Teachers College Journal* Dec. 1957: 37.

Frazier, M. "Inner City Schools that Work." *Readers Digest* June 1980: 24–28.

Glatthorn, A. A. "Little Bit of Rebellion is Good for the Soul, and the School." *Seventeen* Aug. 1969: 324–25.

Handl, J. "Educational Chances and Occupational Attitudes of Women: A Sociohistorical Analysis." *Journal of Social History* 17 (Spring 1984): 463–487.

Hechinger, Grace, and Fred M. Hechinger. "Report Card on Education." *Ladies Home Journal* Sept. 1985: 96.

Hillson, M. "Reorganization in the School: Bringing about a Remission of the Problems Faced by Minority Children." *Phylon* 28 (Fall 1967): 230–45.

Holcomb, J. H. "Can We—Should We Save the Public Schools?" *American Educator* June 1983: 34–37.

"Johnny is Doing a Lot Better." *Life* April 1961: 32.

Kirst, M. W. "How to Improve Schools without Spending Money." *Phi Delta Kappan* September 1982: 6–8.

Klitgaard, R. E., and G. R. Hall. "Are There Unusually Effective Schools?" *Journal of Human Resources* 10 (Winter 1975): 90–106.

Lanier, H. B., and J. Byrne. "How High School Students View Women: The Relationship between Perceived Attractiveness, Occupation, and Education." *Sex Roles* 7 (1981): 145–8.

Lerner, Barbara. "Minimum Competence Testing Movement: Social, Scientific, and Legal Duplications." *American Psychologist* Oct. 1981: 1057–66.

Liazos, A. "School Alienation and Delinquency." *Crime and Delinquency* July 1978: 355–70.

Linton, C. D. "In Defense of a Liberal Arts Education." *Christianity Today* May 1974: 5–8.

"Low Marks for U.S. Education." *Saturday Evening Post* 20 Oct. 1962: 96.

Maynard, F. "What We Can Learn from the Little Red Schoolhouse." *Good Housekeeping* Aug. 1968: 70–1.

McClung, M. "Right to Learn." *Trial* May 1974: 22–25.

Melby, E. O. "Education Is the Ultimate Weapon." *Educational Forum* November 1956: 45–54.

Miles, C. G. "Do Boys and Girls Need Different Schooling?" *Educational Digest* April 1981: 23–25.

Morley, F. "Scientific Triumph of Russia Shows a Paradox in Education." *Nation's Business* Jan. 1958: 21–22.

Morris, J. P. "Principles of Education for a Free Society." *Bulletin of the National Association of Secondary School Principals* Dec. 1954: 99–100.

Petrie, M. A. "Education Without Schools." *Nation* 15 November 1971: 505–6.

Ransom, H. H. "Rediscovery of Teaching." *Texas Quarterly* 8 (Winter 1965): 7–11.

Rothstein, S. W. "Abandonment of the Public Schools." *Crisis* Jan. 1979: 27–31.

"Sex and the Schools." *New Republic* 6 July 1974: 8–9.

Silber, J. R. "Need for Elite Education." *Harpers* June 1977: 22–24.

Smith, M. "Faddishness in Education." *Saturday Review* 21 Aug. 1965: 53.

"Why Our Schools Went Wrong." *Changing Times* May 1978: 25–28.

Will, George F. "D is for Dodo: Grade Inflation." *Newsweek* 19 Feb. 1976: 84.

EXERCISE 32

Each of the passages below has been extracted from a longer article (or, in one case, a book) on the general subject of anorexia and bulimia. These excerpts all deal specifically with the causes and symptoms of these adolescent diseases, and some are especially concerned with teenage anorexics and bulimics.

Carefully examine the distinctive way in which each passage presents its information, noting especially:

A. the amount and kind of evidence that is cited;
B. the expectations of the reader's knowledge and understanding;
C. the relative emphasis on generalizations and abstract thinking;
D. the characteristic tone and vocabulary.

Take into consideration what you may already know about these publications and the audience for each. Then decide whether there would be any difficulty in using these sources together in a single research essay on anorexia and bulimia.

Write a thesis for such an essay, and then decide which three sources you would definitely use in writing your essay. Be prepared to justify your choice.

A. **ANOREXIA NERVOSA**, an-ə-rek′-sē-ə nər-vō′ sə, a psychosomatic illness in which self-inflicted starvation leads to a devastating loss of weight. It occurs chiefly among well-to-do high school and college girls, affecting about one out of every 200 girls in that group. Girls affected with this disorder have a pathological fear of being fat, which leads to a relentless pursuit of excessive slimness coupled with an intense interest in food. Severe personality problems are common. The typical patient is overcompliant in childhood, and thus inadequately prepared for adolescence and independence. Excessive control over weight—to the point of starvation—represents an effort to establish a sense of selfhood and autonomy. Starvation, in turn, creates its own physiological and psychological symptoms and complications.

from *Encyclopedia Americana*

B. *What is anorexia?* Anorexia nervosa is an eating disorder of self-inflicted starvation in which the victim—usually a young woman—loses 25 percent or more of her normal body weight. An anorexic eats little or no food and often exercises vigorously. She feels that she is fat even though she is very thin, and she thinks that eating even a normal amount will make her gain weight. Anorexics often engage in food rituals, such as not allowing food to touch their lips or deciding, If I don't eat by six o'clock, I can't eat at all. They often become emotionally withdrawn.

What is bulimia? How does it differ from anorexia? Bulimia is a seemingly uncontrollable food craving that leads its victims to binge frequently, eating two to three times the amount of food in an average meal—and usually high-calorie foods. Then, in order to rid themselves of the food consumed during these binges, bulimics resort to vomiting, laxative abuse (sometimes using between 40 and 80 doses per day), diuretics and enemas. Bulimics also have distorted body images and weight fluctuations of ten pounds or more, but most maintain a weight that is close to average—and some are even overweight. While bulimics are more socially and sexually involved than anorexics, they are often severely depressed and even suicidal. Bulimia nervosa (also known as bulimarexia) is a disorder with symptoms of both anorexia and bulimia. Victims may lose more than 25 percent of their body weight.

from "Why Women Starve and Binge" McCall's,
April 1985

C. Psychiatrists tell us that the range of odd eating behaviors and attitudes form an "eating arc." At one end are people with *anorexia nervosa*: they have lost at least 25 percent of original body weight, according to official diagnostic criteria, have no known physical illness to account for their weight loss, and "feel fat" even though they are obviously emaciated. About half of these are called *restrictor anorexics*—they maintain their emaciation by simple denial of food. The other half are called *bulimic anorexics*. Their behavior is complicated. Bulimic anorexics practice food denial, but regularly binge, then choose one or more compensatory methods for getting rid of the food, such as self-induced vomiting, laxatives, diuretics, amphetamines, and excessive exercise.

Following the two types of anorexics on the eating arc are bulimics, or bingers of basically "ideal" weight. Normal-weight bulimics regularly go on eating binges and use the same methods of compensation to avoid gaining weight—most commonly vomiting, laxatives and, to a lesser degree, diuretics.

Then there are the *situational purgers* (also called *occasional* or *episodic purgers*) who may use instant-compensation methods (usually self-induced vomiting) for a specific reason, but who are not particularly obsessed with the fear of weight gain and don't hate themselves for their behavior.

Next on the arc, approaching mid-point, are normal-weight people who also binge, but who don't use instant-compensation methods to avoid weight gain; instead, they diet, fast, or use exercise as their methods. They are *bulimic dieters*. Whatever their weight, the urge to binge and the act itself is at first a direct response to the constant hunger of rigid dieting, but over time its function broadens to become an all purpose tension releaser as well as a hunger reliever.

Susan Squire, from The Slender Balance

D. My bout with bulimia began as a diet that got out of hand. It was my freshman year in college, and I had gained 20 pounds. I was 5 feet 8 inches and weighed close to 160 pounds.

In a strange new environment, I felt that if I got to be thin, all my worries would go away. I'd be more successful academically, more popular and more attractive to men.

But I lost the weight too fast—about 35 pounds in a month and a half. I was existing on just an apple and a salad a day and I just couldn't keep it up. I felt I would be fat if I ate any more, so I found myself eating and then deliberately making myself sick.

Visits home were especially hard, because I knew I would have to deal with lots of food. Often, I would say I wasn't hungry or that I'd just eaten. But other times, I'd eat an awful lot and then go back to school and make myself throw up.

Daily habits. The binging and vomiting gradually increased, becoming everyday habits. And it became worse when I moved into an apartment in my senior year. I had a roommate, but we had different schedules and rarely had meals together. Alone, I would find myself not eating at all or binging on ice cream or an entire bag of corn chips.

I was always counting calories, keeping myself strictly regimented. But then the pressures I was putting on myself to be perfect—physically, academically, at work—would get so great that I would binge as a release.

Looking back, what I was doing was eating my feelings. I would begin to binge to block my feelings of loneliness, anger or worry about the future. But then, the food would be gone and I'd panic. "I ate all this," I'd think. "I'm going to be fat and ugly and no one will love me." Then I would feel guilty and get rid of it all. I didn't even enjoy food. I was wasting my time and energy on something that wasn't giving me any satisfaction.

Everyone commented on my loss of weight, but I hid my binge-vomiting from my family and friends. Thinking myself the only person to eat this way, I was ashamed to ask for help.

from *"Binge and Purge: Road Back from Bulimia,"*
U.S. News & World Report, 8 Oct. 1984

E. My experience with bulimarexics contradicts standard psychoanalytic theory. . . . Far from rejecting the stereotype of femininity—that of the accommodating, passive, dependent woman—these young women have never questioned their assumptions that wifehood, motherhood, and intimacy with men are the fundamental components of femininity. I came to understand that their obsessive pursuit of thinness constitutes not only an acceptance of this ideal but an exaggerated striving to achieve it. Their attempts to control their physical appearance demonstrate a disproportionate concern with pleasing others, particularly men—a reliance on others to validate their sense of worth. They have devoted their lives to fulfilling the feminine *role* rather than the individual person. None has developed a basic sense of personal power or of self worth.

Bruch says that these women have a basic *delusion* "of not having an identity of their own, of not even owning their body and its sensations, with the specific inability of recognizing hunger as a sign of nutritional needs." She attributes this to, among other things, "the mother's superimposing on the child her own concept of the child's needs." Thus the child, believing that she is hungry because her mother says so, has little sense of what hunger is about internally. In my experience with these women, the feeling of not having any identity is not a delusion or a misperception but a reality which need not be caused solely by the stereotyped protective mother but by other cultural, social, and psychological pressures as well.

Anne, for example, was a good, generally submissive child. She had lived her life the way "she was supposed to"—precisely her problem. She had been socialized by her parents to believe that society would reward her good looks: "Some day the boys are going to go crazy over you." "What a face! With your good looks you'll never have to worry about getting a job." Clinging and dependent, she could not see herself as a separate person. Our early sessions had an unreal quality. I searched for a glimpse of unique character, but Anne had no identifiable sense of self from which to project a real person. Her dependency on others prevented any development of self. Most of the women in my study had been rewarded for their physical attractiveness and submissive "goodness," while characteristics such as independence, self-reliance, and assertiveness were generally punished by parents, grandparents, teachers, and peers. Peggy said, "I was always a tomboy. In fact at the age of ten to twelve I was stronger and faster than any of the boys. After I won a race against a boy, I was given the cold shoulder by the rest of the boys in my class. The girls teased me and my parents put pressure on me to 'start acting like a girl should.' I did, and stopped having as much fun."

Wulff refers to an intense, unconscious mother hate in these women. In my experience they were, on the contrary, painfully conscious of despising their mothers, most of whom they described as weak and unhappy, women who had abandoned careers in order to raise children. "My mother wanted to be a lawyer but gave it all up when she married my father." Though the mothers are painted as generally ineffectual, they do exercise power in one limited realm: over their children. There, as if they are compensating for their misery elsewhere, they are often suffocating, dominating, and manipulative. Rather than rejecting the passive aggressive behavior of their mothers and with it the more destructive results of such behavior, the women to whom I listened described their struggle for a social acceptance that would allow them to enact their mother's role. Most of them also strongly identified with their fathers, despite the fact that many fathers spent little time with their families. Instead, they concentrated on interests outside the home. Some of the women reported that the fathers were more persistent in their demands for prettiness and feminine behavior than the mothers. Fathers were objects of hero worship, even though they were preoccupied, distant, or emotionally rejecting.

> from "Cinderella's Stepsisters: A Feminist Perspective
> on Anorexia Nervosa and Bulimia," Marlene Boskind-
> Lodahl, *Signs*, Winter 1976

F. Bulimia, an appetite disorder, has been recognized as a significant problem with college-age females. Has this disorder filtered down to the high school level as have other collegiate life styles? This research clearly answers the question in the affirmative.

Bulimia is a newly documented appetite disorder characterized by an uncontrollable urge to eat, consideration of oneself as a binge eater, feelings of guilt coupled with self-deprecating thoughts, actual binging on food, and a fear of not being able to stop eating. The third edition of the *Diagnostic and Statistical Manual* of the American Psychiatric Association (DSM-III, 1980) has recognized bulimia as a distinct disorder when three of these characteristics are present.

This research project, among the first to be conducted with a high school population, surveyed the entire female population of a midwestern suburban high school; 1093 students responded to the Eating Disorder Inventory (EDI). Students identified as Probably Bulimic were present in all age groups (14–18), and all ethnic groups.

Thus it would appear that there is, indeed, a new adolescent problem which needs to be recognized by people who work with adolescents.

There was an interest in bulimia even before the symptoms were first described in the DSM-III. In 1976, Marlene Boskind-Lodahl's study defined bulimarexia as a cyclical eating disorder characterized by binging/purging behaviors and abnormally low self-esteem. In this study, the low self-esteem which affected women was hypothesized to be caused by a society which teaches women to be responsive to the needs of men and to feel the need to be attractive to them.

Stangler and Printz (1980) used the DSM-III to diagnose a college population and found that bulimia was frequently present in this age group:

> The emergence of bulimia as a diagnostic entity and its striking frequency in our sample serves as one example of the complicated sociocultural issues surrounding femininity.

Thirty-four case studies were reported by Pyle et al. (1981), all of which met the criteria set by DSM-III for bulimia. All were white females with a median age of twenty-four; the median age of onset was eighteen; and most had suffered from bulimia for several years without treatment. These patients stated that they had not told anyone of their problem because they feared they would be considered weird.

from "The Presence of Bulimia in High School
Females" Mary Deanna Van Thorre and Francis X.
Vogel, Adolescence, Spring 1985

EVALUATING SEVEN SOURCES: AN EXAMPLE

Assume that you are gathering information for an essay about Ernest Hemingway's life in Paris in 1924 and 1925. From your introductory reading, you have already become familiar with some of the basic facts. You know that Hemingway and his wife, Hadley, traveled to Paris with their infant son, Bumby; that the Hemingways had very little money; that they associated with many of the literary figures who lived in Paris at the time; that they took occasional trips to Spain for the bull-running and to Austria for the skiing; and that Hemingway was working on a novel called *The Sun Also Rises*. Now, through research, you are intending to fill in the details that will enable you to construct a portrait of Hemingway and his Paris experiences. You have selected a preliminary bibliography of seven books. Here is the annotated preliminary bibliography; the comments are based on a rapid examination of each book.

Baker, Carlos. *Hemingway: A Life Story*. New York: Scribner's, 1969. 563 pages of biography, with one hundred pages of footnotes. Everything seems to be here, presented in great detail.

Donaldson, Scott. *Hemingway: By Force of Will*. New York: Viking, 1977. The material isn't organized chronologically; instead, the chapters are thematic, with titles like "Money," "Sex," "War," etc. Episodes from Hemingway's life are presented within each chapter. The introduction calls this "a mosaic of [Hemingway's] mind and personality." Lots of footnotes.

Gurko, Leo. *Ernest Hemingway and the Pursuit of Heroism*. New York: Crowell, 1968. This is part of a series called "Twentieth Century American Writers": a brief introduction to the man and his work. After fifty pages of straight biography, Gurko discusses Hemingway's writing, novel by novel. There's an index and a short bibliography, but no notes. The biographical part is clear and easy to read, but it sounds too much like a summary.

Hemingway, Ernest. *A Moveable Feast*. New York: Scribner's, 1964. This is Hemingway's own version of his life in Paris. It sounds authentic, but there's also a very strongly nostalgic tone, so I'm not sure how trustworthy it is.

Hemingway, Leicester. *My Brother, Ernest Hemingway*. Cleveland: World, 1962. It doesn't sound as if the family was very close. For 1924–1925, he's using information from Ernest's letters (as well as commonly known facts). The book reads like a third-hand report, very remote; but L. H. sounds honest, not as if he were making up things that he doesn't know about.

Hotchner, A. E. *Papa Hemingway*. New York: Random House, 1955. This is called a "personal memoir." Hotchner met Hemingway in 1948, and evidently hero-worshiped him. Hemingway rambled on about his past, and Hotchner tape-recorded much of it. The book is their dialogue (mostly Hemingway's monologue). No index or bibliography. Hotchner's adoring tone is annoying, and the material resembles that of *A Moveable Feast*, which is better written.

Sokoloff, Alice Hunt. *Hadley, the First Mrs. Hemingway*. New York: Dodd, Mead, 1973. This is the Paris experience from Hadley's point of view, most of it taken from her recollections and from the standard biographies. (Baker is acknowledged.) It's a very slight book—102 pages—but there's an index and footnotes, citing letters and interviews that some of the other biographers might not have been able to use.

Examining the Sources

The notes on those seven sources seem to be the outgrowth of two separate processes. In the first place, the student is noting basic facts about each biography—the length of the book, the amount of documentation, the potential bias of the writer (if it is easily recognized), and the way in which the material has been organized. But there are also several comments on tone, impressions of the way in which the information is being presented: "sounds like . . ." or "reads like . . ." How were these impressions formed?

Let's begin with the biography which, according to the annotations, may be the most thorough and complete of the seven. Here is Carlos Baker's account of Ernest and Hadley Hemingway immediately after their arrival in Paris:

> The first problem in Paris was to find an apartment. Ezra's *pavillon* in the rue Notre Dame des Champs was too cold and damp for the baby, but there was another available flat on the second floor of a building farther up the hill. It was a pleasant street sloping down from the corner of the Avenue de l'Observatoire and the Boulevard du Montparnasse, an easy stroll from the Luxembourg Gardens, where Hadley could air the baby, a stone's throw from an unspoiled café called La Closerie des Lilas, and much closer to Gertrude Stein's than the former walk-up apartment in the rue du Cardinal Lemoine. The whole neighborhood was a good deal prettier and more polite than that of the Montagne Ste.-Geneviève, though not much quieter. The Hemingways' windows at Number 113 looked down upon a sawmill and lumberyard. It was owned and operated by Pierre Chautard, who lived with his wife and a small dog on the ground floor. The whine of the circular saw, the chuff of the donkey-engine that drove it, the hollow boom of newly sawn planks being laid in piles, and the clatter of the ancient camions that carried the lumber away made such a medley that Ernest was often driven to the haven of the Closerie des Lilas to do his writing.
>
> In the apartment itself, a dark tunnel of a hall led to a kitchen with a stone sink and a two-ring gas burner for cooking. There was a dining room, mostly filled by a large table, and a small bedroom where Ernest sometimes worked. The master bedroom held a stove and double bed, with a small dressing room large enough for the baby's crib. Hadley quickly rehired the *femme de ménage*, Madame Henri Rohrback, who had worked for her off and on before. Marie was a sturdy peasant from Mur-de-Bretagne. She and her husband, who was called Ton-Ton, lived at 10 bis, Avenue des Gobelins. Her own nickname was Marie Cocotte, from her method of calling the chickens at home on the farm in Brittany. She took at once to the child and often bore him away in a carriage lent by the Straters to see Ton-Ton, who was a retired soldier

with time on his hands. Madame Chautard, the wife of the owner of the sawmill, was a plump and childless woman with brassy hair and a voice so harsh that it made the baby cry. She seemed to be envious of Hadley's motherhood. Watching the child drink his daily ration of orange juice she could only say scornfully, "*Il sera un poivrot comme sa mère.*"* Of the baby's many nicknames—Gallito, Matt, and Joe—the one that stuck was Bumby, which Hadley invented to signify his warm, plump, teddy-bearish, arm-filling solidity which both parents admired and enjoyed.

What makes Baker's description so effective is the impressive amount of detail. One cannot help believing a biographer who offers so much specific information about everyone and everything with even the remotest connection to his subject. One expects to be told what Hemingway ate for dinner and, indeed, in reporting the novelist's skiing trip to Schruns, Baker tells us that the cook prepared "great roasts of beef, with potatoes browned in gravy, jugged hare with wine sauce, venison chops, a special omelette soufflé, and homemade plum pudding." On the other hand, you are sometimes told more than you want to know. There's a house-that-Jack-built effect in the sentences about the Hemingways' nursemaid who was a "sturdy peasant from Mur-de-Bretagne," who had a husband named Ton-Ton, who lived in the Avenue des Gobelins, whose nickname was the result of . . . and so on. Nevertheless, Baker tells a good story and his description of the apartment is effective: notice the description of the sounds that Hemingway must have heard from his windows.

Next, in sharp contrast to all this detail, we have a comparable passage from the biography by Leo Gurko (which the bibliography described as "a summary"). Gurko is dealing with the same material as Baker, in less than one-tenth the space, and naturally offers much less detail:

> Paris in the 1920s was everyone's catalyst. It was the experimental and fermenting center of every art. It was highly sophisticated, yet broke up naturally into small intimate *quartiers.* Its cafés were hotbeds of intellectual and social energy, pent up during the war and now released. Young people from all over the world flocked to Paris, drawn not only by the city's intrinsic attractions but by the devaluation of the franc.
>
> The young Hemingways settled on the Left Bank, and since they were short of money, rented modest rooms in an ancient walk-up. They moved several times, taking flats that were usually on the top floor, five or six flights up, commanding good views of the roofs of Paris. This was somehow in tune with a passion to absorb the city.

*"He'll become a lush like his mother."

Hemingway did much of his writing in cafés, where he would sit for hours over a beer or *Pernod* with paper spread before him. He took long walks through the streets and gardens, lingered over the Cézannes in the Luxembourg Museum, and let the great city permeate his senses.

Baker was trying as much as possible to draw the reader into the scene and to share the Hemingways' own experience of Paris. In contrast, Gurko is *outside* the scene, describing what he, the observer, has seen over the distance of time. He does not hesitate to tell his reader what to think—about Paris, about its expatriate population, and about the Hemingways. Notice in this short passage how Gurko moves from verifiable facts to his own hypotheses:

The Hemingways put themselves on short rations, ate, drank, and entertained as little as possible, pounced eagerly on the small checks that arrived in the mail as payment for accepted stories, and were intensely conscious of being poor. The sensation was not altogether unpleasant. Their extreme youth, the excitement of living abroad, the sense of making a fresh start, even the unexpected joy of parenthood, gave their poverty a romantic flavor.

Gurko's book does not document his sources; the reader is asked to accept Gurko's assertion that being poor in Paris was "not altogether unpleasant" for Hemingway, because of its romantic connotations. Other biographers, however, may not agree with this statement. Remember that Gurko's hypothesis is one man's opinion and is not to be confused with fact or presented as such in a research essay. Acceptance of this opinion depends on Gurko's credentials as an authority on Hemingway and on what other established authorities have to say.

Here's a final excerpt from Gurko's biography, as a starting point for a second group of comparisons. Notice his tendency to generalize and summarize and, especially, to speak for Hemingway. Then contrast Gurko's approach with that of Alice Sokoloff:

He was becoming increasingly devoted to imaginative writing, to the point where his newspaper assignments and the need to grind out journalistic pieces were growing more and more irksome. Another threat to his work was the "arty" atmosphere of Paris. The cafés of the city, he soon recognized, were filled with aesthetes of one kind or another who wanted to be artists, talked incessantly and even knowledgeably about art, but never really produced anything. There were a hundred of these clever loafers and dilettantes for every real writer. Hemingway developed a contempt and even fear of them, perhaps because there was in him, as in most genuine artists, a feeling of uncertainty about his own talent. He drove himself to hard work and avoided the café crowd as much as he could.

Leo Gurko

It was a worldly crowd, full of intellectual and artistic ferment, some of it real, some of it bogus, some of them obsessed with their own egos, a few of them deeply and sincerely interested in Ernest's talent. The Hemingways' finances were as restricted as ever, but these people "could offer them all the amenities, could take them anywhere for gorgeous meals," could produce any kind of entertainment and diversion. Although Ernest accepted it all, Hadley thought that he resented it and always kept "a very stiff upper front to satisfy himself." He did not want "simply to sink back and take all this," but the success and admiration was heady stuff and he could not help but enjoy it.[1] Hadley used to be wryly amused when Ernest and Gertrude Stein would talk about worldly success and how it did not mean anything to them.[2] The fact that this was true for a part of him, and that he despised anything false or pretentious, was a source of inner conflict which sometimes expressed itself in malice.

[1]John Dos Passos. *The Best Times* (New York: New American Library, 1966), p. 143.
[2]Interview with Hadley Richardson Hemingway Mowrer, January 18, 1972.

Alice Sokoloff

Sokoloff's conclusions differ from Gurko's: she points to a conflict in Hemingway's reaction to his Paris acquaintances, and offers footnotes to support her suggestion. In another sense, Sokoloff's commentary is limited: because the subject of her biography is Hadley Hemingway, she is describing events from Hadley's point of view. On the other hand, Sokoloff's presentation makes it fairly easy to figure out where Hadley's version leaves off and the biographer's account begins, and the story is told coherently.

Leicester Hemingway's account of his brother's life is far more confusing; most of his information comes from letters, and he makes little attempt to sort out the contents into a form that the average reader can follow easily:

Things were going very well for Ernest, with his home life as well as with his writing. Bumby was beginning to talk and Ernest was learning that a child could be more fun than fret. With wife and son he took off for Schruns in the Vorarlberg when good skiing weather set in. For months they were deep in the snow up there, working and enjoying the sports, before returning to Paris in mid-March.

Ernest wrote the family that when they camped in the mountains, up above 2,000 meters, there had been lots of ptarmigan and foxes, too. The deer and chamois were lower down.

He said Bumby weighed twenty-nine pounds, played in a sand pile with shovel and pail, and was always jolly. His own writing was going very well. *In Our Time* was out of print and bringing high prices, he said, while his stories were being translated into Russian and German. . . .

Hadley added other details, thanking the family for the Christmas box which had been delayed more than two months in customs, but had arrived without damage to the fruit cake—Mother's one culinary triumph besides meat loaf. She wrote that Bumby had a wonderful nurse who had taken care of him while she and Ernest spent days at a stretch in mountain huts to be near good snow.

Ernest's writing is mixed up with Bumby's pail and shovel and fruitcakes for Christmas. This is certainly raw material. The biography offers no interpretation at all for the reader to discount or accept. The material is stitched together so crudely that one has to spend time sorting out important details from trivia. Certainly, this biography would be a poor choice for the student who was beginning research on this topic; but the details might provide interesting background once the events of 1924–1925 were made more familiar by other biographies.

Finally, here are four descriptions of Hemingway as a baby sitter, odd-job man, and scavenger, all dealing with similar experiences:

Ernest was working fairly hard. He awoke early in the spring mornings, "boiled the rubber nipples and the bottles, made the formula, finished the bottling, gave Mr. Bumby a bottle," and wrote for a time at the dining-room table before Hadley got up. Chautard had not begun his sawing at that hour, the street was quiet, and Ernest's only companions were Mr. Bumby and Mr. Feather Puss, a large cat given them by Kitty Cannell and named with one of Hadley's nicknames. But Ernest was truly domestic only in the early mornings. He took the freedom of Paris as his personal prerogative, roving as widely as he chose. There was a gymnasium in the rue Pontoise where he often went to earn ten francs a round by sparring with professional heavyweights. The job called for a nice blend of skill and forbearance, since hirelings must be polite while fighting back just enough to engage, without enraging, the emotions of the fighters. Ernest had befriended a waiter at the Closerie des Lilas and sometimes helped him weed a small vegetable garden near the Porte d'Orléans. The waiter knew that he was a writer and warned him that the boxing might jar his brains. But Ernest was glad enough to earn the extra money. He had already begun to save up to buy pesetas for another trip to Spain in July.

Carlos Baker

When there were the three of us instead of just the two, it was the cold and the weather that finally drove us out of Paris in the winter time. Alone there was no problem when you got used to it. I could always go to a café to write and could work all morning over a *café crème* while the waiters cleaned and swept out the café and it gradually grew warmer. My wife could go to work at the piano in a cold place and with enough sweaters keep warm playing and come home to nurse Bumby. It was wrong to take a baby to a café in the winter though; even a baby that never cried and watched everything that happened and was never bored. There were no baby-sitters then and Bumby would stay happy in his tall cage bed with his big, loving cat named F. Puss. There were people who said that it was dangerous to leave a cat with a baby. The most ignorant and prejudiced said that a cat would suck a baby's breath and kill him. Others said that a cat would lie on a baby and the cat's weight would smother him. F. Puss lay beside Bumby in the tall cage bed and watched the door with his big yellow eyes, and would let no one come near him when we were out and Marie, the *femme de ménage*, had to be away. There was no need for baby-sitters. F. Puss was the baby-sitter.

Ernest Hemingway

. . . As he grew older (and *A Moveable Feast* was the last book he finished), Hemingway laid increasing stress on the poverty he suffered in Paris. Without question, Ernest and Hadley Hemingway lived on a relatively scant income during those years, but they were never so badly off as the writer, in retrospect, liked to believe.

In any case, poverty is virtually apotheosized in *A Moveable Feast*. As the title hints, a gnawing hunger for food and drink symbolizes Hemingway's indigence. According to the legend constructed in this book, Hemingway worked all day in his unheated garret, too poor to buy firewood or afford lunch. At least he does not tell here the unlikely yarn that appears in A. E. Hotchner's biography: the one about Hemingway catching pigeons in the Luxembourg Gardens in order to satisfy a rumbling stomach. But poverty, and its symbolic hunger, are nonetheless celebrated. "You got very hungry when you did not eat enough in Paris," Hemingway writes, because of the good things on display in the *pâtisseries* and at the outdoor restaurants. Mostly he and Hadley survived on leeks (*poireaux*), but at least so frugal a diet enabled one to savor, truly, the joys of eating well when an unexpected windfall made it possible for them to dine out.

Scott Donaldson

Ernest wanted me to see the neighborhood where he had first lived; we started on Rue Notre-Dame-des-Champs, where he had lived over a sawmill, and slowly worked our way past familiar restaurants, bars and stores, to the Jardin du Luxembourg and its museum, where, Ernest said, he fell in love with certain paintings that taught him how to write. "Am also fond of the Jardin," Ernest said, "because it kept us from starvation. On days when the dinner pot was absolutely devoid of content, I would put Bumby, then about a year old, into the baby carriage and wheel him over here to the Jardin. There was always a *gendarme* on duty, but I knew that around four o'clock he would go to a bar across from the park to have a glass of wine. That's when I would appear with Mr. Bumby—and a pocketful of corn for the pigeons. I would sit on a bench, in my guise of buggy-pushing pigeon-lover, casing the flock for clarity of eye and plumpness. The Luxembourg was well known for the classiness of its pigeons. Once my selection was made, it was a simple matter to entice my victim with the corn, snatch him, wring his neck, and flip his carcass under Mr. Bumby's blanket. We got a little tired of pigeon that winter, but they filled many a void. What a kid that Bumby was—played it straight—and never once put the finger on me."

A. E. Hotchner

Characteristically, Baker describes exactly how the father tended his son, pausing to explain the full name and the origins of their cat. Hemingway himself, years after the event, describes much the same relationship, but with a completely different emphasis and set of details. The two passages are not in conflict; but they are not at all the same kind of writing and, in fact, they provide an excellent illustration of the difficulties of combining two sources written in two different modes for two different kinds of audience. The Hemingway who reminisced for A. E. Hotchner offers a somewhat different version of the same experience, a version criticized in Donaldson's extract, which tries to distinguish between nostalgia and truth. Unlike Gurko's, Donaldson's presentation is detailed; unlike Baker, he has an outsider's perspective, and the combination, backed up by documentation, is quite convincing.

In what order, then, would you consult these seven books for full-scale research? You might begin with Gurko's brief account, to establish the sequence of events, and then fill in the details by reading Baker's longer version. Donaldson gets pushed down the list to third or fourth, primarily because his biography is not chronological; gathering the scattered references to 1924 will be easier once the overall chronology has been made clear by Gurko and Baker. Now, you can also draw on the details to be found in the works by "interested" parties: wife, brother, friend, and the author himself. And, at intervals, you should stop reading and note-taking to compare these various versions of one life and determine which of the sources was in a position to know the truth—the man himself, thirty years later? his correspondence at the time? records left by his wife (whom, in fact, he divorced in 1929)? his biographers, whose information is presented second-hand? a combination of all the sources?

EXERCISE 33

Choose one of the passages listed below and:

A. Find out some information about the author's background and write a paragraph describing his qualifications for writing about this subject.
B. Think about the suggested research topics that accompany the references, and state whether and why the passage would be a suitable source to consult if you were writing an essay on that topic.

1. Bertrand Russell: "The Social Responsibility of Scientists" (Chapter 1, p. 56)
   a) The arms race
   b) The power of the media
2. John Kenneth Galbraith: excerpt from *The Affluent Society* (Chapter 1, p. 7.)
   a) Conspicuous consumption in America
   b) What is the American dream?
3. Andrew Carnegie: excerpt from *The Gospel of Wealth* (Chapter 2, p. 108)
   a) American tycoons at the turn of the century
   b) In support of private charity
4. Margaret Mead: excerpt from *Some Personal Views* (Chapter 1, p. 49)
   a) Origins of neurosis
   b) Problems of the handicapped child
5. Robert K. Merton: "Scientific Fraud and the Fight to be First" (Chapter 1, p. 27)
   a) Plagiarism in scientific research
   b) Competition as a cause of deviant behavior

EXERCISE 34

In the middle of the night of November 29, 1942, a Boston nightclub called the Cocoanut Grove burned down, resulting in the deaths of at least three hundred people. Read the following three accounts of this disaster, and be prepared to discuss the differences in content, organization, tone, purpose, and point of view. What is the thesis of each article? Consider how you would use the three articles in a single research essay dealing with the Cocoanut Grove disaster. Are these three versions interchangeable?

300 KILLED BY FIRE, SMOKE AND PANIC IN BOSTON RESORT—DEAD CLOG EXITS—Terror Piles Up Victims as Flames Suddenly Engulf Nightclub—Service Men to Rescue—Many of Them Perish—Girls of Chorus Leap to Safety—150 Are Injured

BOSTON, Sunday, Nov. 29—More than 300 persons had perished early this morning in flames, smoke and panic in the Cocoanut Grove Night Club in the midtown theatre district.

The estimate of the dead came at 2 A.M. from William Arthur Reilly, Fire Commissioner, as firemen and riggers searched the ruins for additional bodies. It was a disaster unprecedented in this city.

The chief loss of life resulted from the screaming, clawing crowds that were wedged in the entrance of the club. Smoke took a terrific toll of life and scores were burned to death.

At the Boston City Hospital officials said there were so many bodies lined up in corridors that they would attempt no identifications before daybreak.

Commissioner Reilly stated that an eyewitness inside the club said the fire started when an artificial palm near the main entrance was set afire.

Martial law was clamped on the entire fire area at 1:35 A.M. Sailors, Coast Guardsmen, shore patrolmen and naval officers dared death time and again trying to get at bodies that were heaped six feet high by one of the entrances.

Firemen said that many bodies were believed to have fallen into the basement after the main floor collapsed.

A chorus boy, Marshall Cook, aged 19, of South Boston, led three co-workers, eight chorus girls and other floor show performers totaling thirty-five to an adjoining roof from the second-floor dressing rooms and from there they dropped to the ground from a ladder.

Scores of ambulances from nearby cities, the Charlestown Navy Yard and the Chelsea Naval Hospital poured into the area, but the need for ambulances became so great that even railway express trucks were pressed into service to carry away victims. At one time victims, many of them dead, lay two deep in an adjoining garage.

Many of the victims were soldiers, sailors, marines and Coast Guardsmen, some of them junior officers, visiting Boston for a weekend of merrymaking. In the throng were persons who had attended the Holy Cross–Boston College football game.

Scores of dead were piled up in the lobbies of the various hospitals as the doctors and nurses gave all their attention to the 150 injured.

A "flash" fire, believed to have started in the basement, spread like lightning through the dance floor area, and the panic was on. All available nurses and priests were being called into the disaster area.

Among the dead were a marine and one who appeared to be a fireman. Casualties were arriving at hospitals so rapidly that they were being placed in the corridors wherever a suitable place could be found.

It appeared probable that the greatest loss of life was in the newly opened lounge of the night club in Broadway. Here, one policeman said, burned and suffocated persons were heaped to the top of the doors, wedged in death.

The night club was a one-and-a-half story building with a stucco exterior. The blaze was said to have broken out in the basement kitchen at 10:17 P.M. just as the floor show performers were preparing for their next performance. Performers on the second floor were met by terrific smoke and flame as they started downstairs. Their stories were the only ones available, as those who had escaped the dance floor and tables were too hysterical to talk.

A temporary morgue and hospital were set up in the garage of the Film Exchange Transfer Company at the rear of the club in Shawmut Street. At least fourteen persons, suffocated and lying in grotesque positions, were lying on the garage floor at one time, while scores of injuries were cared for by garage workers and others.

The city's Civilian Defense Workers were called to the scene to maintain order and to give first aid to those suffering from burns and smoke inhalation. Every hospital in the area soon was loaded with the victims.

At least thirty-five performers and their friends were rescued by the quick actions of Marshall Cook, a South Boston boy. He was met by a blast of flame as he started down stairs, went back to the dressing room and organized those caught there.

He then smashed his way through a window, carrying away the casing. Through this opening he led a group to an adjoining room, where a small ladder was found. The ladder was not long enough to reach the street, but Cook and several other male performers held the top end over the roof's edge and guided the women over the side. They had to jump about 6 feet to reach the ground.

At the City Hospital bodies were piled on the floors, many so burned that there was no attempt to identify them immediately. Many service men were among the victims, many of whom were partly identified through their uniforms.

Buck Jones, the film star, was believed to be one of the victims.

Among the first at the scene was the Rev. Joseph A. Marcus of Cranwell School, Lenox, who administered the last rites for at least fifty persons. In the meantime, thirty or forty ambulances rushed to the fire, these coming from Lynn, Newton, and Brookline. Despite the hindrances caused by automobiles parked in the streets, some of the dead and injured were taken from nearby buildings, where they had been left covered only by newspapers.

Abraham Levy, a cashier at the Cocoanut Grove, said there were about 400 in the place, including many sailors.

Sailors saved many lives, pulling people through the doors and out of danger. A fireman said that he saw at least thirty bodies lying on the floor, and that he believed some of them were firemen.

Among the spectacular escapes were those of two of the eight chorus girls, who leaped from the second floor and were caught by two of the male dancers. They were Lottie Christie of Park Drive, Boston, and Claudia Boyle. They jumped into the arms of Andrew Louzan and Robert Gilbert. Louzan and Gilbert had climbed out of a window of their dressing room to an adjoining roof and then descended by ladder.

New York Times, 30 November 1942

CATASTROPHE: BOSTON'S WORST

Holy Cross had just beaten Boston College: downtown Boston was full of men & women eager to celebrate or console. Many of them wound up at Cocoanut Grove: they stood crowded around the dimly lighted downstairs bar, filled the tables around the dance floor upstairs. With them mingled the usual Saturday night crowd: soldiers & sailors, a wedding party, a few boys being sent off to Army camps.

At 10 o'clock Bridegroom John O'Neil, who had planned to take his bride to their new apartment at the stroke of the hour, lingered on a little longer. The floor show was about to start. Through the big revolving door, couples moved in & out.

At the downstairs bar, a 16-year-old busboy stood on a bench to replace a light bulb that a prankish customer had removed. He lit a match. It touched one of the artificial palm trees that gave the Cocoanut Grove its atmosphere; a few flames shot up. A girl named Joyce Spector sauntered toward the checkroom because she was worried about her new fur coat.

Panic's Start

Before Joyce Spector reached the cloakroom, the Cocoanut Grove was a screaming shambles. The fire quickly ate away the palm tree, raced along silk draperies, was sucked upstairs through the stairway, leaped along ceiling and wall. The silk hangings, turned to balloons of flame, fell on table and floor.

Men & women fought their way toward the revolving door; the push of bodies jammed it. Nearby was another door; it was locked tight. There were other exits, but few Cocoanut Grove patrons knew about them. The lights went out. There was nothing to see now except flame, smoke and weird moving torches that were men & women with clothing and hair afire.

The 800 Cocoanut Grove patrons pushed and shoved, fell and were trampled. Joyce Spector was knocked under a table, crawled on hands & knees, somehow was pushed through an open doorway into the street. A chorus boy herded a dozen people downstairs into a refrigerator. A few men & women crawled out windows; a few escaped by knocking out a glass brick wall. But most of them, including Bridegroom John O'Neil, were trapped.

Panic's Sequel

Firemen broke down the revolving door, found it blocked by bodies of the dead, six deep. They tried to pull a man out through a side window; his legs were held tight by the mass of struggling people behind him. In an hour the fire was out and firemen began untangling the piles of bodies. One hard bitten fireman went into hysterics when he picked up a body and a foot came off in his hand. They found a girl dead in a telephone booth, a bartender still standing behind his bar.

At hospitals and improvised morgues which were turned into charnel houses for the night, 484 dead were counted; it was the most disastrous U.S. fire since 571 people were killed in Chicago's Iroquois Theater holocaust in 1903. One Boston newspaper ran a two-word banner line: BUSBOY BLAMED. But the busboy had not put up the Cocoanut Grove's tinderbox decorations, nor was he responsible for the fact that Boston's laws do not require nightclubs to have fireproof fixtures, sprinkler systems or exit markers.

Time, 7 December 1942

[COMMENTARY]

On the last Sunday morning of November, 1942, most inhabitants of greater Boston learned from their newspapers that at about the time they had gone to bed the night before the most terrible fire in the history of their city had occurred. The decorations of a crowded night club had got ignited, the crowd had stampeded, the exits had jammed, and in a few minutes hundreds of people had died of burns or suffocation. Two weeks later the list of dead had reached almost exactly five hundred, and the war news was only beginning to come back to Boston front pages. While the Allied invasion of North Africa stalled, while news was released that several transports engaged in it had been sunk, while the Russians and the Germans fought monstrously west of Stalingrad and Moscow, while the Americans bombed Naples and the RAF obliterated Turin and conducted the war's most widespread raids over western Europe, while the Japs tried again in the Solomons and mowed down their attackers in New Guinea, while a grave conflict of civilian opinion over the use of Admiral Darlan developed in America and Great Britain, while the anniversary of Pearl Harbor passed almost unnoticed—while all this was going on the Boston papers reported it in stickfuls in order to devote hundreds of columns to the fire at the Cocoanut Grove. And the papers did right, for the community has experienced an angry horror surpassing anything that it can remember. For weeks few Bostonians were able to feel strongly about anything but their civic disaster.

There is irony in such preoccupation with a minute carnage. In the same fortnight thousands of men were killed in battle. Every day, doubtless, more than five hundred were burned to death, seared by powder or gasoline from bombed dumps, in buildings fired from the sky, or in blazing airplanes and sinking ships. If these are thought of as combatants meeting death in the line of duty, far more than five hundred civilians were killed by military action in Germany, Italy, France, Great Britain, Russia, China, Australia, and the islands of the Pacific. Meanwhile in two-thirds of the world civilians died of torture and disease and starvation, in prison camps and wire stockades and the rubble of their homes—they simply came to their last breath and died, by the thousand. At a moment when violent death is commonplace, when it is inevitable for hundreds of thousands, there is something grotesque in being shocked by a mere five hundred deaths which are distinguished from the day's routine only by the fact that they were not inevitable. When hundreds of towns are bombed repeatedly, when cities the size of Boston are overrun by invading armies, when many hundreds of Boston's own citizens will surely be killed in battle in the next few weeks, why should a solitary fire, a truly inconsiderable slaughter, so oppress the spirit?

That oppression provides perspective on our era. We have been so conditioned to horror that horror must explode in our own backyard before we can genuinely feel it. At the start of the decade our nerves responded to Hitler's murdering the German Jews with the outrage properly felt in the presence of cruelty and pain. Seven years later our nerves had been so overloaded that they felt no such outrage at the beginning of a systematic effort to exterminate an entire nation, such as Poland. By progressive steps we had come to strike a truce with the intolerable, precisely as the body develops immunity to poisons and bacteria. Since then three years of war have made the intolerable our daily bread, and every one of us has comfortably adapted to things which fifteen years ago would have driven him insane. The extinction of a nation now seems merely an integral part of the job in hand. But the needless death of five hundred people in our home town strikes through the immunity and horrifies us.

The fire at the Cocoanut Grove was a single, limited disaster, but it exhausted Boston's capacity to deal with an emergency. Hospital facilities were strained to the limit and somewhat beyond it. If a second emergency had had to be dealt with at the same time its victims would have had to wait some hours for transportation and a good many hours for treatment. If there had been three such fires at once, two-thirds of the victims would have got no treatment whatever in time to do them any good. Boston is an inflammable city and it has now had instruction in what to expect if a dozen hostile planes should come over and succeed in dropping incendiary bombs. The civilian defense agencies which were called on justified themselves and vindicated their training. The Nurses' Aid in particular did a memorable job; within a few hours there was a trained person at the bed of every victim, many other Aids worked to exhaustion helping hospital staffs do their jobs, and in fact more were available than could be put to use. Nevertheless it was clearly demonstrated that the civilian agencies are nowhere near large enough to take care of bombings if bombings should come. There were simply not enough ambulances; Railway Express Company trucks had to be called on to take the injured to hospitals and the dead to morgues. The dead had to be stacked like cord wood in garages because the morgues could take no more; the dying had to be laid in rows in the corridors of hospitals because the emergency wards were full. The drainage of doctors into the military service had left Boston just about enough to care for as many victims as this single fire supplied. Six months from now there will be too few to handle an equal emergency; there are far too few now for one twice as serious. One plane-load of incendiaries would start more fires than the fire department and its civilian assistants could put out. There would be more injured than there are even the most casually trained first-aiders to care for. Hundreds would be abandoned to the ignorant assistance of untrained persons, in streets so blocked by rubble and so jammed with military vehicles that trained crews could not reach them even when trained crews should be free. Boston has learned that it is not prepared to take care of itself. One doubts if any community in the United States is.

Deeper implications of the disaster have no direct connection with the war. An outraged city has been confronting certain matters which it ordinarily disregards. As a place of entertainment the Cocoanut Grove was garish but innocuous and on the whole useful. It had been called "the poor man's Ritz"; for years people had been going there to have a good time and had got what they were looking for. With the naïve shock customary in such cases, the city has now discovered that these people were not receiving the minimum protection in their pleasures to which they were entitled and which they supposed they were receiving.

The name of the night club suggests the kind of decorations that cluttered it; the public supposed that the law required them to be fireproof; actually they burned like so much celluloid. The laws relating to them were ambiguous and full of loopholes; such as they were, they were not enforced. The public supposed that an adequate number of exits was required and that periodic inspections were made; they were not. There were too few exits for the customary crowds, one was concealed, another could not be opened, and panic-stricken people piled up before the rest and died there by the score. The public supposed that laws forbidding overcrowding were applied to night clubs and were enforced; on the night of the fire the place was packed so full that movement was almost impossible, and it had been just as crowded at least once a week throughout the years of its existence. The public supposed that laws requiring safe practice in electric wiring and machinery were enforced; the official investigations have shown that the wiring was installed by unlicensed electricians, that a number of people had suspected it was faulty, and that in fact officials had notified the club that it was violating the law and had threatened to take action—but had not carried out the threat. Above all, the public supposed that an adequate building code taking into account the realities of modern architecture and modern metropolitan life established certain basic measures of protection. It has now learned that the Boston building code is a patched makeshift based on the conditions of 1907, and that though a revision which would modernize it was made in 1937, various reasons have held up the adoption of that revision for five years.

These facts have been established by five official investigations, one of them made by the Commonwealth of Massachusetts in an obvious expectation that the municipal authorities of Boston would find convincing reasons to deal gently with themselves. They have turned up other suggestive facts. The Cocoanut Grove was once owned by a local racketeer, who was murdered in the routine of business. The present owners were so expertly concealed behind a façade of legal figureheads that for twenty-four hours after the fire the authorities were not sure that they knew who even one of them was and two weeks later were not sure that they knew them all. An intimation that financial responsibility was avoided by a technically contrived bankruptcy has not yet been followed up as I write this, and other financial details are still lost in a maze of subterfuges. It is supposed that some of the club's employees had their wagescale established by terrorism. Investigators have encountered, but so far have not published, the customary free-list and lists of those entitled to discounts. Presumably such lists contemplated the usual returns in publicity and business favors; presumably also they found a use in the amenities of regulation. Names and business practices of the underworld have kept cropping up in all the investigations, and it is whispered that the reason why the national government has been conducting one of them is the presence at the club of a large amount of liquor on which the latest increase in revenue taxes ought to have been paid but somehow had not been.

In short, Boston has been reminded, hardly for the first time, that laxity in municipal responsibility can be made to pay a profit and that there can be a remunerative partnership between the amusement business and the underworld. A great many Bostonians, now writing passionate letters to their newspapers and urging on their legislators innumerable measures of reform, have gone farther than that. They conclude that one of the reasons why the modernized building code has not been adopted is the fact that there are ways of making money from the looser provisions of the old code. They suppose that one reason why gaps and loopholes in safety regulations are maintained is that they are profitable. They suppose that one reason why laws and regulations can be disregarded with impunity is that some of those charged with the duty of enforcing them make a living from not enforcing them. They suppose that some proprietors of night clubs find that buying immunity is cheaper than obeying safety regulations and that they are able to find enforcement agents who will sell it. They suppose that civic irresponsibility in Boston can be related to the fact that a lot of people make money from it.

But the responsibility cannot be shouldered off on a few small grafters and a few underworld characters who have established business relations with them, and it would be civic fatuousness to seek expiation for the murder of five hundred citizens in the passage of some more laws. The trouble is not lack of laws but public acquiescence; the damaging alliance is not with the underworld but with a communal reverence of what is probably good for business. Five hundred deaths in a single hour seem intolerable, but the city has never dissented at all to a working alliance between its financial interests and its political governors—a partnership which daily endangers not five hundred but many thousand citizens. Through Boston, as through every other metropolis, run many chains of interests which might suffer loss if regulations for the protection of the public's health and life were rigorously enforced. They are sound and enlightened regulations, but if they should be enforced then retail sales, bank clearings, and investment balances might possibly fall off. The corner grocery and the downtown department store, the banks and the business houses, the labor unions and the suburban housewife are all consenting partners in a closely calculated disregard of public safety.

Since the system is closely calculated it usually works, it kills only a few at a time, mostly it kills gradually over a period of years. Sometimes however it runs into another mathematical certainty and then it has to be paid for in blocks of five hundred lives. At such times the community experiences just such an excess of guilt as Boston is feeling now, uncomfortably realizing that the community itself is the perpetrator of wanton murder. For the responsibility is the public's all along and the certain safeguard—a small amount of alertness, civic courage, and willingness to lose some money—is always in the public's hands. That means not the mayor's hands, but yours and mine.

It is an interesting thing to hold up to the light at a moment when millions of Americans are fighting to preserve, among other things, the civic responsibility of a self-governing people. It suggests that civilians who are not engaged in the war effort, and who feel intolerably abased because they are not, could find serviceable ways to employ their energies. They can get to work chipping rust and rot from the mechanisms of local government. The rust and rot are increasing because people who can profit from their increase count on our looking toward the war, not toward them. Your town may have a police force of no more than four and its amusement business may be confined to half a dozen juke joints, but some percentage of both may have formed a partnership against your interests under cover of the war. Certainly the town has a sewage system, a garbage dump, fire traps, a rudimentary public health code, ordinances designed to protect life, and a number of Joe Doakes who can make money by juggling the relationship among them. Meanwhile the ordinary hazards of peace are multiplied by the conditions of war, carelessness and preoccupation increase, and the inevitable war pestilence is gathering to spring. The end-products do not look pleasant when they are seen clearly, especially when a community realizes that it has killed five hundred people who did not need to die.

Bernard DeVoto, *Harper's,* February 1943

7.
Gathering Materials at the Library: Taking Notes

Copying machines are a tempting alternative to note-taking. However, taking notes remains an important skill. Some sources, like newspaper articles, are difficult to copy clearly; others contain only one or two useful sentences and are not worth the expense of copying.

Moreover, when you have found some sources worth copying, what do you do with the stack of xeroxed pages? You have only moved the raw materials from the library to your desk. How do you turn them into an essay? In order to take inventory and start working on your *essay* (as distinguished from your *research*), you must select the important points and discard the irrelevancies that surround them. Of course, you could plan the organization of your essay by cutting up each page and sorting the vital passages into separate piles; but unless you identify each source clearly on each bit of cut-up paper, you can easily lose track of its origin.

It therefore makes sense to take notes as part of the research process, to express as much of the information as you can in your own words, and, at the same time, to make copies of the most important passages, so that you will have the originals to refer to if your notes let you down. There is no substitute for good notes.

TAKING GOOD NOTES

The following guidelines should help your note-taking:

1. *Try to complete your survey of the library's resources and work out a preliminary bibliography before you start to make copies*

or take notes. Not only will you get a good idea of what materials are available and the probable extent of your research, but your survey can also assure you that your preferred topic is a practical one. If you start taking notes before you are certain of your precise focus, you may waste a good deal of time. You may discover, for example, that there is very little documented information about the gunfight at the O.K. Corral, and thus decide to shift your focus to Wyatt Earp. Or the amount of technical material about Lindbergh's flight in the *Spirit of St. Louis* might overwhelm you, with the result that you switch to Lindbergh's opposition to America's entry into World War II.

2. *Use paraphrase and summary rather than quotation.* If you write down sentence after sentence, word for word from your source, you might as well save time and copy the page. Remember that the longer you use the language of the original author, the more difficult it will be to make the transition to your own writing style. If your first draft reads like an anthology of cannibalized quotations, then you will find it hard to make your essay coherent and intelligible. The pasted-together sources will still be in control. Take the trouble *now* to master each new idea by putting it in your own words.

3. *Make sure that your notes make sense.* Remember that you will have seen a vast number of similar pages by the time you begin to organize your essay and that you won't remember everything. Plan to include a certain number of facts to serve as your supporting evidence. It is not enough to say that "X's father lost his job." What was his job? Why did he lose it? What did he do instead? Later on, you may find that these details are irrelevant and will not fit into the shape of your essay; but if you do need supporting evidence, you will find it easier to look in your notes than to go back to the library.

4. *Differentiate your own ideas from those that you are paraphrasing.* Taking notes is often an intellectually stimulating experience, probably because it requires so much concentration and because your reading rate is slowed down. You are therefore likely to have plenty of comments about the source that you are paraphrasing. As you develop your own ideas and include them in your notes, be careful to differentiate them from contributions of your sources. Later on, you will want to know exactly which ideas were yours and which were your source's. Square brackets ([ ]) for your own ideas are a good way of making this distinction.

5. *Keep a running record of page references.* In your essay, you will have to cite a page number for each reference, and these must be correct pages, not approximate guesses. It is therefore not enough to write "pp. 285–91" at the top of the note card or sheet. Three

weeks later, or three hours later, how will you remember on which of these pages you found the point that you want to cite in your essay? If you are writing a lengthy set of notes that paraphrase your source, make a slash and insert a new page number to indicate exactly where you turned the page. This is especially important for quotations. Of course, it is vital that you immediately put quotation marks around quotations since later on you will never remember who said what.

6. *Keep a master list of your sources, assigning a code number or symbol to each one.* As you take notes, use an abbreviation or code number to identify each new source. When you begin a new card or sheet, you won't have to repeat all the basic information.

Using Note Cards—One Fact per Card

The traditional method of taking notes is to write a single fact or piece of information on one three- by five-inch index card. These single-note cards are easily sorted into stacks; they can also be left at home when you go back to the library. On the other hand, index cards can stray from the pile and become lost. A stack of cards should be kept under control with a sturdy rubber band.

In fact, certain topics lend themselves to note cards, topics that require the collection of small, fragmentary bits of information, like facts or brief descriptions, which fit easily on to an index card. Eight- by ten-inch cards or sheets of paper may be more suitable for an abstract topic that depends on complex sources, with each one discussed at length. Whether you write on small cards or long sheets, make sure that you *write on one side only*, and be careful to label each separate unit of information with its exact source and page number, using abbreviations, symbols, or numbers.

One student, taking notes for an essay describing the 1871 fire that devastated Chicago, used the one-fact-per-card method. At the top of the following page is a typical note card.

The empty space that is left on this card may seem wasteful, but the method enables the writer, later on, to place all the cards that refer to the category *casualties* in a single pile. If the card contained information relating to two different categories, the same card would have to be placed in two separate piles, which would defeat the purpose of the organizational system. Notice that, to keep track of all the notes, the writer has assigned a number to the card.

Notes Grouped by Topic

A second student used a more sophisticated system combining note-taking and preliminary organization. Early in the note-taking process, the student decided that at least one card would be devoted only to

One fact per card

25

Estimate of 1,000 dead

<u>NY Times</u>, 10/15/1871,
p. 1

Notes grouped by topic

10

<u>fire-fighting</u>

all engines and hose carts in city came (<u>NYT</u>, 10/8, p. 5)

water station on fire, with no water to put out
small fires (Hall, p. 228)

all engines out there; fire too big to stop (<u>NYT</u>, 10/8
p. 5)

fire department "demoralized"; bad fire previous
night; men were drinking afterwards; fire
marshal "habitually drunk" (<u>NYT</u>, 10/23, p. 2)

Below, notes grouped by source

<u>Source H</u>

<u>NY Times</u>, 10/15/1871, p. 1

1. city normal again
2. still martial rule; Gen. Sheridan in charge
3. citizens working at night to watch for new outbreak of fire
4. newspapers moved to other locations
5. estimate 1,000 dead
6. earlier reports of looting and loss of life not exaggerated
7. waterworks won't open till next day
8. two-thirds of city still using candlelight
9. suffering mostly among "humbler classes"
10. businessmen are "buoyant"
11. bread is 8¢
12. saloons are closed at 9:00 P.M. for one week

notes about *fire-fighting*. Thereafter, every time the student came across a new point about fire-fighting—no matter what the source—it was added to that card. Such organization requires a list, either written or mental, of possible categories or note topics, which may also be identified by number. (See the second card on the previous page.)

Because the notes are grouped according to topic, this student will find organizing an outline easier than will the first student. But preliminary categorizing during the note-taking stage is practical only with relatively short items. A lengthy presentation of a theory can destroy this tidy system by forcing the note-taker to devote card after card to a single idea from a single source. (Notice that none of the sources on the "fire-fighting" card seems to be offering any lengthy opinions about the fire.) For this reason, when you organize notes by topic, you may prefer to use long sheets of paper, in order to be prepared for any kind of material and not to be cramped for space.

Notes Grouped by Source

Instead of putting one point on each card or one topic on each card, a third student chose to use one source per sheet. This system "uses up" one source at a time and calls for a long sheet of notes in which the information is presented in the order of its appearance in the source. (See the example at the bottom of the previous page.)

Notice that to simplify the essay's organization, this student numbered each item on the sheet and also gave each sheet a code letter. When the time comes to synthesize these notes into paragraph topics, the student can establish a category dealing with, say, *food supplies*, find the relevant references to that topic, and place the code numbers under that heading. While writing the first draft, the writer will find H-11 under the heading *food supplies* and have immediate access to information about the price of bread after the fire. (For further explanation of this process, see Chapter 8, p. 337).

TAKING NOTES FROM ABSTRACT SOURCES

As the sample notes suggest, research on the Chicago fire mostly uncovered factual guidance about incidents that occurred during and after the catastrophe. The research notes are therefore brief, factual summaries. Taking notes becomes quite a different proposition when the source consists of generalizations and evidence used to develop complex ideas; for the note-taker must constantly struggle to understand and paraphrase abstract thinking. To illustrate the difficulties, here is a brief extract from *Victorian Cities*, by Asa Briggs. Assume that the book is being consulted for an essay on "The City One Hundred Years Ago."

The industrial city was bound to be a place of problems. Economic individualism and common civic purpose were difficult to reconcile. The priority of industrial discipline in shaping all human relations was bound to make other aspects of life seem secondary. A high rate of industrial investment might mean not only a low rate of consumption and a paucity of social investment but a total indifference to social costs. Overcrowding was one problem: displacement was another. There were parts of Liverpool with a density of 1,200 persons to the acre in 1884: rebuilding might entail the kind of difficulties which were set out in a verse in *The Builder* of 1851:

> Who builds? Who builds? Alas, ye poor!
> If London day by day "improves,"
> Where shall ye find a friendly door,
> When every day a home removes?

The paragraph may seem hard to understand on first reading because Briggs is developing his image of the industrial city through a series of abstract words combined into phrases—"economic individualism," "common civic purpose," "industrial discipline," and "low rate of consumption."

These difficult abstractions, typical of the social sciences, are included in the paragraph as if everyone understood them. Fortunately, the essential point is repeated in several different ways and supported by some straightforward facts about the density of population in Liverpool. The passage ends with quite a different kind of evidence: the verse-quotation which suggests that, earlier in the century, people were already aware of the dangers of unlimited expansion.

Here are a few attempts at note-taking based on Briggs's paragraph.

Note A: Effective Summary, with Comments

> Briggs, p. 491
>
> If capital is being used for industrial expansion and personal profit, the same money can't be used for social services. [This was before the welfare state.] Because production was paramount, no one worried that living conditions were impossibly crowded or that people were evicted or moved to allow for industrial expansion. Example: Liverpool -- 1,200 per acre in 1884. Fear of improvement ("If London day by day 'improves'") [sounds like urban renewal and the inner city cycle today -- renovating slum brownstones becomes fashionable]

The researcher here has made a point of avoiding the original phrasing, and thus avoided the danger of quoting the author's words without acknowledgment. The researcher's brief comments in square brackets, clearly distinguished from the notes on Briggs, suggest possible points for development in the research essay.

If one does not expect to refer to Briggs in any detail, it would be sufficient to make a note that summarizes his basic point more briefly:

Note B: **Effective Short Summary**

> Briggs, p. 491
>
> Danger of industrialization : profit becomes more important than social values.
> Expansion results in a highly dense population and the need for relocating existing neighborhoods.

In taking good notes, everything depends on achieving a clear understanding of the author's meaning. The following example, however, suggests that the researcher did not bother to puzzle out the complexities of the paragraph and, instead, tried a few wild guesses:

Note C: **Distortion of the Source**

> Briggs, p. 491
>
> A city of crowded business brings chaos. People couldn't find a job. Your rights meant nothing. Industries didn't respect people's real needs. The cities were overcrowded because industrial investments were poor.

With the possible exception of the first sentence, none of these points can be correctly attributed to Briggs, whose meaning has been entirely distorted. On the other hand, the attempt to play it safe by copying out the phrases verbatim is not successful either:

Note D: Meaningless List

Briggs, p 491

Problems of the industrial city:
1. "economic individualism"
2. "Common civic purpose" difficult to reconcile
3. "industrial discipline" takes priority over "all human relations"
4. "high rate of social investment" and "total indifference to social costs"
5. "over-crowding"
6. "displacement"

Although this information is beautifully laid out in outline form, with quotation marks carefully inserted, there is no evidence that the researcher has understood a word of Briggs's paragraph. Moreover, using an outline format makes it hard to recognize the relationships among these concepts. When the time comes to include a reference to Briggs in the research essay, this student will have no idea how the phrases fit together.

Even when a reading is much less abstract and densely argued than the excerpt from Briggs, it is possible to distort the author's meaning by selecting the wrong points to emphasize in your notes. Here are two paragraphs from *Shakespeare of London*, by Marchette Chute, followed by sample notes for an essay on "Shakespeare's Education as a Playwright."

Apart from teaching him Latin, Stratford grammar school taught Shakespeare nothing at all. It did not teach him mathematics or any of the natural sciences. It did not teach him history, unless a few pieces of information about ancient events strayed in through Latin quotations. It did not teach him geography, for the first (and most inadequate) textbook on geography did not appear until the end of the century, and maps and atlases were rare even in university circles. It did not teach him modern languages, for when a second language was taught at a grammar school it was invariably Greek.

What Shakespeare learned about any of these subjects he learned for himself later, in London. London was the one great storehouse in England of living, contemporary knowledge and in that city an alert and intelligent man could find out almost anything he wanted to know. It was in London, for instance, that Shakespeare learned French; and French was taught by Frenchmen who worked in competition with each other and used oral conversational methods that were designed to get colloquial French into the student's head as quickly as possible.

Note E: **Summarizing the Main Point, with Supporting Facts**

> Most of the basic knowledge that Shakespeare needed to write his plays was learned in London, not in school.
>
> Evidence: grammar school taught no math, natural science, history, geography, modern languages

Here, the note-taker has made the necessary contrast between Stratford and London, and the generalization is clearly distinguished from the evidence that Chute cites to support it. In the next example, the focus gets shifted from what Shakespeare did or did not learn to the deficiencies of schools in sixteenth-century England.

Note F: **False Emphasis / Context Disregarded**

> Elizabethan schools were no good; taught only useless subjects.

What the student is missing here is the essential contrast between an ordinary, unsophisticated school in rural England and the resources available to an inquiring young man (no longer a school boy) in the capital city. The note-taker has ignored the *context* of the two paragraphs and the material that surrounds them in the original source. Chute has previously explained the advantages that Shakespeare derived from learning Latin, and is listing what he was unable to learn (partly because books and other teaching materials had not yet been developed), not to condemn Stratford grammar school, but to prepare the reader for the burst of learning that would occur when Shakespeare arrived in London. The context—Shakespeare's development—is ignored in favor of a narrower focus on the blunt statement that he was taught "nothing at all."

EXERCISE 35

In 1937, the German airship *Hindenburg* caught fire near Lakehurst, New Jersey, killing thirty-six people. Two of the many eyewitness accounts were by Leonhard Adelt and Margaret Mather, both passengers on the ship. Read these two passages and then evaluate the following sets of notes prepared by students writing about the *Hindenburg* disaster. Consider the following criteria:

1. Does one get a good sense of the experience from reading the notes?
2. Which sets of notes are reliable? complete?
3. Do any of the notes omit anything important?
4. Which notes quote excessively?
5. Does the note-taker recognize that the two sources often confirm each other's testimony, and indicate when they agree?
6. Would the notes make sense to someone who had not read the original?
7. Which sets of notes would you prefer to work from if you were writing an essay on the *Hindenburg*?

   With my wife I was leaning out of a window on the promenade deck. Suddenly there occurred a remarkable stillness. The motors were silent, and it seemed as though the whole world was holding its breath. One heard no command, no call, no cry. The people we saw seemed suddenly stiffened.

   I could not account for this. Then I heard a light, dull detonation from above, no louder than the sound of a beer bottle being opened. I turned my gaze toward the bow and noticed a delicate rose glow, as though the sun were about to rise. I understood immediately that the airship was aflame. There was but one chance for safety—to jump out. The distance from the ground at that moment may have been 120 feet.

For a moment I thought of getting bed linen from the corridor in order to soften our leap, but in the same instant, the airship crashed to the ground with terrific force. Its impact threw us from the window to the stair corridor. The tables and chairs of the reading room crashed about and jammed us in like a barricade.

"Through the window!" I shouted to my fellow passengers, and dragged my wife with me to our observation window.

Reality ceased with one stroke, as though fate in its cruelty was yet compassionate enough to withdraw from its victims the consciousness of their horror. I do not know, and my wife does not know, how we leaped from the airship. The distance from the ground may have been 12 or 15 feet. I distinctly felt my feet touch the soft sand and grass. We collapsed to our knees, and the impenetrable darkness of black oil clouds, shot through with flames, enveloped us. We had to let go of each other's hands in order to make our way through the confusion of hot metal pieces and wires. We bent the hot metal apart with our bare hands without feeling pain.

We freed outselves and ran through a sea of fire. It was like a dream. Our bodies had no weight. They floated like stars through space.

Leonhard Adelt

I was leaning out of an open window in the dining saloon with many others including the young aviator, who was taking photographs. He told me that he had taken eighty during the trip. When there were mysterious sounds from the engines I glanced at him for reassurance.

At that moment we heard the dull muffled sound of an explosion. I saw a look of incredulous consternation on his face. Almost instantly the ship lurched and I was hurled a distance of fifteen or twenty feet against an end wall.

I was pinned against a projecting bench by several Germans who were thrown after me. I couldn't breathe and thought I should die suffocated, but they all jumped up.

Then the flames blew in, long tongues of flame, bright red and very beautiful.

My companions were leaping up and down amid the flames. The lurching of the ship threw them repeatedly against the furniture and the railing, where they cut their hands and faces against the metal trimmings. They were streaming with blood. I saw a number of men leap from the windows, but I sat just where I had fallen, holding the lapels of my coat across my face, feeling the flames light on my back, my hat, my hair, trying to beat them out, watching the horrified faces of my companions as they leaped up and down.

Just then a man—I think the man who had exclaimed "Mein Gott" as we left the earth—detached himself from the leaping forms, and threw himself against a railing (arms and legs spread wide) with a loud terrible cry of ''Es ist das Ende.''

I thought so too but I continued to protect my eyes. I was thinking that it was like a scene from a medieval picture of hell. I was waiting for the crash of landing.

Suddenly I heard a loud cry: ''Come out, lady!'' I looked and we were on the ground.

Margaret G. Mather

Student A:

All of a sudden there was complete silence and not a sound from the motors of the airship. Everybody in the airship "stiffened." Leonhard Adelt suddenly "heard a dull detonation from above, no louder than a beer bottle being opened." L.A. knew that the "airship was aflame." The only way to save one's life was to jump. This meant the jump was for 120 feet. All of a sudden, "the airship crashed to the ground with terrific" speed. The force was so high that Margaret Mather "was hurled a distance of fifteen to twenty feet against an end wall."

Student B:

"The motors were silent, and it seemed as though the whole world was holding its breath." "At that moment we heard the dull and muffled sound of an explosion." "Almost suddenly the ship lurched and I was hurled a distance of 15 or 20 feet against an end wall." This is the beginning described by two passengers that were on the Hindenburg of 1937. After a long voyage over the Atlantic and being so close to their destiny, this was too much of a shock for them to handle. All the passengers had to escape death. Some were fortunate, others weren't. "I was pinned against a projecting bench by several Germans who were thrown after me. I couldn't breathe, and thought I should die, suffocated, but they all jumped up." Everyone ran for their life.

Student C:

Adelt: "The motors were silent"
Mather: "Dull muffled sound of an explosion"
Adelt: "I turned my gaze towards the bow and noticed a rose glow . . ."
Mather: "The ship lurched and I was hurled a distance of fifteen or twenty feet against an end wall."
Adelt: "its impact threw us from the window to the stair corridor."

Mather: "Then the flames blew in"
Mather: "I saw a number of men leap from the windows."
Adelt: "We leaped from the airship."

Student D:

before crash:
Adelt: "The motors were silent" "I heard a light, dull detonation from above, . . ." "I turned my gaze towards the bow and noticed a delicate rose glow"
Mather: "Mysterious sounds from the engine" "dull muffled sound of an explosion" "then the flames blew in, long tongues of flame, bright red and very beautiful"
after crash:
Adelt: "Through the window!" I shouted to my fellow passengers, . . ." ". . . how we leaped from the airship. The distance from the ground may have been 12 or 15 feet," . . . "impenetrable darkness of black oil clouds, shot through with flames" . . . "a sea of fire."
Mather: ". . . where they cut their hands and faces against the metal trimmings. They were streaming with blood."

Student E:

"I turned my gaze towards the bow and noticed a delicate rose glow, as though the sun were about to rise." The blimp catches on fire: the only means of escape is jumping to the ground. Distance from the ground approximately 12 or 15 feet when couple jumped out of "airship." People "beat the hot metal apart with our bare hands without feeling pain." How mind works when in life and death situation. No pain. People had to run through fire one at a time.
Mather: "mysterious sounds from the engine." She was leaning out of dining saloon, heard sounds of explosion. People thrown 15 or 20 feet after hearing explosion. Flames came into room after people thrown. "lurching of ship threw them repeatedly across furniture and the railings."

Student F:

There was an inexplicable silence followed by a "light, dull detonation from above, no louder than the sound of a beer bottle being opened." Then it was observed that the airship was on fire looking like "the sun were about to rise." There was the realization that the only chance for survival was to abandon the ship. By the time the decision to jump and the action itself was implemented, the ship had crashed (from 120 feet). Upon impact, everything in the ship (chairs, tables, people) was tossed about. Reality became suspended "as though fate in its cruelty was yet compassionate enough to withdraw from its victims the consciousness of their horror."

EXERCISE 36

Reread the three articles dealing with the Cocoanut Grove Fire of 1942 at the end of the previous chapter. Head one group of cards or one sheet of paper "The Causes of the Fire," and take a set of notes on that topic. Head another group of cards or sheet of paper "The Fire's Intensity and Speed," and take a second set of notes on the second topic. Each set of notes should make use of all three sources.

EXERCISE 37

Assume that you are planning an essay about scientific discoveries and that you have come across the following source, published in 1951, in the library. After doing a preliminary evaluation of the passage, take a set of notes for an essay entitled "What motivates the scientist?"

My purpose is to talk about science as it is, practical and theoretical. I define science as the organization of our knowledge in such a way that it commands more of the hidden potential in nature. What I have in mind therefore is both deep and matter of fact; it reaches from the kinetic theory of gases to the telephone and the suspension bridge and medicated toothpaste. It admits no sharp boundary between knowledge and use. There are of course people who like to draw a line between pure and applied science; and oddly, they are often the same people who find art unreal. To them, the word useful is a final arbiter, either for or against a work; and they use this word as if it can mean only what makes a man feel heavier after meals.

There is no sanction for confining the practice of science in this or another way. True, science is full of useful inventions. And its theories have often been made by men whose imagination was directed by the uses to which their age looked. Newton turned naturally to astronomy because it was the subject of his day, and it was so because finding one's way at sea had long been a practical preoccupation of the society into which he was born. It should be added, mischievously, that astronomy also had some standing because it was used very practically to cast horoscopes. (Kepler used it for this purpose; in the Thirty Years' War he cast the horoscope of Wallenstein which wonderfully told his character, and he predicted a universal disaster for 1634 which proved to be the murder of Wallenstein.)

In a setting which is more familiar, Faraday worked all his life to link electricity with magnetism because this was the glittering problem of his day; and it was so because his society, like ours, was on the lookout for new sources of power. Consider a more modest example today: the new mathematical methods of automatic control, a subject sometimes called cybernetics, have been developed now because this is a time when communication and control have in effect become forms of power. These inventions have been directed by social needs, and they are useful inventions; yet it was not their usefulness which dominated and set light to the minds of those who made them. Neither Newton nor Faraday, nor yet Norbert Wiener, spent their time in a scramble for patents.

What a scientist does is compounded of two interests: the interest of his time and his own interest. In this his behavior is no different from any other man's. The need of the age gives its shape to scientific progress as a whole. But it is not the need of the age which gives the individual scientist his sense of pleasure and of adventure, and that excitement which keeps him working late into the night when all the useful typists have gone home at five o'clock. He is personally involved in his work, as the poet is in his, and as the artist is in the painting. Paints and painting too must have been made for useful ends; and language was developed, from whatever beginnings, for practical communication. Yet you cannot have a man handle paints or language or the symbolic concepts of physics, you cannot even have him stain a microscope slide, without instantly waking in him a pleasure in the very language, a sense of exploring his own activity. This sense lies at the heart of creation.

J. Bronowski, from *Science and Human Values*

EXERCISE 38

Read the following excerpt from an essay (printed in the August 3, 1975, issue of *The Observer*, a British newspaper) about the career and personality of George Washington. Then take *four separate sets of notes* from this passage, using four separate cards or sheets, as if you were preparing an essay on *each* of the following topics:

1. The personality of George Washington
2. George Washington's military strategy
3. War atrocities
4. How England lost the Revolutionary War

The verdict of military historians is that Washington was a competent but not a great general. The British were overconfident. The man in charge of the British armies in the field, as Secretary of State for the Colonies, was a Lord George Germain who had been court-martialled for cowardice in 1760, found guilty, and declared 'unfit to serve His Majesty in any military capacity whatever.' George III interfered constantly, and disastrously. In any case, as the great English republican Tom Paine pointed out at the time, it was always 'very absurd' that an island should try to rule a continent.

Even so, the war went on for almost as long as the war in Vietnam. It was 18 June 1775 when Washington wrote from Philadelphia to his wife Martha, at home at Mount Vernon, to tell her of his unwillingness to part with her and the family, 'not doubting but that I shall return safe to you in the fall.' But it was 17 October 1781 before a white cloth appeared on the British ramparts at Yorktown to indicate that General Cornwallis was suing for terms, and an entire British army—7,421 men, with 7,000 muskets, 200 cannon, 450 horses—marched out to stack its arms while the band played 'The World Turned Upside Down.'

Undoubtedly, it was Washington who kept the struggle going. It was a brutal and bloody war: a civil war as well as a war of liberation. When the British were led at night by their Tory spies to a force of sleeping Americans at Paoli, in Pennsylvania, they went in with bayonets, stabbing until their muscles were tired. The British army, whether or not it was incompetent, was certainly not gentle. The 42nd Highlanders, later the Black Watch, went into action not only with muskets and bayonets, but with enormous swords, like claymores. During battles, the Highlanders were liable to throw aside their muskets and lay about them with these monstrous broadswords. To oppose such savage apparitions, Washington was compelled to rely on farmboys, many of whom expected to return to their farms after a few months' service. The rich young Marquis de Lafayette, second-in-command of the French troops in Washington's forces (Lafayette later gave Washington the key of the Bastille that today hangs at Mount Vernon), described a section of Washington's army as follows: 'About eleven thousand men ill-armed, and still worse clothed, presented a strange spectacle. Their clothes were particoloured, and many of them were almost naked. The best clad wore hunting shirts, large grey linen coats.'

Washington kept this rabble in being as a fighting force by no other means than his own force of character. He shared with his men the terrible winter ordeals of Valley Forge and Morristown, hanged deserters selectively, and showed an iron nerve in battle. He also stood up for his troops against the Congressmen who put their own interests before that of the cause. Washington's writing in time of peace was invariably stodgy and temperate, but some of his wartime papers are violent and impassioned. 'I would to God,' he wrote in 1778, 'that one of the most atrocious [speculators] of each State was hung in gibbets upon a gallows five times as high as the one prepared by Haman. No punishment in my opinion is too great for the man who can build his greatness upon his country's ruin.'

This is the heart of the Washington legend—the patriot holding the cause together. And the legend is true. The picture of General Washington that emerges from contemporary writings—especially in Tom Paine's descriptions of him, as a man 'who never appeared to full advantage but in difficulties and action,' a man with 'a mind that can flourish upon care'—is sharp and unequivocal. No one can argue with it; no one has tried.

from "Washington—The Truth Behind the Legend"
by Michael Davie, *Observer Magazine*, 3 August 1975

8.
Presenting the Results of Your Research: Organizing and Writing the Essay

The research essay should be planned and written in exactly the same way that you would work on any other essay. No matter what the topic, you will probably be starting out with written notes—facts, ideas, suggestions, comments, opinions—that serve as the raw materials for your synthesis. From these notes, you establish a sequence of separate generalizations to be used as the focus of your paragraphs; and, in doing so, you work out the basic structure of your essay. What distinguishes the organization of the research essay from that of the essays that you have previously written is the unusually large quantity of notes. The term "notes" here refers to any of the products of your research, such as your own summaries and paraphrases, quotations, xeroxed copies of pages and articles, class lecture notes, and stories clipped from the newspapers, as well as your own ideas about the topic.

TAKING INVENTORY AND DEVELOPING A LIST OF TOPICS

At this stage, you search for ideas worth developing by reviewing all the major points that you have learned and thought about in the course of your research. These ideas form the core of your essay. You select the main ideas of your research essay by carefully reading through all your notes. As you read, you look for and write down any points that seem especially important to understanding and explaining your topic. In other words, you take a *new* set of notes from your old set and thus reduce the accumulated mass of information to a more manageable size. By taking inventory of what you might want to include, you produce a working version of your notes, a list of generalizations that can be rearranged, tried out in different versions, and eventually converted into an outline of topic sentences. This new set of notes is *not* supposed to be a summary of your research, nor should you attempt at this point to summarize any single source.

Your new notes will be a random list of vaguely related items. At this early stage of organization, there is no special reason to place the names of the sources next to your new list of ideas; not every statement in your new list will get included in your essay, and you are not yet at the point where you need to decide which source should be used to support which topic sentence.

This inventory of your research is not only an essential stage in the organization of your essay, but it is also the point at which the essay really becomes the product of your own thinking. Until this stage, most of what you have written down has been extracted directly from the sources; your own individual reactions and opinions have probably been restricted to the occasional comment in square brackets. Now, when you sift this information and evaluate it, you are deciding what you are going to write about. Each point that you jot down, however brief and however fragmentary, should be expressed in your own words; it should be *your* version of the idea. Even if it is a point that has appeared in ten different articles (and has been noted on ten different index cards), you are now, in some sense, making it your own.

Once your tentative list of general ideas has been completed, once you have read through all of your research notes and decided which points are worth writing about, it is time to take inventory again. Evaluate your list. If your new notes take up more than a couple of pages, try to reduce the number of ideas, avoiding duplication and combining similar statements. Some points will be in the mainstream of your research, discussed by several of your sources. Others, however, will seem more peripheral; you may find it difficult to cite a variety of evidence in their support, and you may wish to exclude them from your master outline. Eliminate what seems to be minor or remote from the topic or inconsistent with most of your research notes.

Next, consider what remains on your list. How do these ideas relate to the topic with which you began your research? How do they help to establish a thesis? Are you working with a collection of reasons? consequences? problems? dangers? You are also trying to find an overall strategy for your essay—cause-and-effect? problem-and-solution? explanation of a procedure? evaluation of reasons for an argument? If you are developing a historical or biographical topic, see if your information naturally divides into units that might correspond to the separate parts of your essay. Did the event fall into distinct narrative stages? What aspects of the scene would an observer have noticed? Which of your subject's activities best reveals his personality? In other words, decide what is to be included and what is to be discarded. Finally, when your list of topics is relatively firm, remember to arrange them in a sequence that makes sense, carrying out your strategy and developing your thesis in a clear direction.

CROSS-REFERENCING

When you have developed a list of major topics that will roughly correspond to the paragraphs of your essay, then and only then are you ready to link up that tentative outline with your research notes. Remember to leave plenty of space between the items on your outline, and also remember to assign a number or a letter to each item. Now, once again, slowly reread all your research notes, this time keeping your list of topics right in front of you. Every time you come across something in your notes that might be cited in support of a topic on your outline, immediately:

1. place the number or letter of the point in your outline next to the reference in your notes;
2. place the source's name (and the number of the note-card, if you have used that system, or the page number of your notes) under the item on your outline.

To illustrate cross-referencing, here is an excerpt from the notes for an essay on the Chicago Fire, with cross-references in the margin, followed by three paragraph topics taken from an outline for that essay.

Notes:

Source G

Times, October 11, "The Ruined City," p. 1

1. the fire has stopped and there has been some "blessed rain"
2. 20–30 people have died in their homes
3. plundering everywhere--like a scene of war
   VII   a. a thief suffocated while trying to steal jewelry from a store
        b. people who were caught pilfering had to be released because the jail burned down
   VI 4. water for drinking from the lake
   5. people dying of exposure
   V 6. little food; people searching the ruins
   V 7. difficulties of transporting supplies

VIII. 8. meeting of citizens at church to help protect what was left, to help homeless, and to provide water if further fires broke out

Outline:

V. Feeding the homeless   **Source G, 6, 7**

VI. Providing basic services   **Source G, 4**

VII. Protecting life and property   **Source G, 3, 8**

Cross-referencing enables you to make full use of your notes and avoid time-consuming searches for references later on when you are writing the essay. At the end of this procedure, your outline will have a list of sources to be cited for each main point, and your research notes will have code numbers in most of the margins. Notice that a few of the items on the notes for Source G have no cross-references next to them. Some will be placed under the headings of other topics in this outline, and they have not yet been given their reference numbers. Items 2 and 5 in the notes, for example, would probably come under the heading of Casualties. On the other hand, not all the notes will necessarily get used in the essay; some items will simply not fit into the topics chosen for the outline and will be discarded. In the same way, cross-referencing can be used to organize one-fact-per-card notes, which can be sorted into piles corresponding to your topics.

In the following example, the code number of the source is identified in the upper right-hand corner, the card's own number is placed in the upper left-hand corner, and the number of the topic that this fact will be used to illustrate is indicated on the bottom of the card.

#32   *Source G*

A thief suffocated while trying
to steal jewelry from a store

VII

The outline used for one-fact-per-card notes will have the relevant card numbers placed after each item; it is not necessary to identify the source on the outline.

Outline:

> V. Feeding the homeless

> VI. Providing basic services

> VII. Protecting life and property
> # 32, # 38

The third kind of notes—one-topic-per card/sheet—incorporates much of the cross-referencing process into note-taking. Since you have already grouped your materials by topic, you need only review your notes and shift those points (usually by cutting and pasting) that have accidentally been placed under the wrong topic.

In the next stage, as you prepare to write a paragraph or two about each topic on your outline, you will be able to refer to the exact points in your notes that you need to cite. The more notes that you have collected, the more important it is that you try to be thorough during the preliminary organization. Don't start to write your essay, don't even start to sort your note cards or cut-and-paste your sheets, until you have completed both your basic outline and your cross-referencing.

EXERCISE 39

Read the following set of notes, organized by source, for an essay on the Olympic Games, and:

A. write an outline of topics for an essay to be called "The Future of the Olympics;"

and

B. cross-reference the notes with your outline.

As you consider the information in these notes, remember that, if this were preparation for an assigned essay, you could return to any of the sources, if you wished, and add details or examples to develop a topic that does not have enough supporting information.

Source A

"Behind the Pageantry and Thrills," U.S. News and World Report 2 August, 1976, 16–17.

1. Montreal Olympics: disputes over politics: 30 out of 119 countries refused to participate or left before games began
2. Difficulty maintaining good security--Montreal feared terrorist attacks
3. Incredibly high costs--keeping 16,000 soldiers and police in reserve cost at least 150 million dollars
4. Facilities cost Montreal and Quebec province nearly 1.5 billion
5. Montreal packed with spectators (approx. 95 thousand each day)
6. Tickets originally costing $40. were being sold for $400.
7. Most severe threat to games' continuation is not costs, but politics: "Now everybody is using the Olympics as a political tool." (Monique Berlioux, Director, International Olympic Committee)
8. Canada refused to allow Taiwan to participate in the games if it insisted on calling itself "The Republic of China"
9. African countries boycotted games to protest visit by New Zealand rugby team to South Africa; they wanted New Zealand expelled from the Olympics
10. The International Olympic Committee (IOC) allowed Canada to decide Taiwan issue; was ineffectual in dealing with the African boycott
11. Security made the games grim: helicopters, soldiers on patrol, security screens, troops with rifles
12. Possible solution = keep Olympics in Greece permanently
13. Counterargument = this doesn't fit in with the Olympic spirit

Source B

Roger M. Williams, "Moscow '80--Playing for Political Points," Saturday Review 1 September, 1979, 12–16

1. Moscow preparing for 1980 Olympics by building and redecorating; the city looks much improved
2. 300,000 foreign spectators expected
3. Possible political crises
    a. Arabs may boycott if Israelis come
    b. African nations may boycott if French/English/New Zealand teams come

   c. China may boycott if Taiwan comes
4. Russians trying to prevent dissidents from staging demonstrations during games; many under house arrest or temporarily exiled
5. Rivalry between Soviets and U.S. increasingly important (13)
6. Peking regards Taiwan as "a province of China"; will boycott if any other status given to Taiwan or if it's permitted to have its own flag or anthem (14)
7. French Olympic Committee "declined to intervene" to prevent French rugby team from inviting South African team to France
8. Possible advantages to Russia for holding the games:
   a. gain foreign capital
   b. build useful public facilities to be used later
   c. demonstrate that they can hold such an event as successfully as a Western nation can
9. Russians: sensible planning for games: (15)
   a. renovated whenever possible, instead of building anew
   b. plan permanent uses for newly built facilities
10. Overall Russian expenditure probably less than last few Olympics (although more than the 350 million that Russia claims)
11. Olympic Village will be rental apartment complex; will relieve chronic housing shortage
12. Russia is getting $100 million from NBC for TV rights (16)

Source C

"Five Ideas to Save the Olympics," U.S. News and World Report, 28 May, 1984, 31

1. Establish permanent site, preferably in Greece, where Olympics originated: save having to spend money every four years and prevent political problems, like U.S. (1980) and Soviet (1984) boycotts, every time a new country becomes host--Senator Bill Bradley
2. Insist that a country that boycotts the Olympics never be permitted to participate again. Would need strict enforcement by IOC--John Ferraro (Chairman of Los Angeles Committee, 1984)
3. Sign an international treaty ensuring athlete participation as individuals even if their countries choose to boycott--David Scheffer (Harvard University Center for International Affairs)
4. Divide the Olympics into five types of games and put each in a different country--
   a) decentralization: difficult to create publicity for politics;
   b) games could be moved if host country started creating problems;
   c) costs would be spread over more countries;
   d) give more countries the prestige of being host--Buck Dawson (The International Swimming Hall of Fame)

5. Establish a permanent site (not Greece) instead in a politically neutral country like Switzerland
(Note: IOC rejects that idea; believes Olympic spirit requires sharing responsibilities of being host)
at least, limit games to a few noncontroversial sites, (e.g. Tokyo, Montreal, and Munich)
--John Lucas (Professor of Physical Education, Penn State)

Source D

Pete Axthelm, "Should the Games Go On?" Newsweek 21 May 1984, 22-24

1. After Arab terrorists killed 11 Israeli athletes at Munich (1972), Avery Brundage (of IOC) insisted that the games continue. Axthelm: Brundage was wrong
2. Risk of bloodshed and political upheaval not worth gains-- nationalistic, commercial, or athletic
3. Even bloodless Olympics at Montreal resulted in a) boycotts and b) a loss of one billion for city of Montreal (23)
4. Moscow Olympics ruined by boycott of Americans
5. Probable boycott of South Korean Olympics in 1988 (24)
6. Decentralization = weak idea--more glamorous sports would get all the publicity
7. Olympics as political tool has advantages: one country can chastise another without declaring war and shedding blood

Source E

Roger Rosenblatt, "Why We Play These Games," Time 30 July 1984, 34-37

1. Boycotts not a threat to future Olympics, as many predicted--more countries are sending athletes (e.g. 1984: Chinese delegations; unusually large Egyptian and Italian delegations)
2. Some countries (e.g., Lebanon, Northern and Southern Ireland) participate despite civil war (35)
3. Nationless Olympics, with athletes not competing for their countries but only against each other, won't work--impossible to ignore nationality (37)
4. Olympics provide a bond between nations--one of "few historical experiences that the world holds in common."

Source F

" 'Olympic Movement Has Grown Stronger' Despite Boycotts," U.S. News and World Report 20 August, 1984, 27 (Interview with Juan Antonio Samaranch, President of the International Olympic Committee)

1. Encourages business community to get involved and provide financial support
2. Olympics stronger than ever is underlined by increased competition among nations to host future Olympics
3. Security problems not a deterrent: "Security--and the high costs of providing it--are the high price you must pay for putting on the greatest event in the world."
4. Boycotts haven't "tarnished" the Olympics--"Just imagine how great the 1988 games will be if all countries will take part."
5. The IOC is "considering" penalizing boycotting countries--but punishing countries isn't the answer--instead, persuade them that boycotts hurt Olympic ideals
6. A permanent site won't work: "the games belong to all the world" besides, countries might still boycott, even if in Greece
7. There is no reason to limit displays of nationalism, which is both natural and understandable

Source G

J. M. Leiper, "Political Problems in the Olympic Games," Olympism eds. Jeffrey Segrave and Donald Chu, Champaign, Ill.: Human Kinetics, 1981, 104-17

1. Present problems partly caused by IOC, which has refused to consider that politics could have any bearing on Olympic ideal, yet failed to introduce any educational campaigns to make countries understand this ideal; "abdicated responsibility" to the various national committees (105)
2. Olympics now a political tool; a "conspicuous theatre" and "useful stage on which to mount a political position." (106)
3. Nationalism built into the IOC's original statements (1894) saying that the success of the games would depend on the support of individual nations and that athletes participating would be regarded as representatives of their countries (108)
4. The various rituals that encourage nationalism (parade of the nations at opening ceremonies, playing of national anthems of winners) were included in the games by Pierre de Coubertin, founder of the modern games
5. IOC's effectiveness dependent on those elected to the committee and their commitment to the interests of their own governments
6. Only way for IOC to have prevented excluding Taiwan in 1976 = moving the games from Montreal--too drastic--IOC had no choice but to yield (112)
7. Permanent site: hard to finance--host country (e.g., Switzerland) would depend on contributions from participants--example of United Nations shows that this system works badly

8. Decentralization: would dilute impact of games and wouldn't necessarily prevent boycotts

---

ASSIGNMENT 16

Below are two sets of subjects for a research essay, with a list of readings for each set. You are to work on one of these subjects. First, read through all of the relevant passages. (In a full-scale research project, these readings would form a substantial part, but not all, of your sources.) Then, develop a tentative list of main ideas, based on these sources, that ought to be discussed in an essay dealing with your subject. Include also your own ideas on the subject. Each point in your list should suggest the focus of a paragraph or group of paragraphs in the essay. As you work on your list consider possible theses for the essay and, later on, the strategy that will best fit your thesis and materials. After you have a substantial list of topics and a tentative thesis to pursue, re-read the passages, cross-referencing the topics on your list with the relevant paragraphs from the essays. While you do not have to "use up" everything in all of the readings, you should include all relevant points. Later, you will develop this outline into an eight- or ten-page essay.

Set A:

How can our society more effectively prevent violence and crime?

or

Can punishment be made to fit the crime?

Readings for Set A:

- Marcia Chambers, "End of Secrecy in Youth Courts Urged" 242 -245
- Jan Gorecki, from *A Theory of Criminal Justice* 345-348
- *Hetrick v. Martin* 235
- Michael T. Kaufman, "Facing Violence" 19-21
- Selwyn Raab, "Holdup Man Tells Detectives How to Do It" 51-54
- Jesus Rangel, "2-year House Arrest Instead of Jail Term Is Ordered for Fraud" 54-56
- Charles Silberman, from *Criminal Violence, Criminal Justice* 155-162
- Gresham M. Sykes, from *Society of Captives: A Study of Maximum Security Prisons* 349-352

Set B:

How can violence at sporting events be prevented?

or

What social function is served by sports?

Readings for Set B:

Brenda Jo Bredemeier and David J. Shields, "Values and Violence in
    Sports Today"
Daniel Goleman, from "Brutal Sports and Brutal Fans"
H. Graves, from "A Philosophy of Sport"
Christopher Lasch, from "The Corruption of Sports"
Douglas Martin, "Sports Violence Seen as Ritual Amid the Chaos"
George Stade, "Football—The Game of Aggression"
Paul Weiss, from *Sport: A Philosophic Inquiry* 366

FROM: A THEORY OF CRIMINAL JUSTICE

In their search [for the causes of criminal behavior] the American
criminologists have identified a large number of social determinants of
criminal behavior. One important school stresses, in a variety of ways,
bad companions—association with criminals, especially in youth peer
groups. Numerous writers stress deficient upbringing, in particular,
difficult childhood in broken families. Others add density of population and impersonal relations in urban areas, high mobility, social
change, cultural conflicts, emergence of large cohorts of young people
following periods of high birth rate, declining role of religion, and so
forth. Still others stress economic inequality and poverty—frustrations
of being deprived, unemployed, or of living in a slum. An influential
school treats inequality, within a broader framework of the anomie
theory, as a cause of many crimes: Americans are taught to compete
for wealth and status, but economic inequality deprives many of lawful access to either; therefore, to achieve wealth and status, some of
the deprived reject legal norms and resort to crime. The Marxists go
further in pursuit of generality of the economic explanation: they consider private investment property and the resulting class structure of
the society as the determinant of all criminal behavior.

There is a strong determinist component in many of these notions:
their inventors consider criminal behavior to be produced unavoidably, or almost unavoidably, by the social forces beyond the criminal's
control. (Positivists and many psychoanalysts also opt for a determinist stand: the respective biological or mental influences operating in
some men inevitably make criminals of them.) Thus, on the part of
someone who has been exposed to their impact, the forces leave little
or no room for the use of will to avoid commitment of crime. In this
manner the metaphysics of the entirely free will of the classical school
has been replaced by the metaphysics of extreme social determinism
(or biological or "mental" determinism).

The implications of the replacement are obvious. If the criminal, rid-
den by forces he is unable to control, has no choice, ascribing guilt to
him is nonsense, and punishing him is both morally wrong and purposeless. How can anybody be punished for having bad parents, being

born in poverty, growing up in the slum, or being, since early child-hood, discriminated against? The more so that all these and many other criminogenic influences have been brought about by the general society, that is by all of us; we are at fault rather than the criminal whom we produced. How, then, can we, the guilty society, punish him, the innocent victim of our institutions? The only humane and rea-sonable policy would be to abandon sanctioning crime and to remove the root causes, in particular, all the social ills that generate crime—poverty, economic inequality, racial discrimination, family irresponsi-bility, and others.

The impact of this ideology in the United States is astounding. It may have something to do with the widespread complex of guilt—for the plight of the blacks, the Indians, the poor. The ideology is being pro-claimed by a variety of journalists, clergymen, politicians and policy makers, sociologists and social philosophers, and this is just a sample of the proclamations. The "ills within our ghettos, the burdens of our socially and economically deprived and our system's inability to deal with the underlying problems . . . cause most criminality." If thus "a criminal does what he must do . . . it is obviously both futile and un-just to punish him as if he could go straight and had deliberately cho-sen to do otherwise." "The only way in the world to abolish crime and criminals is to . . . [m]ake fair conditions of life. Give men a chance to live. Abolish the right of private ownership of land, abolish monop-oly, make the world partners in production, partners in the good things of life. . . . There should be no jails." "We need, above all, to give far more attention to prevention of crime by attacking its causes and breeding grounds through an intensified battle to eliminate pov-erty, unemployment, inadequate housing, inferior education. . . . What we need is to build a good society [and] . . . to move away from the punishment ideology and objective."

This philosophy, "widespread among the most influential and artic-ulate contemporary leaders of public opinion," has considerable im-pact on the legal profession. The President's Commission on Law En-forcement and Administration of Justice claims that "unless society does take concerted action to change the general conditions and atti-tudes that are associated with crime, no improvement in law enforce-ment and administration of justice . . . will be of much avail," and this means an "action designed to eliminate slums and ghettos, to improve education, to provide jobs, to make sure that every American is given the opportunities and the freedoms that will enable him to assume his responsibilities. We will not have dealt effectively with crime until we have alleviated the conditions that stimulate it." In the words of a for-mer Attorney General of the United States, "[i]f we are to control crime, we must undertake a massive effort to rebuild our cities and ourselves, to improve the human condition, to educate, employ, house and make healthy." In this atmosphere it is feasible for some judges (and prosecutors, defense attorneys, and other participants in the criminal process) to assume "that the institution of prison probably must end" and, for many more, to find the practice of intermittent enforcement of criminal law not only expedient, but also legitimate and respectable.

This ideological support of poor law enforcement is unfortunate. To be sure—and the point could hardly be overstated—efforts to solve broad social problems and the suffering they bring are worthwhile for obvious reasons and irrespective of whether the suffering generates criminal behavior. But an attempt to control crime exclusively or mainly by solving the problems is hopeless.

First, the degree to which persistence of criminal behavior depends on each of the problems is unclear. In any society (and the more so if the analysis exceeds narrow spatiotemporal limitations) the term *crime* denotes many kinds of very different behavior. Owing to this heterogeneity, the number of social determinants of criminal behavior is almost unlimited, even at a close level of the causal distance, and it grows while we draw back along the causal paths. That is why the social problems listed here constitute but a small fraction of the many determinants, and it is dubious whether solving them would prevent all or even the majority of crimes. The Marxist fallacy is a case in point here. If Marxist belief in private investment property as a necessary condition for all crimes had been true, the removal of the property would have brought about a crimeless or nearly crimeless society. Nevertheless, the Soviet crime rate is, more than six decades after the revolution, embarrassingly high—so much so that Soviet criminologists felt compelled to invent an auxiliary explanation: criminal behavior in the Soviet Union is an outcome of "survivals" of the bourgeois past in the Soviet minds.

However, even if removal of all these social ills were effective in preventing crime, we would be unable to remove the majority of them anyway and none of them easily and quickly. In particular, in view of the amount of crime in the United States, it is hardly possible to insulate everyone from associations with criminals and juvenile delinquents. It is equally impossible to "supply the missing 'parental affection' and restore to the child consistent discipline supported by a stable and loving family." However much anomie, as claimed by Merton, may be responsible for a high proportion of criminal behavior, it would be difficult to "ask lower-class people to teach their children to strive for lower-class jobs only," to introduce a "caste system," or "to level all occupations." If the Marxists had been correct—if a radical change of the socioeconomic system had been able to bring a crimeless society—it would be difficult to convince the American public that we can implement the ideal without destruction of free institutions. Thus, the attempt to solve the crime problem by removing broad "social causes" of criminal behavior is utopian. It was long ago ridiculed by Popper: "How far should we get if, instead of introducing laws and police force, we approached the problem of criminality 'scientifically,' i.e., by trying to find out what precisely are the causes of crime. . . . It is as if one insisted that it is unscientific to wear an overcoat when it is cold; and that we should rather study the causes of cold weather, and remove them. Or, perhaps, that lubricating is unscientific, since we should rather find out the causes of friction and remove them."

There is only one method of efficient and prompt dealing with the crime problem, and this is proper administration of criminal justice. Somewhat paradoxically, this method eliminates the "causes" of crime as much as any one of the social reforms just mentioned. After all, the poverty of justice administration is an important "cause"—a factor contributing to many, if not all, kinds of criminal behavior. The factor operates mainly through the medium of the psychological process analyzed in the first part of this book: it destroys the educative power of criminal punishments. (It also operates, though much less forcefully, by destroying their deterrent power.) There is one critical difference, however, between this factor and the many others: it can be removed in a relatively easy way—it is much easier to improve the system of criminal punishments than to eliminate such assumed determinants of crime as lack of parental love, anomie, private property, social inequality, racial discrimination, unemployment, or density of population in urban areas. That is why the idea of eliminating all these determinants instead of improving criminal justice is not only fallacious but harmful; by influencing attitudes of judges, prosecutors, and others who carry out the criminal process, it undermines the educative force of criminal law and thus contributes to the great amount of crime. The implications of the fallacy go further than that, however. High crime rates are themselves a force hindering solution of many grave social problems. As I said earlier, they greatly increase the amount of suffering; are an important factor in the socioeconomic decline of the cities; make lives of the urban poor particularly deplorable (especially in the slum and the ghetto); and, by arousing widespread fear, bring setbacks in the process of racial integration. Thus, it is not only wrong to assume that solution of general social problems is the optimal implement for crime control. Rather the opposite is true. We can best control crime by improving criminal justice, and once we succeed in this, the decrease of crime will itself become a major step towards an alleviation of the broader social ills.

Jan Gorecki

FROM: THE SOCIETY OF CAPTIVES:
A STUDY OF MAXIMUM SECURITY PRISONS

Of all the painful conditions imposed on inmates, none is more immediately obvious than the loss of liberty. The prisoner must live in a world shrunk to thirteen and a half acres and within this restricted area his freedom of movement is further confined by a strict system of passes, the military formations in moving from one point within the institution to another, and the demand that he remain in his cell until given permission to do otherwise. In short, the prisoner's loss of liberty is a double one—first, by confinement to the institution and second, by confinement within the institution.

The mere fact that the individual's movements are restricted, however, is far less serious than the fact that imprisonment means that the inmate is cut off from family, relatives, and friends, not in the self-isolation of the hermit or the misanthrope, but in the involuntary seclusion of the outlaw. It is true that visiting and mailing privileges partially relieve the prisoner's isolation—if he can find someone to visit him or write to him and who will be approved as a visitor or correspondent by the prison officials. Many inmates, however, have found their links with persons in the free community weakening as the months and years pass by. This may explain in part the fact that an examination of the visiting records of a random sample of the inmate population, covering approximately a one-year period, indicated that 41 percent of the prisoners in the New Jersey State Prison had received no visits from the outside world.

It is not difficult to see this isolation as painfully depriving or frustrating in terms of lost emotional relationships, of loneliness and boredom. But what makes this pain of imprisonment bite most deeply is the fact that the confinement of the criminal represents a deliberate, moral rejection of the criminal by the free community. Indeed, as Reckless has pointed out, it is the moral condemnation of the criminal—however it may be symbolized—that converts hurt into punishment, i.e., the just consequence of committing an offense, and it is this condemnation that confronts the inmate by the fact of his seclusion.

Now it is sometimes claimed that many criminals are so alienated from conforming society and so identified with a criminal subculture that the moral condemnation, rejection, or disapproval of legitimate society do not touch them; they are, it is said, indifferent to the penal sanctions of the free community, at least as far as the moral stigma of being defined as a criminal is concerned. Possibly this is true for a small number of offenders such as the professional thief described by Sutherland or the psychopathic personality delineated by William and Joan McCord. For the great majority of criminals in prison, however, the evidence suggests that neither alienation from the ranks of the law-abiding nor involvement in a system of criminal value is sufficient to eliminate the threat to the prisoner's ego posed by society's rejection. The signs pointing to the prisoner's degradation are many—the anonymity of a uniform and a number rather than a name, the shaven head, the insistence on gestures of respect and subordination when addressing officials, and so on. The prisoner is never allowed to forget that, by committing a crime, he has foregone his claim to the status of a full-fledged, *trusted* member of society. The status lost by the prisoner is, in fact, similar to what Marshall has called the status of citizenship—that basic acceptance of the individual as a functioning member of the society in which he lives. It is true that in the past the imprisoned criminal literally suffered civil death and that although the doctrines of attainder and corruption of blood were largely abandoned in the eighteenth and nineteenth centuries, the inmate is still stripped of many of his civil rights such as the right to vote, to hold office, to sue in court, and so on. But as important as the loss of these civil rights may be, the loss of that more diffuse status which defines the individual as someone to be trusted or as morally acceptable is the loss which hurts most.

In short, the wall which seals off the criminal, the contaminated man, is a constant threat to the prisoner's self-conception, and the threat is continually repeated in the many daily reminders that he must be kept apart from "decent" men. Somehow this rejection or degradation by the free community must be warded off, turned aside, rendered harmless. Somehow the imprisoned criminal must find a device for rejecting his rejectors, if he is to endure psychologically. . . .

There are admittedly many problems in attempting to compare the standard of living existing in the free community and the standard of living which is supposed to be the lot of the inmate in prison. How, for example, do we interpret the fact that a covering for the floor of a cell usually consists of a scrap from a discarded blanket and that even this possession is forbidden by the prison authorities? What meaning do we attach to the fact that no inmate owns a common piece of furniture, such as a chair, but only a homemade stool? What is the value of a suit of clothing which is also a convict's uniform with a stripe and a stenciled number? The answers are far from simple, although there are a number of prison officials who will argue that some inmates are better off in prison, in strictly material terms, than they could ever hope to be in the rough-and-tumble economic life of the free community. Possibly this is so, but at least it has never been claimed by the inmates that the goods and services provided the prisoner are equal to or better than the goods and services which the prisoner could obtain if he were left to his own devices outside the walls. The average inmate finds himself in a harshly Spartan environment which he defines as painfully depriving.

It is true that the prisoner's basic material needs are met—in the sense that he does not go hungry, cold, or wet. He receives adequate medical care and he has the opportunity for exercise. But a standard of living constructed in terms of so many calories per day, so many hours of recreation, so many cubic yards of space per individual, and so on, misses the central point when we are discussing the individual's feeling of deprivation, however useful it may be in setting minimum levels of consumption for the maintenance of health. A standard of living can be hopelessly inadequate, from the individual's viewpoint, because it bores him to death or fails to provide those subtle symbolic overtones which we invest in the world of possessions. And this is the core of the prisoner's problem in the area of goods and services. He wants—or needs, if you will—not just the so-called necessities of life but also the amenities: cigarettes and liquor as well as calories, interesting foods as well as sheer bulk, individual clothing as well as adequate clothing, individual furnishings for his living quarters as well as shelter, privacy as well as space. The "rightfulness" of the prisoner's feeling of deprivation can be questioned. And the objective reality of the prisoner's deprivation—in the sense that he has actually suffered a fall from his economic position in the free community—can be viewed with skepticism, as we have indicated above. But these criticisms are irrelevant to the significant issue, namely that legitimately or illegitimately, rationally or irrationally, the inmate population defines its present material impoverishment as a painful loss.

In modern Western culture, material possessions are so large a part of the individual's conception of himself that to be stripped of them is to be attacked at the deepest layers of personality. This is particularly true when poverty cannot be excused as a blind stroke of fate or a universal calamity. Poverty caused by one's own mistakes or misdeeds represents an indictment against one's basic value or personal worth, and there are few men who can philosophically bear the want caused by their own actions. It is true some prisoners in the New Jersey State Prison attempt to interpret their low position in the scale of goods and services as an effort by the state to exploit them economically. Thus, in the eyes of some inmates, the prisoner is poor not because of an offense which he has committed in the past but because the state is a tyrant which uses its captive criminals as slave labor under the hypocritical guise of reformation. Penology, it is said, is a racket. Their poverty, then, is not punishment as we have used the word before, i.e., the just consequence of criminal behavior; rather, it is an unjust hurt or pain inflicted without legitimate cause. This attitude, however, does not appear to be particularly widespread in the inmate population, and the great majority of prisoners must face their privation without the aid of the wronged man's sense of injustice. Furthermore, most prisoners are unable to fortify themselves in their low level of material existence by seeing it as a means to some high or worthy end. They are unable to attach any significant meaning to their need to make it more bearable, such as present pleasures foregone for pleasures in the future, self-sacrifice in the interests of the community, or material asceticism for the purpose of spiritual salvation.

The inmate, then, sees himself as having been made poor by reason of his own acts and without the rationale of compensating benefits. The failure is *his* failure in a world where control and possession of the material environment are commonly taken as sure indicators of a man's worth. It is true that our society, as materialistic as it may be, does not rely exclusively on goods and services as a criterion of an individual's value; and, as we shall see shortly, the inmate population defends itself by stressing alternative or supplementary measures of merit. But impoverishment remains as one of the most bitter attacks on the individual's self-image that our society has to offer and the prisoner cannot ignore the implications of his straitened circumstances. Whatever the discomforts and irritations of the prisoner's Spartan existence may be, he must carry the additional burden of social definitions which equate his material deprivation with personal inadequacy.

Gresham M. Sykes

BRUTAL SPORTS AND BRUTAL FANS

New research prompted by increased violence among sports fans in recent years is challenging some long-held notions about the link between some highly competitive games of aggression and the observers they enthrall.

Many psychologists and sociologists now conclude that the violence that often occurs in physical-contact sports has a tendency to spur aggression off the field. "There is a direct psychological connection between violence on the field and violence in the stands," said Michael Smith of York University in Toronto, one of many researchers who are studying sports violence.

That view is vigorously denied by sports figures who contend that what they see as sporadic violence among fans is but a reflection of an increasingly violent society.

Psychologists, though, argue that there are factors in sports that make violence more likely, over and above the unruliness to which crowds of any sort are prone.

They agree that sports contests are peaceful events for most people and that watching them contributes to their enjoyment of life and their sense of well-being. And they acknowledge that violence in the stands or on the streets after the game is restricted for the most part to a youthful minority. Nor do these behavioral scientists place blame solely on either the games themselves or these fans; rather, problems of violence are found to occur as a result of the volatile interaction of the two.

The emerging view is that the particularly brutal and angry aggression that is a virtually integral part of some forms of competitive athletics increases the likelihood of imitative violence among crowds dominated by young adult males. One theory holds, for example, that anonymity and excitement allow fans to put aside more readily the inhibitions that would keep them from being openly aggressive in other situations. Violence on the playing field then holds out to them an example they are more likely to follow. Drinking adds to that likelihood.

This theory runs counter to the view proposed by Freud and others that aggressive competitive sports are a means to contain human aggression, for both those who participate and those who watch. The notion was that harsh physical contact on the field tends to let off steam, to relieve frustrations, to defuse aggressiveness. On a grander scale, international games would serve as a substitute for warfare.

Stimulant to Violence

That argument was used for years, by such Olympics officials as Avery Brundage in promoting international sporting events as a kind of cathartic alternative for wars among nations, and as a way to build individual character. Indeed, it remains an important belief among many athletes and sports administrators, along with the idea that international games promote good will and understanding.

Yet, psychologists who have done experiments to test the notion that aggressiveness is relieved by physical-contact sports now say that it does not seem to hold up. To the contrary, combative sports, such as football, "serve to teach and stimulate violence," said Jeffrey Goldstein, a psychologist at Temple University who is at the forefront of the new work on sports violence.

Dr. Goldstein, in his book "Sports Violence" (Springer-Verlag), reviews a series of findings, all of which indicate that aggressive sports has a role in increasing the aggressiveness of those who participate, as well as at least some of those who watch.

Research with high school and college athletes has found that participants in more combative sports, such as hockey and football, are quicker to anger than athletes in noncontact sports such as swimming. Since football athletes might be more aggressive to start with, the telling point in this research is that, as the season goes on, these athletes grow more hostile and aggressive, and remain so in the off-season. That result was not found with swimmers.

Rehearsal of Anger

The reason, in Dr. Goldstein's view, is that engaging in aggressive sports is a rehearsal of anger and aggression. An equivalent effect holds among spectators, in his view. In a study of fans at an Army-Navy football game, for example, male spectators were found to be more hostile after the game than they had been before, even among fans of the winning side, Army, and among those who said they did not care who won. There was no such increase in hostility, though, among fans at a nonaggressive sport, gymnastics.

"It is not competition per se that leads to an increase in hostility," he said, "but, apparently, the aggressive nature of the competition."

As yet, psychologists are unable to pinpoint exactly which fans are most likely to become violent. "Fans who get caught up in outright violence," Dr. Goldstein said, "do not seem to be psychologically different from most other fans, but the one difference is that they are almost universally young men, some of whom come to sports events in the hope of a battle." Then the violence in the game itself builds on this predisposition, he said.

The most extensive survey of violence among American spectators is being conducted by Jerry M. Lewis, a sociologist at Kent State University. He is studying more than 300 incidents of violence, in which 10 or more people were involved, from 1982 to 1983.

Baseball was the sport with the most such incidents. Though it may have less built-in body contact than some other sports, it nevertheless has its inevitable moments—those accompanying bean balls, broken-up double plays or what might politely be called disagreements with the umpires, for example. It is closely followed by football, basketball, ice hockey and boxing. The fewest incidents of fan violence occurred in such events as horse racing, golf tournaments, wrestling and tennis.

Daniel Goleman, New York Times, 13 August 1985

FOOTBALL—THE GAME OF AGGRESSION

There are many ways in which professional football is unique among sports, and as many others in which it is the fullest expression of what is at the heart of all sports. There is no other major sport so dependent upon raw force, nor any so dependent on a complex and delicate strategy; none so wide in the range of specialized functions demanded from its players; none so dependent upon the undifferentiated athletic *sine qua non*, a quickwitted body; none so primitive; none so futuristic; none so American.

Football is first of all a form of play, something one engages in instinctively and only for the sake of performing the activity in question. Among forms of play, football is a game, which means that it is built on communal needs, rather than on private evasions, like mountain climbing. Among games it is a sport; it requires athletic ability, unlike croquet. And among sports, it is one whose mode is violence and whose violence is its special glory.

In some sports—basketball, baseball, soccer—violence is occasional (and usually illegal); in others, like hockey, it is incidental; in others still, car racing, for example, it is accidental. Definitive violence football shares alone with boxing and bullfighting, among major sports. But in bullfighting a man is pitted not against another man, but against an animal, and boxing is a competition between individuals, not teams, and that makes a great difference. If shame is the proper and usual penalty for failures in sporting competitions between individuals, guilt is the consequence of failing not only oneself and one's fans, but also one's teammates. Failure in football, moreover, seems more related to a failure of courage, seems more unmanning than in any other sport outside of bullfighting. In other sports one loses a knack, is outsmarted, or is merely inferior in ability, but in football, on top of these, a player fails because he "lacks desire," or "can't take it anymore," or "hears footsteps," as his teammates will put it.

Many sports, especially those in which there is a goal to be defended, seem enactments of the games animals play under the stimulus of what ethologists, students of animal behavior, call *territory*—"the drive to gain, maintain, and defend the exclusive right to a piece of property," as Robert Ardrey puts it. The most striking symptom of this drive is aggressiveness, but among social animals, such as primates, it leads to "amity for the social partner, hostility for the territorial neighbor." The territorial instinct is closely related to whatever makes animals establish pecking orders; the tangible sign of one's status within the orders is the size and value of the territory one is able to command. Individuals fight over status, groups over *lebensraum*[1] and a bit more. These instincts, some ethologists have claimed, are behind patriotism and private property, and also, I would add, codes of honor, as among ancient Greeks, modern Sicilians, primitive hunters, teen-age gangs, soldiers, aristocrats, and athletes, especially football players.

The territorial basis of certain kinds of sports is closest to the surface in football, whose plays are all attempts to gain and defend property through aggression. Does this not make football *par excellence* the game of instinctual satisfactions, especially among Americans, who are notorious as violent patriots and instinctive defenders of private property? . . . Even the unusual amity, if that is the word, that exists among football players has been remarked upon. . . . And what is it that corresponds in football to the various feathers, furs, fins, gorgeous colors by means of which animals puff themselves into exaggerated gestures of masculine potency? The football player's equipment, of course. His cleats raise him an inch off the ground. Knee and thigh pads thrust the

---

[1]Literally, living space. The word is most often associated with the territory thought by the Nazis to be essential to Germany's political and economic security.

force lines of his legs forward. His pants are tight against his rump and the back of his thighs, portions of the body which the requirements of the game stuff with muscle. . . . Even the tubby guard looks slim by comparison with his shoulders, extended half a foot on each side by padding. Finally, the helmet, which from the esthetic point of view most clearly expresses the genius of the sport. Not only does the helmet make the player inches taller and give his head a size proportionate to the rest of him; it makes him anonymous, inscrutable, more serviceable as a symbol. The football player in uniform strikes the eye in a succession of gestalt[2] shifts; first a hooded phantom out of the paleolithic past of the species; then a premonition of a future of spacemen.

In sum, and I am almost serious about this, football players are to America what tragic actors were to ancient Athens and gladiators to Rome: models of perenially heroic, aggressive, violent humanity, but adapted to the social realities of the times and places that formed them.

[2]I.e., perceptual.

from "Game Theory," by George Stade, *The Columbia Forum*

FROM: SPORT: A PHILOSOPHIC INQUIRY

The athlete must have a strong urge to defeat his opponent, and must carry out that urge in the form of actions which will enable him to outdistance all. This requires him to be aggressive. Man's aggression, as has already been remarked, is thought by some to exhibit in a vigorous but harmless form an inescapable but dangerous aggressiveness characteristic of us all. Aggression, on this view, is part of man's very nature, rooted deep in the unconscious, in the history of the race, and in the early experiences of the child. It is always and inevitably expressed; mankind is fortunate in having found ways for releasing it without much injury to anyone.

So much aggression seems to be expressed in games that to many an observer a game appears to be like a war, that outstanding example of aggressiveness. Though some sports seem to have been invented to promote physical fitness, skill, and dexterity, or for the purpose of using up surplus energy enjoyably, others—archery, fencing, shooting, judo, evidently, and conceivably boxing, wrestling, dressage, running, weight lifting, and the relay—have instead a military origin or a military objective. These, and perhaps others, refine and promote activities which are parts of the art of war. The fact has tempted some to think of games as a substitute for war. If they were, hopefully they might some day usurp the place that war has assumed in what we like to call "the civilized world." Unfortunately, it does not appear that there is much ground for their expectation, in part because war and game are quite distinct in nature, and in the role they give to aggressiveness.

Both war and game aim at victory. Both usually end in a clearly evidenced superiority of one side over the other, though draws and stalemates are not unknown. Only games *must* conform to rules, though in modern times we try to make wars conform to them too. But it is paradoxical to expect both sides in a war to submit to common rules. Each side seeks to annihilate the other; it would be foolish for either to allow its efforts to be restrained or blocked by an effort to conform to rules it has agreed, with its enemy, to abide by. A genuine war is a ruthless affair, paying for victory with the lives of men and the destruction of property and works of art. Omnivorous, it sweeps away for the time any meaning to a common acceptance of any rule, and jeopardizes every civilized value. If the antagonists could agree upon anything one would expect them to agree to stop the war; when advantage is thought of in terms of what life is and what gives it value, war is evidently to the advantage of neither. It is because they can find no basis for agreement that they go to war seriously, with the intent to render the enemy impotent and sometimes even to destroy him utterly. Wars begin with a disagreement precluding the acceptance of common rules.

Men poised to destroy one another cannot, except foolishly and futilely, agree on conforming to certain rules. There is no punishment which the violators of rules need fear. If they win no one will punish them, and if they lose their loss is inseparable from whatever punishment they thereby suffer. The loser could be punished, over and above what is normally the case, because of his violations of a supposed agreement made in happier days, but since the punishment is meted out by the victor, as he sees fit, it is arbitrary to claim that a closer adherence to the rules would have resulted in a less severe punishment. Only where it is the object of a war to restrain or warn is there much point in keeping to common rules.

It is possible, and it may even be desirable, to act aggressively toward others in a game, but one must, to play with them, act with good will. An intent to cripple and destroy goes counter to the purpose of a game. The aggressiveness exhibited in it is an aggressiveness which conforms to rules, or one is doing violence to the game.

The soldier seeks victory. He must be aggressive. Of course, without a strong desire to defeat his opponent, no athlete can have much hope of victory either. He, too, insists on himself. But there is too much self-sacrifice, humility, team play, together with an acceptance of official neutral decisions and a conformity to objectively stated and applied prescriptions, to make the expression of aggression represent the primary or essential goal, or the motive for athletic activity.

Paul Weiss

INTEGRATING YOUR SOURCES INTO PARAGRAPHS

Writing a research essay is rather like putting a mosaic together. Each paragraph has its basic design, determined by its topic sentence. To carry out the design, you might present a group of reasons or examples to illustrate the main idea, or provide an extended explanation to develop that idea in greater detail, or compare two elements introduced in the topic sentence. These are the same paragraphing patterns that you use in all of your writing. What makes the research essay different is the way that the materials are assembled from many sources, *not* the way in which they are organized or presented.

Imagine that the notes that you have taken from several different sources are boxes of tiles, each box containing a different color. You may find it easier to avoid mixing the colors and to work only with red tiles or only with blue, or to devote one corner of the mosaic to a red pattern and another to a blue. In the same way, you may find it both convenient and natural to work with only one source at a time and to avoid the decisions and the adjustments that must be made when you are combining different styles and ideas. But, of course, it is the design and only the design that dictates which colors should be used in working out the pattern of the mosaic, and it is the design or outline of your essay that dictates which evidence should be included in each paragraph. Whichever topic you have decided to discuss in a given paragraph, you must work with *all* the relevant information that you have gathered about that topic, whether it comes from one source or from many. Of course, there may be an abundance of materials; you may find it impossible to fit everything into the paragraph without overloading it with excessive repetition. These rejected pieces may not fit into another part of the essay; instead, they will go back into their boxes as a backup or reserve fund of information.

At the same time, the criteria for judging the quality of a paragraph remain the same—clarity, coherence, and unity. Try to integrate your materials so that your reader will not be distracted by their different origins or made aware of any breaks or disharmony between the various points. On the other hand, your materials should not be so completely assimilated that you fail to provide appropriate acknowledgment of your sources. As you will learn in the next chapter, the documentation that you insert will act as a running record of your research. Observing the names and page numbers of your sources in parentheses, your reader becomes aware of the diverse origins of these smoothly integrated pieces of information.

Here, then, are the basic rules for paragraph construction, adjusted to fit the requirements of the research essay:

1. Each paragraph should possess a single main idea, usually expressed in the topic sentence. That topic or design controls the ar-

rangement of all the information in the paragraph. Everything that is included should develop and support that single idea, without digressions.

2. The body of the paragraph will probably contain a combination of information taken from a variety of sources. The number of different sources that you will include in any one paragraph depends partly on the number of authors in your notes who have touched on that point and partly on the contribution each can make to the development of your topic.

Providing a Clear Account of Your Evidence

Worth noting again is that you may find yourself with so much information that you run the risk of overcrowding your paragraph. You may have collected four or five examples from several different sources, all illustrating your topic sentence; each of these examples in its original text may have filled several sentences or several paragraphs or several pages. Interesting as they all may be, giving each the same amount of space is impractical. You must select a few examples and either disregard or briefly refer to the others. But if you go to the other extreme and your examples are too brief and abrupt, your reader will not understand their significance and your reasons for including them. Your goal is to supply just enough information about each example to make your reader appreciate its interest and its relevance to your topic.

In the following complete paragraph, the examples are presented as afterthoughts:

> Advertising uses women amorally. This condition should be publicized, and the sooner the better for every member of the reading public. For the past half century, the giant and not-so-giant corporations have succeeded in portraying an image of women that ranges from downright stupidity (Parker Pen: "You might as well give her a gorgeous pen to keep her checkbook unbalanced with") to the object of sadistic sex (Vogue's "The Story of Ohhh . . ." which included shots of a man ramming his hand into a woman's breast). Women today are being awakened to these debasing and degrading tactics.

The parentheses here are being used to wedge the examples into an already overloaded sentence. This writer is counting on having an exceptionally patient reader, who will pause long enough to interpret the significance of what is in parentheses.

In contrast, here is a paragraph from an essay about the novelist F. Scott Fitzgerald, in which four different explanations of an incident are presented, each at suitable length. Formal documentation of the sources has been omitted; but, to emphasize the variety and complexity of the research, the names of the sources and the attributing verbs and phrases have been italicized. The writer is describing an affair between Fitzgerald's wife, Zelda, and Edouard Jozan, a young Frenchman.

> There is a lack of agreement about the details of the affair as well as its significance for the Fitzgeralds' marriage. According to one of Fitzgerald's biographers, Jozan and Zelda afterwards regarded it as "nothing more than a summer flirtation." But Ernest Hemingway, in his memoirs, wrote much later that Scott had told him "a truly sad story" about the affair, which he repeated many times in the course of their friendship. Gerald and Sara Murphy, who were present that summer and remembered the incident very well, told of being awakened by Scott in the middle of a September night in order to help him revive Zelda from an overdose of sleeping pills. The Murphys were sure that this incident was related to her affair with Jozan. Nancy Milford, Zelda's biographer, believes that the affair affected Zelda more than Scott, who, at that time, was very engrossed in his work. Indeed, Milford's account of the affair is the only one which suggests that Zelda was so deeply in love with Jozan that she asked Scott for a divorce. According to an interview with Jozan, the members of this triangle never engaged in a three-way confrontation; Jozan told Milford that the Fitzgeralds were "the victims of their own unsettled and a little unhealthy imagination."

This paragraph gives a brief but adequate account of what is known about the events of that summer of 1924. The writer does not try to rush through the four accounts of the affair, nor does he reduce each one to a phrase, as if he expected the reader to have prior knowledge of these people and their activities. Placed in the context of the whole essay, the paragraph probably provides enough information for the reader to judge whose interpretation of the affair is closest to the truth.

DOING JUSTICE TO YOUR SOURCES

Perhaps the greatest disservice that you can do your sources is to distort them so that your reader is left with a false impression of what they have said or written. One way of shading an argument to suit your own ends is to misrepresent the strength of the opposition. Let us assume that you are working with a bibliography of ten articles. Three clearly support your point of view, but four of the others are openly opposed, and the remaining three avoid taking sides, emphasizing related but less controversial topics. If your essay cites only the three favorable articles and the three neutral ones, and if you avoid any reference to the views of the opposition, you have presented the issue falsely. Such ostrichlike tactics will not convince your reader that your opinions are right; on the contrary, your unwillingness to admit the existence of opposing views can only suggest that your point of view must have some basic flaw. If you omit the troublesome sources from your bibliography, then your reader, who may be familiar with some of the arguments on both sides, will wonder at your inability to locate and cite sources that represent the other side. Thus, a one-sided presentation will either make you appear to be wholly biased or damage your credibility as a thorough researcher. If the sources are available and if their views are pertinent, then they should be represented and, if you wish, refuted in your essay.

Sometimes, distortions occur accidentally, because you have presented only a *partial* account of a source's views. In the course of an article or a book, an author may examine and then reject or accept a variety of views before making it clear which are his own conclusions. Or he may have mixed opinions about the issue and see merit in more than one point of view. If you choose to quote or paraphrase material from only one section of such a work, then you must find a way to inform your reader that these statements are not entirely representative of the writer's overall views.

When ideas get distorted, the reason is usually the researcher's misunderstanding or careless note-taking or hasty reading. Remember to check through the entire section of the article or all your notes *before* you attribute an opinion to your source, to make sure that you are not taking a sentence out of context or ignoring a statement in the next paragraph or on the next page that may be more typical of the writer's thinking. Remember that a common argumentative strategy is to set up a point with which one basically disagrees in order to shoot it down shortly thereafter. Don't confuse a statement made for the sake of argument with a writer's real beliefs.

Occasionally you may be tempted to distort a source deliberately because you are so eager to uphold your point of view that you will cite any bit of material that looks like supporting evidence. To do so, however, you will probably have to twist the words of the source to fit your ideas. This is one of the worst kinds of intellectual dishonesty—and one of the easiest for a suspicious reader to detect: one has only to look up the source. If you cannot find sufficient arguments and if your sources' evidence does not clearly and directly support your side, then you should seriously consider switching sides or switching topics.

Here is a fairly clear instance of such distortion. In an essay on the need for prison reform, Garry Wills is focusing on the general deficiencies of our society's penal system, not the death penalty (or lack thereof). But the student who is citing Wills in his research essay is writing specifically in support of capital punishment. To make Wills's arguments fit into the scheme of this essay, the student has to make some suspiciously selective references. Here is a paragraph from the research essay, side by side with the source:

Although the death penalty may sound very harsh and inhuman, is this not fair and just punishment for one who was able to administer death to another human being? A murderer's victim always receives the death penalty. Therefore, the death penalty for the murderer evens the score, or, as stated in the Bible, "an eye for an eye, and a tooth for a tooth." According to Garry Wills, "take a life, lose your life." Throughout the ages, society has demanded that man be allowed to right his wrongs. Revenge is our culture's oldest way of making sure that no one "gets away with" any crime. As Wills points out, according to this line of reasoning, the taking of the murderer's life can be seen as his payment to society for his misdeed.

Revenge: The oldest of our culture's views on punishment is the *lex talionis*, an eye for an eye. Take a life, lose your life. It is a very basic cry—people must "pay" for their crimes, yield exact and measured recompense. No one should "get away with" any crime, like a shoplifter taking something unpaid for. The desire to make an offender suffer equivalent pain (if not compensatory *excess* of pain) is very deep in human nature, and rises quickly to the surface. What is lynching but an impatience with even the slightest delay in exacting this revenge? It serves our social myth to say that this impatience, if denied immediate gratification, is replaced by something entirely different—by an impersonal dedication to justice. Only lynchers want revenge, not those who wait for a verdict. That is not very likely. Look at the disappointed outcry if the verdict does not yield even delayed satisfaction of the grudge.

The importance of revenge is seen in the fact that the demand for a death penalty is often greatest in cases where no other motive can be observed—with the psychotic or deranged killer or rapist or child-abuser; with those who have committed crimes of passion, where deterrence of the similarly afflicted is not possible. Such cries for redress have little to do with social utility—especially when it is an outsider or outcast who is being punished (an Indian on the frontier, a black in the old South). One cannot pretend to be instilling respectability in a people denied that respectability from the outset.

In the essay, the writer is citing only the preliminary part of Wills's argument and thus makes him appear to be a supporter of capital punishment. Wills is being misrepresented because (unlike the writer) he considers it fair to examine the views of the opposing side before presenting his own arguments. The ideas that the student cites are not Wills's, but Wills's presentation of commonly accepted assumptions about punishment. It is not entirely clear whether the writer of the research essay has merely been careless, failing to read past the first few sentences, or whether the misrepresentation is intentional.

INTEGRATING YOUR SOURCES: AN EXAMPLE

To illustrate the need for careful analysis of sources before you write your paragraphs, the following example uses a group of passages, all direct quotations, which have been gathered for a research essay on college athletics. The paragraph developed from these sources must support the writer's thesis: colleges should, in the interests of both players and academic standards, outlaw the high-pressure tactics used by coaches when they recruit high school players for college teams. The first three statements come from college coaches describing recruiting methods that they have observed and carried out; the last four are taken from books that discuss corruption in athletics.

> I think in the long run, every coach must recognize this basic principle, or face the alumni firing squad. Recruiting is the crux of building a championship football team.
>
> Steve Sloan, Texas Tech

> Athletics is creating a monster. Recruiting is getting to be cancerous.
>
> Dale Brown, Louisiana State University

> You don't out-coach people, you out-recruit them.
>
> Paul "Bear" Bryant, University of Alabama

> It is an athletic maxim that a man with no special coaching skills can win games if he recruits well and that a tactician without talented players is a man soon without a job.
>
> Kenneth Denlinger

> There is recruiting in varying degrees in every intercollegiate sport, from crew to girls' basketball and from the Houston golf dynasty that

began in the mid-50's to Southern California importing sprinters and jumpers from Jamaica.

J. Robert Evans

The fundamental causes of the defects in American college athletics are too much commercialism and a negligent attitude towards the educational opportunity for which the college exists.

Carnegie Foundation, 1929

[*Collier's* magazine, in 1905, reported that] Walter Eckersall, All-American quarterback, enrolled at Chicago three credits short of the entrance requirement and his teammate, Leo Detray, entered the school before he even graduated high school. In addition the University of Minnesota paid two players outright to play in a single game (Nebraska: 1902). A quarterback and an end also from Minnesota admitted shaving points during the 1903 Beloit game.

Joseph Durso

Your paragraph will focus on recruiting high school stars as opposed to developing students who enter college by the ordinary admissions procedure. Which of these ideas and observations might help to develop this paragraph? In other words, which statements should be represented by paraphrase or perhaps by direct quotation?

I think in the long run, every coach must recognize this basic principle, or face the alumni firing squad. Recruiting is the crux of building a championship football team.

This very broad generalization initially seems quotable, largely because it sums up the topic so well; but, in fact, because it does no more than sum up the topic, it does not advance your argument any further and need not be included if your topic sentence makes the same point. (In general, you should write your own topic sentences rather than letting your sources write them for you.) The phrase "alumni firing squad" might be useful to cite in a later paragraph, in a discussion of the specific influence of alumni.

Athletics is creating a monster. Recruiting is getting to be cancerous.

Coach Brown's choice of images—"cancerous" and "monster"—is certainly vivid; but the sentence as a whole is no more than a generalized opinion about recruiting, not an explanation of *why* the situation is so monstrous. To be lured into quoting this for the sake of two words would be a mistake.

> You don't out-coach people, you out-recruit them.

This is the first statement that has advanced a specific idea: the coach may have a *choice* between building a winning team through recruiting and building a winning team through good coaching; but recruiting, not coaching, wins games. Coach Bryant, then, is not just making a rhetorical point, as the first two coaches seem to be. His seven-word sentence is succinct, if not elaborately developed, and would make a good introduction to or summation of a point that deserves full discussion.

The remaining four statements suggest a wider range of approach and style.

> Walter Eckersall, All-American quarterback, enrolled at Chicago three credits short of the entrance requirement and his teammate, Leo Detray, entered the school before he even graduated high school. In addition, the University of Minnesota paid two players outright to play in a single game (Nebraska: 1902). A quarterback and an end also from Minnesota admitted shaving points during the 1903 Beloit game.

This passage is as much concerned with corruption as recruiting and indicates that commercialism is nothing new in college athletics. Although the information is interesting, it is presented as a list of facts, and the language is not worth quoting.

> The fundamental causes of the defects in American college athletics are too much commercialism and a negligent attitude towards the educational opportunity for which the college exists.

In contrast, this extract from the 1929 Carnegie Foundation study is phrased in abstract language that is characteristic of foundation reports and academic writing in general. This style can be found in most of the textbooks that you read (including this one) and in many of the sources that you use in college. The foundation presents its point clearly enough and raises an important idea: an athlete recruited to win games (and earn himself fame and fortune) is likely to ignore the primary reason for going to college—to acquire an education. Nevertheless, there is no compelling reason to *quote* this statement. Remember that you include quotations in your essay to enhance your presentation; the quotation marks automatically prepare the reader for special words and phrasing. But the prose here is too colorless and abstract to give the reader anything to focus on; a paraphrase is preferable.

> There is recruiting in varying degrees in every intercollegiate sport, from crew to girls' basketball and from the Houston golf dynasty that

began in the mid-50's to Southern California importing sprinters and jumpers from Jamaica.

This statement presents a quite different, more detailed level of information; it contains a list of sports, including some not known for their cutthroat recruiting practices. But details do not necessarily deserve quotation. Will these references be at all meaningful to the reader who is not familiar with the "Houston golf dynasty" or the Jamaican track stars? To know that recruitment is not limited to "cash" sports, such as football, is interesting, but the specifics date quickly: in a few years, they may no longer be a useful frame of reference for most readers.

> It is an athletic maxim that a man with no special coaching skills can win games if he recruits well and that a tactician without talented players is a man soon without a job.

Largely because of parallel construction, the last comment sounds both sharp and solid. In much the same way as Coach Bryant's seven words, but at greater length, Kenneth Denlinger sums up the contrast between coaching and recruiting, and suggests which one has the edge. Because the statement gives the reader something substantial to think about and because it is well phrased, Denlinger is probably worth quoting.

Should the writer include both the statements, by Bryant and by Denlinger, which say essentially the same thing? While Bryant's first-hand comment is commendably terse and certainly authoritative, Denlinger's is more complete and self-explanatory. A solution might be to include both, at different points in the paragraph, with Bryant cited at the end to sum up the idea that has been developed. Of course, the other five sources need not be excluded from the paragraph. Rather, if you wish, all five may be referred to, by paraphrase or brief reference, with their authors' names cited.

Here is *one* way of integrating this set of statements into a paragraph:

> In college athletics, what is the best way for a school to win games? Should a strong team be gradually built up by training ordinary students from scratch, or should the process be shortened and success be assured by actively recruiting players who already know how to win? The first method may be more consistent with the traditional amateurism of college athletics, but as early as 1929, the Carnegie Foundation complained that the focus of college sports had shifted from education to the material advantages of winning. Even earlier, in 1903, there were several instances of players without academic qualifications who were "hired" to guarantee victory. And in recent years excellence of recruiting has become the most important skill for a coach to possess. Kenneth Denlinger has observed, "It is an athletic

maxim that a man with no special coaching skills can win games if he recruits well and that a tactician without talented players is a man soon without a job." It follows, then, that a coach who wants to keep his job is likely to concentrate on spotting and collecting talent for his team. Coaches from LSU. Alabama, and Texas Tech all testify that good recruiting has first priority throughout college athletics. According to Bear Bryant of Alabama: "You don't out-coach people, you out-recruit them."

SELECTING QUOTATIONS

Now that you are working with a great variety of sources, it may be more difficult to limit the number of quotations in your essay and to choose quotable material. If you are doubtful about when and what to quote, review the guidelines for quotation in Chapter 1 and Chapter 4. As a rule, the more eminent and authoritative the source, the more reason to consider quoting it; but make sure that eminence does not bring with it a complexity of style that makes it unreadable. Never quote something just because it sounds impressive. The style of the quotation—the level of difficulty, the choice of vocabulary, and the degree of abstraction—should be compatible with your own style. Don't force your reader to make a mental jump from your own characteristic voice and wording to a far more abstract or flowery or colloquial style. Of course, the need for a consistent voice does not mean that your essay should lack all variety; nor are you expected to exclude significant but difficult quotations by authors whose style is so distinctive that it cannot be paraphrased.

When the time comes to decide whether and what to quote, stop and observe your own reactions. After an interval, rapidly reread what you intend to quote. If you find any quotation difficult to understand on the first try, then either attempt to paraphrase the point, or leave it out entirely. If your mind becomes distracted or confused or blank, your reader's will be, too. In the long run, the writers that you will want to quote will be the ones whom you understand and enjoy.

When you are working on a biographical or historical research essay, you will probably encounter special problems deciding whether or not to quote. Primary sources often have a special claim to be quoted. You would be more likely to include one of Hemingway's descriptions of Paris in 1925, without alteration, than a comparable sentence by one of his biographers. A person who witnessed the Chicago Fire has a better claim to have his original account presented verbatim than does a historian decades later.

When quoting primary sources, it is essential to make the exact source of the quotation quite clear to your reader. Here, for example, is an excerpt from a student essay describing Charles Dickens on holiday in France in 1853:

> On first beholding Boulogne, Dickens was enraptured. He immediately wrote home to a friend expressing his delight in the beauty of the French countryside and of the town. "He raved about the rustic qualities of the people. . . ." He raved about the "fresh sea air" and about the "beauty and repose of his surroundings."

The first "He raved" tells us at once that the biographer, not Dickens, is being quoted, and the reader cannot be sure which of the two is responsible for "fresh sea air" and "beauty and repose," since the biographer may, in fact, be quoting from Dickens's letters. Single quotation marks inside the double quotation marks might have been used to show who wrote what.

The placement of the quotation marks in the next excerpt makes it clear that the words are Dickens's own; on the other hand, they may not be worth quoting. The novelist is describing the house that he has rented, the Chateau des Moulineux:

> Dickens rattled off a list of phrases in his attempt to describe this idyllic place. It was to become his "best doll's house," "our French watering place," and "this abode of bliss." More than anything else it would become a "happy, happy place."

Such a list of separately quoted phrases creates an awkward, disconnected effect, which, if used too often, will become tedious for your reader.

Descriptions are often more difficult to paraphrase than ideas and therefore tend to be presented in such a sequence of quoted phrases. If your source states that the walls of the room were painted sea-green and the furniture was made out of horsehair and covered with light-brown velvet, you may find it next to impossible to summon up appropriate synonyms to paraphrase these standard descriptive terms. "Crin de chevel" covered with fuzzy beige fabric? Mediterranean colors decorating the walls? The result is hardly worth the effort. If the man's eyes are described as dark blue, don't alter the phrase to "piercing blue" or "deep azure" or "ocean pools." If you place "dark blue" in a sentence that is otherwise your own writing, you may omit the quotation marks.

EXERCISE 40

The unfinished student paragraphs below are followed by brief excerpts from sources.

1. Decide which of the excerpts contains the most appropriate sentence for quotation. (It is not necessary to quote the entire excerpt.) For the purposes of this exercise, assume that all the sources are qualified authorities.
2. Paraphrase the other excerpts.
3. Complete the paragraph by using both paraphrase and quotation, citing two *or* three sources. Maintain a consistent tone and (except for the quotation) a single voice. Do not digress too far from the topic sentence.

Student Paragraph A:

> Although, in democratic countries, freedom is usually regarded as an unalienable right, it is possible to waste or even abuse one's freedom. There is a difference between being free <u>from</u> tyranny or oppression and being free <u>to</u> do something constructive with one's liberty. Freedom can even bring responsibilities . . .

Sources

I am free only in so far as I recognize the humanity and respect the liberty of all the men surrounding me.

Mikhail Bakunin

As soon as man apprehends himself as free and wishes to use his freedom, his first activity is play.

Jean-Paul Sartre

Freedom is a food which must be carefully administered when people are too hungry for it.

Lech Walesa

Freedom exists only where the people take care of the government.

Woodrow Wilson

Student Paragraph B:

> It is not clear whether John D. Rockefeller saw accumulating wealth as an end in itself or as a means to a more worthwhile end. At times, he seemed to be obsessed with adding to his financial empire, and money seemed to be his only object in life. . . .

Sources

John D. Rockefeller can be fully described as a man made in the image of the ideal money-maker. . . . An ideal money-maker is a machine the details of which are diagrammed on the asbestos blueprints which paper the halls of hell.

Thomas Lawson, quoted in Jules Abel,
The Rockefeller Millions

I believe the power to make money is a gift of God . . . to be developed and used to the best of our ability for the good of mankind. Having been endowed with the gift I possess, I believe it is my duty to make money and still more money, and to use the money I make for the good of my fellow man according to the dictates of my conscience.

John D. Rockefeller, quoted in Matthew Josephson,
The Robber Barons

I'm bound to be rich! Bound to be rich!

John D. Rockefeller, quoted in Allen Nevins,
Study in Power

I had an ambition to make a fortune. More money-making has never been my goal. I had an ambition to build.

John D. Rockefeller, quoted in Allen Nevins,
Study in Power

ASSIGNMENT 17

Write an essay of at least seven pages based on the outline developed in Assignment 16.

9.
Presenting the Results of Your Research: Acknowledging Your Sources

When you engage in research, you are continually coming into contact with the ideas and the words of other writers; as a result, the opportunities to plagiarize—by accident or by intention—increase tremendously. You must therefore understand exactly what constitutes plagiarism.

Plagiarism is the unacknowledged use of another person's work, in the form of original ideas, strategies, and research, as well as another person's writing, in the form of sentences, phrases, and innovative terminology.

Plagiarism is the equivalent of theft; but the stolen goods are intellectual rather than material. And, like other acts of theft, plagiarism is against the law. The copyright law, which governs publications, requires that authorship be acknowledged and (if the "borrowed" material is long enough) that payment be offered to the writer.

Plagiarism also violates the moral law that people be allowed to take pride in, as well as profit from, the fruits of their labor. Put yourself in the victim's place. Think about the best idea that you ever had, or the paragraph that you worked hardest on in your last paper. Now, imagine yourself finding exactly the same idea or exactly the same sentences in someone else's essay, with no mention of your name, with no quotation marks. Would you accept the theft of your property without protest?

Plagiarists are not only guilty of robbery; they are also guilty of cheating. People who bend or break the rules concerning authorship, who do not do their own work, will be rightly distrusted by their classmates, teachers, and future employers, who may equate a history of plagiarism with laziness, incompetence, or dishonesty. One's future rarely depends on getting a better grade on a single assignment; on the other hand, one's reputation may be damaged if one resorts to plagiarism in order to get that grade.

But plagiarism is dangerous for a more immediate and practical reason. As you observed in Exercise 13, an experienced teacher can usually detect plagiarized work quite easily. If you are not skilled enough to write your own essay, you are unlikely to do a good enough job of adapting someone else's work to your needs. Plagiarism represents a confession of failure, an inability to do—even to attempt to do—the job. Remember that anyone can learn to write well enough to make plagiarism an unnecessary risk.

Finally, you will not receive greater glory by plagiarizing. On the contrary, most teachers believe that students who successfully understand and digest the ideas of others, apply them to the topic, and place them in their own words deserve to receive the highest grade for their mastery of the basic skills of academic writing. There are, however, occasions when your teacher asks you not to use secondary sources and thus makes it impossible for you to acknowledge your debt. In such cases, you would be wise to do no background reading at all, so that the temptation to borrow or steal will not arise.

ACKNOWLEDGING YOUR SOURCES

Acknowledging your sources—or documentation—means telling your reader that someone other than yourself is the source of ideas and words found in your essay. Acknowledgment can take the form of quotation marks and citation of the author's name, techniques that are by now familiar to you, or more elaborate systems of indicating the source, which will be explained later in this chapter. There are guidelines to help you decide what can and what cannot safely be used without acknowledgment, and these guidelines mostly favor complete documentation.

Documenting Information

By conservative standards, you should cite a source for all facts and evidence in your essay that you did not know before you started your research. Knowing when to acknowledge the source of your knowledge or information largely depends on common sense. For example, it is not necessary to document the fact that there are fifty states in the United States or that Shakespeare wrote *Hamlet* since these are points of common knowledge. On the other hand, you may be presenting more obscure information, like facts about electric railroads, which you have known since you were a child, but which may be unfamiliar to your readers. Technically, you are not obliged to document that information; but your audience will trust you more and will be better informed if you do so. In general, if the facts are not unusual, if they can be found in a number of standard sources, and if they do not vary from source to source, from year to year, then they can be considered common knowledge, and the source need not be acknowledged.

Documenting Ideas Found in Your Source

Your object is both to acknowledge the source and to provide your reader with the fullest possible background. Let us assume that one or more of the ideas that you are writing about was firmly in your mind—the product of your own intellect—long before you started to work on your topic. Nevertheless, if you come across a version of that idea during your research, you should cite the source, even though the idea was as much your own as the author's. Of course, in your acknowledgment, you might state that so-and-so is confirming *your* theories and thus indicate that you had thought of the point independently.

Documenting the Source of Your Own Ideas

Perhaps, in the course of working on an essay, you develop a new idea of your own, stimulated by one of your readings. You should make a point of acknowledging the source of inspiration and, perhaps, describing how and why it affected you. (For example: "My idea for shared assignments is an extension of McKeachie's discussion of peer tutoring.") The reader should be made aware of your debt to your source as well as your independent effort.

Plagiarism: Stealing Ideas

If you present another person's ideas as your own, you are plagiarizing even if you used your own words. Here is an illustration: The paragraph on the left, by Leo Gurko, is taken from a book, *Ernest Hemingway and the Pursuit of Heroism*; the paragraph on the right comes from a student essay on Hemingway. Gurko is listed in the bibliography and is cited as the source of several quotations elsewhere in the essay. But the student does not mention Gurko anywhere in *this* paragraph.

The Hemingways put themselves on short rations, ate, drank, and entertained as little as possible, pounced eagerly on the small	Despite all the economies that they had to make and all the pleasures that they had to do without, the Hemingways rather

checks that arrived in the mail as payment for accepted stories, and were intensely conscious of being poor. The sensation was not altogether unpleasant. Their extreme youth, the excitement of living abroad, the sense of making a fresh start, even the unexpected joy of parenthood, gave their poverty a romantic flavor.

enjoyed the experience of being poor. They knew that this was a more romantic kind of life, unlike anything they'd known before, and the feeling that everything in Paris was fresh and new, even their new baby, made them sharply aware of the glamorous aspects of being poor.

Leo Gurko

The language of the student paragraph does not require quotation marks, but unless he acknowledges Gurko in a note, the student will be guilty of plagiarism. These impressions of the Hemingways, these insights into their motivation, would not have been possible without Gurko's biography—and Gurko deserves the credit for having done the research and for having formulated the interpretations. After reading extensively about Hemingway, the student may have absorbed these biographical details so thoroughly that he feels as if he had always known them. But the knowledge is still second-hand, and the source must be acknowledged.

Plagiarism: Stealing Words

When you quote a source, remember that the quoted material will require *two* kinds of documentation: *the acknowledgment of the source of the information or ideas* (through a system of documentation that provides complete publication information about the source and possibly through the citation of the author's name in your sentence) and *the acknowledgment of the source of the exact wording* (through quotation marks). It is not enough to supply the author's name in parentheses (or in a footnote) and then indiscriminately to mix up your own language and that of your sources. The author's name tells your reader nothing whatever about who is responsible for the choice of words. Here is an excerpt from a student essay about Henrik Ibsen, together with the relevant passage from its source:

When writing [Ibsen] was sometimes under the influence of hallucinations, and was unable to distinguish between reality and the creatures of his imagination. While working on *A Doll's House* he was nervous and retiring and lived in a

While Ibsen was still writing A Doll's House, his involvement with the characters led to his experiencing hallucinations that at times completely incapacitated his ability to distinguish between reality and

world alone, which gradually became peopled with his own imaginary characters. Once he suddenly remarked to his wife: "Now I have seen Nora. She came right up to me and put her hand on my shoulder." "How was she dressed?" asked his wife. "She had a simple blue cotton dress," he replied without hesitation. . . . So intimate had Ibsen become with Nora while at work on *A Doll's House* that when John Paulsen asked him why she was called Nora, Ibsen replied in a matter-of-fact tone: "She was really called Leonora, you know, but everyone called her Nora since she was the spoilt child of the family."

P. F. D. Tennant,
Ibsen's Dramatic Technique

the creations of his imagination. He was nervous, distant, and lived in a secluded world. Gradually this world became populated with his creations. One day he had the following exchange with his wife:

Ibsen: Now I have seen Nora. She came right up to me and put her hand on my shoulder.
Wife: How was she dressed?
Ibsen: (without hesitation) She had a simple blue dress.

Ibsen's involvement with his characters was so deep that when John Paulsen asked Ibsen why the heroine was named Nora, Ibsen replied in a very nonchalant tone of voice that originally she was called Leonora, but that everyone called her Nora, the way one would address the favorite child in the family (Tennant 26).

The documentation at the end of this passage may refer the reader to Tennant's book, but there is no indication at all of the debt that the student owes to Tennant's phrasing and vocabulary. Phrases like "distinguish between reality and the creatures of his imagination" must be placed in quotation marks, and so should the exchange between Ibsen and his wife. Arranging these sentences as dialogue is not a solution.

In fact, the problem here is too complex to be solved by the insertion of a few quotation marks. The student, who probably intended a paraphrase, has substituted some of her own words for Tennant's; however, because she keeps the original sentence structure and many of the original words, she has only succeeded in obscuring some of her source's ideas. At times, the phrasing distorts the original idea: the student's assertion that Ibsen's hallucinations "incapacitated his ability to distinguish between reality and the creatures of his imagination" is very different from "[Ibsen] was sometimes under the influence of hallucinations and was unable to distinguish between reality and the creatures of his imagination." Many of the substituted words change Tennant's meaning: "distant" does not mean "retiring"; "a secluded world" is not "a world alone"; "nonchalant" is a very different quality from "matter of fact." Prose like this is neither quotation nor successful paraphrase; it is doubly bad, for it both plagiarizes the source and misinterprets it.

EXERCISE 41

Here are two excerpts from two books about the Industrial Revolution in England. Each excerpt is followed by a passage from a student essay that makes use of the ideas and the words of the source, without any acknowledgment at all. Compare the original with the plagiarized passage; insert the appropriate quotation marks; underline the paraphrases.

Source A

Materially the new factory proletariat was likely to be somewhat better off [than domestic workers who did light manufacturing work in their own homes]. On the other hand it was unfree, under the strict control and the even stricter discipline imposed by the master or his supervisors, against whom they had virtually no legal recourse and only the very beginnings of public protection. They had to work his hours or shifts, to accept his punishments and the fines with which he imposed his rules or increased his profits. In isolated areas or industries they had to buy in his shop, as often as not receiving their wages in *truck* (thus allowing the unscrupulous employer to swell his profits yet further), or live in the houses the master provided. No doubt the village boy might find such a life no more dependent and less impoverished than his parents'; and in Continental industries with a strong paternalist tradition, the despotism of the master was at least partly balanced by the security, education, and welfare services which he sometimes provided. But for the free man entry into the factory as a mere 'hand' was entry into something little better than slavery, and all but the most famished tended to avoid it, and even when in it to resist the draconic discipline much more persistently than the women and children, whom factory owners therefore tended to prefer.

E. J. Hobsbawm, *The Age of Revolution 1789–1848*

Student Essay

The new factory proletariat was likely to be better off materially than those who did light manufacturing in their homes, but it was unfree. There was strict control and discipline imposed by the owner and his supervisors. They had no legal recourse and only the very start of public protection. The despotism of the master was at least a

little bit set off by the security, education, and welfare services
that he sometimes provided. But entry into the factory as a hand
wasn't much better than slavery.

Source B

Most of the work in the factories was monotonously dreary, but that
was also true of much of the work done in the homes. The division of
labor which caused a workman to perform over and over only one of
the several processes needful for the production of any article was intensified by the mechanical inventions, but it had already gone so far
in the homes that few workers experienced any longer the joy of creation. It was, indeed, more of a physical strain to tend a hand loom than
a power loom. The employment of women and children in the factories finally evoked an outcry from the humanitarians, but the situation
was inherited from the domestic system. In the homes, however, most
of the children worked under the friendly eyes of their parents and not
under the direction of an overseer. That to which the laborers themselves most objected was "the tyranny of the factory bell." For the
long hours during which the power kept the machines in motion, the
workers had to tend them without intermission, under the discipline
established by the employer and enforced by his foreman. Many domestic laborers had to maintain equally long hours in order to earn a
bare subsistence, but they were free to begin, stop and rest when they
pleased. The operatives in the factories felt keenly a loss of personal independence.

W. E. Lunt, *History of England*

Student Essay

Factory work was monotonous and dreary, but that was also true of
work at home. Humanitarians cried out against the employment of women
and children, but that was inherited from the domestic system. What
annoyed the laborers the most was the dictatorship of the factory
bell. The workers had to stay at the machines without intermission,
maintaining long hours to earn a bare subsistence. Those who worked in
their homes were free to begin, stop, and rest whenever they felt like
it. Factory workers keenly felt a loss of personal freedom.

USING DOCUMENTATION

In addition to using quotation marks and citing the author's name in
your text, you also need to provide your reader with more detailed information about your sources. This documentation is important for two

reasons. First, when you show where you found your information, you are providing proof that you did your research. Including the source's publication history and the specific page on which you found the information assures your reader that you have not made up fictitious sources and quotations. The systems of documentation that are described below and in Appendix B enable your reader to distinguish your ideas from those of your sources, to know who was responsible for what, just by skimming over the essay and observing the parenthetical notes or numbered notes.

Documentation also enables your readers to learn more about the subject of your essay. Methods of documentation originally developed as a way for serious scholars to share their findings with their colleagues—while making it entirely clear who had done the original research. The reader of your research essay should be given the option of going back to the library and locating the basic materials that you used in writing about the topic. Of course, the essay's bibliography can serve this purpose, but not even the most carefully annotated bibliography guides readers to the book and the precise page that will provide the information that they need. Documentation, then, serves as a direct link between an interesting sentence in the paper and the source in the library that will satisfy your readers' interest.

Using Endnotes

Until very recently, documentation for most research essays was provided by footnotes or endnotes. In this system, a sequence of numbers in your essay is keyed to a series of separate notes containing publication information, which appear either at the bottom of the page or on a separate page at the end of the essay. (A standard bibliography would also be part of the essay.) Since some of your teachers, especially in the fields of history, philosophy, and political science, may still require you to document your essays with footnotes or endnotes, there is a comprehensive description of this system in Appendix B. Here, in a brief excerpt from a biographical essay about Ernest Hemingway, is what the footnote system looks like.

Hemingway's zest for life extended to women also. His wandering heart seemed only to be exceeded by an even more appreciative eye.[7] Hadley was aware of her husband's flirtations and of his facility with women.[8] Yet, she had no idea that something was going on between Hemingway and Pauline Pfeiffer, a fashion editor for Vogue magazine.[9] She was also unaware that Hemingway delayed his return to Schruns from a business trip to New York, in February 1926, so that he might spend some more time with this "new and strange girl."[10]

[7]Ernest Hemingway, <u>A Moveable Feast</u> (New York: Scribner's, 1964), p. 102.

[8]Alice Hunt Sokoloff, <u>Hadley: The First Mrs. Hemingway</u> (New York: Dodd, Mead, 1973), p. 84.

[9]Carlos Baker, <u>Ernest Hemingway: A Life Story</u> (New York: Scribner's, 1969), p. 159.

[10]Hemingway, p. 210. Also Baker, p. 165.

Using Parenthetical Notes

The new system of documentation that is gradually replacing footnotes/endnotes is based on the insertion directly into your essay of the author's name and the page on which the information can be found, placed in parentheses. There are no separate notes. Instead, readers who want to know more about the source can turn to the bibliography, which provides all the necessary publication information. Documenting through parenthetical notes is much less cumbersome than preparing an additional page of endnotes. It is also simpler for your reader to learn who the source is while reading the essay instead of having to turn to a separate page at the back. On the other hand, as you will see, parenthetical notes can make the page look somewhat crowded, especially if you have a great deal of source information to include. Here is what the same excerpt from the Hemingway essay would look like using this new form of documentation (often called New MLA after the Modern Language Association, which instituted the change). Notice that the paragraph is followed by a bibliography. The parenthetical notes are meaningless unless the reader can refer to an accurate and complete bibliography.

> Hemingway's zest for life extended to women also. His wandering heart seemed only to be exceeded by an even more appreciative eye (Hemingway 102). Hadley was aware of her husband's flirtations and of his facility with women (Sokoloff 84). Yet, she had no idea that something was going on between Hemingway and Pauline Pfeiffer, a fashion editor for <u>Vogue</u> magazine (Baker 159). She was also unaware that Hemingway delayed his return to Schruns from a business trip in New York, in February 1926, so that he might spend more time with this "new and strange girl" (Hemingway 210; Baker 165).

> Works Cited

> Baker, Carlos. <u>Ernest Hemingway: A Life Story</u>. New York Scribner's, 1969.
> Hemingway, Ernest. <u>A Moveable Feast</u>. New York: Scribner's, 1964.
> Sokoloff, Alice Hunt. <u>Hadley: The First Mrs. Hemingway</u>. New York: Dodd, 1973.

Inserting Parenthetical Notes

Many of the basic rules for using MLA parenthetical notes are apparent in the previous example. Here are some points to observe:

1. **Format.** The placement of the parenthetical note within your sentence is governed by a set of very precise rules, established by conventional agreement. Like the rules for quotation, these must be followed without any deviation.

   a. The parenthetical note is intended to be a part of your sentence, which should not end until the source has been cited. For this reason, final punctuation (period, semicolon, or comma) should be placed *after* the parenthetical note.

   b. If the parenthetical note follows a quotation, the quotation should be closed *before* you open the parentheses. Remember that the note is not part of the quotation and therefore has no reason to be inside the quotation marks.

   c. Any terminal punctuation that is part of the quotation (like a question mark or an exclamation point) remains inside the quotation marks. Remember also to include a period at the end of the sentence, after the parenthetical note.

   d. When you insert the parenthetical note, leave one space before it and one space after it—unless you are ending the sentence with terminal punctuation (period, question mark), in which case you leave the customary two spaces between the end of that sentence and the beginning of the next one.

2. **Placement.** The parenthetical note comes at the *end* of the material that is being documented, whether that material is quoted, paraphrased, summarized or briefly mentioned. By convention, your reader will assume that the parenthetical note signals the end of the material from that source. Anything that follows is either your own idea, independently developed, or taken from a new source that will be documented by the next parenthetical note a little further along in the text.

3. **Frequency.** Each new point in your essay that requires documentation should have its own parenthetical note. Under no circumstances should you accumulate references to several different sources for several sentences and place them in a single note at the end of the paragraph. All the sources used in the Hemingway paragraph cannot be covered by one parenthetical note at the end.

4. **Multiple Notes in a Single Sentence.** If you are using a large number of sources and documenting your essay very thoroughly, you may need to

cite two or more sources at separate points in the same sentence. Here is another excerpt from the Hemingway essay in which two notes appear in the same sentence:

> Even at this early stage of his career, Hemingway seemed to have developed a basic philosophy of writing. His ability to perceive situations clearly and to capture the exact essence of the subject (Dos Passos 153; Loeb 218) might have stemmed from a disciplined belief that each sentence had to be "true" (Hemingway 12) and that a story had to be written "as straight as you can" (Hemingway 183).

The reference to Dos Passos and Loeb has to be inserted in midsentence because they are responsible only for the information about Hemingway's capacity to focus on his subject and capture its essence, not for the quoted material at the end of the sentence. The placement of the notes tells you where the writer found which information. The inclusion of each of the next two parenthetical notes tells you that a reference to "true" sentences can be found on page 12 of the Hemingway book and a reference to "straight" writing can be found on page 183.

5. Multiple Sources for the Same Point. If you have two sources to document the same point, you can demonstrate the completeness of your research by placing both in the same parenthetical note. Thus, the inclusion of Dos Passos *and* Loeb in the same note tells you that much the same information can be found in both sources. Should you want to cite two sources but believe that one is preferable to the other, you can indicate your preference by using "also" (Dos Passos 118; also, Loeb 153). There is, of course, a limit to how many sources you can cram into a single pair of parentheses; common sense will tell you what is practical and what is distracting to your reader. Usually, one or two of your sources will have more complete or better documented information; those are the ones to cite. If you wish to discuss the quality of information to be found in your various sources, their advantages and disadvantages, then you can use an explanatory endnote to do so (see p. 386 later in the chapter).

6. Referring to the Source in the Text. In the previously cited examples, the writer of the Hemingway essay has chosen not to cite any of her sources in the text itself. That is why each parenthetical note contains a name as well as a page number. If, however, you do refer to your source as part of your own presentation of the material, then there is no need to use the name twice; all you need to insert in the parenthetical note is the page number.

During the time in Paris, Hemingway had begun to experiment with storytelling. Silas Huddleston writes of the young Hemingway's aspirations:

> I happened to be the president of an association to which he [Hemingway] belonged, and at its meetings he would chat with me about his ideals and his ambitions. He was seeking a simple, realistic style. He wanted to set down life as he saw it. Conversation in novels was too highfalutin. He intended to make it as he supposed it to be. (144)

Because Huddleston's name is cited in the text, it need not be placed in parentheses; the page number is enough. Huddleston's book would, of course, be included in the list of works cited. Notice, too, that the parenthetical note works just as well at the end of a lengthy, indented quotation, but that, because there are no quotation marks to signify the end of the quotation, it terminates with a period placed *before* the parenthetical note, which follows separated by *two* spaces.

  7. **Including the Source's Title.** Occasionally, your bibliography will include more than one book by the same author or two authors with the same last name. To avoid confusion and specify your exact source, use an abbreviated title inside the parenthetical note. Had the author of the Hemingway essay included more than one work by Carlos Baker in her bibliography, her parenthetical note would look like this:

> Yet, she had no idea that something was going on between Hemingway and Pauline Pfeiffer, a fashion editor for <u>Vogue</u> magazine (Baker, <u>Life Story</u> 159).

If you are working from a newspaper or periodical article that does not cite an author, use an abbreviation of the title in your parenthetical note (unless you have referred to the title in your text, in which case you need only include the page number in your note).

These rules are quite practical and, after a while, the forms will become automatic. But you will not be able to document your essay and provide an accurate list of Works Cited if you do not have all the necessary information about your sources. Whether you take notes or provide yourself with pages from a copying machine, remember always to write down the information that you will need for your notes and bibliography. Look at the front of the book or periodical and jot down the publishing history. And, as you work on the first draft of your essay, include the author's name and the relevant page number in parentheses after every reference to one of your sources, to serve as a guide when you document your essay. Even in this early version, your essay will resemble the finished product, with MLA documentation. Finally, when the essay is ready for its final typing, read through it again, just to make sure that each reference to a source is covered by a parenthetical note.

Signaling the Transitions Between Sources

The student who wrote the research essay on Ernest Hemingway had enough confidence to write about her subject by citing sources in her parenthetical notes, not in her own sentences. However, since most students go to considerable trouble to find and select the right materials to support their ideas, they tend to paraphrase and quote from their sources and, by using their names, keep them before the reader's eye. Of course, citations should appear only when necessary, so that the reader is not distracted by the constant appearance of certain names.

In general, the citation of the author's name serves as the standard signal to your reader that you are starting to use new source material; the parenthetical note signals the point of termination for that source. If the name is not cited, at the beginning, the reader may not be aware that a new source has been introduced until he reaches the parenthetical note. Here is a brief passage from an essay that illustrates this kind of confusion:

> 1946 marked the beginning of the postwar era. This meant the demobilization of the military, creating a higher unemployment rate because of the large number of returning soldiers. This also meant a slowdown in industry, so that layoffs also added to the rising rate of unemployment. As Cabell Phillips put it: "Motivation [for the Employment Act of 1946] came naturally from the searing experience of the Great Depression, and fresh impetus was provided by the dread prospect of a massive new wave of unemployment following demobilization" (Phillips 292-3).

Here, the placement of the citation creates a problem. The way in which the name is introduced into the paragraph firmly suggests that Cabell Phillips is responsible for the quotation and only the quotation. (The fact that the quotation is nothing more than a repetition of the first three sentences, and therefore should not have been included in the essay, may also have occurred to you.) Anyone reading the essay will assume that the note covers only the material that starts with the name and ends with the number; the coverage is not expected to go back any further than the beginning of the sentence. Thus, in this passage, the first three sentences are not documented. Although it is highly probable that the writer got all the information from Phillips, *The 1940's* is not being acknowledged as the source. "Probably" is not an adequate substitute for clear documentation. Phillips's name should be cited somewhere at the beginning of the paragraph (the second sentence would be a good place); alternatively, an "umbrella" note could be used (see pp. 390–391). But, as was pointed out on page 381, you may need to insert a parenthetical note in midsentence if that single sentence contains references to two different sources. For example, you might want to place a note in midsentence to indicate exactly where the source's opinion leaves off and your own begins:

> These examples of hiring athletes to play in college games, cited by Joseph Durso (6), suggest that recruiting tactics in 1903 were not as subtle as they are today.

If the page number were put at the end of the sentence, the reader would assume that Durso was responsible for the comparison between 1903 and the present; but he is not. It is only the examples that must be documented, not the conclusion drawn from these examples. In this case, the *absence* of a parenthetical note at the end of the sentence signals to the reader that this conclusion is the writer's own.

Here is a passage in which the techniques of documentation have been used to their fullest extent and the transitions between sources are clearly indicated. This example is taken from Jessie Bernard's "The Paradox of the Happy Marriage," an examination of the woman's role in American marriage. At this point, Bernard has just established that more wives than husbands acknowledge that their marriages are unhappy:

> These findings on the wife's marriage are especially poignant because marriage in our society is more important for women's happiness than for men's. "For almost all measures, the relation between marriage, happiness and overall well-being was stronger for women than for men," one study reports (Bradburn 150). In fact, the strength of the relationship between marital and overall happiness was so strong for women that the author wondered if "most women are equating their marital happiness with their overall happiness" (Bradburn 159). Another study based on a more intensive examination of the data on marriage from the same sample notes that "on each of the marriage adjustment measures . . . the association with overall happiness is considerably stronger for women than it is for men" (Orden and Bradburn 731). Karen Renne also found the same strong relationship between feelings of general well-being and marital happiness: those who were happy tended not to report marital dissatisfaction; those who were not, did. "In all probability the respondent's view of his marriage influences his general feeling of well-being or morale" (64); this relationship was stronger among wives than among husbands (Renne

63).** A strong association between reports of general happiness and reports of marital happiness was also found a generation ago (Watson).

**Among white couples, 71 percent of the wives and 52 percent of the husbands who were "not too happy" expressed marital dissatisfaction; 22 percent of the wives and 18 percent of the husbands who were "pretty happy" expressed marital dissatisfaction; and 4 percent of the wives and 2 percent of the husbands who were "very happy" expressed marital dissatisfaction.

This paragraph contains six parenthetical notes to document the contents of seven sentences. Four different works are cited, and, where the same work is cited twice consecutively (Bradburn and Renne), the reference is to a different page. The material taken from page 64 of Renne covers a sentence and a half, from the name "Karen Renne" to the parenthetical note; the remainder of the sentence comes from page 63. Finally, there is no page reference in the note citing Watson, since Bernard is referring the reader to the entire article, not a single part of it.

Bernard quotes frequently, but she never places quotations from two different sources together in the same sentence, and she is careful to use her own voice to provide continuity between the quotations. Notice, too, that one is never in doubt as to the source of information. Although Bernard does not always cite the name of the author, we are immediately told in each case that there *is* a source—"one study reports"; "the author wondered"; "another study based on a more intensive examination of the data on marriage from the same sample"; "Karen Renne also found." These phrases not only acknowledge the source but also provide vital transitions between these loosely related points.

EXERCISE 42

The following paragraph, taken from a research essay about the Industrial Revolution, is based on source materials that can be found in Exercise 41. Compare the paragraph with its sources, and then decide where the parenthetical notes should be placed. Insert the notes, making sure that you distinguish the source material from the writer's own contributions to the paragraph.

The Industrial Revolution caused a major change in the working environment of most people in England. Historians have described the painful transition from working in the home and on the farm to working in the factory. E. J. Hobsbawm points out that most factory employees were at the mercy of the master and his foremen, who controlled their working hours with "draconic discipline." According to W. E. Lunt,

those who previously did spinning and weaving in their homes had
worked as long and as hard as the workers in the new textile factories,
but they had been able to maintain more control over when and how they
performed their tasks. It was the male workers who especially resented their loss of freedom and tended to be more resistant to discipline, and so manufacturers found it desirable to hire women and children, who were more passive and obedient. The long hours and bleak and
unhealthy environment of the factories must have been particularly
hard on the women and children who worked in them. Indeed, Lunt observes that it was their plight that "finally evoked an outcry from
the humanitarians." Ultimately, then, an improvement in working
conditions came about because of respect for the frailty of women and
children, not because of respect for the rights of all workers.

Using Explanatory Notes

You will have noticed that, following the second parenthetical reference to Renne, there is a double asterisk, which calls the reader's attention to a separate note appearing at the bottom of the paragraph. (In the
actual essay, the note would appear either at the bottom of the page or,
together with other notes, on a separate sheet at the end of the essay.)
Jessie Bernard is using an explanatory note as a way of including information that does not quite fit into the text of her essay.

If your research has been thorough, you may find yourself with more
material than you know what to do with. It can be tempting to use up
every single point on your note cards and cram all the available information into your essay. But, if you include too many extraneous points,
your sentences will bulge with random facts, and your reader will find it
hard to concentrate on the real topic of your paragraph. To illustrate this
point, here are two paragraphs dealing with the domestic life of Charles
Dickens: one is bulging; the other is streamlined. The first contains an
analysis of Dickens's relationship with his sister-in-law; in the second,
he decides to take a holiday in France.

Another good friend to Charles Dickens was his sister-in-law.
Georgina had lived with the family ever since they had returned from
an American tour in June, 1842. She had grown attached to the children
while the couple was away (Pope-Hennessy 179-80). She now functioned
as an occasional secretary to Dickens, specifically when he was writing A Child's History of England, which Pope-Hennessy terms a "rather
deplorable production." Dickens treated the history of his country
in a very unorthodox manner (311). Dickens must have felt close to
Georgina since he chose to dictate the History to her; with all his
other work, Dickens always worked alone, writing and correcting it by

himself (Butt and Tillotson 20–21). Perhaps a different woman would have questioned the relationship of her younger sister to her husband; yet Kate Dickens accepted this friendship for what it was. Pope-Hennessy describes the way in which Georgina used to take over the running of the household whenever Kate was indisposed. Kate was regularly too pregnant to go anywhere. She had ten children and four miscarriages in a period of fifteen years (391). Kate probably found another woman to be quite a help around the house. Pope-Hennessy suggests that Kate and her sister shared Charles Dickens between them (287).

In 1853, three of Dickens's closest friends had died (Forster 124),[5] and the writer himself, having become even more popular and busy since the publication of David Copperfield (Maurois 70), began to complain of "hypochondriacal whisperings" and also of "too many invitations to too many parties" (Forster 125). In May of that year, a kidney ailment that had plagued Dickens since his youth grew worse (Dickens, Letters 350), and, against the advice of his wife, he decided to take a holiday in Boulogne (Johnson 757).[6]

[5]The friends were Mr. Watson, Count d'Orsay, and Mrs. Macready.
[6]Tillotson, Dickens's doctor, who had been in Boulogne the previous October, was the one to encourage him to go there.

The first paragraph obviously contains too much information that is unrelated to its topic. Pope-Hennessy's opinion of the History of England and the history of Kate's pregnancies are topics that may be worth discussing, but not in this paragraph. Whether this extraneous material should be shifted to other paragraphs of the essay, placed in explanatory notes, or simply omitted is a decision that cannot be made without examining the entire essay and its structure. But the second, much shorter paragraph suggests that some related but less important detail can usefully be put into explanatory notes where, if wanted, it is always available. Readers of the second paragraph are being given a choice: they can absorb the essential information through the paragraph alone, or they can examine the topic in greater depth by referring also to the explanatory notes.

EXERCISE 43

Read each of the following paragraphs, paying special attention to unity and coherence. Draw a line through any material that you find entirely unrelated to the topic. Any information that seems loosely related to the paragraph's focus should be placed in explanatory note(s).

A. Since Dickens tried to pack so much activity into each day of his holiday, one wonders when he had time for his nine children-- Charles, born in 1837; Kate, 1839; Francis, 1844; Sydney, 1847; Mary, 1838; Walter, 1841; Alfred, 1845; Henry, 1849; and Edward, 1852 (Johnson Genealogical Chart 5). Since July 3, the children had been with their parents, and on that day, their father wrote to a friend in London that the children had arrived "all manner of toad-like colors" from their trip across the channel (Johnson 759). In this description and in other references to them in letters to his wife, we can see evidence of Dickens's feeling for his children: very often he refers to them as "the darlings," sends them his love (Dexter 159-60), and refers to them by nicknames that perhaps only another father might appreciate: "Keeryleemoo" (either Walter or Francis); "the jolly post boy" (Henry); "Lucifer Box" (Kate); and "Plornishghenter" (Edward) (Dexter 167; Johnson 751; Dexter 175). Many of the boys had been named for great literary men of the time, which suggests their father's hopes for their future: Edward Bulwer-Lytton, Henry Fielding, Sydney Smith, and Alfred Tennyson (Pope-Hennessy 373).

B. A day after the major league strike of June 1981, baseball was not as much concerned about hits and runs as about concepts that are more relevant to labor unions. According to Pete Axthelm, "deadlocked negotiations and empty ball parks and a hopelessly disputed clause in the collective bargaining agreement between players and management began to dominate headlines" (57). Axthelm paints a good picture of how baseball was before the strike. The head-to-head confrontation between Rose and Ryan is what makes baseball so special. This was the final stage of a long and controversial struggle between the owners and players that dated back to the beginning of baseball. The strike was caused by a disagreement between players and owners on how to compensate teams that lose free agents. (Axthelm 57). In 1975, pitchers Dave McNally and Andy Messersmith had challenged baseball's reserve clause and declared themselves free agents. Before their action, all players were bound to the teams that they first signed with until they were either traded or retired from baseball (Phillips 55). In 1971, Curt Flood also tried to do the same thing as McNally and Messersmith, but he failed to succeed. These two pitchers triumphed over a reserve clause that had stood for 92 years. The reserve clause meant that once a player completed his contract he was free to offer his services to the highest bidder. This gave the owners a chance to go out and spend their money on the best players available with hopes that they could win a World Series (Falls 17). Falls, whose articles appear in the Detroit Free Press, disapproves of buying world championships by buying players. The owners began plunking down tremendous amounts of money to secure ballplayers who had become free agents.

Avoiding Excessive Notes

Complex research was needed to gather the numerous details found in the biographical essays about Ernest Hemingway and Charles Dickens, and the writers of these essays use numerous notes to document their sources. Here is a brief example:

> Dickens's regular work habits involved writing at his desk from about nine in the morning to two in the afternoon (Butt and Tillotson 19; Pope-Hennessy 248), which left a good deal of time for other activities. Some of his leisure each day was regularly spent in letter-writing, some in walking and riding in the open air (Pope-Hennessy 305, quoting Nathaniel Sharswell). Besides this regular routine, on some days he would devote time to reading manuscripts which Wills, his sub-editor on Household Words, would send to him for revision and comment (Forster 65; Johnson 702).

In this passage, three notes are needed for three sentences because a different biographer is the source for each piece of information. To combine all the sources in a single note would confuse, rather than simplify, the acknowledgments. In addition, the writer of this essay is not only making it clear where the information came from, but is also providing her reader with a choice of references. She has come across the same information in more than one biography, has indicated the duplication of material in her notes, and has decided to demonstrate the thoroughness of her research by citing more than one reference. Since the sources are given equal status in the notes (by being placed in alphabetical order and separated by a semicolon), one assumes that they are equally reliable. Had the writer thought that one was more thorough or more convincing than another, she would either have omitted the secondary one or indicated its status by placing it after "also" (Johnson 702; also, Forster 65).

But an abundance of parenthetical notes does not always indicate sound research. As the following example demonstrates, excessive documentation only creates clutter.

> In contrast to the Dickenses' house in London, this setting was idyllic: the house stood in the center of a large garden complete with woods, waterfall, roses (Forster 145), and "no end of flowers" (Forster 146). For a fee, the Dickenses fed on the produce of the estate and obtained their milk fresh from the landlord's cow (Forster 146). What an asset to one's peace of mind to have such a cooperative landlord as they had (Pope-Hennessy 310; Johnson 758; Forster 147) in the portly, jolly Monsieur Beaucourt (Forster 147)!

Clearly, this entire passage is taken from three pages in Forster's biography of Dickens, and a single note would serve to document the entire

390 · WRITING THE RESEARCH ESSAY

paragraph. What information is contained in the sentence leading up to the triple parenthetical note that justifies citing three sources? And what does the last note document? Is it only Forster who is aware that Monsieur Beaucourt is portly and jolly? To avoid tiring and irritating his readers, the writer here would have been well advised to ignore the supporting evidence in Pope-Hennessy and Johnson, and use a single reference to Forster, or possibly include an explanatory note to indicate why all three are so important. The writer was undoubtedly proud of his extensive research, but he seems more eager to show off his hours in the library than to provide a readable text for his audience.

Using Umbrella Notes

As the previous example indicates, sometimes the logical sequence of your ideas or information requires you to cite the same source for several sentences or even for several paragraphs at a stretch. Instead of repeating "Forster 146" again and again, you can use a single note to cover the entire sequence. These notes are sometimes called "umbrella" notes, because they cover a sequence of sentences as an umbrella might cover more than one person. Umbrella notes are generally used in essays where the sources' names are not often cited in the text, and so the reader cannot easily figure out the coverage by assuming that the name and the parenthetical note mark the beginning and ending points. An "umbrella" simply means that you are leaving the reader in no doubt as to how much material the note is covering.

Because an umbrella note consists of an explanation of how much material is being covered by a source, it is too long to be put in parentheses within the text and generally takes the form of an explanatory note placed outside the body of your essay. Here is an example:

> *The information in this and the previous paragraph dealing with Dickens's relationship with Wilkie Collins is entirely derived from Hutton, <u>Dickens-Collins Letters</u> 41-49.

Inside your essay, the asterisk referring the reader to this note would appear right after the *last* sentence that uses material from Hutton to discuss Dickens and Wilkie Collins.

Of course, umbrella notes only work when you are using a single source for a reasonably long stretch. If you use two sources, you have to distinguish between them in parenthetical notes, and the whole point of the umbrella—to cut down on the number of notes—is lost. Umbrella notes must also be used with caution when you are quoting. Because the umbrella is providing the reference for a long stretch of material, the citation usually includes several pages; but how will the reader know on

which page the quotation appears? Sometimes you can add this information to the note itself:

> *The information in this and the previous paragraph is entirely
> derived from Hutton, <u>Dickens-Collins Letters</u>, 41–49. The two quota-
> tions from Dickens's letters are from pages 44 and 47 respectively.

However, if you end up using too many umbrella notes, or if you expect
a single note to guide your reader through the intricacies of a long paragraph, you will have abused the device. Your essay will have turned into
a series of summaries, with each group of paragraphs describing a single
source. That is not what a research essay is supposed to be.

EXERCISE 44

Improve the documentation of the following paragraphs by eliminating
unnecessary notes, placing the remaining notes in the proper places, and
introducing umbrella notes if they seem appropriate. If necessary, eliminate repetition and rearrange the sequence of information in the text.

> A. Many students are highly uncertain about their future ca-
> reers. Sometimes, they change their career goals many times while
> they are undergraduates. Some who enter college with a career already
> chosen later discover that they are really interested in new and dif-
> ferent professions (Van Doren 119). Even students who have graduated
> from college or graduate school and have entered their chosen profes-
> sion may find themselves doing completely different work 25 years
> later (Van Doren 119). Mark Van Doren observes that "most undergradu-
> ate students cannot predict . . . what careers they will follow, what
> turns those careers will take, or what specialized preparation they
> will need for their later opportunities" (Van Doren 121). For this
> reason, the best security for the future lies in a broad liberal arts
> education, which is the best way for young students to prepare for the
> professions that await them (Van Doren 119–121).

> B. Japanese students receive a very thorough education because
> they are so well disciplined. For one thing, students in Japan spend
> more time in school than Americans do. "Japanese adolescents are in
> school sixty days more each year than are their American counter-
> parts" (Rohlen 274). Even their weekends are cut short because they
> have to go to school on Friday nights (Rohlen 274). Students in the
> United States are usually partying on a Friday night, and the thought
> of going to school instead would seem hilarious to them. The sixty
> days spent in school by Japanese students are used as holidays and

vacations by American students. What is so amazing about the students
in Japan is that, although they spend a tremendous amount of time in
school throughout the year, they have an average attendance rate of no
less than 99% in the elementary and lower secondary schools (Cogan
464). They also spend a great deal of time studying, an average of two
hours a night and three hours on Sunday, in contrast to the American
average of less than one hour a night (Rohlen 276). Even the top five
percent of our students do less homework than the average Japanese
(Rohlen 277)! Clearly, in Japan, studying and going to school become
"the unequivocal central pivot of a student's existence" (Rohlen
161).

THE FINAL BIBLIOGRAPHY

While the bibliography is always an essential part of the research essay, it becomes especially important when you use New MLA documentation, since it is the only place where your reader can find publication
information about your sources. Which works you include in your final
bibliography may depend on the wording and intention of your assignment. There is an important difference between a list of works that you
have *consulted or examined* and a list of works that you have *cited or
actually used in the writing of your essay*. Many instructors restrict the
bibliography to "Works Cited," but you may be asked to submit a list of
"Works Consulted." Remember that one purpose of a "Works Consulted" bibliography is to help your readers to find appropriate background information, not to overwhelm them with the magnitude of
your efforts. Don't present a collection of thirty-five titles if, in your essay, you actually cite only five sources.

On the whole, a sensible final bibliography of "Works Consulted" for
an undergraduate essay consists of all the sources that you examined (in
other words, actually held in your hand and looked at) that proved to
have a clear bearing on your topic, whether you actually used them in
your essay or not. If you consulted a book *in the hope* that it contained
some relevant information, and if it provided no pertinent material,
should you include it in your final bibliography? You might do so to prevent your readers from repeating your mistake and attempting to consult works with misleading titles in the belief that they might be useful,
but only if your bibliography is annotated and the book's lack of usefulness can be pointed out. Finally, if you have been unable to locate a
source and have thus never yourself examined it, you may not ordinarily
include it in your final bibliography, however tempting the title may be.

The Correct Format for Your Final Bibliography

Here are the guidelines for bibliographical entries:

1. The bibliography is always listed on a separate sheet at the end of your research essay. The title should be centered, one-half inch from the top of the page.
2. Each entry is double-spaced, with double spacing between entries.
3. Each bibliographical entry starts with the author's last name at the margin; the second line of the entry (if there is one) starts five spaces in. This format enables the reader's eye to move quickly down the list of names at the left-hand margin.
4. The bibliography is in alphabetical order, according to the last name of the author. If there are two authors, only the first has the last name placed first: "Woodward, Robert, and Carl Bernstein." If an author has more than one work included on your list, do not repeat the name each time: alphabetize or arrange chronologically by publication date the works by that author, place the name at the margin preceding the first work, and for the second (and further) title(s), replace the name with three hyphens, followed by a period and two spaces.

> Freud, Sigmund. <u>Civilization and Its Discontents</u>. London: Hogarth, 1930.
> ---. <u>Moses and Monotheism</u>. New York: Knopf, 1939.
> May, Rollo. <u>Love and Will</u>. London: Souvenir, 1970.

A work that has no author should be alphabetized within the bibliography according to the first letter of the title, which is placed at the margin as the author's name would be.

5. A bibliographical entry for a book is read as a list of three items—author, title (underlined), and publication information—with periods between each piece of information. Each period is followed by *two* spaces. All the information should always be presented in exactly the same order that you see in the model bibliography above. Place of publication comes first; a colon separates place and name of publisher; a comma separates publisher and date.
6. A bibliographical entry for a periodical starts with author and article title (in quotation marks), each followed by a period and two spaces; the name of the periodical, followed by one space (and no punctuation at all). What comes next depends on the kind of periodical you are citing. For quarterly and monthly journals, you include the volume number, followed by a space, and then the year in parentheses, followed by a colon. For weekly or biweekly jour-

nals, you include only the full date—day, month, and year—followed by a colon. All periodical entries end with the inclusive pages of the article, first page to last, followed by a period.

> Tobias, Sheila, and Carol Weissbrod. "Anxiety and Mathematics: An Update." Harvard Educational Review 50 (1980): 61-67.

> Winkler, Karen J. "Issues of Justice and Individual's Rights Spur Revolution in Political Philosophy." Chronicle of Higher Education 16 April 1986: 6-8.

7. Each entry of the bibliography ends with a period.

Note: For models illustrating more complex kinds of bibliographical entries, see Appendix B.

The Annotated Bibliography

Annotating your bibliography (which was described in Chapter 5, pp. 274–75 is an excellent way to demonstrate the quality of your research. But, to be of use, your comments, though brief, must be informative. The following phrases do not tell the reader very much: "an interesting piece"; "a good article"; "well-done": "another source of well-documented information." What is well done? Why is it interesting? What is good about it? How much and what kind of information does it contain? A good annotated bibliography will answer some of these questions.

Examine the following bibliography carefully, noting the way it presents the basic facts about author, title, and publication, as well as some evaluative information. If the annotations were omitted, these entries would still be perfectly correct, for they conform to the standard rules for bibliographical format. Without the annotation, one would simply have to change the heading to "Works Consulted" or an equivalent title.

ANTON CHEKHOV IN 1912: AN ANNOTATED BIBLIOGRAPHY

> Bruford, W. H. Chekhov and His Russia. London: Paul, Trench, Trubner, 1948. Excellent material about Russia and the social background which helped to influence Chekhov's writings.
> Edwards, Christine. The Stanislavsky Heritage. New York: New York University Press, 1965. Edwards seems to be very well acquainted with her subject. The book is interesting and valuable

in understanding the impact of the Moscow Art Theatre on Chekhov's craft.

Gillés, Daniel. <u>Chekhov: Observer Without Illusion</u>. Translated by Charles Lam Markmann. New York: Funk and Wagnalls. 1968. A very lively biography, written with enthusiasm for his subject.

Gorky, Maxim. "Anton Chekhov: Fragments of Recollections." <u>Reminiscences of Tolstoy</u>, <u>Chekhov and Andreev</u>. London: Hogarth, 1948. Not useful for biographical facts, but supplies very descriptive details about Chekhov's personality and out- look upon life.

Hingley, Ronald. <u>Chekhov: A Biographical and Critical Study</u>. London: George Allen & Unwin, 1950. A very good biography. A unique feature of this book is the appendix, which has a chrono- logical listing of all English translations of Chekhov's short stories.

Macdonald, Alexander. "A. Chekhov: The Physician and the Major Writer." <u>Journal of the American Medical Association</u> 229 (1974): 1203-4. A two-page appreciation of Chekhov's career as a doctor. This is interesting reading with apt quotations from Chekhov, especially the references to Chekhov fighting the cholera epidemic.

Magarshack, David. <u>Chekhov: A Life</u>. 2nd ed. 1953; rpt. Westport, Conn.: Greenwood Press, 1970. A valuable biography by an author who is also an accomplished translator of Russian literature.

EXERCISE 45

Correct the errors of form in the following bibliography:

Becker, Howard S, Geer, Blanche, and Everett C. Hughes. Making the Grade: New York (1968) Wiley.

Dressel, Paul L.. College and University Curriculum, Berkeley (Cali- fornia): McCutcheon, 1971

(same)—Handbook of Academic Evaluation. San Francisco (Califor- nia): Jossey-Bass: 1976.

J. F. Davidson, "Academic Interest Rates and Grade Inflation," <u>Edu- cational Record</u>. 56, 1975, pp. 122-5

(no author). "College Grades: A Rationale and Mild Defense." AAUP Bulletin, October 1976, 320-1.

New York Times. "Job Plight of Young Blacks Tied to Despair, Skills Lack," April 19, 1983: Section A page 14.

10.
The Research Essay

An effective research essay depends on the integration of the many variables that have been explored throughout this book as overlapping stages in the writing process. However, a research essay must also conform to a few basic mechanical rules:

1. Type your essay. Use a dark ribbon and double-space throughout.
2. Use 8½-by-11-inch paper, and type on only one side of the page.
3. Leave one-inch margins on all sides.
4. Number each page after the first.
5. Proofread your essay and insert any corrections neatly, in ink.

Check with your instructor for any other special rules that may apply to the assignment.

THREE SAMPLE RESEARCH ESSAYS

Following are three student research papers on three very different subjects, using three different kinds of documentation.

The first writer uses a narrative structure, with a great deal of precise detail, to describe a historical event—the opening of the Crystal Palace Exhibition in London in 1851. This essay will help you to understand why many history instructors—and also instructors in some of the other humanities disciplines—continue to prefer the traditional footnote or endnote form of documentation. The writer frequently refers to several sources to support specific points, and also presents a great deal of background information that cannot be included in the body of the paper. The separate endnotes provide enough room to cite all of the sources and explain some of the points that they are making.

The second writer is analyzing an issue, rather than describing a single event that actually happened. In presenting some of the reasons why some people advocate and others condemn the practice of euthanasia, the writer is also constructing an argument: his essay is intended to persuade his readers that terminally ill people should have the right to choose the time of their deaths. Although the number of sources in the bibliography is about the same as those in the Crystal Palace essay, they are used differently, with New MLA documentation. The writer summarizes, paraphrases, or quotes one source at a time, which makes it practical to use brief and unobtrusive parenthetical notes at the ends of the sentences. Almost everything that the writer wants to say is said within the body of the essay, so there is no need to have many endnotes.

The third writer combines narrative and analysis by describing the aftermath of the strange event that must have happened in 1908 at Lake Tunguska in Siberia and then analyzing some of the many theories that have been used to explain that event over the last seventy years. The bibliography for this essay contains fewer sources, which are cited less frequently than they are in the first two essays. The writer's purpose is to help his readers understand what might have happened at Lake Tunguska and to clarify the scientific explanations. He is not using numerous sources to reconstruct the event in complete detail, or trying to convince his readers, by citing authorities, that his conclusions are the right ones. Like many essays in the behavioral sciences, this paper uses the author/year variation of parenthetical note documentation. (This method, often called APA after the American Psychological Association, is described in Appendix B, on pp. 452–453.) Having the date, as well as the author, included within the body of the essay is especially useful when you are reading about scientific theories developed over a span of sixty years.

A Research Essay Checklist

As you read these essays, keep some of the following questions in mind. Then, when you have completed the next-to-the-last draft of your own research paper, check the list again to see if you can answer "yes" to most of these questions.

1. Does the essay have a single focus which is clearly established and maintained throughout?
2. Does the writer have a thesis or a consistent point of view about the events being described?

3. If it is a narrative essay, does the narration have a beginning, middle, and end?
4. Does the essay begin with an informative introduction?
5. Does the essay end on a conclusive note?
6. Does each paragraph have a clear topic sentence?
7. Does each paragraph contain one and only one topic?
8. Are the paragraphs long enough to be convincing? Does each point get supported by facts and information?
9. Does the development of the essay depend entirely upon the dry listing of facts and events, or does the writer offer explanations and relevant commentary?
10. Does the writer use transitions to signal the relationship between separate points?
11. Does the reader get a sense of the relative importance of the sources being used?
12. Does the writer use one source for very long stretches at a time?
13. Is there the right number of notes rather than too many or too few?
14. Is it clear how much material is covered by each note?
15. In essays containing endnotes, do notes provide important explanatory information?
16. Are the quotations well-chosen?
17. Is paraphrase properly used? Is the style of the paraphrase consistent with the style of the writer of the essay?
18. Does the writer use enough citations? Does the text of the essay make it clear when the writer is using a specific source, and who that person is?
19. Is the essay convincing? Did you believe what you read?

Phyllis Schall

History 101

May 15, 1983

The Opening of the Crystal Palace

At the mid-point of the nineteenth century, the government of Great Britain decided to hold a giant international exhibition to demonstrate to the world its manufacturing and commercial leadership. Prince Albert, Queen Victoria's husband, is generally credited with initiating the idea for the exposition, which was finally held in London in 1851. He saw to it that funds were raised, with the Queen heading the list of subscribers.[1] The site decided upon was a twenty-six acre vacant lot in Hyde Park between Rotten Row and the Kensington Road. A Royal Commission was established to make arrangements for the exhibit, which was officially entitled "The Great Exhibition of the Works of Industry of All Nations."[2]

The most remarkable and distinctive feature of the Great Exhibition was the glass building in which it was housed. Joseph Paxton, formerly employed as the chief gardener to the Duke of Devonshire, was the architect of this highly original structure.[3] In actuality, the building was nothing more than a gigantic greenhouse. Cast iron columns and girders provided the skeleton of the building while the walls and roofing were entirely of glass.[4] After plans for the building were made public, it was dubbed "The Crystal Palace" by Paxton's friend,

Douglas Jerrold.[5] In its entirety, the building took six months to construct, at a cost of 150,000 pounds.[6]

The Crystal Palace was built in the shape of a huge cathedral cross. Its overall length, known as the nave, was 1,851 feet, with four parallel aisles that were each 456 feet wide. In the middle, where the arms of the cross met, was a vaulted transept that was 108 feet high, high enough to shelter several huge elm trees that had been growing in Hyde Park before the structure was built.[7] In addition to several large doors, adjustable louvers provided more ventilation.[8]

The construction of this building was radical for its day since its components were mostly prefabricated, manufactured in various factories and then assembled in London.[9] Statistics vary as to the impressive number of iron columns (approximately three thousand), girders (approximately two thousand), and square feet of glass (approximately one million).[10] In the interior, unbleached calico blinds were placed under the roof to protect spectators from the glare of the sun. The underside of the girders was painted red and the columns yellow and blue.[11] According to those who first saw this remarkable edifice, "the eye rested with delight upon that charming variety of colors and those harmonious proportions which give to this place of industry so remarkable and fairy-like a character."[12]

In preparation for the opening ceremony on May 1, 1851, a dais for the Queen was erected at the intersection of the nave and the transept. It was covered with carpet that had been hand-worked by 150 ladies. Upon this was a chair of state covered with a velvet robe of crimson and gold. Overhead was suspended an octagonal canopy trimmed with blue satin and draperies of blue and white.[13] Seats were reserved near the throne for ministers, officers of state, and foreign exhibitors. There were also some seats provided for ladies in the galleries and below. A robing room was installed for the Queen.[14]

A few days before the first of May it was announced that, instead of the originally scheduled public event, the Queen would inaugurate the Exhibition in a private ceremony in the morning, and that the general public would not be admitted until the afternoon. This news was greeted by an avalanche of protest from the indignant press as well as from the 25,000 insulted season-ticket holders who had originally paid three pounds ($15.75) for men and two pounds ($10.50) for women to enjoy this privilege. The power of the press, as well as the Queen's responsiveness to public opinion, is illustrated by the immediate change of plans: all season-ticket holders were permitted to attend the ceremony.

Meanwhile, the preparations for the exhibits continued well into the night of April 30. At that point, many of the foreign exhibits were still incomplete; the French section, for example, had nothing in it at all. These last-minute preparations created so much litter that two companies of the Grenadier Guards had to be called in to clean it up.[15]

Those responsible for the exhibition, as well as those attending it, had many pre-opening fears which later proved unfounded, but which were quite understandable under the circumstances. Many were afraid that the lightness of the glass structure would be dangerous, that, for example, the noise of the cannon salute would shatter the glass, or a hailstorm or stiff wind would break the glass, that the vibration of the organs would shake the panes of the glass out of its fittings, or that the structure itself would buckle under the weight of the people in the galleries. Others feared that the opening would provide an occasion for riots, rebellions, and conspiracies, or that the presence in London of so many foreigners might be the occasion for some kind of increase in crime, the foreigners being a tempting prey for robbers.[16] Notwithstanding all these doubts, the glass building itself received almost unanimous praise, and the opening ceremonies took place with almost incredible order and harmony.[17]

It had rained almost daily for weeks before the opening day,[18] but the first of May was a crisp, sunny day, except for a passing morning shower which "served but to lay the dust" before the Queen's appearance.[19] Since early morning, people had been pouring into town by every road and railway. The South Eastern Railway, with the cooperation of the Northern Railway Company of France, had brought London within an eleven hours' continuous journey of Paris. As a result, strange bearded foreigners were seen on the streets, perhaps confirming the fears of those who anticipated riots and anarchy.[20]

For the English, this day was virtually a national holiday. The church bells were all ringing; most shops were closed. At 6:00 A.M. the gates of Hyde Park were opened, and streams of people pressed their way into the park. It was estimated that half a million people finally gathered together in the park and its vicinity to cheer, dance, picnic, and sleep. Little boys filled the trees, vying for the highest branches. The music of military bands resounded across the waters of the Serpentine Lake. Charles Spencer, a noted balloonist, prepared to ascend in a balloon that was being inflated in readiness for the occasion.[21] Carriages of the season-ticket holders extended far along the Strand, past Trafalgar Square; in single file, the row of carriages would have been nearly twenty miles long.[22]

At 9:00 the doors of the Crystal Palace were opened, and the season-ticket holders crowded in like "a great pent-up tide," with "a rushing stream of spectators, mad with excitement . . . desperately bent upon getting the best possible seats." Some of the temporary barriers placed around the throne were pushed away by the crowd. Nevertheless, police had very little difficulty establishing order. Observers present noted that "the utmost good-humor prevailed, and what appeared

5

most to impress strangers was the perfect order and security, with the utter absence of any apparent force to maintain it."[23]

About 10:30, the notables started to appear. The Duke of Wellington arrived and was warmly greeted by the spectators, especially since it was known to be his 82nd birthday. As was usually the case, he was soon encircled by a group of beautiful ladies. At one point, a Chinese mandarin, wearing a splendid costume, approached the Duke and made a salaam to him, extending his hand. The mandarin also bowed to the Marquis of Anglesea, and it was explained that this was the Mandarin Hesing of a royal Chinese junk anchored in the Thames for the inspection of the English. When he made a grand salaam to the Queen, she asked her staff to make sure that he had a good place in the royal procession, next to the Archbishop of Canterbury. Unfortunately, it was subsequently learned that this "mandarin" was a sailor from a Chinese junk that had been anchored off the East India docks for some time.[24]

Next, the diplomatic corps and foreign commissioners arrived, and then the members of the Cabinet, with the Lord Mayor and Alderman arriving almost last. Just before 11:00, a huge mass of people struggled to make their way in, but soon after, the doors were closed.[25] Lord Palmerston observed that, despite the crowds, "it was impossible for the invited guests of a lady's drawing room to have conducted themselves with more perfect propriety than did this sea of human beings."[26]

The royal family left Buckingham Palace at 11:40, attended by a suite of nine carriages. Her Majesty's Life Guards and some police guarded the way. They proceeded up Constitution Hill and along Rotten Row to the northern entrance of the Crystal Palace. The roofs of every house that commanded a view of the procession were crowded with enthusiastically cheering people. The royal party traveled very quickly, however, giving the people who lined the streets little opportunity to cheer the Queen as much as they would have liked.

At 11:45, the band played "God Save the Queen" as the royal party approached the entrance, and the cannon stationed on the banks of the Serpentine fired a salvo of artillery. From every elevated point was displayed the Union Jack, as well as the 101 flags of all the nations participating in the exhibit. A flourish of trumpets greeted the Queen as she entered the building. Although she went immediately to the robing room, she reappeared very quickly and entered the main part of the building, accompanied by Prince Albert, the Prince of Wales, the Princess Royal, and her attendants. Queen Victoria wore a pink satin dress, brocaded in gold and set with precious stones, all crowned by a diamond tiara on her head. Her consort wore a field-marshal's uniform, the Prince of Wales (age 9) sported highland dress, and the Princess Royal (age 11) had on a white lace dress with a wreath of flowers around her head. When the royal party had assembled on the dais, the national anthem was played again, this time on the gigantic organ in the north transept, accompanied by a chorus of several hundred singers from the royal and cathedral choirs, the pupils of the Royal Academy, and the band of the Sacred Harmonic Society.[27]

Prince Albert then gave a speech addressed to the Queen, praising her majesty's granting of the site, Mr. Paxton's structure, and the 15,000 exhibitors (of whom nearly half were British), representing forty foreign countries. He explained that the exhibits were divided into four major categories, namely Raw Materials, Machinery, Manufactures, and Sculpture and Fine Arts. He also described the geographical organization of the exhibit, with countries in warm latitudes allocated sites near the center of the building, and the cooler countries placed at the extremities.[28]

There appears to have been a small controversy as to
whether the Queen was seated during Prince Albert's address. An
illustration reproduced from the Illustrated London News shows
her seated,[29] and she is described as being seated in a contemporary account,[30] but, in her diary, the Queen insists that she
never sat on the chair.[31] What is well established is that she
then read (while standing) a brief reply to the Prince Consort's speech, expressing her satisfaction with the Exhibition
and her hopes that it would be conducive to the welfare of her
people as well as to

> the common interests of the human race, by encouraging the
> arts of peace and industry, strengthening the bonds of
> union among nations of the earth, and promoting a friendly
> and honorable rivalry in the useful exercise of those fac-
> ulties which have been conferred by a beneficent Provi-
> dence for the good and happiness of mankind.[32]

To her subjects, seeing the Queen was "a noble sight," and the
occasion itself confirmed Britain's superiority to the rest of
the world.[33]

Next, the Archbishop of Canterbury offered up a prayer
invoking God's blessing on the undertaking. Then the organs and
choir joined in performing the "Hallelujah Chorus" from Han-
del's Messiah. The music heightened the feelings of the spectators,[34] whose sensibilities were already much moved by the
great variety of uniforms and costumes worn by the nobles,
church dignitaries, statesmen, and representatives of foreign
countries, as viewed against the backdrop of the elaborately
decorated building. After this, the royal party, including Mr.
Paxton, made a tour of the entire Exhibition, the route of
which had been covered with matting made of coconut fiber to
protect the red carpets. After passing through the Fine Arts
Court and the Manufacturing section, they reached the western

entrance and found themselves reflected in the immense mirror that had been placed at this point. Then they proceeded down the south side of the nave, reached the transept, and swept into the Foreign area, which was skillfully decorated to disguise the incompleteness of the exhibits. All along the route, the Queen was greeted with cheers and handkerchief waving.[35] The French organ poured forth as they rounded the eastern end of the building and returned along the north side of the nave to the throne in the transept.[36] Back at the dais, the Marquis of Breadalbane, Lord Chamberlain of the Household, announced that the Queen had declared, "The Exhibition is open." Then, with a flourish of trumpets, the royal party departed to return to Buckingham Palace. The ceremony had taken one hour, and was judged by many to have been a grander sight than the coronation.[37]

Once the Queen had left and the boundary ropes were removed, chaos reigned. The crowds of people pushed, squeezed, and crammed through the building. Everybody struggled to see the much publicized attractions, the chief of which were the throne, the Crystal Fountain (made entirely of glass), and the Koh-i-Noor or Mountain of Light, said to be the largest diamond in the world, which rested in a gilded cage beside the fountain.[38] Yet, even now, while there was much jostling and elbowing, the tone remained good humored. The Times reported that "hardly a blow was struck or a temper ruffled during the whole day," calling this a tribute to "the deep fund of good nature and self-government in the mass of the people."[39]

The refreshment rooms were constantly filled with people clamoring for ices and jellies. There was also available a large variety of soft drinks, cold meats, bread, cheese, fruit, and pastries. The builders had also thought of other necessities: 14% of visitors to the Exhibit paid for the use of the "waiting rooms" available, and "no account was kept" of the number of gentlemen who made use of the urinals.[40]

It has been estimated that thirty visits were necessary to completely view the Exhibition.[41] The Queen herself returned for several hours, day after day, visiting each separate section "and selecting from many of them such objects as gratified her taste, or were, for other reasons, considered to possess claims upon her attention."[42] Among those attracting the greatest attention was the Austrian exhibit in the side court, which had a fountain constantly streaming forth eau de cologne. Ladies were encouraged to carry away its fragrant moisture on their handkerchiefs.[43] Other exhibits represented the ingenuity of the age: the modern locomotive, intricate textile machinery, Shepherd's electric clock, Rosse's telescope, Nasmyth's steam hammer, and Applegarth's vertical printing machine. Exhibits from the United States included false teeth, artificial legs, Colt's pistol, Goodyear rubber goods, and chewing tobacco.[44]

In the artistic sections, the bad taste of the age was also on display. Visitors could view furniture covered with carved scrollwork, the legs of which were in the shape of a bear or lion's paw, atrocious statuary, "real artificial" flowers placed in the hands of a marble "veiled Vestal," and everywhere cupids holding up candelabra, centerpieces, or cornices.[45] There were two sculptures by Americans, "The Greek Slave" and "The Dying Indian"; Horace Greeley remarked that it was very strange indeed that both American sculptors had chosen for the subject matter a slave and a dying Indian.[46] One wholly negative reaction was that of John Ruskin, the critic, who felt that the time and money spent on the Crystal Palace would have been better applied to the preservation of the art of antiquity: "We shall wander through our palaces of crystal, gazing sadly on copies of pictures torn by cannon-shot, and on casts of sculpture dashed to pieces long ago."[47]

The Duke of Wellington may have spoken for the majority of visitors when, on the one hand, he wondered "whether the show [would] ever be of any use to anybody," yet also asserted that "of this I am certain--nothing [could] be more successful."[48] More than six million people actually visited the Crystal Palace, including about seventeen percent of the population of Great Britain,[49] and it brought its sponsors a profit of 186 thousand pounds.[50] Some 75,000 pounds were spent by hungry spectators for assorted cold foods and non-intoxicating beverages in the refreshment rooms.[51] London itself saw an increase of approximately four million pounds in income during the six-month period that the Exhibition was open to the public.[52]

The opening day ceremony and the Exhibition itself provided the British people with a great feeling of national pride. The day after the ceremony, the _Times_, which previously had been highly critical of the venture, paid tribute to the efforts of the Royal Commissioners and spoke in glowing terms of their enormous achievement.[53] Poems and hymns filled with extravagant praise were composed for the occasion by William M. Thackeray, who wrote a "May-Day Ode," and Martin Tupper, whose "Hymn for All Nations" was translated into 25 languages. On May 1, in her diary, Queen Victoria herself wrote:

> One felt--as so many did whom I have spoken to--filled with devotion--more so than by any service I have ever heard. The tremendous cheers, the joy expressed in every face, the immensity of the building, the mixture of palms, flowers, trees, statues, foundations--the organ (with 200 instruments and 600 voices, which sounded like nothing), and my beloved husband, the author of this "Peace-Festival," which united the industry of all nations of

the earth--all this was moving indeed, and it was and is a
day to live for ever [sic].[54]

Underlying all the extravagant ceremony was the belief
that the Exhibition would foster mutual understanding and
brotherhood among nations. Lady Charlotte Guest affirmed that
"it was a proud moment for our Queen, for England! While the
nations of the earth were convulsed [in war], she has called
into existence this peaceful meeting, the most gigantic ever
known."[55] The Crimean War, which began a decade later, under-
lines the pathetic hopelessness of this belief. The Exhibition
had a far more lasting influence as "a lesson in industrial
and social geography."[56] The Crystal Palace certainly did contain a representative accumulation of the "Industry of All Nations." No exhibition or event before it had ever been "devoted to the advancement and diffusion of the Useful Arts
throughout the world."[57]

The Crystal Palace thus played a lasting role as the first
of a series of World's Fairs, each one billed as more magnificent than the previous one. When John Ruskin questioned the
worth of such a World's Fair, he could not have known what a
long line of descendents the Crystal Palace would have, a fact
which undoubtedly would have pained him even more than the artistic exhibits. Nevertheless, from the pictures on the cave
men's walls to the capsules we bury in the ground at our
present day expositions, man appears to be compelled to record
his achievements for posterity. It seems to me that the best
purpose of a World's Fair is to serve as a true picture of the
age. The Great Exhibition and its Crystal Palace certainly fulfilled this criterion. It represented, in microcosm, the
achievements, the values, and the artistic taste--or lack of
it--of Victoria's age.

Notes

[1]"Exhibitions and Fairs," Encyclopaedia Britannica, 8th ed. (1964), 958. France had held several national exhibitions of its manufactures, but nothing had been done on an international scale.

[2]J. W. Dodds, The Age of Paradox (New York: Rinehart, 1952), pp. 444-45. There had been considerable opposition to any building being put up in Hyde Park because it was necessary to cut down some of the trees. Punch expressed the general apprehension:

> Albert! spare those trees
> Mind where you fix the show;
> For mercy's sake, don't please
> Go spoiling Rotten Row.

Quoted from Punch, Dodds, p. 445.

[3]Over 240 suggested designs had been turned down as ugly or impractical by the Royal Commission before Prior submitted his plans; the Commission was in the embarrassing position of seeing the entire project collapse when Paxton's name was suggested. Dodds, p. 444.

[4]"Paxton, Sir Joseph," Encyclopaedia Britannica, 8th ed. (1964), 409.

[5]Christopher Hobhouse, 1851 and The Crystal Palace (New York: Dutton, 1937), p. 37.

[6]"The Exhibition," Littell's Living Age, 29 (May-June 1851), 560.

[7]Littell, 524. See also Anthony Wood, Nineteenth Century Britain (London: Longmans, Green, 1960), p. 174; and "Exhibitions and Fairs," 958.

[8]Horace Greeley, The Crystal Palace and Its Lessons: A Lecture (New York: DeWitt and Davenport, 1851), pp. 5-6.

[9]"Paxton," 409. The parts could be disassembled with relatively small effort and a high salvage value. Dodds, 445.

[10]The Crystal Palace Exhibition: An Illustrated Catalogue (1851; rpt. New York: Dover, 1970), p. xxii. According to contemporary accounts, "it was one of the most imposing sights that had ever been witnessed in this country." Catalogue, p. xxv.

[11]Beard et al., Tallis's History and Description of the Crystal Palace, and the Exhibition of the World's Industry in 1851 (London: John Tallis and Co., [n.d. 1852?]), I, 22.

[12]Littell, 523.

[13]Beard, p. 22.

[14]Littell, 524.

[15]The information in this and the preceding paragraph comes from Hobhouse, p. 62.

[16]Quoted from the diaries of Lady Charlotte Guest and Lord Palmerston, in They Saw It Happen, ed. T. Charles-Edwards and B. Richardson (New York: Macmillan, 1958), pp. 254-55. The catalog of the Exhibition notes that "the first impression conveyed to the mind of a visitor, inexperienced in the science of architecture, on entering the building, is a sense of insecurity, arising from the apparent lightness of its supports as compared with the vastness of its dimensions. But this feeling is soon dissipated when he is informed how severely the strength of every separate part has been tested, and with what extreme care the connexion of all the supports with each other has been considered, so as to present the greatest possible combination of strength." Catalogue, p. xxii. Tests showed that the girders would be able to bear four times the anticipated strain, p. xx.

[17]"Paxton, Sir Joseph," 409.

[18]Greeley, p. 6.

[19]Littell, 523.

[20]Dodds, p. 449. Dodds also notes that The Morning Chronicle "ran articles in parallel columns in English, French and
German."

[21]Hobhouse, p. 63.

[22]Littell, 523.

[23]Littell, 523. The quotation in the last sentence appears
on 526.

[24]Littell, 524-25.

[25]Beard, 22-23.

[26]Quoted in They Saw It Happen, p. 253.

[27]The description of the arrival of the Royal Party in
this and the preceding paragraph comes from Littell, 523 and
Beard, 21-23. The details of the royal family's dress are taken
from Beard.

[28]Littell, 523.

[29]Hobhouse, p. 66.

[30]Beard, 23.

[31]Quoted in Hobhouse, 69. See also Lady Charlotte Guest,
in They Saw It Happen, p. 256.

[32]Littell, 524-25.

[33]Lady Charlotte Guest and Lord Palmerston, in They Saw It
Happen, pp. 253-55.

[34]Those who could hear it, at any rate. It had been discovered that sound did not travel well in the building.
Greeley, p. 8.

[35]Littell, 523-24. Lady Charlotte Guest explains that she
and her party, seated near the throne, at first believed the
crowds were greeting the procession in silence, but finally
deduced from the violent gestures and hand wavings of the distant audience that they were indeed cheering the Queen. They
Saw It Happen, p. 257.

[36]Littell, 523-26.

[37]Lady Charlotte Guest in They Saw It Happen, p. 256. See also History through "The Times," ed. James Marchant (London: Cassell, 1937), p. 136.

[38]Greeley, pp. 11-12.

[39]Marchant, p. 138. See also Littell, 526.

[40]Dodds, p. 447. Drinks consisted of soda water, lemonade, and ginger beer. No intoxicating beverages were served.

[41]Marchant, p. 137.

[42]Catalogue, p. xxv.

[43]Littell, 526.

[44]Dodds, pp. 462-63. The printing machine turned out ten thousand sheets of the Illustrated London News each hour before the amazed eyes of the spectators.

[45]Dodds, p. 463.

[46]Greeley, p. 10.

[47]John Ruskin, The Opening of the Crystal Palace (London: Smith, Elden, 1854), p. 22. The quotation is on pp. 17-18.

[48]Quoted in Hobhouse, p. 79.

[49]"Exhibitions and Fairs," 961.

[50]Wood, p. 175.

[51]Dodds, p. 447.

[52]C. B. Norton, World's Fairs from London 1851 to Chicago 1893 (Chicago: Milton Weston, 1890), p. 14.

[53]Marchant, p. 137.

[54]Dodds, pp. 469-70.

[55]Lady Charlotte Guest, quoted in They Saw It Happen, p. 255.

[56]Marchant, p. 138.

[57]Greeley, p. 2.

Bibliography

Beard et al. Tallis's History and Description of the Crystal
    Palace, and the Exhibition of the World's Industry in
    1851. Vol. I. London, John Tallis and Co., [n.d. 1852?].
Charles-Edwards, T., and B. Richardson, eds. They Saw It
    Happen. New York: Macmillan, 1958.
The Crystal Palace Exhibition: An Illustrated Catalogue. 1851;
    rpt. New York: Dover, 1970.
Dodds, John W. The Age of Paradox. New York: Rinehart, 1952.
"The Exhibition," Littell's Living Age, 29 (May-June 1851),
    523-26; 558-59.
"Exhibitions and Fairs." Encyclopaedia Britannica. 8th ed.
    (1964).
Greeley, Horace. The Crystal Palace and Its Lessons: A
    Lecture. New York: DeWitt and Davenport, 1851.
Hobhouse, Christopher. 1851 and The Crystal Palace. New York:
    Dutton, 1937.
Marchant, James, ed. History through "The Times." London:
    Cassell, 1937.
Norton, C. B. World's Fairs from London 1851 to Chicago
    1893. Chicago: Milton Weston, 1890.
"Paxton, Sir Joseph." Encyclopaedia Britannica. 8th ed.
    (1964).
Ruskin, John. The Opening of the Crystal Palace. London: Smith,
    Elden, 1854.
Wood, Anthony. Nineteenth Century Britain 1815-1914. London:
    Longmans, Green, 1960.

Jorge Catto

English 102

Spring, 1986

Euthanasia:

The Right to Die

Someone you love is suffering from terminal cancer. He asks you to inject a lethal drug into him so that he can die without prolonged agony. Would you do it? Should you? Incidents such as this one, in which one person asks another for help to die, are called euthanasia. At the center of this problem is the right of a person to die with the least suffering and the most dignity and comfort. In this essay, I will explore some of the reasons why euthanasia has become such a controversial issue.

Euthanasia is usually divided into two kinds: active and passive. Active euthanasia involves directly causing the death of another person through an intended action (Cawley 859). Administering a fatal drug to a dying person, injecting an air bubble into the bloodstream, or giving him some other means to shorten his life are examples of active euthanasia.

Passive euthanasia can be described as helping someone to die by doing nothing. It is also called "cooperating with the patient's dying" (Cawley 959). Failing to resuscitate a patient who has suffered a massive heart attack is one example of passive euthanasia. Another is deciding not to feed a terminally ill patient who is unable to feed himself. In contrast, removing the feeding tube from a patient who is being fed that way would be considered active euthanasia.

The professional people who care for the sick and dying think that there is a great difference between active and passive euthanasia. In a survey taken in 1975, 73% of the nurses questioned were in favor of withholding treatment that would prolong the lives of dying patients who don't want their lives sustained in that way--in other words, passive euthanasia. But only 17% were in favor of using active means to end the lives of dying patients who request euthanasia ("Taking Life" 40).

In the past, euthanasia was not such a topic for public speculation and censure. In part, this was because death did not usually take place in a public place, and therefore no one was likely to know whether the patient was or wasn't helped to die. Also, doctors lacked the knowledge and the means to try to prolong a dying person's life. But, Sonia Rudikoff points out, this acceptance that death was inevitable and not to be avoided may also have been related to the idea that death was a significant and sacred event and even a welcome one, because it was the prelude to a better existence in the afterlife (62).

Today, as a result of advances in medical science, it has become both possible and, many say, desirable to try to prolong a dying person's life. Indeed, it is considered criminal not to try to do so. Ten years ago, Peter Hammerli, a doctor in Switzerland, was arrested for "murdering" his patients. He was accused of not taking steps to prolong the lives of the terminally ill people that he was treating.[1] Thus, most controversies over euthanasia center around the issue of who, if anyone, has the right to end a sick person's life. Those concerned in this issue include the patient, the patient's family, and the doctor and nursing staff, all of whom may be affected by their differing conceptions of God or divinity or fate.

***

In a Gallup Poll in 1975, slightly over 50% of Americans said that they do not believe that an individual has the right to end his or her own life ("Taking Life" 40). Most of these people probably share the belief that life is a gift from God and that our bodies and lives are not our private possessions, but are held in trust (Cawley 869). As Sonia Rudikoff puts it, they believe that "the breath of life in each of us is a part of a spirit or life, or a community of spirit over which we do not exert ultimate control" (63). To these people, only God has enough knowledge and power to have the right to take away life. They associate euthanasia with murder, and quote Biblical phrases such as "Thou shalt not kill" and "The Lord giveth and the Lord taketh away" as the basis for their belief (Rudikoff 66). They argue that no human being--not even the dying person--can ever be certain when death is about to happen or whether euthanasia is really necessary. So, they want to turn the matter over to God, to whom they attribute perfect objectivity and omniscience.

Advocates of euthanasia think that this argument is a way of avoiding human responsibility. The ideals of our society include the belief that we are all individuals capable of self-determination. A Catholic theologian has observed that, in this respect, man is different from the rest of living creation, because he is "the only animal who knows he is going to die and who also knows he can bring about his own death" (Maguire 57). Before becoming ill, most patients were free to choose their style of life, to decide when to eat, when to sleep, and how to take care of themselves. Why, then, should they not have the right to choose whether to live or to die? (Rudikoff 63). In discussing a decision he once made to end his life if his illness grew more serious, Edward M. Brecher makes the point that it is perfectly acceptable for veterinarians to put extremely sick animals out of their misery, but the same privilege is not usually extended to human beings (72). It is as if man's ability to reason and make moral choices no longer matters when someone is dying.

This issue is a particularly painful one to discuss because, very often, the dying person is experiencing great suffering. Peter Hammerli became a practitioner of euthanasia because he could not bear to prolong the misery of the patients whom he saw suffering ("Hammerli Affair" 1273). Similarly, a licensed practical nurse reported that she had "seen an elderly terminal patient bite through his I.V. tubing to prevent prolonging of the inevitable. I think it was horrible that we drove that man to such extremes" ("Taking Life" 40). On the other hand, such incidents may be the exceptions, and these reactions may, to some extent, be extreme and unnecessary. According to a report made by the British Medical Association, most people, no matter how serious their illnesses are, do not die in agony, but rather peacefully and with dignity ("Against Euthanasia").

The right to die with dignity is regarded as almost as important as the right to die without suffering excessive pain. In earlier times, people of all ages died at home, in a natural and familiar setting, with their loved ones about them. As recently as 35 years ago, more than half the deaths that took place in the United States occurred at home (Tifft 68). Today, however, four out of five Americans die in institutions ("Right to Choose" 22). Patients and their families are especially frightened by "the frantic commotion and turmoil that

5

surround a dying patient." Those who aren't used to the new equipment and the hospital procedures intended to prolong lives think that what goes on is a form of torture inflicted on helpless victims (Fackelmann 232).

***

The person making unpleasant decisions about euthanasia is often not the patient nor one of the patient's relatives, but rather the patient's doctor. The majority of doctors are strongly opposed to both passive and active euthanasia, arguing that the Hippocratic Oath, which they must swear when they receive their medical degrees, pledges them to save lives, not to end them. Few would approve of Dr. Walter W. Sackett, a general practitioner in Miami, who has publicly stated that he has prescribed euthanasia for hundreds of his patients during thirty years of medical· practice (Maguire 64).[2] Most doctors tend to share the attitude of the British Medical Association: "No doctor or nurse should be asked to hold responsibility for deciding when euthanasia may properly be administered, or for administering it" ("Against Euthanasia").

One reason that doctors frequently cite for their refusal to accept any form of euthanasia is that an error may have been made, that the case may not be hopeless, and that, as the British Medical Association puts it, "errors of judgment in euthanasia cases would be irreversible" ("Against Euthanasia"). Some patients with symptoms that suggest a terminal illness have been known to survive for months or years. If euthanasia were an accepted practice, how could such patients be protected from a possible premature death? By prolonging life and postponing death, doctors are also buying time in the hope that a cure might soon be found for a disease that appears to be hopeless (St. John-Stevas 422; Fackelmann 233). To some extent, this concern over possible errors and possible cures may be connected to a fear of being sued. Each year more and more lawsuits are being brought against doctors who have supposedly failed to use every possible means to ensure that the dying live as long as possible ("Right to Choose" 23). If it can be proven that a doctor has failed to do everything possible to prolong life, then he may be faced with a malpractice suit, and the resulting bad publicity could seriously affect his future career (Lamm 21).[3]

Another strong professional objection to euthanasia is based on the special relationship that is supposed to exist between doctor and patient. People trust doctors because they assume that a doctor's sole object is to save lives. Daniel C. Maguire makes the point that doctors are not supposed to differentiate between good death and bad death: "As medicine has developed, it is geared to promoting life under all circumstances. Death is the natural enemy of the healing science" (59). According to Norman St. John-Stevas, it is vital that patients continue to regard doctors as a force for life, not as a potential giver of death (422). The British Medical Association confirms that "to be a trusted physician is one thing; to appear as a potential executioner is quite another" ("Against Euthanasia"). But there are those who criticize this attitude, suggesting that doctors get considerable personal satisfaction from their almost god-like ability to keep people from dying.[4] Some nurses have criticized the almost proprietary attitude of doctors and other health-care professionals toward their patients:

> In a sense aren't we playing God? If God has called a patient to meet his Maker, what right does a nurse or doctor have to prolong his suffering if there is no hope?
>
> A patient does not belong to the nurses or to the physician.

We saved him, if you can call it that. What it amounts to
is an ego trip for us. ("Taking life" 41)

These statements suggest that doctors and nurses may be reluctant to practice or even permit any form of euthanasia because
of their own fear of failing to carry out their mission (Fackelmann 232).

One important point is that the mission of the medical
profession may have changed as a result of new advances in medical science and technology. The Hippocratic Oath was relatively simple to maintain centuries, even decades ago, before
drugs, equipment, and techniques were invented that could prolong the natural course of a patient's life. An article in Science News describes "the high-tech atmosphere" existing in
most hospitals today, especially in intensive care units, that
supports the idea that science is stronger than death, and that
encourages doctors to think of death as "an unacceptable outcome of medical therapy" (Fackelmann 232). Some hospital teams
seem to regard patients as the objects of scientific experiment: Lamm cites the case of a dying woman who was resuscitated
70 times in one 24-hour period (22). Professor George J. Annas
of the Boston University School of Medicine considers whether a
patient has the right to refuse to have his life prolonged and
concludes that "the proper role of medical technology" is at
the center of the debate over euthanasia: "Is technology going
to be our master or our servant? Is technology going to take on
a life of its own such that we give it rights of its own? Or
are we going to to reassert our dominant role in controlling
technology and using it for human ends?" ("Symposium").[5]

An important factor here is the high cost of these technological miracles. Maintaining a comatose patient can cost hundreds of thousands of dollars. Even if much of the financial
burden is placed on health insurance agencies or the government, the gain may not be worth the cost. Noting that, in 1983,
the national bill for health care was $355 billion, Lamm ob-

serves that "the time is not far off when there will be a direct conflicts [sic] between the health of the individual and the health of the society" (21). Given the limited amount of money available to pay for chronic and terminal illnesses, it may be necessary to make some unpleasant choices. Providing the latest medical equipment for one patient may drain resources that might be used to pay for more nursing personnel and a more pleasant environment for other patients. There are also those who believe that available resources should be spent on preventive medicine: according to one doctor writing in The New England Journal of Medicine, "the costs of trying to preserve the life of one cirrhotic patient with bleeding esophageal varices might be used to treat and prevent alcoholism in many persons" (Lamm 21).

The final argument against euthanasia that must be given serious consideration is that it is dangerous for any society to legalize the killing of a certain class of its citizens. According to those who reject euthanasia, it is too easy to enlarge the category of people marked for euthanasia to include the handicapped, the mentally ill and retarded, those convicted of serious crimes, and other groups rejected by society. St. John-Stevas expresses concern about euthanasia as a social policy and points to the terrible precedent of Nazi Germany and the eugenics movement, which attempted to eliminate everyone who did not meet a certain standard of social excellence and desirability (421). Sonia Rudikoff fears that we will create "euthanasia mills," which would make the termination of life a routine matter (66). It is true that, as one psychiatrist put it, euthanasia can never be "a logical decision. It is not one that you can make by a computer model" (Fackelmann 233). It is important to have some degree of personal involvement in each decision, to consider each case individually, and to assert, as Dr. Peter Hammerli did, that "I have never done anything to my patients that I would not do for my own mother and father . . . if they were in such a position" ("Hammerli Affair" 1272).

***

If euthanasia is going to become acceptable social policy, it is important to have some guidelines so that hospitals and nursing homes will understand when and by whom each decision will be made. Otherwise, Ladd points out, euthanasia will take place at random: "Sometimes someone, no one knows who it is, will turn off the ventilator or will turn it on again after it has been turned off, because he thinks that one ought to let the patient die or ought not to let him die." These communication breakdowns can happen easily enough when everyone thinks it is his or her particular duty to intervene--or to stop someone else from intervening. Eventually, Ladd continues, "the patient becomes a football tossed around among those with different and competing interests and ideologies" (138).

One solution to this problem is, whenever possible, to allow the individual to assume the responsibility for deciding when he is ready to die (Modell 908). The report of the Presidential Commission in 1983 determined that the dying patient, if competent to make a decision, should be informed of all the available options and that "those who decline life-prolonging therapy should not be denied other forms of care needed to relieve pain and to maintain dignity" ("Right to Choose" 23). But doctors may not always be sure when patients are competent to make a responsible decision or whether they may have been coerced by family members for whom a lingering illness may be a continued burden (Rudikoff 66-67). For this reason, supporters of the right to euthanasia frequently recommend that each individual write a "living will" relatively early in life while still healthy and undeniably competent to make decisions (Rudikoff 64; "Hammerli Affair" 1272). Such a legal document would state that, should the person be incapable of making such a decision, he or she is establishing certain preferences among the options that might be available for his or her care. Typically, such wills, which have been adopted by 14 states since 1976, instruct doctors not to start or to stop any procedures intended to sustain life if the condition is terminal (Modell 908).

Of course, a living will is no assurance that the patient would still choose euthanasia. What if the patient has changed his mind since he wrote the living will? (Fackelmann 233; Rudikoff 66). A nurse who frequently cares for the dying notes that many patients do change their minds--sometimes more than once-- as death approaches. "Since the patient may be unresponsive by this time, and since hearing is the last thing to go, I have wondered if it wouldn't be a terrible thing to be laying [sic] there and each time someone came in, wondering if they were coming to kill you" ("Taking Life" 42). That is, of course, a horrifying picture. But so, too, is the picture of a patient lying there longing for death and unable to convince anyone to carry out that wish.

Today, for most of us, the dread of death is so great that we go to any lengths to avoid it for those we love, as well as for ourselves. However, death in the right circumstances is everyone's right. It may be that the right to choose euthanasia would never have become a vital issue if death were a more integral part of our lives and if the circumstances in which death took place were easier to bear. St. John-Stevas argues against euthanasia by asserting that "dying can be a vital period in a person's life, reconciling him to life and death and giving an interior peace" (422). But this kind of ideal acceptance of death is possible only if there is a lot of care and love provided by all those in charge of the patient. At

11

present, we seem to be more concerned with keeping people alive than with the quality of the lives that are being prolonged. Until we can have some assurance of a compassionate death-- without unbearable cost to others and to society--we should not be intimidated by the church, the law, or the medical profession. Just as we choose the way we live, so should we be able to choose the way we die.

Notes

[1]When there seemed to be no hope at all of a return to
consciousness for those elderly people who were being kept
alive by artificial feeding, Hammerli and his staff decided
against continued treatment. Defending his actions, Hammerli
insisted that he did not "believe in giving extensive treatment to a patient who is hopelessly ill: sometimes it is better
to allow a person to die in peace" (26).

[2]Dr. Sackett suggests that, whether they admit it or not,
75% of all doctors have acted similarly at some point in their
careers.

[3]The President of a Presidential Commission of the question of euthanasia is concerned that this fear of legal action
may affect doctors' medical judgment. He imagines "a future
horror scene in which a dying patient looks up from his death-
bed to see the doctor flipping through a thick docket of legal
cases" (Fackelmann 233).

[4]Of those few (17%) nurses who favored active euthanasia,
only half would allow patients themselves the means to end
their own lives; the other half believe that only professionals
should be allowed to make and carry out that decision ("Taking
Life" 40).

[5]The case of Elizabeth Bouvia is a good illustration. A
quadriplegic who is regarded as mentally competent, Ms. Bouvia
has been prevented from carrying out her expressed wish to end
her own life by hospital staff, who insist on force-feeding
her. Ernest van den Haag compares this with force-feeding convicts who go on hunger strikes, and argues that it is acceptable to force food on convicts since they are not entitled to

13

the same liberties that free people are. "A hospital . . . may be liable for failing to artificially feed patients who cannot eat by normal means, or are incompetent. But not a patient who will not eat. He has a perfect right to decline food, or medicine, or an operation, if he so wishes and is competent to understand the consequences" (45-46).

Works Cited

"Against Euthanasia." The Lancet 30 Jan. 1971: 220.

Brecher, Edward. "Opting for Suicide." The New York Times Magazine 18 March 1979: 72-80.

Cawley, Michelle Anne. "Euthanasia: Should It Be a Choice?" American Journal of Nursing May 1977: 859-61.

Fackelmann, Kathy. "A Question of Life or Death." Science News 9 Oct. 1982: 232-33.

"The Hammerli Affair: Is Passive Euthanasia Murder?" Science 26 Dec. 1975: 1271-74.

Ladd, John. "Euthanasia, Liberty, and Religion." Ethics Oct. 1982: 129-38.

Lamm, Richard D. "Long Time Dying." The New Republic 27 Aug. 1984: 20-23.

Maguire, Daniel C. "Death By Chance, Death by Choice." Good Housekeeping Jan. 1975: 57-65.

Modell, Walter. "A 'Will' to Live." The New England Journal of Medicine 18 April 1971: 907-8.

"The Right to Choose." The Economist 26 March 1983: 22-23.

Rudikoff, Sonia. "The Problem of Euthanasia." Commentary Feb. 1974: 62-68.

St. John-Stevas, Norman. "Euthanasia: A 'Pleasant Sounding Word.'" America 31 May 1975: 421-22.

"Symposium: When Sophisticated Medicine Does More Harm Than Good." The New York Times, 30 March 1986: E6.

"Taking Life Away." Nursing75 October 1975: 40-50.

Tifft, Susan. "Debate on the Boundary of Life." Time 11 April 1983: 68-70.

van den Haag, Ernest. "A Right to Die?" National Review 4 May 1984: 45-46.

David Morgan

Natural Science I

December 15, 1986

Explaining the Tunguskan Phenomenon

The Tunguska River Valley in Siberia has always been an area of swamps and bogs, forests and frozen tundra, sparsely populated, and remote and inaccessible to most travelers. It was at dawn on June 30, 1908 that witnesses in the Tungus observed a light glaring more brightly than anything they had ever seen. This cosmic phenomenon, they said, was bluish-white in color and gradually became cigarlike in shape. Just as terrifying to the few people inhabiting that part of Siberia was the tremendous noise that accompanied the light, a noise that was reported to have been heard 1000 kilometers from the site (Parry, 1961). Some who were in the vicinity were deafened, while others farther away apparently became speechless and displayed other symptoms of severe trauma. The Tungus community refused to go near the site or speak of the occurrence, and some even denied that it had ever happened (Crowther, 1931). The event was so frightening to these simple peasants that many believed it had been an act of divine retribution, a punishment by a god demanding vengeance (Baxter & Atkins, 1976).

Since 1921, when the first perilous expedition to the Tungus region confirmed that a remarkable event had indeed taken place, scientists have attempted to explain what it was and why it happened. Almost 80 years later, the various theories devel-

oped to explain the explosion in the Tunguska Valley have become almost as interesting a phenomenon as the original occurrence. Like doctors trying to diagnose a disease by examining
the symptoms, scientists have analyzed the fragmentary evidence
and published theories that supposedly account for it. However,
no theory has been entirely convincing. The purpose of this
essay is to provide a brief description of some of the major
interpretations of the Tunguska occurrence and to suggest that,
in their efforts to substantiate their theories, scientists can
be fallible.

At dawn on that day in June, 1908, a huge object evidently
came from space into the earth's atmosphere, breaking the sound
barrier, and, at 7:17 a.m., slammed into the ground in the central Siberian plateau. Moments before the collision, a thrust
of energy caused people and animals to be strewn about, structures destroyed, and trees toppled. Immediately afterwards, a
pillar or "tongue" of fire could be seen in the sky several
hundred miles away; others called it a cylindrical pipe. A
thermal air current of extremely high temperature caused forest
fires to ignite and spread across forty miles, melting metal
objects scattered throughout the area. Several shock waves were
felt for hundreds of miles around, breaking windows and tossing
people, animals, and objects in the air. Finally, black rain
fell from a menacing-looking cloud over a radius of 100 square
miles. It is no wonder that the peasants of the Tunguska River
Valley thought that this was the end of the world (Krinov,
1966; Baxter & Atkins, 1976).

For a variety of reasons, this devastating occurrence remained almost unknown outside Russia--and even outside central
Siberia--for many years. The Tungus was extremely remote, even
for Russia, which is such a vast country that transportation
and communication between places can be slow and difficult. The
few people living in the area who actually witnessed what hap-

pened were mostly peasants and nomadic tribesmen, and did not have much opportunity or inclination to talk about what they had seen. There was little publicity, and what there was was limited to local Siberian newspapers (Krinov, 1966). During that summer, there was a lot of discussion in the newspapers of the European capitals about peculiar lights and colors seen in the northern skies, unusually radiant sunsets, some magnetic disturbances, and strange dust clouds (Cowan et al., 1965). But, since news of the events at the Tungus River had hardly yet been heard even in Moscow, there was no way for scientists in other countries to see a connection between these happenings.

It was only in 1921, when Russia was relatively stable after years of war, revolution, and economic problems, that the first expedition to investigate the event at Tunguska actually took place (Crowther, 1931). That it occurred then at all was largely because an energetic Russian scientist, Leonid Kulik, had become fascinated by meteorites. He read in an old Siberian newspaper that, in 1908, a railway train had been forced to stop because a meteorite fell in its path--a story that was quite untrue. Kulik thought that he might become the discoverer of the greatest meteorite ever found on earth and determined to search for evidence that such a meteorite existed. Authorized by the Soviet Academy, Kulik led a series of expeditions to the Tungus River. In 1921, he did not even reach the site, for the route was almost impassable. In 1927, and annually for the next few years, Kulik did, indeed, explore the devastated area and was able to study the evidence of what had happened and listen to the oral accounts of the event provided by those inhabitants who were still alive and who were willing to talk to him. Finally, in 1938-39, Kulik traveled to the Tungus for the last time, for the purpose of taking aerial photographs that might confirm his meteorite theory (Baxter & Atkins, 1976).

Kulik and his fellow investigators believed that whatever had happened at the Tungus River had been caused by a meteorite. So, what they expected to find was a single, vast crater to mark the place where the meteorite had landed. Such a crater, however, was simply not there (Cowan et al., 1965). Instead, he found a vast devastated and burned area, a forest of giant trees with their tops cut off and scattered around (Crowther, 1931). In 1928, without the benefit of an aerial view of the region, Kulik concluded from his various vantage points on the ground that, around the circumference of the area where the meteorite had landed, there was a belt of upright dead trees, which he named the "telegraph pole forest." Scattered around the perimeter of the frozen swamp, which he called the "cauldron," were groups of fallen trees, with their tops all pointing away from the direction of where the blast had occurred (Cowan et al., 1965). None of this was consistent with Kulik's meteorite theory, and he could only attribute the odd pattern of upright and fallen trees to a shock wave or "hot compressed-air pockets," which had missed some trees and affected others (Baxter & Atkins, 1976). The account of his discovery in the Literary Digest of 1929 states that "each of the falling meteoric fragments must have worked, the Russian scientists imagine, like a gigantic piston," with compressed air knocking trees down like toothpicks ("What a meteor," p. 34). Kulik continued to insist that the fire and the resultant effect on the trees was the result of a meteorite explosion. But the Russian scientist V. G. Fesenkov estimated that such destruction could only have been caused by an object of at least several hundred meters, and that, if anything of this size or force had hit the ground, it would have left a crater (Baxter & Atkins, 1976).

Kulik found other evidence that could not easily be explained by the meteorite theory. Although there was no trace of a single large crater (Cowan et al., 1965), there were numerous shallow cavities scattered around the frozen bog (Olivier, 1928). For several years, Kulik attempted to bore into the ground, seeking evidence that these pits and ridges were formed by lateral pressure caused by gases exploding from the meteorite's impact. Kulik described the scene as "not unlike a giant duplicate of what happens when a brick from a tall chimney-top falls into a puddle of mud. Solid ground actually must have splashed outward in every direction." In this account, the supposed meteorite became "the great swarm of meteors" that "must have traversed" the atmosphere for several hundred miles, pushing ahead of it a "giant bubble of superheated atmosphere" that was "probably responsible" for the burned countryside ("What a meteor," 1929, p. 33). All the "must have's" and "probably's" make a good narrative, but are not scientifically convincing.

Similarly, Kulik endeavored to explain eyewitness accounts of the huge fireball in the sky that burned one observer's shirt off his back and threw him off his porch (Cowen et al., 1965). Such extreme heat waves had never before been known to have accompanied the fall of a meteorite, but Kulik decided that this meteorite was much larger than those previously recorded and that therefore it would have released much more energy upon impact and that would account for such radiant heat (Baxter & Atkins, 1976). So obsessed was Kulik with the idea that somewhere buried in the Tungus swamp was a phenomenal meteorite that he focused the efforts of all the expeditions to the area during his lifetime on digging beneath the frozen tundra and to some extent neglected the examination of other evidence that might have further threatened the theory that he was determined to prove (Parry, 1961). Initially, he was successful in convincing the scientific community that his theory was correct. It is most interesting to read excerpts from The American Weekly of 1929 flatly asserting that a meteorite had fallen in Siberia and that Professor Kulik had brought back photographs of the giant crater that he found, as well as small samples of meteoric materials. The article is accompanied by a photograph of Professor Kulik measuring "the main crater, where the largest mass of this celestial visitor buried itself in the earth" (Quoted in "What a meteor," p. 34).

While Kulik's expeditions were still searching for evidence of a meteorite, other scientists were hypothesizing that the Tunguska explosion might have been caused by a small comet, which would account for the absence of a crater. Comets are composed of ice, frozen gases, and dust, and as they travel around the sun, they develop a long tail. Upon impact, a comet might give off a trail of gases and dust which would create a bright and colorful night sky similar to that observed after the explosion. This would not be true of a meteorite, which has no gaseous trail and thus leaves no trace in the atmosphere. It has also been suggested that the observed direction of the object's travel was more typical of a comet than of a meteorite (Florensky, 1963). If the comet had blown up approximately two miles above the site, that would explain why some trees survived while others did not (Parry, 1961). On the other hand, there is no evidence that a comet had ever crashed on earth before, or caused a comparable change in magnetic and atmospheric phenomena, or even come so close without being sighted (Baxter & Atkins, 1976). Those scientists supporting the comet theory have suggested that, although it is unusual for any comet to come that close to earth without anyone sighting it, the one landing at Tunguska might have been small enough to go by unnoticed. But that idea is contradicted by Fesenkov's estimate that, to cause such destruction, the nucleus of the Tunguskan comet--if there was one--would have been only slightly smaller than those of well-documented comets that were visible at great distances (Cowan et al., 1965).

The next major explanation for the cosmic phenomenon at Tunguska could only have been formulated after World War II, when the scientific community had learned how to make atomic explosions and had become familiar with their aftermath. Aleksander Kazantsev, a Russian scientist and (equally important) science-fiction writer, had visited Hiroshima after the atom bomb explosion and had studied the data describing its impact and aftermath. Because of certain similarities in the blast effects--the burnt yet upright trees, the mushroom cloud, the black rain--Kazantsev and other scientists concluded that the blast of 1908 was an atomic explosion estimated at a minimum of ten times the strength of the one at Hiroshima (Parry, 1961). Witnesses had described the blinding flash and withering heat at Hiroshima in much the same way that the Siberian peasants described the frightening blast at Tunguska. The melting heat that Kulik found so inconsistent with his meteorite theory was more consistent with an atomic explosion (Baxter & Atkins, 1976). It is worth pointing out that scientists went on to develop the hypothesis that a nuclear explosion had occurred at Tunguska even though their theorizing was largely based on stories told by ignorant peasants, believers in devils and wrathful gods, who could quite easily have exaggerated what actually happened to improve their stories. Even though these eyewitness accounts were gathered twenty or more years after the actual event, and had quite possibly entered the folklore of the countryside (Krinov, 1966), they were still regarded as the purest evidence.

To test whether a nuclear explosion might have occurred, scientists examined the trees for radioactivity and for any unusual increase in normal growth patterns, shown by greater

spacing between the age lines, that might have been the result
of radioactivity. What they found was that some trees at the
site grew to be four times greater than what would normally
have been expected. Similarly, scabs that appeared on the hides
of local reindeer were explained as being the result of radio-
active contamination (Baxter & Atkins, 1976). This evidence, by
no means conclusive (Florensky, 1963), was cited as proof that
such an atomic explosion had taken place, just as Kulik had
cited the existence of shallow pits in the terrain as proof
that a meteorite had exploded.

Assuming that what happened at Tunguska was the result of
an atomic blast, and faced with the fact that nuclear fission
was not within man's grasp before the 1940s, Kazantsev and his
colleagues concluded that the phenomenon must have involved
extraterrestrial beings and that the explosion was caused by a
UFO, propelled by atomic energy, that crashed (Parry, 1961).
The pattern of devastation on the ground, as seen from the air,
suggested that the object took a zigzag path, changing its direction as it came closer and closer to earth. Advocates of the
UFO theory argue such a change in direction would not have been
possible with a natural object like a meteorite or comet, and
that the object--a spacecraft--was driven by intelligent beings
who were trying to land without hitting a more densely populated area. They hypothesize that the craft had some mechanical
problem that made it necessary to land but that the initial
angle of its trajectory was too shallow for landing and would
only have bounced the craft back into space. So the navigators
tried to maneuver and correct the angle, but swerved, came down
too sharply, and exploded (Baxter & Atkins, 1976). On the other
hand, it seems just as possible that a natural object swerved
or that debris from a nonatomic explosion was thrown in zigzag
directions than that navigators from outer space ran into mechanical troubles and crash-landed. If probability is going to

be disregarded in order to support one theory, then the same suspension of the natural order of things can be used to confirm an equally unlikely theory.

In the late 1950s, an exploratory team examined the Tunguska site with an advanced magnetic detector and, in 1962, scientists magnified the soil and found an array of tiny, colored, magnetic, ball-shaped particles, made of cobalt, nickel, copper, and germanium (Baxter & Atkins, 1976). According to extraterrestrial-intelligence specialists, these could have been the elements used for electrical and technical instruments, with the copper used for communication services and the germanium used in semiconductors (Parry, 1961). However, controlled experiments would be necessary to make this atomic-extraterrestrial argument convincing.

Scientists who find the UFO and extraterrestrial explanations less than credible have turned to the most recent theories of physics and astronomy to explain what might have happened in the Tungus. Some (including Kazantsev) argue that such an explosion might have been caused by antimatter, which exploded as it came in contact with the atmosphere (Parry, 1961). Alternatively, the explosion might have been caused by a "black hole" hitting the earth in Siberia and passing through to emerge on the other side. Those opposing these theories point, again, to the absence of a crater and to the numerous eyewitness accounts that describe the shape of the object and the sound of the blast, all of which would be inconsistent with antimatter or black-hole theories (Baxter & Atkins, 1976). However, a 1973 article in Nature asserts that a black hole would not, in fact, leave a crater, but would simply enter the earth at a great velocity and that a shock wave and blast might possibly accompany its entrance (Jackson & Ryan).

What is most fascinating about the Tunguska Valley phenomenon is that, despite all the advances in science over the past

80 years, investigators cannot now be any more certain of the cause of the blast than they were in 1921, when Kulik first came near the site. None of the theories presented is wholly convincing, for all of them rely to some extent on human observers, whose accounts of events are notoriously unreliable, or hypotheses based on ambiguous evidence, without the support of controlled tests and experiments. The formulation of a radically new body of scientific knowledge might provide a new theoretical context for examining the evidence and establishing a more convincing explanation. But, as it is, with the trail getting colder, finding a solution to this mystery seems to become more and more unlikely.

Examining these explanations about what did or did not land and explode in Siberia does teach us that scientific theories are sometimes based on the selective interpretation of evidence and that scientists, like everyone else, tend to believe their own theories and find the evidence that they want to find. Although the language that they use is very different, the accounts of what happened at Tunguska according to Kulik, Kazantsev, and their other scientific colleagues are not so very different from what the local peasants say that they saw. Both have a closer resemblance to science fiction than science fact.

List of References

Baxter J., & Atkins, T. (1976). The Fire Came By: The Riddle of the Great Siberian Explosion. Garden City, N.Y.: Doubleday.

Cowen, C., Atluri, C.R., & Libby, W.F. (1965, May 29). Possible antimatter content of the Tunguska meteor of 1908. Nature (London), pp. 861-65.

Crowther, J.G. (1931). More about the great Siberian meteorite. Scientific American, 144 (5), 314-17.

Florensky, K.P. (1963, November). Did a comet collide with the earth in 1908? Sky and Telescope, pp. 268-69.

Jackson, A.A., & Ryan, M.P. (1973, September 14). Was the Tungus event due to a black hole? Nature (London), pp. 88-89.

Krinov, E.L. (1966). Giant Meteorites. London: Pergamon, pp. 125-265.

Olivier, C.P. (1928). The great Siberian meteorite. Scientific American, 139 (1), 42-44.

Parry, A. (1961). The Tungus mystery: Was it a spaceship? In Russia's Rockets and Missiles. London: Macmillan, pp. 248-67.

What a meteor did to Siberia. (1929, March 16). Literary Digest, pp. 33-34.

Appendix A.
Some Useful
Reference Sources

Here are some points to remember when you use the reference works listed on the following pages:

1. You can find sources for your essays by looking in the *subject card catalog,* by looking in the *bibliographies of standard works* on your subject, by looking at the brief bibliographies at the end of *encyclopedia articles,* by looking under the broad subject headings in *general-interest bibliographies* and *periodical indexes,* and by looking in the *indexes and abstract collections* that deal with the specific subject of your research.
2. Some reference sources are entirely bibliography: they consist of long lists of articles and (sometimes) books, each followed by the essential publication information. These indexes are usually arranged by topic. You may have to check several broad headings before you find the articles that you need. If, for example, you are doing research on educational television, you would look up "education," "television," and the names of some of the programs that you intend to write about. Most indexes are cross-referenced.
3. Some reference sources are called "abstracts" because they contain abstracts or paragraph summaries of many (but not all) of the articles published each year in that discipline. Abstracts often have two sections: the first contains a series of summaries of articles, chosen for their special interest or excellence and arranged by subject; the second contains a list of all the articles published in that field in that year. (Occasionally, you will find a modified form of abstract, in which several articles are each given a one-sentence

summary.) First you look up the specific subject that you are interested in and glance at the summaries. Then you get the publication information about the articles relevant to your research by looking up their *authors* in the second section of the reference work. Although abstracts give you a convenient preview, you will find that many of the articles are highly technical and may therefore be difficult to read and write about.

4. Some of the periodical articles that you want to consult may be available only on microfiche, or microcards. Ask the reference librarian to help you to use the system and its apparatus. With the proper explanations, even the most unmechanical people can become adept at using these tools of the modern library.

5. If you can't find a specific reference work or if you are not sure which one to use, check with a librarian. As long as you can tell librarians the broad or (preferably) the narrow subject of your research, they will be willing and able to help you.

GENERAL ENCYCLOPEDIAS

Collier's Encyclopedia. 24 vols. with annual supplements. New York: Crowell-Collier, 1981. Easier to read and understand than the old *Britannica* or *Americana.*

Encyclopedia Americana. 30 vols. with annual supplements. New York: Americana Corporation, 1978. Use the index volume to locate your subject within the longer encyclopedia.

Encyclopaedia Britannica. 14th ed. 24 vols. with annual supplements and periodic revisions (through 1973). Chicago: Encyclopaedia Britannica, 1929. Dated and more sophisticated than the 15th edition, but retained by many libraries for the excellence of its articles.

New Columbia Encyclopedia. 4th ed. 1 vol. New York: Columbia University Press, 1975. A single-volume encyclopedia, especially good as a starting point.

New Encyclopaedia Britannica. 15th ed. 30 vols. with annual supplements and periodic revisions. Chicago: Encyclopaedia Britannica, 1974. Use the "Micropaedia" to find your subject in the 19-volume "Macropaedia." A disappointing successor to earlier editions; the "Micropaedia"/"Macropaedia" arrangement can be inconvenient to use.

SPECIALIZED ENCYCLOPEDIAS

Encyclopedia of American Art. Chanticleer Press. New York: Dutton, 1981.

Encyclopedia of Biological Sciences. Ed. Peter Gray. 2nd ed. New York: Van Nostrand Reinhold, 1970.

Encyclopedia of Computer Science and Technology. 14 vols. New York: Dekker, 1980.

Encyclopedia of Education. Ed. Lee C. Deighton et al. 10 vols. New York: Macmillan, 1971.

The Encyclopedia of Human Behavior: Psychology, Psychiatry, and Mental Health. Ed. Robert M. Goldenson. 2 vols. New York: Doubleday, 1974.

Encyclopedia of Physics. Ed. Robert M. Besancon. 2nd ed. New York: Van Nostrand Reinhold, 1974.

Encyclopedia of Psychology. Ed. H.J. Eysenck. 2nd ed. 3 vols. New York: Continuum, 1979.

Encyclopedia of Sociology. Ed. Gayle Johnson. Guilford, Conn.: Dushkin Press, 1974.

Encyclopedia of World Art. 15 vols. New York: McGraw-Hill, 1959–68.

An Encyclopedia of World History: Ancient, Medieval, and Modern Chronologically Arranged. Comp. and ed. William Leonard Langer. 5th ed. Boston: Houghton Mifflin, 1972.

International Encyclopedia of the Social Sciences. Ed. D.L. Sills, 17 vols. New York: The Free Press, 1972.

McGraw-Hill Encyclopedia of Science and Technology. 15 vols. 4th ed. New York: McGraw-Hill, 1977.

McGraw-Hill Encyclopedia of World Drama. 4 vols. New York: McGraw-Hill, 1972.

New Grove Dictionary of Music and Musicians. Ed. Stanley Sadie. 20 vols. Washington, D.C.: Grove's Dictionaries of Music, 1980.

VNR Concise Encyclopedia of Mathematics. Ed. W. Gellert et al. Florence, Ky.: Reinhold, 1977.

GENERAL INDEXES

Book Review Digest. New York: H. W. Wilson, 1905–present. Includes excerpts from reviews as well as lists of references.

Book Review Index. Detroit: Gale Research Co., 1965–present. Lists reviews of books on literature, art, business, economics, religion, and current affairs.

Editorials on File. New York: Facts on File, 1970–present. Selected editorials on subjects of contemporary interest, with each editorial preceded by a summary of the issue being discussed.

Facts on File. New York: Facts on File, 1941–present. Summaries of issues and events, with selected bibliographies.

Milner, Anita Check, *Newspaper Indexes: A Location and Subject Guide for Researchers,* Metuchen, N.J. and London: The Scarecrow Press, Inc., 1977.

New York Times Index. New York: New York Times, 1851–present.

Popular Periodical Index. Camden, N.J.: Popular Periodical Index, 1971–present. Includes magazines such as *New York*, *Playboy*, *Rolling Stone*, and *TV Guide.*

Readers' Guide to Periodical Literature. New York: H. W. Wilson, 1905–present. Includes listings of articles in many general-interest magazines, especially news magazines and women's magazines.

Vertical File Index. New York: H. W. Wilson, 1932/1935–present. Lists pamphlets on all subjects.

BIOGRAPHICAL SOURCES

Annual Obituary. New York: St. Martin's, 1980–present. Annual collection of profiles of prominent individuals who died during the year (1980–present), arranged by month of death date.

Biography Index. New York: H. W. Wilson, 1947–present. Organized like the *Readers' Guide,* listing articles about contemporary celebrities.

Current Biography. New York: H. W. Wilson, 1940–present. Consists of full-scale articles (like encyclopedia entries) about prominent people. Use the index to find the right year for the person that you are researching.

Dictionary of American Biography. 10 vols. New York: Scribner's, 1980. Articles contain basic information about notable figures in American history. (Do not use this source for contemporary figures.)

New York Times Obituary Index 1858–1968. New York: New York Times, 1970.

SEMISPECIALIZED INDEXES
AND ABSTRACTS

Humanities

Art Index. New York: H. W. Wilson, 1929–present.

Humanities Index. New York: H. W. Wilson, 1974–present. Annual volumes include reviews of books and performances as well as a listing of articles on issues and new developments in all the humanities.

MLA International Bibliography of Books and Articles in the Modern Languages and Literature. New York: Modern Language Association, 1921–present.

Music Index. Detroit: Information Service, 1949–present. Includes reviews listed under composer and title.

The Philosopher's Index. Bowling Green, Ohio: Bowling Green State University, 1967 to present. Articles on philosophy and its relation to art, religion, the humanities in general, and history.

Salem, James. *A Guide to Critical Reviews.* 5 vols. New York: The Scarecrow Press, Inc., 1966. Theater reviews, listed by playwright, with title index.

Physical and Biological Sciences

Applied Science and Technology Index. New York: H. W. Wilson, 1958–present. Includes references to a large number of scientific and technological periodicals.

Biological and Agricultural Index. New York: H. W. Wilson, 1964–present.

Chemical Abstracts. Easton, Pa.: American Chemical Society, 1907–present.

Engineering Index. New York: Engineering Index, 1934–present.

Lasworth, Earl. *Reference Sources in Science and Technology.* Metuchen, N.J.: The Scarecrow Press, Inc., 1972.

Science Abstracts. London, England: Institute of Electrical Engineers, 1898–present. Summaries of articles about physics.

Social Sciences

Almanac of American Politics. Ed. Michael Barone. Boston: Gambit, 1972–present. Lists sources for information about local and national public affairs.

America: History and Life. Santa Barbara, Calif.: American Bibliographical Center, Clio Press, 1964–present. Includes references to 2,000 publications dealing with past, recent, and present history. Part A consists of abstracts; Part B consists of one-sentence summaries of articles, grouped under topic headings.

Guide to U.S. Government Serials and Periodicals. McLean, Va.: Documents Index, 1964–present. A cumulative index directs the user to the correct volume.

Historical Abstracts. Santa Barbara, Calif.: American Bibliographical Center, Clio Press, 1955–present. Part A deals with modern history from 1450 to 1940; Part B deals with mid–twentieth-century history. The index is in the Winter issue.

International Bibliography of Economics. Chicago: Aldine, 1952–present.

International Political Science Abstracts. Paris, France: International Political Science Assn., 1951–present. Summaries of articles on political science and international relations.

Psychological Abstracts. Lancaster, Pa.: American Psychology Assn., 1927–present. Use the three-year cumulative subject and author indexes; for example, the years 1978–1980 are indexed together.

Public Affairs Information Service Bulletin. New York: P.A.I.S., 1915–present. Includes pamphlets and government documents and reports as well as periodical articles. Covers an unusually large number of periodicals. Emphasizes factual and statistical information.

Sage Public Administration Abstracts. Beverly Hills, Calif.: Sage Publications, 1979–present. Summaries of books, articles, government publications, speeches, and research studies.

Social Sciences Index. New York: H. W. Wilson, 1974–present.

Sociological Abstracts. New York: Sociological Abstracts, Inc., 1953–present. Includes articles on mass communications, ecology, and women's studies.

INDEXES AND ABSTRACTS
FOR PROFESSIONAL STUDIES

Business

Accountants' Index. New York: American Institute of Certified Public Accountants, 1944–present. Lists articles about accounting, data processing, financial management, and taxation.

Business Periodicals Index. New York: H. W. Wilson, 1958–present. Lists articles from over a hundred periodicals dealing with new developments and methods in business management.

Personnel Literature. Washington, D.C.: U.S. Civil Service Commission, 1969–present. Lists articles about administration, supervision, management relations, and productivity.

Education

Current Index to Journals in Education. New York: Macmillan, 1969–present.

Education Index. New York: H. W. Wilson, 1929–present.

Law

Index to Legal Periodicals. New York: H. W. Wilson, 1908–present. In addition to a listing of articles by subject and author, there is a table of cases and a group of book reviews.

Library Science

Library and Information Science Abstracts. London, England: The Library Association, 1970–present. Materials about information dissemination and retrieval, as well as library services.

Nursing and Health

Index Medicus. Bethesda, Md.: National Library of Medicine, 1961–present. Lists articles of medical interest and includes a bibliography of medical book reviews.

International Nursing Index. New York: American Journal of Nursing, 1966–present.

Cumulative Index to Nursing and Allied Health Literature. Glendale, Calif.: Nursing and Allied Health Corp., 1956–present. Articles listed include health education and social services as they relate to health care.

Social Work

Human Resources Abstracts: Beverly Hills, Calif.: Sage Publications, 1965–present. Summarizes developments in areas such as poverty, manpower, and distribution of human resources.

Journal of Human Services Abstracts. Rockville, Md.: Project Share, 1976–present. Summarizes articles concerning the provision of public services as they relate to public administration, education, psychology, environmental studies, family studies, nutrition, and health services.

Sage Family Studies Abstracts. Beverly Hills, Calif.: Sage Publications, 1979–present.

Social Work Research and Abstracts. Albany, N.Y.: National Association of Social Workers, 1965–present. Selected research articles as well as abstracts of other articles in the field of social welfare.

INDEXES TO STATISTICAL COMPILATIONS

American Statistics Index: A Comprehensive Guide and Index to the Statistical Publications of the U.S. Government, Washington, D.C.: Congressional Information Service, 1973–present.

Statistical Yearbook. New York: United Nations Department of Economic and Social Affairs, 1949–present. International statistics.

Appendix B.
Some Basic Forms
For Documentation

These are the most common forms for compiling your list of Works Cited when you write an essay using New MLA parenthetical documentation.

Book by a Single Author

> Veysey, Laurence R. The Emergence of the American University.
> Chicago: U of Chicago P, 1965.

Book by Two Authors

> Postman, Neil, and Charles Weingartner. Teaching as a Subversive
> Activity. New York: Dell, 1969.

Book by Several Authors

> Riesman, David, Nathan Glazer, and Reuel Denney. The Lonely Crowd.
> New Haven: Yale UP, 1950.

Essay from a Collection Written
by Different Authors

> Webb, R.K. "The Victorian Reading Public." In From Dickens to
> Hardy. Ed. Boris Ford. Baltimore: Penguin, 1958. 205-26.

Book Published in Several Volumes

Tocqueville, Alexis de. Democracy in America. Ed. Phillips Bradley. 2 vols. New York: Knopf, 1945.

Book Published in a Reprinted Edition

Orwell, George. Animal Farm. 1946; rpt. New York: Signet, 1959.

Book That Is One Volume in a Series

Scouten, Arthur H. ed. The London Stage 1729-1747. Vol. 3 of The
London Stage 1600-1800. 4 vols. Carbondale, Ill.: Southern
Illinois UP, 1961.

Gaff, Jerry G. Institutional Renewal through the Improvement of
Teaching. New Directions for Higher Education, No. 24. San
Francisco: Jossey-Bass, 1978.

Article in an Encyclopedia

"American Architecture." Columbia Encyclopedia. 3rd ed. (1963).

Publication of a Corporation, Foundation, or Government Agency

Carnegie Council on Policy Studies in Higher Education. Three Thousand Futures, The Next Twenty Years for Higher Education. San
Francisco: Jossey-Bass, 1980.

Article in a Periodical Numbered by Volume

Plumb, J.H. "Commercialization of Childhood." Horizon 18
(1976): 16-29.

Article in a Monthly Periodical

Loye, David. "TV's Impact on Adults." Psychology Today April
1978: 87+.

[Note: The plus sign after the page number indicates that the article is
not printed consecutively, but skips to other pages.]

Article in a Weekly Periodical

Meyer, Karl E. "Television's Trying Times." Saturday Review 16
Sept. 1978: 19-23.

Article in a Newspaper

Price, Hugh. "Leave School Gates in Place." New York Times 26
March 1982: A16.

Article without an Author

"How to Get Quality Back into the Schools." U.S. News & World Report 12 Sept. 1977: 31-34.

Lecture

Auchincloss, Louis, Erica Jong, and Gloria Steinem. "The 18th Century Woman." Symposium at the Metropolitan Museum of Art, 29
April 1982.

Film

Dr. Strangelove. dir. Stanley Kubrick. Columbia Pictures, 1963.
Kubrick, Stanley, dir. Dr. Strangelove. Columbia Pictures, 1963.

Television Program

Serge Pavlovitch Diaghilev 1872-1929: A Portrait. Prod. Peter Adam
(BBC), Hearst/ABC, 12 July 1982.

OTHER METHODS OF DOCUMENTATION

Endnote / Footnote System

In Chapter 9, on pp. 378–379, you read a brief description of the
endnote/footnote system, in which the documentation of sources is
placed away from the text, either at the bottom of the page or in a separate group at the end of the essay. Numbers are used to link up the
source references in the essay with the footnotes (bottom of the page) or
endnotes (end of the essay). If your instructor asks you to use this
method of documentation, do not put parenthetical source references
anywhere within the text of the essay. Instead, at the end of the material
to be documented, at the point where you would insert a parenthetical
reference, place a number to indicate to your reader that there is a corresponding footnote or endnote.

When *inserting the numbers,* follow these rules:

1. The note number is raised slightly above the line of your essay. To
   do this, you move the typewriter roller up one half-turn or, if you

are using a word processing program that has no mechanism for note insertion, you leave a space and insert the number neatly by hand, slightly above the line, once the essay is finished. Skip two spaces after each number.

2. The notes are numbered consecutively: if you have twenty-six notes in your essay, the number of the last one should be 26. There is no such thing as "12a." If "12a" appears at the last moment, then it becomes "13," and the remainder of the notes should be renumbered.

3. Every note should contain at least one separate piece of information. Never write a note that states only, "See footnote 3." The reader should be told enough to make it unnecessary to consult footnote 3.

4. While a note may contain more than one piece of information (for example, the source reference as well as some additional explanation of the point that is being documented), the note should have only one number. Under no circumstances should two note numbers be placed together, like this: [6,7]

When you prepare the documentation for your essay, you will have two lists to make: the bibliography of works cited or consulted, and the list of notes.

The *format of the bibliography* closely resembles the "Works Cited" format for parenthetical documentation that was described in Chapter 5 and Chapter 9: the sources are alphabetized by last name, with the second line of each entry indented. The entries themselves closely resemble the forms listed at the beginning of this appendix, with slight differences in punctuation.

The *format of the list of notes* is almost like the bibliography in reverse: the first line of the note is indented five spaces, with the second line at the margin; the note begins with a raised number, corresponding to the number in the text of the essay; the author's name is in first name/last name order; author and title are separated by commas, not periods; publication information is placed in parentheses; and the note ends with the page reference (preceded by p. or pp., except for books and periodicals that are a part of a series of volumes) and a period. Notes should be double-spaced throughout.

Here is a list of five notes, illustrating the most common forms, followed by a bibliography consisting of the same five sources:

Notes

[1] Helen Block Lewis, *Psychic War in Men and Women* (New York: New York UP, 1976), p. 43.

[2] Gertrude Himmelfarb, "Observations on History and Human-

ism, " in <u>The Philosophy of the Curriculum</u>, ed. Sidney Hook et al. (Buffalo: Prometheus, 1975), p. 85.

[3] Harvey G. Cox, "Moral Reasoning and the Humanities, " <u>Liberal Education</u>, 71, No. 3 (1985), 196.

[4] Lauro Martines, "Mastering the Matriarch, " <u>Times Literary Supplement</u>, 1 February 1985, p. 113.

[5] Carolyn See, "Collaboration with a Daughter: The Rewards and Cost, " <u>New York Times</u>, 19 June 1986, p. C2.

Bibliography

Cox, Harvey G. "Moral Reasoning and the Humanities, " <u>Liberal Education</u>, 71, No. 3 (1985), 195-204.

Himmelfarb, Gertrude. "Observations on Humanism and History. " In <u>The Philosophy of the Curriculum</u>. Ed. Sidney Hook et al. Buffalo: Prometheus, 1975, pp. 81-88.

Lewis, Helen Block. <u>Psychic War in Men and Women</u>. New York: New York UP, 1976.

Martines, Lauro. "Mastering the Matriarch. " <u>Times Literary Supplement</u>, 1 February 1985, p. 113.

See, Carolyn. "Collaboration with a Daughter: The Rewards and Cost. " <u>New York Times</u>, 19 June 1986, p. C2.

Another kind of endnote or footnote, known as the *short form,* should be used when you are citing the same source more than once in your essay. The first time you cite a new source, you use the long form, as illustrated above, which contains detailed information about publication history. The second time you cite the same source, and all subsequent times, you write a separate note, with a new number, but now you use the short form, consisting of the author's name and a page number:

[6] Lewis, p. 74.

The short form can be used here because there is already a long-form entry for Lewis on record in a previous note. If your bibliography contained two works by Lewis, then you would have to include an abbreviated title in the short form of the note:

[6] Lewis, <u>Psychic War</u>, p. 74.

The short form makes it unnecessary to use any Latin abbreviations, like *ibid.* or *op. cit.,* in your notes.

For an example of the use of endnote documentation in a full-length essay, see "The Opening of the Crystal Palace" in Chapter 10.

Other Methods of Documentation: Notes Plus Page Numbers in the Text

If you are using only one or two source-references in your essay, it is a good idea to include one footnote at the first reference and, thereafter, cite the page number of the source in the text of your essay.

For example, if your essay is exclusively about Sigmund Freud's *Civilization and Its Discontents,* document your first reference to the work with a complete note, citing the edition that you are using:

> * Sigmund Freud, <u>Civilization and Its Discontents</u> (Garden City, New York: Doubleday, 1958), p. 72. All further citations refer to this edition.

This single note explains to your reader that you are intending to use the same edition whenever you cite this source. All subsequent references to this book will be followed by the page reference, in parentheses, usually at the end of your sentence.

> Freud has asserted that "the greatest obstacle to civilization [is] the constitutional tendency in men to aggression against one another . . ." (p. 101).

This method is most useful in essays on literary topics when you are focusing on a single author, without citing secondary sources.

Other Methods of Documentation: Parenthetical Author-Year (APA)

This kind of documentation, which is used in the behavioral sciences, closely resembles the standard system of bibliography with parenthetical references to author and page, which was described in Chapter 9. The chief difference is that, in the APA system (named for the American Psychological Association), you include the work's date of publication after the author's name, both within parentheses.

> America's colleges began to make room for the individual sciences in 1711 when William and Mary [College] established a professorship of natural philosophy and mathematics (Rudolph, 1977).

The reader then uses Rudolph's name to turn to the bibliography and find complete publication information about this book.

If you cite the author's name in your own sentence, it is not necessary to repeat it in parentheses. (This is also true of the date of publication.) When you quote from your source, you must place the page number in the parentheses (with or without author and date), with "p." preceding the page number.

> Bowen and Schuster point out that, in the past 40 years, "American higher education has undergone massive growth and profound changes, and these have affected . . . the work environment of faculties and their motivations, satisfactions, and compensation" (1986, p. 4).

Check with your instructor to determine whether you need to cite a page number when you summarize or paraphrase.

Your bibliography remains similar to New MLA format, with a few differences. Chapter and article titles need no quotation marks around them or underlining. The date (in parentheses) is placed immediately after the author's name. And, since the identification of sources greatly depends on the dates that you cite, you must be careful to clarify the dating, especially when a single author has published two or more works in the same year. Here, for example, is an excerpt from a bibliography that carefully distinguishes between three sources published in 1972:

> Carnegie Commission on Higher Education. (1972a). The Campus and the City: Maximizing Assets and Reducing Liabilities. New York: McGraw.
> Carnegie Commission on Higher Education. (1972b). The Fourth Revolution: Instructional Technology in Higher Education. New York: McGraw.
> Carnegie Commission on Higher Education. (1972c). The More Effective Use of Resources: An Imperative for Higher Education. New York: McGraw.

And here is how one of these sources would be documented in the essay:

> In its report on The More Effective Use of Resources, the Carnegie Commission on Higher Education recommended that "colleges and universities develop a 'self-renewal' fund of 1 to 3 percent each year taken from existing allocations" (1972c, p. 105).

For an example of the use of APA author-year documentation, look at "Explaining the Tunguskan Phenomenon," the third research essay in Chapter 10.

Other Methods of Documentation: Numbered Bibliography

In this method, used primarily in the abstract and engineering sciences, you number each entry in your bibliography. Then, each citation in your essay consists of only the number of the work that you are referring to, placed in parentheses. Remember to include the page number if you quote from your source.

> Theorem 2 of Joel, Shier, and Stein (2) is strengthened in the following theorem:

> The following would be a consequence of the conjecture of McMullen and Shepher (3, p. 133):

Depending on your subject, you may arrange your bibliography in alphabetical order (Biology or Mathematics) or in the order in which you cite the sources in your essay (Chemistry, Engineering, or Physics). Consult your instructor or a style sheet that contains the specific rules for your discipline.

Remember: The choice of documentation for your essay is not really yours. Ask your instructor which method is appropriate for your course and your paper topic.

Appendix C.
Writing Essay
Examinations

The purpose of an essay examination is to make sure that you have read and understood the assigned reading, to test your analytical skills, and to find out if you can integrate what you have read with the ideas and information that you have learned about in lectures and class discussion.

Since, as a rule, the object is not to test your memory, essay examinations are often open-book, allowing you to refer freely to the source. But in any exam, even a take-home assignment, there is likely to be some time pressure. To prepare, you should have read all the material carefully in advance and outlined, underlined, or annotated the text.

Reading the Question

You determine your strategy by carefully examining the wording of the question that you are being asked before you begin to plan and write your essay. First of all, it is vital that you accept that someone else is providing the topic for your essay. The person who wrote the question wants to pinpoint a single area to be explored and thus may offer you very little scope. However restrictive it may seem, you have to stay within the boundaries of the question. If you are instructed to focus on only a small section of the text, summarizing the entire work from beginning to end is inappropriate. If you are asked to discuss an issue that is raised frequently throughout the work, paraphrasing a single paragraph or page is pointless. Do not include extraneous information just to demonstrate how much you know. In fact, most teachers are more impressed with aptness and conciseness than with length.

The writer of the question is really saving you the trouble of devising your own topic and strategy. The controlling verb of the question will usually provide you with a key. Different verbs will require different approaches. You are already familiar with the most common terms:

summarize; state; list; outline; condense; cite reasons

What is sometimes forgotten under pressure is that you are expected to carry out the instructions literally. "Summarize" means condense: the reader expects a short but complete account of the subject specified. On the other hand, "list" should result in a sequence of short entries, somewhat disconnected, but not a fully developed series of paragraphs.

Other directions may be far more broad:

describe; discuss; review; explain; show; explore; determine

Verbs like these give you a lot of scope. Since they do not demand a specific strategy, be careful to stay within the set topic, so that you do not explain or review more than the readers want to know about.

Still other verbs indicate a more exact method of development, perhaps one of the strategies that you have already worked with in Assignment 4 in Chapter 3:

compare and contrast; illustrate; define; show the reasons; trace the causes; trace the effects; suggest solutions; analyze

Notice that none of the verbs so far have provided an opportunity for personal comment. You have been asked to examine the text, to demonstrate your understanding of its meaning and its implications, but you have not been asked for your opinion. However, several verbs do request commentary:

evaluate; interpret; criticize; justify; prove; disagree

Although these verbs invite a personal response, they do not give you freedom to write about whatever you choose. You are still confined to the boundaries of the set subject, and you would still be wise to devote as much of your essay as possible to demonstrating your understanding of what you have read. A brilliant essay that ignores the topic rarely earns the highest grade; usually, the reader insists on being convinced that you have mastered the material. And, in fact, if you have worked hard to prepare for the essay, you would be foolish to ignore the question. Don't reinterpret the directions in order to write about what is easiest or what would display your abilities in order to write about what is easiest or what would display your abilities to best advantage or what you figured out earlier would be asked. Just answer the question on the page.

Planning and Developing the Essay

Even when you have worked out what you are expected to write about, you are still not ready to start writing. Your reader will also judge the way in which your essay is constructed, so organize your thoughts before you begin to write. No elaborate outline is necessary. As you would in longer essays, make a list of some of the main points that come into your head; reduce the list to a manageable number; and renumber the sequence. Only then are you ready to write. This process does not take very long and it can prevent unnecessary repetition, unintentional omissions, mixed-up sequences, and overemphasis. These are the guidelines for developing your topic:

1. *Develop each point separately.* Don't try to say everything at the same time. Consult your list; say what is necessary about each item; and then move on to the next.
2. *Develop each point adequately.* Each reason or cause or criticism deserves convincing presentation. Unless you are asked for a list, don't just blurt out one sentence and rush away to the next item. You will write a more effective essay by including some support for each of your points. Do not make brief, incomplete references to ideas which you assume that the reader will know all about. It is your responsibility to explain each one so that it makes sense by itself.
3. *Refer back to the text.* Whenever possible, demonstrate that you can cite evidence or information from the reading. If you think of two possible examples or facts, one from the source and one from your own experience or knowledge, and if you haven't enough time to include both, the safe choice will come from the source. However, you must always mark the transition between your own presentation of ideas and your reference to the source by citing its title, or the name of its author, or both.

Analyzing an Essay and an Essay Question

Carefully read through George Stade's "Football—The Game of Aggression," on p. 354 in Chapter 8. Assume that you have previously read this essay and that you have been given between 45 minutes and an hour to answer the following question:

Although he acknowledges that it can be violent, George Stade suggests that football may serve a constructive social function. Considering some of his descriptive comments about the sport, explain why football may not be as healthy for society as Stade implies.

Answering the Question

At first, you may have some difficulty determining the focus of your essay since the question includes more than one key word to serve as a clue to your strategy. For your purposes, the main verb is "explain." You are being asked to account for something, to help your reader understand what may not be entirely clear. "Explain" also implies persuasion: your reader must be convinced that your explanation is valid.

If the question asked you to explain something that is confusing in Stade's essay, your task would be to provide an interpretive summary of some part of the text. For example, you might have been asked to explain the differences, with illustrations, between violence that is occasional, incidental, and accidental, discussing the implications of these distinctions for sports in general. If the question asked you to explain some related point that Stade omits from his discussion, your task would be to extend his reasoning, perhaps to discuss causes or effects, or to contrast and compare. For example, you might have to explain why football lends itself to a greater degree of violence than other sports, or explain the parallel between the way football players and animals defend their territory. Or the question may be asking you to evaluate the author's reasoning in forming his conclusions.

In fact, the last possibility suggests the most promising approach to this essay. You are being asked to examine Stade's "almost serious" conclusions and to demonstrate—explain—the limitations of his arguments and examples. The question raises the point that Stade may have underestimated the harmful effects of football, whose violence could undermine the social benefits that the sport otherwise provides. To answer the question, then, you must accept the assumption that Stade may be overenthusiastic about football, whether you agree or not, and proceed to point out the implications and the shortcomings of his analysis. In a sense, writing a good essay depends upon your flexibility and your willingness to allow your views to be shaped by the examiner's, at least for the duration of the exam.

The question defines the *limits* as well as the strategy of your essay. It does not permit you to dispute Stade on grounds that are entirely of your choosing; you are firmly instructed to focus your attention on the conflict between violence and social benefit. It would be foolish to ignore these instructions and write only about the glories of football, or condemn the sport for reasons unrelated to the violence of its play.

What should you be evaluating in your essay, and how many comments are "some"? Stade makes the following points in support of his ultimate view that football can be a useful social ritual: it fosters individual strength and determination; it develops cooperation and teamwork; it teaches players how to acquire and defend territory and thus encourages nationalism and the patriotic defense of one's country; it provides players and spectators with the opportunity to act out their aggressions in a controlled and relatively harmless way. These points should certainly be on the list of paragraph topics that you jot down as you plan your essay. Since the main ideas are embedded within the paragraphs of Stade's essay, you should use your own ordering principle—least violent to most (potentially) violent might be a good choice. Each of your paragraphs should begin with a description of one characteristic of the sport as Stade presents it, followed by your own explanation of the social disadvantages or benefits that might result.

Resist the temptation to devote too much space to a single aspect of the sport. For example, if you spend too much time discussing Stade's comments about uniforms and the extent to which the football player is magnified and dehumanized by his padding and his helmet, you may not be able to develop your discussion of whether football encourages patriotism or a more divisive and dangerous nationalism. You will also be unable to do justice to the question of vicarious activity as a way of controlling our less desirable instincts. Stade predicates his essay on the belief that people participate in sports as a way of expressing passions and impulses that have no place in our normal daily occupations. He implies that, if this outlet is eliminated, our instincts for violence may spill over into activities where they would be far more dangerous. This argument has often been used to justify violence as depicted on television and in the movies. While you are not expected to analyze the issue with the expertise of a trained psychologist or sociologist, your essay should reflect your awareness of and your views on Stade's conception of football as the ritualized experience of aggression.

Introducing Your Topic

Examination essays, like all essays, require an introduction. Before beginning to explore some of the issues inherent in George Stade's analysis, you should provide a short introduction that defines the author's topic and your own. Your later references to his ideas will need a well-established context; therefore, try to define Stade's conception of football (which might differ from someone else's) right at the outset of your essay. Although the introduction need not be longer than two or three sentences, *cite your source*—the name of the author and the name of the essay, both properly spelled—and state exactly what it is that you and your author are concerned about. To demonstrate the frustration of reading an introduction that is shrouded in mystery, look at the first paragraph from a student essay answering the question that has just been analyzed:

> The attitude of the author of this esssay is highly supportive of a sport that may be the most violent in the world. It is true that players acquire a lot of skills and learn about teamwork, as well as receiving huge sums of money and becoming public idols. However, there are also risks and dangers that result, for spectators and those watching on television, as well as for those on the field wearing team uniforms, which he fails to point out in the course of this brief essay.

"He," of course, is George Stade, and the sport under discussion is football. The student had read and understood the source essay, but is so eager to begin commenting on Stade's ideas that she fails to establish a context for her arguments. Here is a more informative introduction:

> In "Football--The Game of Aggression," George Stade presents the game of football as a necessary evil and a useful social ritual. He does not deny that the game, more than most sports, is based on a potentially lethal kind of aggression, but, contrasting football with other sports, he finds that it also encourages a sense of teamwork and an instinct for patriotism, which can be valuable both to the individual and to society. Left unclear is whether ritualizing violence through sports does, in fact, result in a less violent society, or whether watching football players maul each other in weekly combat only encourages spectators to imitate their heroes.

Presenting Your Essay to the Reader

During in-class examinations, students often waste vital minutes by painstakingly transcribing a new copy from their rough draft. While it is crucial that your handwriting be legible, it is not necessary to hand in a clean copy. Teachers expect an exam essay to have sentences crossed out and words inserted. They are used to seeing arrows used to reverse sentences and numbers used to change the sequence of paragraphs. It makes no sense to write the last word of your first draft and then, without checking what you have written, immediately take a clean sheet of paper and start transcribing a copy to hand in. And, because transcription is such a mechanical task, the mind tends to wander and the pen makes errors that were not in the original draft. Use extra time to proofread your essay, to locate grammatical errors and fill in gaps in continuity. As long as your corrections and changes are fairly neat and clear, your teacher will not mind reading the first draft and indeed, in most cases, will be pleased by your efforts to improve your writing.

Students often choose to divide their time into three parts. For example, if you have forty minutes during which to write an essay, spend ten minutes analyzing the question and planning a strategy, twenty minutes writing the essay, and ten minutes proofreading and correcting.

Carlos Baker, excerpted from *Ernest Hemingway: A Life Story*. Copyright © 1969 Carlos Baker and Mary Hemingway. Reprinted with the permission of Charles Scribner's Sons.

"300 Killed by Fire, Smoke and Panic in Boston Resort," *The New York Times*, November 30, 1942. © 1942 by The New York Times Company. Reprinted by permission.

"Boston's Worst." Copyright 1942 Time Inc. Reprinted by permission from *Time*.

"The Easy Chair" by Bernard De Voto. Reprinted from *Harper's*, February 1943, by permission of Mrs. Bernard De Voto, owner of copyright.

Excerpt from *Science and Human Values* by J. Bronowski. Copyright © 1956 by J. Bronowski, renewed © 1984 by Rita Bronowski. Reprinted by permission of Julian Messner, a division of Simon and Schuster, Inc.

"Washington—The Truth Behind the Legend" by Michael Davie. Reprinted by permission of *The Observer*.

Excerpt from *A Theory of Criminal Justice* by Jan Gorecki. Copyright 1979. Reprinted by permission of Columbia University Press.

Gresham M. Sykes, *The Society of Captives: A Study of a Maximum Security Prison*. Copyright © 1958 by Princeton University Press. Chapter 4 reprinted with permission of Princeton University Press.

"Brutal Sports and Brutal Fans" by Daniel Goleman, *The New York Times*, August 13, 1985. Copyright © 1985 by the New York Times Company. Reprinted by permission.

Excerpt from "Game Theory" by George Stade reprinted by permission from *The Columbia Forum*. Copyright 1966 by The Trustees of Columbia University in the City of New York. All rights reserved.

From *Sport: A Philosophic Inquiry*, by Paul Weiss. Copyright © 1969 by Southern Illinois University Press, Carbondale. Reprinted by permission of the publishers.

Index